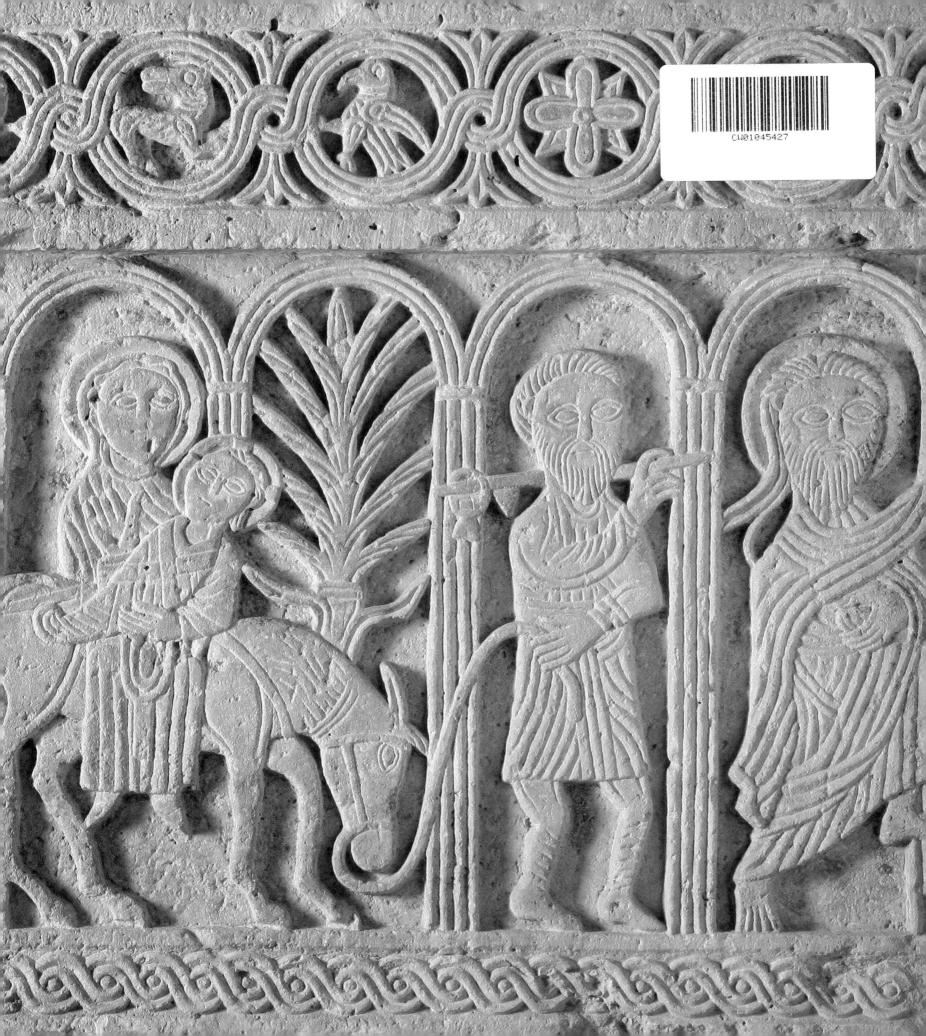

CROATIA

ASPECTS OF ART, ARCHITECTURE AND CULTURAL HERITAGE

CROATIA

ASPECTS OF ART, ARCHITECTURE AND CULTURAL HERITAGE

With an introduction by
JOHN JULIUS NORWICH

FRANCES LINCOLN LIMITED
PUBLISHERS

INA Industrija nafte d.d., the Croatian oil and gas company, has been pleased to support the publication of this remarkable book. This collection of scholarly essays, written by world renowned specialists on art and architecture, will give readers an insight into the rich cultural heritage of Croatia, which is not as widely appreciated as it should be.

Many thanks to Jadranka Beresford-Peirse, who won the 1999 INA award for the promotion of Croatian culture in the world, for all her efforts to make the publication of this book a reality.

Dr Tomislav Dragičević
President of the Management Board

Frances Lincoln Limited
4 Torriano Mews
Torriano Avenue
London NW5 2RZ
www.franceslincoln.com

Croatia
Copyright © Frances Lincoln Limited 2009 and the authors

British Library Cataloguing in Publication Data
A catalogue record for this book is available from the British Library

ISBN 978-0-7112-2921-1

Printed in China

9 8 7 6 5 4 3 2 1

ENDPAPERS Pluteus from a chancel screen, mid-11th c. Limestone, 98 x 183 cm Zadar, Archaeological Museum, from the church of St Nediljica (Sta Domenica) in Zadar. Photo: Goran Vranić.

PAGE 1 Blaž Jurjev, *Virgin and Child with Angels* (the 'Madonna of the Rose Garden'), *c.* 1437, Museum of the church of St John the Baptist, Trogir. Photo: Živko Bačić.

PAGE 2 Missal of George of Topusko, MR 170, fol. 95v, State Archives, Zagreb. Photo: courtesy of the Croatian State Archives and the Metropolitan Library.

OPPOSITE Nikola Božidarević, altarpiece of the *Annunciation* from the Dominican church in Dubrovnik. Photo: Živko Bačić.

CONTENTS

PREFACE
Jadranka Beresford-Peirse

The idea for this book goes back to 1994 when, eagerly leafing through the then just published and hefty tome, *The Civilization of Europe in the Renaissance* by the late Professor John Hale, I could find no reference to any works of art in my country, Croatia. That was at a time when Croatia was under attack after the dissolution of Yugoslavia and many of its artistic treasures were endangered; some perished for ever and many were damaged. I realised that there was a general lack of knowledge and a clear need for scholarly writing by English speaking and world-renowned specialists, to try and fill this evident gap in knowledge about our shared cultural heritage. Even today, at the recent and resplendent 'Renaissance Faces' exhibition at the National Gallery in London, Croatia forms no part. And yet, for example, how well the sublime portrait of Bishop Tommaso Nigris in Split by Lorenzo Lotto, painted in the same year as his portrait of the collector Andrea Odoni and discussed by Timothy Clifford in one of his chapters, would have fitted this exhibition!

This collection of essays is by no means comprehensive or fully representative of the rich cultural heritage of Croatia. It is an attempt to present an insight into some aspects of art and architecture which may be unfamiliar to a wider audience outside of Croatian borders, and some which may be understudied. It is our hope, therefore, that it will inspire further research and serve as a reference for both specialists and all those who are interested in the arts in Croatia and their wider context and who may take pleasure in walking in the footsteps of the authors. Some chapters were indeed conceived with precisely this in mind, and the book may well have its uses, if not as a guidebook, as a vade-mecum for visitors who wish to see more of Croatia than its exquisite Dalmatian coast and holiday resorts. If we achieve this, our purpose will have been fulfilled.

Many people and organisations have contributed to this book and they deserve my gratitude. First and foremost, I would like to thank the authors, all renowned experts in their fields, who so kindly and with such good will agreed to write their chapters at no financial gain. They took time out of their busy schedules to travel and closely examine their chosen subject. Using their vast experience and knowledge, they then presented their findings in these highly informative and enjoyable essays. Their commitment and dedication to their task, and their subsequent help to me, have been exemplary.

I am most grateful to our sponsor, INA industrija nafte d.d., and to Dr Tomislav Dragičević and Mr Darko Blagović, without whose understanding and generous support this book would never have been published.

I also thank the photographers, most particularly Živko Bačić, and institutions in Croatia who kindly provided the illustrations, some taken especially for this purpose, free of charge. I thank John Nicoll and Frances Lincoln Publishers, and especially Nancy Marten, for their guidance and sound advice.

It would not have been possible to publish this book without the help of many people in Croatia. I take this opportunity to thank them all, beginning with the Minister of Culture, Božo Biškupić, and the head conservator, Miljenko Domijan, and the regional departments in Split, Trogir, Zadar, Osijek, Varaždin, Šibenik and Pula. The Croatian National Tourist Board and Croatian Airlines provided tickets and accommodation for some of the authors. The Archaeological Museums in Zagreb, Split and Zadar were most helpful, as were also the Museum of Croatian Archaeological Monuments in Split, the National Museum in Zadar, the Croatian Academy of Sciences and Arts, the State Archives, and the Metropolitan and the National and University Libraries in Zagreb and, in Dubrovnik, the Dominican and Franciscan convents and the Dubrovnik museums. It is, however, Professor Ferdinand Meder, head of the Croatian Conservation Institute, and Joško Belamarić, head of the Conservation Department of the Ministry of Culture in Split, who were crucial at all stages of the book. Professor Meder, apart from helping in many other ways, assigned to me a young art historian, Nena Meter, who worked tirelessly to obtain the illustrations. Joško Belamarić planned and organised the visits by Sir Timothy Clifford and Professor David Ekserdjian and was a source of help and inspiration all along.

I would like to thank Dr Ivan Mirnik for kindly offering his home in Zagreb to visiting scholars. Professor Mladen and Dr Bojana Obad Šćitaroci organised the visit by Marcus Binney and Zdenka Predrijevac helped with his programme in Slavonia. The conservators from Villa Stay, the Dubrovnik branch of the Croatian Conservation Institute, provided illustrations, looked after visiting scholars and gave sound advice.

I would like to extend my thanks to Slobodanka Antičić, Kate Bagoje, Jadranka Baković, Mrg. Juraj Batelja, Mario Braun, Boris Bui, Niko Bulić, Zrinka Buljević, Radoslav Buzančić, Biserka Cimeša, Don Tomislav Ćubelić, Bruno Diklić, Dr Ljerka Dulibić, Vedrana Gjukić Bender, Sanja Grković, Slavija Jačan Obratov, Mladen Klemenčić, Ivan Kosić, Vanja Kovačić, Katarina Kusijanović, Vesna Kusin, Silvija Ladić, Tugomil Lukšić, Padre Vladimir Magić, Dražen Maršić, Tihomil Maštrović, Jagoda Meder, Nataša Nefat, Fra Stipe Nosić, Ana-Maria Ocvirk, Milan Pelc, Hrvoje Perica, Ivana Peškan, Sister Lina Plukavec, Vlaho and Mara Pustić, Fra Kristijan Raić, Eva Sedak, Samir and Sanja Serhatlić, Ivan Sikavica, Sagita Sunara, Tea Srdić, Milo Sršen, Tomislav Šeparović, Ana Šverko, Nives Tomasović, Pavica Vilać, Igor Zidić, Venetian Heritage Inc., among others.

In this country, my special thanks are due to Dr Robin Harris for his continuous advice and invaluable help with translations from Croatian and to Professor Michael Vickers for editing the chapter by Dr Branko Kirigin. I thank Dr Anthea Brook of the Witt Library, on whose knowledge, support and practical help I could always rely, and Dr Donal Cooper for writing a short summary of the chapters for the publisher. I thank HE The Croatian Ambassador Mr Joško Paro, Flora Turner, Dr David Davison, Dr Dorothy King, Dr Sean Kingsley, Susan Morris and Jane Price of Waterstone's Bookshops, who introduced me to John Nicoll. The Croatian National Tourist Office in London helped with illustrations. Brian Sewell was exceptionally kind with advice and encouragement from the beginning. My own family, here and in Croatia, have given me much needed support at all times.

The International Trust for Croatian Monuments, Registered Charity No. 1040187, was established in 1991 and continues its work today. I am eternally grateful to our trustees, Sherban Cantacuzino, John Julius Norwich, Captain Ante Jerković and my husband, for their unfailing help and advice throughout these years. I cannot think of a better place to record my thanks to all our supporters than in the preface to this book. Maestro Ivo Pogorelich gave two piano recitals, in the Royal Festival Hall in 1992 and in 1999, and a concert in Brussels with the Belgian Philharmonic Orchestra in 1994, which provided the much needed funds for major reconstruction works. I thank Their Royal Hignesses The Duke and The Duchess of Gloucester and the Committees of Honour for these concerts for their moral and financial support and the people who sponsored them, particularly Zagrebačka and Privredna Banks, Atlantska Plovidba and Inter Ina. The following people and trusts, especially The Headley Trust, have generously given us their support: The Attingham Trust, The Prince of Wales's Charities Foundation, The Swan Trust, The Peter Stormonth Darling Foundation, The Margaret Thatcher Foundation, The Rothschild Foundation, the late Sir John Smith, The Sandy and Zorica Glen Charitable Settlement, The Samuel Storey Charitable Trust, The Weinstock Fund, American Express, Icomos, World Monuments Fund, Bankgesellschaft Berlin AG, The Carpenters' and Mercers' Companies Charitable Trusts, Weymouth College, Mrs Lesley Lewis, Dr and Mrs Frederick Davies, the late Lord Tweeddale, Nina Campbell, Geoffrey Wooler, Mr and Mrs Anthony Suchy, Mr and Mrs Marvin Carsley, Col. and Mrs A. E. F. Cowan, Joan Dillon and many others. Alan and Marija Templeton have provided a home for a number of Croatian students during their studies in London and my grateful thanks are due to them. I would also like to record here the initial help and support of the late Sir Roger de Grey, who was a trustee until his untimely death. I thank the Royal Academy of Arts and many British artists – in particular, Norman Ackroyd, Anthony Eyton, Ken Howard, the late Paul Hogarth, Donald Hamilton Fraser, Leonard McComb and Brendan Neiland – who responded to our initial plea in 1993 and made it possible to undertake important restoration works. My thanks are due to Bonhams for holding the 'Art for Art' auction in 1994 and for their subsequent support. I would also like to thank Professor Anthony Hobson, Pat Clegg, Alex Kidson, Jane Sellars, Dr Nicholas Pickwoad, Robert Child, Stephen and Pamela Allen, Bond Tours and Matthew Wrigley for their support for many years now.

Their legacy in Croatia will always remain in the form of restored church, cathedral and museum roofs and repairs to many other monuments. In addition, a new generation of young conservators, to whom they have given the opportunity to gain knowledge and expertise in their chosen fields, bears witness to their generosity.

Today Croatia has seven UNESCO World Heritage Sites: Dubrovnik, Plitvice Lakes, Poreč, Šibenik, Split, Starigradsko polje and Trogir. Other applications are in preparation.

I would like to thank most particularly the following people who have assisted us so wholeheartedly and given us their photographs so generously:

Zoran Alajbeg, Milan Babić, Živko Bačić, Vidoslav Barac, Goran Bekina, Frane Beusan, Siniša Bilić Dujmušić, Toto Bergamo Rossi, Mario Braun, Srećko Budek, Zvonko Buljević, Dino Cetinić, Marko Ćolić, Boris Cvjetanović, Nedeljko Čaće, Boris Čargo, V. Červenka, Miljenko Domijan, Miro Dvorščak, Damir Fabijanić, S. Forenbaher, Božo Gjukić, Ćiril Metod Iveković, Pawel Jaroszweski, Daniel Katz, Jovan Kliska, Aleksandar Kotlar, Miljenko Marohnić, Dražen Maršić, Bet McCleod, Luka Mjeda, Nataša Nefat, Zoran Osrečak, Nikolina Oštarijaš, Milan Pelc, Ivo Pervan, Ivana Peškan, Viktor Popović, Vlaho Pustić, Mario Romulić, Tonći Seser, Ivan Sikavica, Jurica Skudar, Davor Šarić, Mladen Šćerbe, K. Tadić, Željko Tutnjević, Goran Vranić,

Jadranka Njerš Beresford-Peirse
Founder and Trustee
The International Trust for Croatian Monuments
www.croatianmonuments.org

THE INTERNATIONAL TRUST FOR CROATIAN MONUMENTS

INTRODUCTION

John Julius Norwich

To the traveller arriving in Croatia from across the Adriatic, the land seems indeed to have been blessed by providence. Nowhere in the whole Mediterranean will you find an interplay of land and sea more breathtakingly lovely than along the Dalmatian coast. Occupying some 400 miles of the eastern littoral of the Adriatic, it actually comprises – thanks to its countless bays, inlets and islands – no less than 3,600 miles of shoreline. Behind, there rises protectively a backdrop of majestic mountains – the Dinaric Alps. The climate is a constant benediction. And man has even improved on nature: from one end to the other the architecture is superb, ranging from the sixth-century Byzantine basilica at Poreč, the Roman amphitheatre at Pula and Diocletian's Palace in Split to the exquisite formerly Venetian cities of Zadar, Šibenik and Trogir and the pink-roofed perfection of Dubrovnik.

But there is much more to Croatia than its coastline. The country is shaped like a boomerang, the other arm of which – known to the Romans as Pannonia but to us as Slavonia – runs from the north-west corner of the coast eastwards for another 400 miles or so to the Serbian frontier. This is a land of broad, flat plains broken by ranges of gently undulating hills – admittedly less spectacular than Dalmatia but quietly beautiful nonetheless, and possessing all the rich fertility that the coast so obviously lacks. Many of its villages are still essentially unspoilt (when I first saw them, half a century ago, most of their inhabitants, young and old, wore national dress), and quite apart from the capital, Zagreb, there are several elegant baroque towns – though perhaps the most elegant of them all, Vukovar, was cruelly destroyed during the war following the declaration of Croatian independence in 1991.

For Croatia is a new country and one which has undergone, quite literally, a baptism of fire. What we may call the Yugoslav experiment – the attempted merging after the First World War of all the South Slavs into the 'Kingdom of the Serbs, Croats and Slovenes' (sensibly renamed Yugoslavia in 1929) – enjoyed a period of success under the firm and formidable hand of the Croatian-born Marshal Tito, but ultimately proved a failure. The constituent peoples – apart from the three mentioned above, they included the Bosnians, Hercegovinans, Montenegrins and Macedonians – were too disparate ever to be happily united. Croatia and Slovenia had been part of the Austro-Hungarian Empire and were Roman Catholic; Serbia, Montenegro and Macedonia had been subject to the Ottomans and were Orthodox. Bosnia and Hercegovina were largely Muslim. The country had been split down the middle during the past war. The

Croats, Serbs and Montenegrins spoke basically the same language but used two different alphabets to write it in; the Slovenes and Macedonians had languages of their own. Yugoslavia was, in short, doomed from the start; and when it finally collapsed, it brought catastrophe in its train.

But this was only the most recent of many disasters. Croatia's tragedy was that although it had always merited full independence, it had not enjoyed it for the best part of a millennium. In 1097 the Hungarian King Koloman defeated the last Croatian King Petar at Petrova Gora; thereafter, for nearly 900 years, Croatia was – in fact though not in theory – a subject nation: subject first to the Hungarians, then to the House of Anjou, then to the Habsburgs and finally to the Serbs. This, it may be objected, is a simplification, and it is true that each change was in theory the free choice of the Croatians. But it is also true that the Croatians always insisted on a union between two equal partners – and that such a union in practice never occurred.

Moreover, the very land itself was fragmented. Frontiers were fluid; in the early centuries the coastal cities were largely cut off by the mountains from the Slavonian plain in the north – and, to a considerable degree, from each other as well. Many of them, together with many of the larger islands, treasured the autonomy granted them by Koloman: Korčula drew up its own statutes as early as 1265, Dubrovnik in 1272. But their very autonomy weakened them, and it was not long before they fell, one by one, to the infinitely more powerful Venice. Only one of them was able to resist – Zadar, which defeated a Venetian fleet in 1190. But its triumph was short-lived. Just twelve years later, Venice was to use the army of the Fourth Crusade to recover the city. Then in 1408 the Angevin King Ladislas the Magnanimous sold his rights to Zadar and its hinterland to the Serenissima for 100,000 gold ducats, and by 1420 Venice controlled the entire coast from there as far as (but not including) Dubrovnik – most of which remained Venetian until the end of the republic in 1797. The land of Croatia was now confined to the Slavonian plain.

And Venice was not the only foreign threat. By the late fourteenth century the Ottoman Turks were advancing rapidly across the Balkan peninsula. Bosnia fell in 1463; its neighbour Croatia was now open to direct attack. The Dalmatian coast was partially protected by the mountains – though the Turks penetrated in several places and Dubrovnik paid regular tribute money to the Sultan – but Slavonia was hard hit. A series of Turkish victories preceded the great battle of Mohács in 1526, which resulted in the death of the Hungarian King Louis II and, as an indirect consequence, the absorption of Hungary and Croatia into the Holy Roman Empire.

Hungary, Venice, the Holy Roman Empire, the Ottomans – with such giants around them, how could the poor Croatians possibly assert their independence? And even these were not all: in 1806 the French had their turn when Dalmatia was seized by

Napoleon to become his 'Provinces Illyriennes'. The decision by the Congress of Vienna ten years later to return it to the Habsburgs may have been a disappointment to many, but at least it meant that the two halves of the country were once again reunited.

The last country which attempted – and with some success – to get its hands on Croatia was the Kingdom of Italy. In 1915, in a burst of barely believable arrogance, the allied powers had bribed Italy to join them with the promise of a generous portion of the Dalmatian coast. Italy accepted and ended on the winning side – Croatia, as part of the Austrian Empire, on the losing one. As a result, by the Treaty of Rapallo in 1920, the whole province of Istria, several islands, the city of Zadar and a sizable part of Slovenia were handed over to Italy. Suddenly, some half a million Croats and Slovenes found themselves under Italian – very shortly to be fascist – rule. This continued until the middle of the Second World War when, after the capitulation of Italy in 1943, the Italians were replaced by the Germans.

It is astonishing to think that, less than a century ago, well-meaning world statesmen, meeting together to decide upon the future of Europe, should have been capable of blunders on such a scale as these. The newly born Kingdom of Yugoslavia had quite enough problems already; it had no need of huge and entirely anomalous foreign enclaves in the middle of its own territory. It coped with the situation as best it could, but it was not until 1947, after the coming to power of Marshal Tito, that Zadar was formally reunited with the country to which it so clearly belonged.

And now Yugoslavia itself has disintegrated, the war with the Serbs under Slobodan Milošević that followed the disintegration was finally brought to an end in 1995, Croatia adopted a new constitution (shifting power gently away from the president to parliament) and is now at last a truly independent democratic republic. It is a member of the United Nations – indeed, at the time of writing it has just joined the Security Council – and of the Council of Europe; in April 2008 it received an invitation to join NATO. Membership of the European Union is only a question of time, being confidently predicted by 2010. Ten million tourists visit it every year. In short, Croatia is now at last enjoying the freedom and prosperity that it has for so many centuries deserved and so seldom managed to achieve. Long may it continue to do so.

A SURVEY OF CROATIAN HISTORY

Stjepan Ćosić

Translated by Robin Harris

The geographical framework within which the history of Croatia has developed over the past thirteen centuries was formed by the river Drava to the north, the river Drina to the east, and the eastern shore of the Adriatic to the south. This region was where a small European nation emerged and engaged in a continuing struggle for existence. Even during the early Middle Ages, the Croats found themselves living within a complex geopolitical environment, for the lands they settled lay at the intersection of the great powers' spheres of influence. Moreover, the eastern shores of the Adriatic – Istria and Kvarner to the north and Dalmatia and the islands to the south – differ from the Adriatic's western shores in being rich in inlets and suitable for navigation. This was the fundamental reason for the centuries-long, bitter struggle for control over these parts of Croatia.

EARLY CROATIA

The Greeks in early antiquity founded their colonies and emporia along this coast, creating a series of maritime and commercial bases which permitted them to navigate the full length of the Adriatic. This was Illyria, inhabited by the diverse Illyrian tribes, whose interests in the mid-third century BC clashed with those of an increasingly powerful Rome. After long (and never entirely successful) attempts to bring the strongest Illyrian tribes into submission, in 168 BC Roman authority was extended over the eastern shores of the Adriatic and into the interior as far as the river Sava. This newly created province of Illyricum represented a strategically and economically important territory for the Roman Empire. By the beginning of the first century, it stretched north of the Sava to the southern edge of the Pannonian plain. While respecting the natural boundaries, the Romans soon split the province into two lesser units – Dalmatia and Pannonia. The name 'Illyria', though, would persist until modern times. Napoleon used it to designate his 'Illyrian Provinces', and the Croats would call their movement for cultural integration in the first half of the nineteenth century the 'Illyrian Movement'.

Historical sources do not reveal very much of the earliest history of the Croats, nor do they offer many reliable facts about the etymology of their un-Slavic name. It is known, however, that, before their arrival in south-east Europe, the Croats inhabited the region of White Croatia, in the southern part of today's Poland,

the areas around Krakow. At the time of the great migrations of peoples and the blows which shattered the ancient frontiers, the Croats offered military help to the Byzantine Empire, then under attack by the Avars. In the first half of the seventh century, the Croats settled the Romanised territories of the province of Dalmatia. They thus came to share in the culture of the Greeks and later of the Romans.

In the course of the eighth century, the Croats formed an ethnic and political group along the Adriatic coast and its immediate hinterland between the rivers Raša to the west and Cetina to the east. This was a mountain chain punctuated by a line of isolated and protected Karst plains. But, of course, this region was not completely cut off from the Dalmatian littoral and towns, where a restricted Roman, Latin, Christian world continued to exist. The Croats gradually absorbed the cultural influences of the Roman-Dalmatian coast, and through the process of assimilation of the newcomers with other Slavs, Romans and Illyrians, the Croatian medieval identity emerged. Their first public institutions, called Sklavinije (literally, 'Lands of the Slavs'), thus enjoyed their own existence alongside the developed and cultured Dalmatian cities or 'communes' under the protection of Byzantium.

Once the Croats had accepted Christianity and definitively become part of the European cultural sphere, they threw off Byzantine rule and at the start of the ninth century relied on the Franks as their protectors. This political decision itself served to confirm their orientation towards Latin and Western European civilisation. But the Croats also created within their new environment a full range of distinctive cultural values. Among these was the existence of the Croats' own script (called 'Glagolitic') and their use of the vernacular in church services (carried on predominantly in the Latin rite). Yet the Croats never, in the course of their history, cut themselves off from the Roman pontiff and the Catholic Church, nor created their own church organisation, as did the Eastern (Orthodox) peoples. The Latin language, alongside Croatian, nurtured the first works of Croatian literature. The earliest Croatian texts are in Latin, while those in Glagolitic/Croatian appear somewhat later.

In Croatian history as a whole up to the present times, one can observe time and again a vacillation between the great powers of Europe, whose spheres in part directly overlapped on Croatian soil. This clash – together with the spasmodic struggle of Croatia to tear itself away from the domination of the opposing powers, while opting for western culture and values – enabled the Croatian princes (prince = Cr. *knez*) to shape an independent, strong, influential Croatia. The Croatian state of the day received a kind of international recognition in the form a letter of 879 from the pope to Knez Branimir. Papal recognition and influence had a decisive influence on the direction of Croatia's cultural and political development. In 925, the Croatian ruler Tomislav managed to repel an attack by the Hungarians and force them back north of the river Drava, which then became the historic frontier between

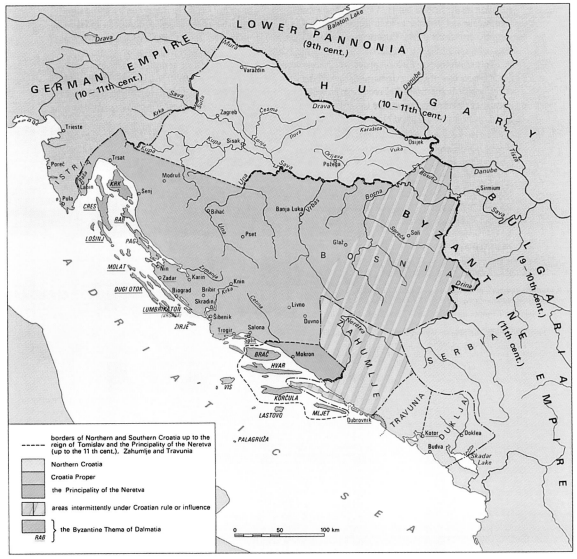

Croatia until the twelfth century.

The map shows the territory of Croatia (in red). In 925 King Tomislav forced the Hungarians back north of the river Drava and united the two earlier Croatian principalities (kneževine). The rivers Bosna and Usora became the kingdom's eastern frontier; in Dalmatia, Croatian territory reached the river Cetina; and to the west, in Istria, it stretched to the river Raša. The map also shows the later extension of territory into Bosnia, up to the river Drina, which occurred under King Petar Krešimir IV in about 1073. The southern border advanced to the Neretva river and to the islands of Brač, Hvar and Vis. When Croatia entered its personal union with Hungary in 1102, the Croatian frontier withdrew westwards in Bosnia to the rivers Bosna and Usora, and the territory in Istria was lost.

the two countries. In doing this, Tomislav included within his control the northern (Pannonian) part of Croatia, and for the first time he received from Byzantium administration of its Dalmatian towns. The papal chancery honoured Tomislav with the title of king, and Croatian historiography considers him the founder of the Croatian Kingdom ('Regnum Croatiae'), in other words the first Croatian king.

The following century saw the alternating rise and fall in strength of the Croatian state, which long had strained relations with Venice, the new power of the Adriatic. Under Kings Petar Krešimir IV (1058–74) and Dimitrije Zvonimir (1075–89), Croatia reached its greatest territorial extent and became a major political and military entity in the region. At this time, the Croatian rulers achieved their most important political goal – the integration within their state of the old Dalmatian cities, well-developed commercial and mercantile communes. From that time dates the name which was always attached to Croatia in diplomacy, 'Regnum Dalmatiae et Croatiae' (the Kingdom of Dalmatia and Croatia).

However, the death of Zvonimir and still obscure internal disorders marked a turning point in the history of the Croatian state, which was left politically divided and without a legitimate king. Marriage alliances and the realities of military power finally led to the historic agreement (Cr. *sporazum* or Lat. *Pacta conventa*) of the Croatian nobility with the king of Hungary of the Árpád dynasty. This constituted a union of the Crown of Dalmatia and Croatia with that of Hungary by which both states, united under the Crown of Saint Stephen, in other words with the rank of kingdoms, maintained their separateness and individuality. This historic Croatian-Hungarian union survived the ebb and flow of events until its destruction in 1918.

The political turmoil in Croatia at the end of the eleventh century led to a strengthening of the autonomy of the Dalmatian city-communes, which meant a general weakening of the Hungarian-Croatian Kingdom on the coast of the eastern Adriatic. This in turn encouraged an aggressive policy by the Serenissima, which culminated in 1202 with the Venetian doge, assisted by French and Flemish crusaders, seizing Zadar.

The weakness of the central government of the Hungarian-Croatian state also allowed the Croatian nobility to enjoy a more or less independent existence. Of the old Croatian noble families, the Šubić princes of Bribir gained in strength and in the course of the thirteenth century became the effective rulers of Croatia. Indeed, at the end of the century they involved themselves in the dynastic disputes which accompanied the extinction of the ruling Hungarian royal family, and in 1301 they brought to the Croatian-Hungarian throne the Anjou dynasty. But then the Šubićs, as the real masters of Dalmatia (with the exception of Zadar, held by Venice) and of Croatia, fiercely opposed the Angevin attempt at centralisation. Louis the Great of Hungary (1342–82) waged a bitter armed struggle against the Šubićs and drove them off the stage of Croatian history for a century. (Settling in the north, in the remote town of Zrin, their descendants, as counts (Cr. *grof*) of Zrin – thus known as Zrinski – became powerful once more in the sixteenth century and took a leading role in Croatian politics.) A second powerful Croatian noble family which became very strong in the late medieval period was the counts of Krk, who cleverly used their dual relationship with Hungary and Venice, and in the fourteenth century they took the name of the Roman Frankopan family to become the most powerful Croatian house of the day.

The transition from the fourteenth to the fifteenth century in Croatia was marked by complex shifts and entanglements which were exploited by Croatia's neighbours. There appeared a strong Bosnian state under King Tvrtko I, who at the end of the fourteenth century tried to gather Croatian and Serbian lands around a Bosnian nucleus. The internal difficulties of the Hungarian-Croatian state, whose throne was occupied by successive foreign dynasties, were also exploited by Venice, which purchased Dalmatia from the last Angevin, Ladislas of Naples. As ruler of Istria and, after 1420, of most of Dalmatia, the Serenissima became for centuries master of the east Adriatic coast. Only the small, though commercially powerful, Dubrovnik Republic succeeded in holding out and competing with Venice. But soon a new aggressive danger faced the whole of southeast Europe – the Ottomans.

In 1463 neighbouring Bosnia fell under Turkish rule. For the next 130 years the Ottoman Empire would expand and, step by step, subjugate and destroy parts of Croatia. The Croatian Kingdom underwent its 'first ruin' on Krbavsko Polje (Krbava Field), when the Ottomans completely vanquished the Croatian army and massacred the Croatian political and ecclesiastical elite. The southern, Dalmatian estates of the Croatian magnates during the following thirty years almost entirely fell under Turkish sway. A second great catastrophe followed defeat at the battle of Mohács in 1526, when the Ottomans conquered the whole of Pannonia.

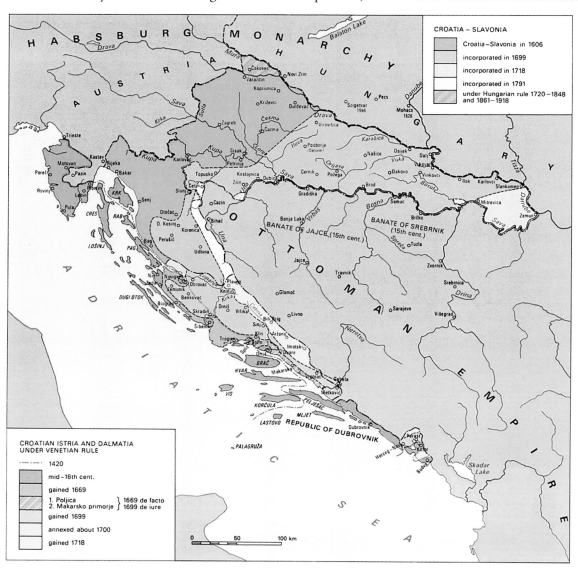

Territorial changes from the sixteenth to the eighteenth centuries
Croatia's territory was gradually squeezed from the end of the fifteenth century by the rise of Bosnia and of Venice. Then in 1463 the Ottoman Empire conquered Bosnia. It destroyed a Croatian army in 1493 at Krbava. It crushed a Croatian-Hungarian force at Mohács in 1526. There followed a series of other defeats, and by the sixteenth century Croatia was reduced to what was known in Latin as Reliquiae reliquiarum (the 'remains of the remains'). But the battle of Sisak in 1593 marked a turning point. During the ensuing 'Long Turkish War', Ottoman expansion was decisively halted. Croatian territory then expanded eastwards during the hostilities concluded with the Peace of Srijemski Karlovci (Carlowitz) in 1699. The Peace of Požarevac (Passarowitz) in 1718 rounded off Croatian territory by inclusion of the regions of Slavonia and Srijem.

CROATIA IN THE PERIOD OF OTTOMAN EXPANSION

The complete collapse of the Hungarian-Croatian state after Mohács presented the Hungarian and Croatian political elite with a huge dilemma – how to survive in the face of the powerful Ottoman Empire directing its aggressive force at Central Europe. Part of the nobility judged that saving their lives and possessions was more important than formal independence, assured by the decision of the Diet at Rákos in 1505 that no foreigner could be chosen as king of Hungary-Croatia. As pragmatists, these nobles looked to a series of agreements which the Habsburgs from the time of Matthias Corvinus had made with a view to eventually acquiring the Hungarian-Croatian throne. Now that the Hungarian-Croatian state had practically ceased to exist, lacked a legitimate king, was militarily crushed and politically riven, the Crown of St Stephen was within the Habsburgs' grasp – and the conditions for acquiring it better than ever before. Apart from that, security reasons pushed Austria's rulers towards vigorous engagement in Hungary and Croatia, on whose eastern frontiers Austrian military forces had for years been stationed against the threatened Ottoman advance. So the aristocracy of Hungary-Croatia and Austria, conscious of the danger that threatened from the east, ratified in 1527 the fateful agreement that would impose its mark on almost four centuries of Central European and Croatian history.

Croatia was at this time a dual kingdom composed of the remains of the ancient Kingdom of Dalmatia and Croatia and the remains of the Kingdom of Slavonia: that is, its northern, Pannonian parts. Each of these kingdoms had its own Ban (regent/governor) and its own aristocratic assembly or Estates called Sabor. Each would also go its own political way. Slavonia, lying between the Drava and the Sava, was for geographical reasons more closely linked to Hungary.

The archival sources relating to the choice of Austrian Archduke Ferdinand I as Croatian king in 1527 at Cetin demonstrate the difficult and divided conditions which obtained during these months. Although the Frankopan family was represented in the electoral Sabor and signed the document choosing the Habsburgs, the royal messengers in their report allege that on their way back to Vienna along the roads across Croatia they had to elude ambushes by the Frankopans in order to save the prized document. Of the highest importance in Croatian constitutional history, this charter is confirmed with seven seals, of which the middle one, the Seal of the Kingdom, bears for the first time the Croatian coat of arms with its sixty-four alternating white and red squares.

As in the *Pacta conventa* of 1102, so on the occasion of its election of the House of Austria in 1527, the Croatian nobility sought from its king the preservation of Croatian distinctness and its independent position within the union. It also expected military help to defend the country against the Turks. The fateful Croatian-Austrian partnership was far from ideal. Just ten years after the election, the Croatian Estates delivered a protest to the king, seeking the return of the 1527 electoral charter because of his failure to fulfil his promises to protect the country. In truth, ten years was too short a time to repair the situation on the frontier with the Ottoman Empire. The stubborn Croatian nobility preferred ruin to voluntarily surrendering its fortified places, towns and lands to Austrian military commanders. The Zrinskis dared openly to show who were the real lords of the land, even putting on trial one of the Austrian generals after a military defeat on suspicion of treason. But the Zrinskis also understood full well that the fragmented approach favoured by the lesser and middling Croatian nobles could not continue, and Nikola Zrinski in his war with the Ottomans did not hesitate to use political and military force against them in the lands around the Sava, Kupa and Una. This same Nikola Zrinski has entered European history as the fearless defender of Siget in 1566, who fell before the walls in a desperate and suicidal break-out from the fortress.

In 1558 at Steničnjak on the Croatian border, the Croatian Estates met for the last time independently and separately from those of Slavonia. That year marks the disappearance of the remains of the old medieval Dalmatian-Croatian state. Its champions escaped to the north, bringing with them the Croatian name and taking over the old Slavonian structures. From that time there passed into customary use the already ancient diplomatic name of the Triune Kingdom: Dalmatia, Croatia and Slavonia.

Only after fifty years did the Croatian-Austrian alliance yield its first obvious results in the struggle to stop the Ottomans. This took the form of large investments from the Austrian interior (Styria, Carinthia and Cariniola), in conjunction with a huge mobilisation of the Croatian population, in building an effective defensive system along the whole Croatian border with the Ottoman Empire. But for Croatia this process was a two-edged sword. The gradual transfer of frontier fortifications and their surrounding territories to Austrian military control eventually resulted in the separation of this region from the authority of the Ban and Sabor – as decreed at the imperial Estates of Bruck an der Mur in 1578. Although this division was described as temporary, it was clear that it would last as long as the danger. The process of fortifying the Croatian frontier was completed that same year with the foundation of a strong fortress at Karlovac, named after its founder, the Austrian Archduke Charles. In 1593 the Ottoman Empire suffered its first great defeat, at the battle of Sisak. The 'Military Frontier' (Vojna Krajina) fulfilled its purpose and prevented further Ottoman incursions into Central Europe. The attempt to have the Military Frontier reunited once again with Croatia became a theme of Croatian history over many centuries.

In the seventeenth century, there was a gradual stabilisation of the frontier after the so-called Long Turkish War. There was also a redefinition of the Croatian political elite, which from this point was led by the Zrinski and Frankopan families. They made marriage alliances with each other and also with Hungarian enemies of the Habsburgs, plotting to break free of rule from Vienna. The leading noble conspirators, Petar Zrinski, Fran Krsto Frankopan and Ferenc Nádasdy, were tried and executed as traitors in 1671. There ensued a period of state terror and absolute rule in Croatia, in the course of which all the estates of the Zrinskis and Frankopans were confiscated and divided among nobles loyal to the court.

TERRITORIAL INTEGRATION

One of the reasons for the conspiracy of 1671 was dissatisfaction among the Croatian leaders at the delay in waging war decisively against the Ottomans. The most powerful Croatian magnates lost their lives and estates because of the conspiracy, and in 1683 the long expected Ottoman raid into south-east Europe began. But the decisive siege of Vienna was turned from potential catastrophe into triumph by Leopold I, whose armies in the next fifteen years of exhausting warfare liberated large parts of Hungary and Croatia. As a member of the allied coalition, Venice also took much of coastal Croatia and the eastern Adriatic hinterland.

In the late seventeenth and early eighteenth centuries, thanks in large part to Prince Eugene of Savoy, Habsburg arms made further progress against the Ottoman Empire at the battles of Senta (1697), Petrovaradin (1716) and Belgrade (1717). This meant reassurance for the security of the previously liberated areas of Croatia between the Sava and Drava. Venice also enlarged its possessions in Dalmatia. These gains were ratified in 1718 by the Treaty of Požarevac (Passarowitz). The wars, though, continued, and with mixed results. In 1739 at Belgrade all the acquisitions made by Austria at Požarevac were lost, with the exception of Banat. Belgrade too fell and the Croatian frontier was withdrawn to the limits formed by the Una and Sava. In 1740, the death of Emperor Charles VI, with no male heirs, opened up new uncertainties.

The Croatian political elite had been supportive of attempts to solve this long expected problem. Two years before the death of Emperor Leopold I in 1703, his sons Joseph and Charles made an agreement about the succession. In case of the extinction of the male line of the dynasty, the agreement envisaged succession through the female line. As in 1527, so in 1712, the Croatian 'political nation', foreseeing the threat posed by the much stronger Hungarian nobility, sought help and protection from the court in Vienna. Rejecting the conclusion reached by the joint Hungarian-Croatian Sabor of 1687 – which affirmed the free choice of a ruler in the event of extinction of the Habsburg dynasty in the male line – the Croatian Sabor, gathered in the court of the bishop of Zagreb, instituted the famous legal provision known as 'Article VII'. This declared Croatia's acceptance of a ruler from the female line to rule over Austria and its provinces of Styria, Cariniola and Carinthia. Thanks to this law there began in 1712 the process of fundamental constitutional changes within the Habsburg monarchy whose final result was recognition of the so-called 'Pragmatic Sanction' of Charles III of 1713. Austria succeeded through a series of agreements in gaining recognition of the new constitution and new rule of succession from numerous European countries. But when on the death of Charles III the moment arrived to activate the Pragmatic Sanction, the European great powers enthusiastically attacked Austria, now under the young Maria Theresa.

In the difficult situation faced by the imperial armies, Croatian officers distinguished themselves – having for generations been accustomed to the daily realities of war on the Ottoman frontier. The best known of them in Croatian history is the adventurer, Baron Franjo Trenk, son of a Prussian officer, who bought numerous estates in liberated Slavonia and recruited his volunteers there. In the course of the War of Austrian Succession, these soldiers distinguished themselves by their brave, albeit brutal, exploits in Silesia, the Czech lands, Bavaria and France, for which Trenk eventually finished up before a court, dying in prison in 1749.

In the spirit of enlightened absolutism, Maria Theresa introduced a series of reforms which fundamentally transformed all aspects of the monarchy. In Croatia, she resolved the complex forty-year-old question of the 'reincorporation' of Slavonia and Srijem, liberated from the Ottoman Empire. She placed this vast area under the joint control of the Court Military Council and the Chamber (Treasury), the former responsible for war and the latter finance. The armies that at the end of the seventeenth and the beginning of the eighteenth centuries conquered and then abandoned these regions left behind a desert – villages destroyed, towns lost in the flames, almost the whole population dispersed or killed, with the few that remained hiding in forests. The infrastructure was completely destroyed, the essentials for life reduced to a minimum.

Moreover, the question of sovereignty was still open. In historical and legal terms, Slavonia was part of the 'triune' Croatian Kingdom. The Croatian Estates, therefore, right from the start demanded the return of these areas to their own authority, while the Hungarians, on the other hand, pressed for their incorporation into the Hungarian constitutional framework. But the army was not ready to give up the resources of Slavonia and Srijem, nor was the Chamber, which shared control over the newly liberated areas and divided up the estates between deserving families: that is, those who had financed the anti-Ottoman wars.

As she had promised at her coronation as queen of Hungary-Croatia four years earlier, Maria Theresa in 1745 renewed Croatian civil authority over three Slavonian counties (županije). The territory along the Sava towards the Ottoman Empire, however, remained under military authority as part of the huge cordon which from that time ran from the Adriatic to Transylvania. The Military Frontier constituted an entirely militarised territory organised in three 'generalships' with a total of twelve 'colonelships', which carried on the whole civil and military administration.

This military region became a powerful instrument of imperial-royal authority and a guarantee of external security. From it in the century and a half that followed were recruited the monarchy's most loyal and able officers. The Military Frontier confirmed its importance during the renewed struggle with Frederick the Great of Prussia in the Seven Years War (1756–63) in which Croatian troops played an outstanding role. Careers in the army offered scores of Croatian peasant families the means to rise in society.

After thirty years of service as officers and at least three military campaigns, a first generation of Croats under Maria Theresa was raised to the status of nobility, and in the second and third generations, as well-known barons of the Military Frontier, they occupied the most important positions in the imperial-royal army.

In 1780, forty years after coming to the Habsburg throne, Maria Theresa died and was succeeded by her son Joseph II. He tried to create a Germanised and centralised state with an effective bureaucratic apparatus and army and obedient subjects, sweeping away a host of ancient rules and traditions. The last years of his reign witnessed increasing discontent. He was succeeded by his younger brother, Leopold II. Faced with the dangers of revolution in France, he tried to bring stability to his domains and to smooth over relations with Hungary and Croatia, whose autonomy he recognised. Meanwhile, the Croats themselves engaged in a struggle against Magyarisation. On his early death in 1792, Leopold was succeeded by his son Francis, who in fear of Napoleon proclaimed the Austrian Empire in 1804 and finally abolished the old Holy Roman Empire two years later. Throughout these changes the Croatian – like the Hungarian – nobility held fast to their own royal tradition. So the new Austrian emperor was for the Croats simply their king.

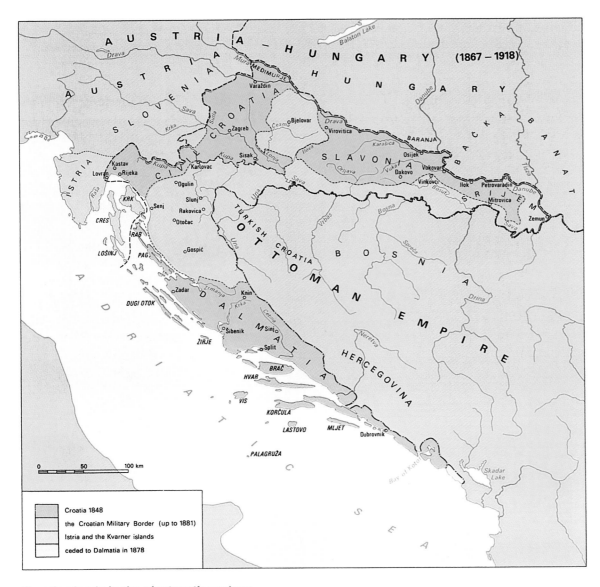

Croatian lands in the nineteenth century
Venice fell in 1797 and for a short while Austria ruled Dalmatia. In 1808 Napoleon abolished the Dubrovnik Republic, and it joined what had been Austrian territory as part of the French Illyrian Provinces. After Napoleon's defeat, Dalmatia was awarded once more to Austria, which it ruled until 1918. In the eighteenth century, the Military Frontier was formally established by the Austrians, and its lands were not reunited to the rest of Croatia until 1881. During that period, both the Croatian and Slavonian elements of the kingdom were divided into military and civil administration.

NATIONAL INTEGRATION
The period of Romanticism in Croatia lay between two great revolutionary European movements, beginning with the French Revolution of 1789 and ending with that of 1848 – itself a watershed in Croatian history. The core of the Croatian national idea in the nineteenth century was the territorial integration not only of the historic Croatian Kingdom of Dalmatia, Croatia and Slavonia, but also of Bosnia and Hercegovina, where a large Catholic Croat population lived under Turkish rule, and parts of the Austrian lands west of Croatia, which had a majority Slovene population. These lands

were divided, under different jurisdictions, and lacked a single national policy. Consequently, an important role in the ideology of national integration was played by the building up of a standardised Croatian language based on the most widespread of the three dialects.

The centre of the national movement was Zagreb, from where numerous political, cultural and economic initiatives were launched in all the ethnically Croatian lands. The ideologues of Illyrianism, at their head Count Janko Drašković and Ljudevit Gaj, saw the ancient Illyrians as the ancestors of the Croats. In fact, based on the old ideas of Pavao Ritter Vitezović at the end of the seventeenth century, until the 1860s this initially 'Illyrian' and later 'national' (*narodni*) Croatian movement created the programme for Croatian unification and also for the unification of the other southern Slavs. In its later phase, after the failure of the wider Illyrianist idea, through the activities of political parties the movement became directed towards specifically Croatian national goals.

The Hungarians, with whom the Croats had lived since 1102 in a unified state, did not welcome this turn of events. Discontent smouldered and national and social tensions built up under state repression until the crisis of March 1848. The disorders began in Vienna not far from the Imperial Palace and in a short while spread to almost all parts of the monarchy. For the Hungarians, the 1848 Revolution was a revolt against the Viennese court; for the Croats it was a revolt against the chauvinism of the Hungarian government. A natural alliance between Vienna and Zagreb had been created on the territory of the Croatian Military Frontier, where thousands of armed Croats were under the direct command of Vienna. At this moment of crisis, their military commander, Josip Jelačić, was appointed Croatian Ban, commander of the whole Military Frontier and later governor of Dalmatia. After the summoning of the first citizens' Sabor and the abolition of serfdom, Ban Jelačić summoned the Croatian army in September 1848 and crossed the Croatian-Hungarian border on the Drava. His march to Budapest and support for the court of Vienna were decisive for the outcome of the struggle. Military operation lasted a year, and the Hungarian revolt was then extinguished with Russian assistance.

Although nowadays many people take an unfavourable view of Jelačić's reaction to the revolutionary movements of 1848, his war against the Hungarians was a war for Croatia's own existence, and because of Hungarian ambitions the preservation of Croatia's autonomy was only possible in alliance with the Viennese court. Amid the constellation of national contradictions in the Danube basin, the survival of the monarchy meant the survival of Croatia, which was threatened by the growing nationalism of the Hungarian people, who were much more numerous than the Croats. So Jelačić stands out as one of the central figures of Croatian history.

The years that followed did not, however, see the fulfilment of the promises which the

Croatia in the Yugoslav state in 1918
After the fall of Austria-Hungary in 1918, the South Slav lands of the monarchy (Croatia and Dalmatia, Bosnia and Hercegovina, and the Slovene regions of Cariniola with southern Styria and part of Carinthia) joined with the Kingdoms of Serbia and Montenegro in a South Slav union under the name of the Kingdom of the Serbs, Croats and Slovenes (later the Kingdom of Yugoslavia). Italy obtained the largest share of Istria, the islands of Cres and Lošinj, Lastovo and Palagruža and the city of Zadar. Rijeka became an independent (Italian) state. From Hungary the new South Slav state received the historic Croatian region of Međimurje, part of Baranja and Vojvodina.

court had given. Under the leadership of the young, militant and duplicitous Emperor Franz Josef I – who had come to the throne at the age of eighteen – the court introduced a new absolutism, in deadly fear of a reawakening of Hungarian nationalism. But it was also a period of preparation for the great process of modernisation which gained momentum after the solution of the fundamental constitutional problem of the monarchy in 1867. After Austria lost its war for Venice and Lombardy at the end of the 1850s, and was defeated in its war with Prussia in 1866, the court turned to resolving its own problems and was forced into a final compromise with the Hungarians. By the Austro-Hungarian Agreement (Nagodba) of 1867, Austria-Hungary was created as a dual state, with Croatia representing the unique exception to this dualism. The following year the Croats concluded their own agreement with Hungary, the so-called Croatian-Hungarian Nagodba, which affirmed the special status in public law of Croatia and a certain degree of administrative and financial autonomy within the vast Habsburg dominions.

But Croatia had not yet achieved its territorial integrity. The Dalmatian region remained a separate realm, with Austrian law and the Italian language, and belonging to the Austrian part of the monarchy. The reason for this lay in the fact that the dualistic principle, which underpinned the new state, depended on a delicate political and economic balance between the two entities. It was the same story after the Austro-Hungarian army occupied Bosnia and Hercegovina – to be administered jointly by the Austrian and Hungarian political elites. The country was modernised, particularly its infrastructure, and numerous reforms were undertaken in the educational system and in ecclesiastical matters. But the Austrian and Hungarian presence in Bosnia was primarily of strategic and economic significance.

After resolving its constitutional issues in 1867 and 1868, Croatia could turn to sorting out its enormous social problems. Ban Ivan Mažuranić, who had previously been Croatian chancellor at the court in Vienna, became Croatia's first governor drawn from a non-noble, citizen family. His administration was distinguished by important economic and social reforms. After the occupation of Bosnia and Hercegovina, the huge region constituted by the Military Frontier became superfluous and it was administratively joined to Croatia. This was a very important victory for Croatian policy with a far-reaching impact on the future economic development and national integration of the Croatian lands. The process was twofold: on one side, the Catholic population integrated with the Croats and, on the other, the Orthodox (who in some areas of the Military Frontier constituted a majority) integrated with the Serbs. It was not long before there arose the first national conflicts, encouraged by the third – that is, the Hungarian – side in the arrangement.

With the installation of Ban Dragutin Khuen-Héderváry, whose term would last two full decades (1883–1903), Hungary found the best exponent of its interests and a loyal executor of its policy in Croatia. Khuen cleverly manipulated politics, sowing disharmony between the Croatian political parties and the elite and encouraging a hatred by the Croats of the Serbs whom he favoured, as a minority, against the majority Croats. When Croatian students, on the occasion of a visit to Zagreb by Franz Josef I in 1895, burnt the Hungarian flag in protest against the regime of Ban Khuen, many were expelled from Croatian universities. Some of them, like Stjepan Radić, continued their studies in Prague, where they encountered the Pan-Slav and liberal ideas of Tomáš G. Masaryk and brought them back to Croatia. Finally, in 1903 discontent with Ban Khuen-Héderváry reached such a level that he had to leave Zagreb, never to return, becoming minister-president of Hungary.

From then on, Croatian political life rapidly modernised. The opposition parties managed to articulate a common national programme, and the Croats and Serbs formed a joint coalition. The period saw the rise of the brothers Antun and Stjepan Radić, the future national tribune, whose political ideology was based on the peasants' movement, involving the mass inclusion of the peasant majority into public life.

In 1903 there was a coup in Serbia and the Karadjordjević dynasty came to the throne. Serbia proceeded to extend its territories during the bloody Balkan Wars of 1912 and 1913 to include former Ottoman possessions of Macedonia and Kosovo. Finally, after the killing of the Austro-Hungarian heir to the throne, Franz Ferdinand, in Sarajevo in 1914, Austria-Hungary declared war on Serbia. The system of European security, based in large part on the old balance of power, collapsed overnight and thrust Europe into the First World War.

TWENTIETH-CENTURY CROATIA: INDEPENDENCE LOST AND REGAINED

Although Croatian lands were not directly caught up in military action during the First World War, Croatian units sustained heavy losses on many battlefields, especially in Eastern Europe and in the Italian campaign. Nothing, though, could prevent the collapse of the dual monarchy in the autumn of 1918, as the German and non-German peoples of the empire began one after the other to abandon the Habsburgs. At its session of 29 October 1918, the Croatian Sabor decided to break all constitutional relations with Austria and the Hungarian kingdom and to transfer authority to the National Council of Slovenes, Croats and Serbs. With the way open for a breakthrough by Italian troops on the east Adriatic coast, and as Serbian forces pressed ahead to the west, the state of the Slovenes, Croats and Serbs was created in the south-eastern region of Austria-Hungary. Lacking both international support and military strength, on 1 December 1918 this state united with the Kingdom of Serbia (which had previously more or less annexed Montenegro) to become the Kingdom of the Serbs, Croats and Slovenes under the Serbian royal house.

For Croats this was the beginning of a long period of

Serbian domination that would result in intense inter-ethnic struggles throughout the whole of the twentieth century. Croatia legitimately expected that the joint South Slav state should be based on equal rights for its constituent peoples, while Serbia under the leadership of its adroit Prime Minister Nikola Pašić understood the Kingdom of the Serbs, Croats and Slovenes exclusively as the creation of a Greater Serbia to advance the economic interests of the Serbian elite. Greater Serbia was not a romantic patriotic dream but rather a very concrete political programme, which was sketched out in the first half of the nineteenth century and whose ideology was based on simplified linguistic and ethnic theories about Serb superiority. At the same time, the Croats founded their national programme of unification of the South Slavs on the very different concept of Illyrianism. From this, in the second half of the nineteenth century, was born the Yugoslav idea, also known as cultural Yugoslavism. So it was that the influential Croatian Bishop Josip Juraj Strossmayer in 1866 founded the Yugoslav Academy of Arts and Sciences (Jugoslavenska Akademija Znanosti i Umjetnosti), which was conceived as the central learned institution of all the South Slav peoples, including the Bulgarians.

The first years of the new joint state were marked by bitter political disputes about its organisation. Serbian policy was to press its unitary and centralised features, and this found many supporters among the Serbs of Bosnia and Hercegovina and Croatia. But it also found numerous opponents in Croatia, which still enjoyed a certain kind of independence and broad autonomy. Finally, at the so-called Constituent Assembly (Ustavotvorna Skupština) the unitarist majority prevailed. The Croatian people faced an increasingly difficult situation, the royal Yugoslav regime placed its opponents under great pressure, and mutual national intolerance increased. It reached its peak in 1928 with an unprecedented attack in parliament, when the Serb MP, Puniša Račić, shot the Croatian leaders. Pavle Radić and Djuro Basariček died on the spot, while the opposition leader Stjepan Radić died soon afterwards in Zagreb. The world press expressed its shock at the assassinations.

There followed the period known as the 'dictatorship of King Alexander', at the start of which the Kingdom of Serbs, Croats and Slovenes was renamed Yugoslavia. The regime in Belgrade became ever more savage in its persecution of Croatian political dissidents; in 1931 the Croatian historian and politician Milan Šufflaj was killed. Albert Einstein and Heinrich Mann launched public protests. The Croats themselves turned bitterly against any future existence within Yugoslavia, and in 1934 an assassin killed King Alexander in Marseilles.

Political conditions became still worse, for in Italy, and supported by the Italian fascists, there gathered around Ante Pavelić an aggressive expatriate movement called the Ustaša (literally, 'insurgent'). With the fall of Yugoslavia in April 1941, the Nazi regime installed them in power as the government of the newly proclaimed Independent State of Croatia (NDH – Nezavisna Država Hrvatska), which included today's Croatia and Bosnia-Hercegovina. On the orders of Berlin, racial laws were introduced, the Jewish population was almost completely destroyed, and both Serbs and Roma suffered huge losses. The Ustaša's reign of terror permitted no internal opposition, and from 1941 in Croatia, and later in other parts of Yugoslavia, there formed a strong partisan movement under the leadership of Josip Broz Tito. Until the end of the war a hard communist core dominated the anti-fascist movement with Tito at its head.

In 1945, Yugoslavia found itself under the control of Tito's regime, which strengthened the country economically and militarily. Its totalitarian ideology also successfully suppressed national problems for thirty-five years, sweetened by federalism in the form of six republics and two autonomous regions. Despite the Yugoslav communist system's successful shifting between East and West during the Cold War, periodic economic crises and the constant Serb urge for dominance led towards its fall. After Tito's death, problems in the system and the unresolved national questions, alongside the rise of Serbian nationalism under Slobodan Milošević, resulted in the bloody collapse of the state.

Under its first democratically elected president, Franjo Tudjman, Croatia duly seceded from Yugoslavia in the summer of 1991. But the prospects of the new state were immediately threatened. There were revolts by most of the country's ethnically Serb population, covertly armed and then openly supported by the Yugoslav People's Army (JNA) controlled from Belgrade. The international community, still hoping to keep the old Yugoslavia together, was reluctant to assist. Even after international recognition came in 1992, much of the country was under enemy military occupation. It remained so until 1995. The successful military and police operations of that year saw Croatia recover its territory, as well as helping to end the genocidal warfare in Bosnia. Since then, Croatia has been engaged in restoring the heavy damage done to the country's infrastructure and in the equally difficult process of transition to a developed market economy and fully law-based state. The country's progress is recognised as crucial for the stability of south-east Europe as a whole, not least by the European Union, which Croatia is now an early candidate to join.

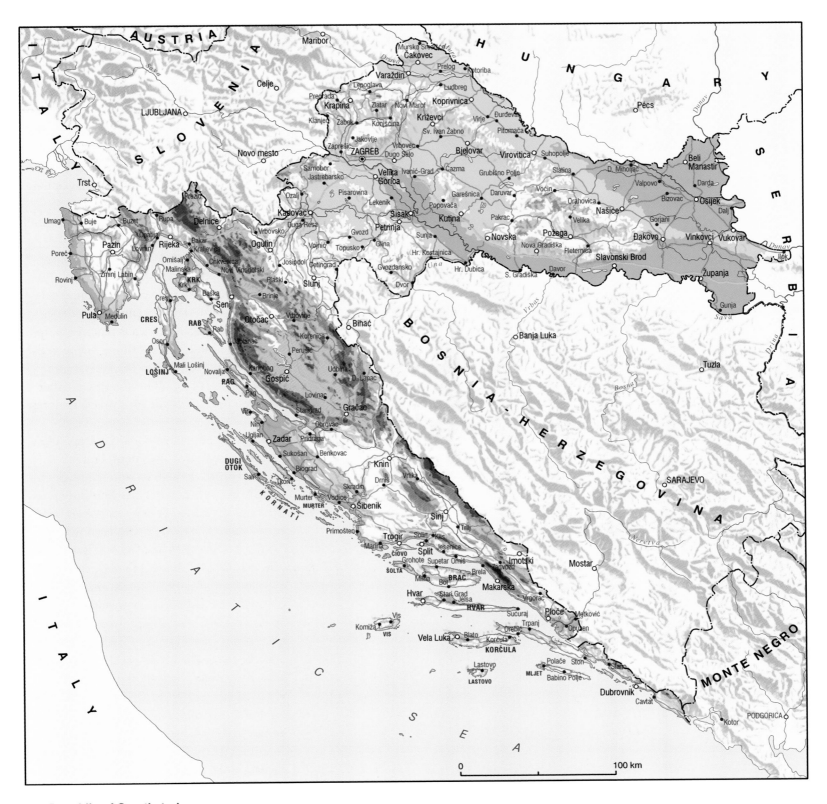

The Republic of Croatia today

Croatia today comprises the territory attributed to it after the Second World War as a member of federal Yugoslavia. That new Croatia was extended to the west to include almost the whole of Istria, and it retained the whole eastern shore of the Adriatic (down to Boka Kotorska) with all the east Adriatic islands. To the east, Croatia lost Boka Kotorska (today in Montenegro) and eastern Srijem (today in Serbia), while to the north it retained Međimurje and a part of Baranja. It is administratively divided into twenty counties and the region of Zagreb.

Maps reproduced by permission of The Miroslav Krleža Lexicographical Institute. Maps on pp11, 12, 15 and 16 are from *A Concise Atlas of the Republic of Croatia* (Zagreb 1993). All were kindly scanned by Mladen Klemenčić.

ANCIENT GREEKS IN CROATIA

Branko Kirigin

Edited by Michael Vickers

The Croatian coast and its islands attracted the attention of Greeks in antiquity. Although there is evidence of Greek presence all along the Adriatic coast, actual settlements only exist on the Albanian coast, the central Dalmatian islands and in the coastal parts around Split. Elsewhere in Croatia, Greek finds are sporadic but indicative of trade or exchange with native communities. In the hinterland Greek finds are rare or non-existent, which is in contrast with Italy across the Adriatic and Albania to the south-east, where Greek finds are abundant not only on the coast but also in the hinterland. This is mainly because the eastern Adriatic coast did not have much to offer the Greeks, since what is in effect a shield of rugged mountains comes straight down to the sea, providing little in the way of fertile land or other natural resources.

The island of Brač in central Dalmatia has produced evidence of contact with Greece as early as the twelfth century BC (the equivalent of the late Mycenaean period): this evidence includes amphora fragments from Škrip, a native hill fort, but an unusual one with unique fortification walls that are similar to, but much smaller than, those of Smyrna; there is also a tholos type tomb (a tomb with a central chamber) at the Monkodonja site in Istria that has been interpreted as reflecting Mycenaean influence.

Several more centuries passed, however, before the Hellenes (as the Greeks called themselves) discovered the Adriatic and its potential (fig. 2.1). In the meantime, they were more interested in other parts of the Mediterranean and the Black Sea, where some 700 colonies were founded. Coming into an unknown sea, they gave some sites a veneer of security by building them into their existing framework of myth and legend. Aeschylus refers to the Adriatic in his play *Prometheus Bound* as the Bay of Rhea, the wife of Cronus, father of Zeus. The Argonauts are said to have sailed along the Croatian coast in the verses of Apollonius of Rhodes, who wrote in the third century BC. Cadmus and Harmonia, the legendary Theban heroic couple, emigrated in their old age to dwell among the Illyrian tribe of the Enchelei, who lived in the area around modern Montenegro. The Trojan hero Antenor had connections with the Croatian island of Korčula, and Diomedes, who was perhaps the best-known hero of the Trojan War after Odysseus, was worshipped on the island of Palagruža on Cape Ploča, and on several sites on the Italian Adriatic coast. The only material evidence of any of these traditions found to date has been in the shrines of Diomedes on Palagruža and at Cape Ploča (see below).

2.1 Map of the Adriatic representing Greek colonisation movement and native populations by Branko Kirigin and Viktor Popović.

Nevertheless, such stories and finds of Greek artefacts in the Adriatic combine to confirm the existence of links between native communities and Greek traders and colonists. They bear witness to a new drive towards urbanisation and social development that was not always easy or harmonious. Between the sixth and early fourth centuries BC (the archaic and classical periods), Greek finds are concentrated mostly on the Italian side of the Adriatic. In fact, it is safe to say that 99 per cent of the more than 4,000 Greek figured vases found on the shores of the Adriatic have been found in Italy – and most of them in the northern Adriatic where the towns of Adria (which gave the name to the sea: from the Greek *aitria*, meaning 'clear, bright') and Spina flourished thanks to trade in such commodities as grain, amber, metals, marble, polychrome glass, slaves and the known Venetian horses.

PALAGRUŽA –
THE ISLAND OF DIOMEDES

In those days sailing the Adriatic required great nautical skills since weather conditions, as nowhere else in the Mediterranean, are hard to predict. Tiny Palagruža at the heart of the Adriatic was a crucial point of orientation for sailors. It lay almost halfway between Corfu (ancient Kerkyra) and Adria and Spina, and halfway between Monte Gargano and the islands of Sušac, Lastovo and Vis. The Athenians were primarily interested in grain from the north Adriatic area, and during the summer many of their cargo ships sailed the Adriatic. This activity is attested to by the existence of fragmentary dedications to Diomedes incised on fine Attic pottery that explicitly mention Greek sailors. One refers to a certain 'Aristokrates', and another only recently found on Palagruža reads 'Soleios anatheke'. This is the only completely preserved graffito from Palagruža, and means 'Soleios dedicated [this]'. Even more interesting is that the same name occurs on a pot of the same date found in Adria way to the north. This is strong evidence of the reconstruction of the Adriatic sea route, and that Greek mariners were engaged in this trade.

More than a hundred such dedications have been found on Palagruža, but most are extremely fragmentary and thus difficult to reconstruct (fig. 2.2). Unfortunately, no architectural remains of the original shrines of Diomedes survive on account of later building and land erosion. It stood sixty metres above sea level, from where one can observe both sides of the Adriatic mainland and islands and see what kind of weather is coming. Only the numerous imported artefacts, which now number more than 12,000, bear witness to the cult activity that lasted from the late sixth century BC to the first or second centuries AD, at first on Palagruža and then from the mid-fourth century BC on Cape Ploča – 'Promonturium Diomedes' as it was called by Pliny the Elder. Pottery was not the only form of dedication. Coins of various cities of the Mediterranean were found, together with gems, finger rings, dice, fibulae, pins, bronze needles for weaving nets, fragments of terracotta figurines and lamps, but few amphorae or cooking pots, which suggests that offerings of wine were made with drinking cups (such as *kylikes*, *skyphoi*), wine-mixing bowls (craters) and jugs (*oinochoai*).

The fragments of figured vases from Palagruža are closely connected with those found at Spina and Adria: pots by the same hands have been found on all three sites (fig. 2.3). This open sea

2.2 Fragment of an Attic kylix with the name of Diomedes, fifth century BC. Photo: B. Kirigin.

2.3 Fragment of an Attic hydria with a Greek god, Semele painter, late classical period. Photo: B. Kirigin.

trade route probably led to the first contacts of Greeks with the native communities on the islands of Croatia. These natives probably instructed the Greeks on how to sail their waters; it is not at all an easy task to navigate among 1,000 islands large and small, not to mention rocks, reefs and shallow canals.

'BLACK CORCYRA' –
THE ISLAND OF KORČULA

Melaina Kerkyra was the name given to the Greek colony said to have been founded in the sixth century BC by colonists from Knidos in Asia Minor on the island of Korčula. The story has come down to us in the works of later Greek and Roman writers (Skymnos, Strabo and Pliny), who record that the Knidians, in support of Kerkyra proper (Corfu) against Periander of Corinth, established a colony in the Adriatic on an island which they named Melaina Kerkyra or 'Black Corcyra' in honour of their ally Kerkyra. The victorious Periander after defeating the Kerkyraians had captured 300 noble youths with a view to presenting them to Alyattes, the Lydian king, for castration. But the Knidians rescued the boys on the island of Samos and returned them to Kerkyra. In return, the Kerkyraians enabled the Knidians to settle at Korčula. Recent systematic archaeological field surveys on Korčula, however, have failed to find any traces of this polis. It could be that that the ancient authors were simply recording a legend rather than a real situation. What the survey did show is that Korčula was well dotted with Bronze and Iron Age hill forts that controlled the fertile zones on the island and that the natives had trade contacts with the Greeks from the sixth century BC onwards. The most important hill fort on Korčula appears to be the one on the site of Kopila in the interior of the island near the village of Blato. Significant imported finds of Corinthian pottery and an extraordinary multicoloured glass fragment (fig. 2.4) were recorded there earlier, but it is only recently that systematic excavations have begun. The Issaeans from the island of Vis did found a settlement on Korčula on the site of Lumbarda in the third century BC (see below).

WHERE IS HERAKLEIA?

Herakleia is one of the most frequent names given to new colonies that the Greeks founded in the Mediterranean and the Black Sea. Heracles was very popular among the Greeks. He symbolises the strength and perseverance which the new colonists really needed

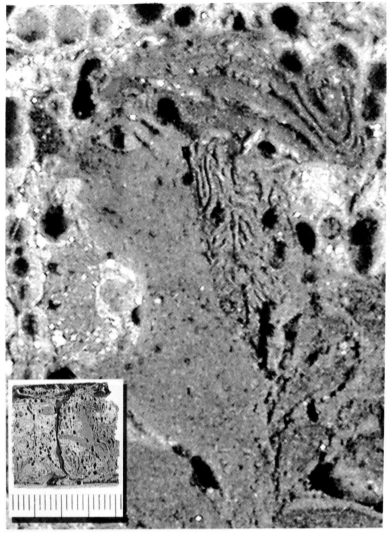

2.4 Multicoloured glass with a representation of a female figure in profile, archaic period. Photo: Dino Cetinić.

THE ISLAND OF HVAR/PHAROS

It seems that the Greek philosopher and poet Xenophanes, who lived at the turn of the sixth and fifth centuries BC, visited the island of Hvar where he saw fossils of fish. Xenophanes, who lived to be over 90, travelled for most of his life. He observed shells and fossilised fish on land, and concluded that the sea must once have covered the earth. Fossilised fish are indeed found on Hvar, in the area where a Greek colony was later founded. Greek archaic painted pottery has also been found at this site, suggesting that some sort of settlement existed and that Xenophanes did not come to a 'No Man's Land'.

An outstanding question is where the colony of Anchiale might have stood. Anchiale is only mentioned by Stephanus of Byzantium, the Greek geographer and grammarian who lived in the sixth century AD and who wrote an extensive lexicon of geographical names under the title *Ethnike*. Under the entry for Anchiale he says: 'Anchiale, a coastal town of Cilicia … There is also another town in Illyria, a settlement of the Parians, next to it is a bay called Enestedon in which is Scheria.' Scholars often quote this as evidence for an earlier Parian colonisation of the island of Hvar. They claim that the 'Bay of Enestedon' is a misspelled 'Bay of Nestoi', the Nestoi being an Illyrian tribe that lived on the mainland opposite the island of Hvar, and consequently that Anchiale should be on Hvar. It is much more likely, however, that the Parian colony of Anchiale lay further south, since the mythical Scheria is often identified with the island of Corfu.

An extensive field survey on the island of Hvar has registered more than 600 archaeological sites, or roughly four sites per square kilometre. Most of these are Bronze and Iron Age, which clearly shows that the island was densely inhabited by the native population. The most important native site was a settlement situated at the modern town of Hvar. Its position on the main east

when founding a settlement. The Adriatic Herakleia is only mentioned in one ancient source, namely Pseudo-Skylax of the mid-fourth century BC, who does not, however, clearly state where Herakleia actually is. Some scholars claim that it stood near the island of Corfu and others that it lay somewhere in Dalmatia. Rogoznica near Šibenik, and the islands of Brač, Hvar and Korčula have all been suggested at different times. Remarkably, bronze coins bearing the name of Herakleia were struck at the same time as coins of Pharos, the Greek colony on the island of Hvar. These coins depict, on one side, the head of Heracles wearing his lion skin and, on the other, his symbols, a bow and a club, as well as the Greek inscription ΗΡΑΚΛ, an abbreviation of 'Herakleia'. Most of the 200 known coins of Herakleia (fig. 2.5) were found at Stari Grad on the island of Hvar, where the colony of Pharos stood. A few have been found at Nin (the ancient Aenona) and on the island of Murter (ancient Colentium), both important sites of the Liburnians, who lived in north Dalmatia. Others have been found at Solin (ancient Salona) and on the islands of Brač, Korčula and Vis. The coins suggest that the town was short-lived, but we still do not know where Adriatic Herakleia originally stood.

2.5 Front and back sides of a bronze coin of Herakleia, fourth century BC. Photo: Tonći Seser.

2.6 A silver coin from Pharos representing Zeus on one side and a goat on the other with the letters ΦΑΡΙ, an abbreviation of ΦΑΡΙΩΝ, meaning a coin of the citizens of Pharos, fourth century BC. Photo: Tonći Seser.

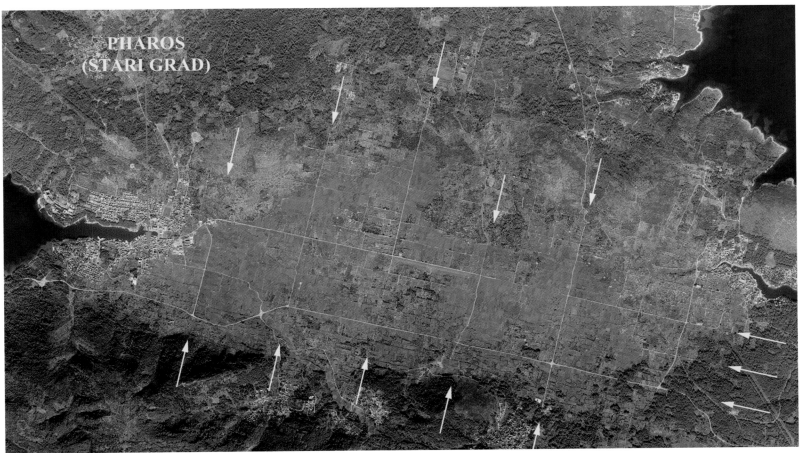

PHAROS (STARI GRAD)

2.7 Aerial view of the Stari Grad plain (north-central part of the island of Hvar) with remains of the regular Greek land division system (rectangles of 906 x 181 metres). Photo: courtesy INFOKARTA – Split.

Adriatic route, its good harbour, a good supply of water and plenty of arable land, were crucial for its development. Judging by finds made there, the site was pre-eminent among similar sites on the island, and imported luxury goods were arriving here before the Greeks ever showed an interest in the Adriatic. It was presumably the native community of the ancient town of Hvar who negotiated with the Parians to settle on the island.

In 385–4 BC, after the 99th Olympiad, a thousand inhabitants from the rich Cycladic island of Paros in the centre of the Aegean

2.8 The Greek watchtower at Tor. Photo: Pawel Jaroszweski.

founded Pharos (ΦΑΡΟΣ) on the north side of the island of Hvar, on the site of modern Stari Grad ('Old Town') on the edge of the largest fertile plain on any Adriatic island. The site was recommended by an oracle, most probably that of Apollo at Delphi, with which Paros had close relations. A year after the Parians built walls around their new town, a conflict occurred with the local Illyrians. Ten thousand Illyrians from the island and the nearby mainland attacked Pharos. The Greeks won the battle thanks to the help of the fleet of Dionysius I of Syracuse, the most powerful Greek ruler in the Mediterranean of the day. This was all recorded by the historian Diodorus (who flourished at the turn of the Christian era). We have very little information concerning the later history of Pharos since not much excavation has been carried out within the site of the colony. Nothing can be said about the layout of the town, public or private spaces, streets, temples or the port. We know that Pharos struck coins in silver (fig. 2.6) and bronze during the three centuries of its existence, we know that it had a democratic government, and we know that it had contacts with the other cities, including its mother city, but details remain a mystery.

One of the most remarkable discoveries of the last few decades is that the regular land division of the Stari Grad plain was laid down by the Pharians soon after the conflict with the Illyrians (fig. 2.7). The plan is so well preserved that it is visible even on satellite

2.9 View of bay of Vis with the sites of ancient cities of Issa Martvilo, Gradina and Prirovo. Photo: Boris Čargo.

images. It is the best preserved, if the smallest, Greek land division system of the few that are known, having remained unchanged for more than two millennia. This massive engineering achievement of the ancient Greeks has recently been listed as a UNESCO monument of landscape architecture. It used to be thought that the land division was of Roman origin, but careful inspection has shown that it is Greek. The basic foot measure employed was 30.21 centimetres, and the basic land unit that each colonist received was a rectangle of 906 x 181 metres (5 x 1 stadia), or a plot of 16.4 hectares. Between the fields were public roads that led to Pharos. The plain and territory of Pharos – the *chora* – was protected from Illyrian raids by watchtowers at Malinovik and Tor (fig. 2.8). Grain was the main subsistence crop of ancient Greeks, and it has been estimated that Pharos could produce a surplus of between 300 and 977 tons, from which they might earn between 7 and 26 talents, or the equivalent of up to half a million euros. But the Pharians must also have produced olive oil, wine and vegetables in quantities that could guarantee them a safe existence in years that were not so productive.

It is scarcely surprising, therefore, to find that Pharos had trading relations with other centres. Pharian amphoras and coins of the third and second centuries BC were found at the hill fort at Ošanići in east Hercegovina, the capital seat of the Illyrian tribe of the Daorsoi. What the amphoras contained is uncertain, but they provide physical evidence of trading contacts. Other Illyrian centres – even those on Hvar itself – so far lack any such evidence.

Pharos and its *chora* occupied only one-eighth of the total territory of the island. The conflicts that began at the start of the colony seem to have prevented further interaction between two rather different cultures.

Demetrius of Pharos is the only inhabitant of Pharos mentioned in ancient literary sources. He played an important role in the course of the two Illyrian Wars which ended in Roman victories in 229 and 219 BC. Demetrius was at first an ally of Agron, the Illyrian king who controlled the territory from Kerkyra to Pharos. After Agron died, Demetrius joined Teuta, Agron's wife. In 230 BC she appointed him the governor of Kerkyra after successful attacks plundering Epirus and the Peloponnese. The Illyrians, being in possession of Kerkyra, blocked the Straits of Otranto, causing Rome to cross the Adriatic for the first time and attack Kerkyra. Demetrius surrendered to the Romans, turning his back on Teuta who lost almost all her territory, and Demetrius was appointed by Rome to govern the area. Ten years later Demetrius was plundering the region, and even attempted to raid the Cyclades. Rome was forced to stop him and began the Second Illyrian War. Demetrius was at Pharos with 6,000 soldiers, but was attacked by Aemilius Paulus, the Roman consul, who defeated him and razed the city to the ground. Demetrius meanwhile fled to Philip V, the Macedonian king, encouraging him to make an alliance with Hannibal and to fight against the Romans. Demetrius later died in an unsuccessful attack on Messenia in the Peloponnese in 214 BC.

Archaeologists have not found any traces of the Roman destruction of Pharos. Both the archaeological evidence and the ancient literary sources attest to Pharos's existence as an independent town under the protection of Rome well into the mid-first century BC, when it was incorporated into the Roman province of Dalmatia.

Two fragments of a public inscription – a *psephisma* – make it clear that after the destruction of Pharos by the Roman army in 219 BC, the Pharians sent a delegation to their mother city Paros to seek help to rebuild the town. They were well received by the assembly of Paros, and a certain Praxiepis was sent to help them in rebuilding their town.

More than half of this inscription is unfortunately missing, but the preserved parts

2.10 South Italian red figured hidira with a farewell funeral scene, mid-fourth century BC. Photo: Boris Čargo.

2.11 Clay lamp with representations of Issis and Serapis with a cornucopia, snake and a bowl, second century BC. Photo: Živko Bačić.

reveal an amazing knowledge of Greek language, style, diplomatic, legal and social regulations and formulas, indicating that the community of Pharians, after the misfortunes under Demetrius, who had finally deserted them, preserved and maintained a highly civilised way of life in this remote part of the Greek world, surrounded by less than friendly neighbours.

The details of the last days of Pharos as an independent Greek city are uncertain, but at some time towards the end of the first century BC, in the period of Augustus, a large Roman villa was built over the Greek remains. Until new excavations are undertaken, we will not know when Greek Pharos became Roman Pharia.

ISSA – THE ISLAND OF VIS

It is a rather different story with the Dorian (Syracusan) colony of Issa on the neighbouring smaller island of Vis that was founded, according to the archaeological evidence, a few decades after Pharos. The Syracusans assisted the Parians to found Pharos, and it seems likely that they founded a settlement on Vis after that.

Similar to Korčula and Hvar, Issa also had a strong native community in the Iron Age. Of five hill fort settlements, the most important and largest was at Talež in the south-eastern part of the island overlooking the expanse that includes Palagruža, Lastovo, Sušac, Korčula and Hvar. Talež is interesting not simply because it is associated with imported painted pottery (Greek and south Italian), but also because this hill fort is very close to the largest barrow on the island – Vela Gomila ('Great Mound') – where there were large numbers of surface finds of local and imported sherds of all periods between the Bronze Age and early Roman.

Judging by the pottery finds, Talež seems to have been abandoned when the Greek urban settlement was founded on the north side of the island at the end of the largest and safest natural bay on any of the central Dalmatian islands (fig. 2.9). It would appear that the settlement at Talež controlled the whole of the island of Vis during the fifth century BC, and it seems to be a key site for our understanding of precolonial Greek contacts in the central Adriatic, for it flourished at the same time as the ascendancy of Adria and Spina to the north.

The Vela Gomila barrow seems to have been a special cult

centre for Vis throughout late prehistory and into the Greek and early Roman periods. It continued to function even when the settlement at Talež was abandoned. Further research will show whether Talež and Vela Gomila could have anything to do with Ionios, a native of Issa, who ruled in this area and is considered to have given his name to the Ionian Sea.

Several ancient literary sources mention Ionios as a native of Issa. Strabo, for example, quotes the eminent fourth-century BC historian Theopompus as saying that the Ionian Sea is named after 'Ionios, a native of Issa who once ruled over the region'. The name of Ionios appears on early issues of bronze coins from Issa. One side of the coin bears an image of a male head in profile inscribed 'IONIO', while the other side shows a dolphin. These coins are dated to the beginning of the second half of the fourth century BC. Some numismatists connected the literary sources and the coins, and proposed that Ionios on the coins was a real historical figure, a local dynast who took power after the fall of Dionysios the Elder of Syracuse. Others disagree and take IONIO (no coin has IONIOS) to be not the name of a contemporary ruler, but that of a mythical person employed by the Issaeans to mark their sphere of interest (the central Dalmatian islands and the nearby coast). Some Ionio coins were overstruck by the mint of Pharos (with the head of Zeus, and a goat and the inscription 'ΦΑΡΙ[ΩΝ]') (See fig. 2.6).

Ionio is also mentioned on a badly preserved Greek inscription from Issa where we can read that Vis was called the island of Ionios, rather as Kerkyra was called the island of Alkinoos. This suggests that Ionios was worshipped on the island of Vis as a local hero and that his burial mound might be at Vela Gomila. Many Greek poleis, whether in Greece proper or overseas, connected their origins with mythical heroes or protectors, and they could be local or derived from Greek mythology.

The polis of Issa was erected on the west side of the north bay of Vis on the slope of the Gradina hill (see fig. 2.9). In contrast with Pharos, the dimensions of the city are well known since the

2.12 Two terracottas of pomegranate with pigeons, symbols of Aphrodite, third century BC. Photo: B. Čargo.

2.13 (left) Terracotta of Eros and Psyche, third/second century BC. Photo: Živko Bačić.

west, north and east Hellenistic fortification walls are preserved, although they have never been excavated, and nothing is known of the internal arrangements of the city. The city covered an area of some ten hectares, which makes it the largest Greek settlement so far known in Dalmatia. Before the city lies the peninsula of Prirovo, which makes a good shelter for ships. Remains of the port a kilometre long can be seen underwater. Natural water springs occur along the front of the city. Two pottery kilns were unfortunately destroyed by local developers, but the vast amount of pottery waste that was found indicates an intensive production of amphorae, pithoi, tiles, loom weights, and various fine wares.

Most of the archaeological data come from the cemeteries that lie on the south-west site in an area called Martvilo ('Place of Death') and on the north-east side at Vlaška njiva ('Field of the Water Basin'). Rescue excavations at these sites produced more than fifty graves from the period of Issaean independence. Most of the graves are family chamber tombs. In each chamber there are two or more adult skeletons; children were buried separately and with different grave offerings. It appears that the same vase types were offered with every burial in family chamber tombs: typical shapes are the *oinochoe*, *pelike*, *skyphos* (all connected with the consumption of wine), miniature *stamnos*, and the *unguentarium* (for perfume). Other imported offerings occur

sporadically (fig. 2.10), except perhaps for lamps (fig. 2.11), terracottas (figs 2.12–2.13), coins and strigils (body scrapers). The early tombs have vases that were imported from different parts of southern and northern Italy, Sicily and Greece, indicating widespread trade. Later tombs contain local fine-ware pottery with original mixtures of ornaments from Greece and shapes from south Italy (fig. 2.14), but for the most part that is much less elaborate than the earlier grave goods, a common feature in other parts of the Hellenistic world. The burial practice with multiple skeletons in a single chamber (fig. 2.15) has not been observed anywhere else in the Greek world. It is possible that it was derived from local Dalmatian burial customs, of which there is evidence at several sites from the sixth to the fourth centuries BC. The epigraphic evidence of tombstones confirms the situation in the family chamber tombs (fig. 2.16). Of thirty-nine preserved inscriptions, nineteen have more than two names, and in one case there are as many as twelve names on a single tombstone. Apart from pure Greek names, there are Illyrian names as well as names that are characteristic of southern Italy, Thebes or the Peloponnese. Among the grave offerings there are unique and exceptional works of Hellenistic art (figs 2.10–2.17). In fact, the site of Issa is the only Greek colony in Croatia that it is possible to excavate and present to the public.

The main economic base of this island was the production of wine. Grapes, wine-mixing bowls (craters) and drinking cups (*kantharoi*) frequently occur as the designs on the bronze coinage of ancient Issa. There is also strong evidence for the cult of

2.14 (above) Local Issaean wine jug (*oinochoe*), third/second century BC. Photo: Boris Čargo.

2.15 Typical chamber tomb from Issa, fourth/third century BC. Photo: Branko Kirigin.

Dionysus on Issa, many of the Issaeans being named after him, as can be seen from surviving tombstones. The local burial custom involving vases associated with wine also confirm a Dionysian scenario. Important testimony relating to Issa can be found in an ancient literary source. The Alexandrian historian and geographer Agatharchides is reported by Athenaeus as saying that 'in Issa, an island in the Adriatic, wine is made that has been found by comparison to be better than other wines'.

Latest research suggests that during the period of Issa's independence between the fourth and first centuries BC, the island of Vis may have produced some two million litres of wine per year. Amphora fragments have been found everywhere on the island, especially on the fringes of its fertile plains where many farmsteads have been recorded, but also within the area of the ancient city of Issa. The fertile area situated between the mountains is divided into numerous fields that cover an area of some 1,000 hectares. The storage and transport of two million litres of wine would have required around 80,000 amphoras, each one containing 26 litres, and perhaps 120 cargo ships of the day, each one capable of carrying 25 tons. The same types of amphora have been found at many sites on the Adriatic and even in Alexandria, but are extremely rare in the hinterland of central Dalmatia. Wine could be expensive. It has been estimated that two million litres of wine might have earned the Issaeans 93 talents, or more than four times what the Pharians made producing grain. It is not surprising that a remarkable bronze head of Artemis (fig. 2.17), strongly influenced by Praxiteles, was found at Issa. Such magnificent works of art suggests that at Issa there were persons who were aware of current artistic production in Greece and that they could afford to buy such very expensive objects of art: a complete statue might cost some 3,000 drachmas, or enough to buy fifteen slaves.

Survival was a difficult matter in these waters. One of the most touching documents from Issa is the inscribed tombstone of a certain Kallias. It was written in verse in the Ionic dialect in the fourth century BC and reads:

> From this town, that so admires your courage,
> You sailed away,
> You fought against an Illyrian ship
> And were killed,
> Leaving little Harmo an orphan.
> Kallias, you left behind much valour.

ISSAEAN EXPANSION

Cape Ploča is a long, narrow and flat barren rock promontory that divides central and northern Dalmatia, where the Illyrian communities of the Hilloi and Boulinoi lived. Pliny's 'Promonturium Diomedes' was already identified by the historian Ivan Lucić in the seventeenth century to be at Cape Ploča, the only place where the Dalmatian coast faces the open sea (fig. 2.18). Strangely, it was not until our excavations of 1996–8 that the site attracted the attention of archaeologists.

2.16 Tombstone of Teimasion Dionisius' family from Issa, second/first century BC. Photo: Živko Bačić.

2.17 Bronze head of Artemis from Issa, fourth century BC. Photo: B. Kirigin.

The site offers no shelter, and is directly exposed to the wind and the sea. There is no fresh water and no arable soil. Its strategic geographical position is well known, as it is a landmark for those who sail along the Dalmatian coast. Its position and function are similar to the promontory of Tianaron, the central tip on the south Peloponnese where the sanctuary of Poseidon stands. The sudden changes of winds at Cape Ploča are well known, and force slow cargo ships to anchor in the nearby bays of Rogoznica or Stari Trogir, where they can wait in safety, usually for a day or two, for favourable winds. Safety was provided not only by the natural benefits of these bays but through native co-operation. It is possible that this area was, like Palagruža, a kind of No Man's Land. From these bays one could easily walk towards Cape Ploča and make offerings to Diomedes. Apart from artefacts, traces of two dry-stone walls in a very bad state of repair were discovered some fifteen metres from the seaside. These may well represent the architectural remains of the sanctuary.

Most of the finds discovered next to the dry-stone wall were of pottery: some 130,000 small sherds heavily corroded through the action of salt. Most of them belonged to drinking vessels such as *skyphoi*, *kantharoi*, small bowls, and possibly some *kylikes* and plates. There are a few sherds that could belong to jugs or storage jars. Several amphorae and amphorae lids were found, and possibly a few fragments of smaller *pithoi*, as well as coins mostly from the eastern Mediterranean, fibulae, finger rings and gems. We also discovered several sherds of different kinds of lamp, but no tiles, loom weights or terracottas. It is interesting that there were no sherds of local native pottery, which suggests that only

seamen or traders from the Hellenised parts of the Adriatic visited this site. The time span of the pottery found at Cape Ploča indicates that the sanctuary was founded in the later fourth century BC (Gnathia ware) and that it was in use until the first century AD (the pottery resembles that from Palagruža and Nakovana cave).

The rest of the Gnathia sherds have rims and painted decoration, and some are inscribed by votaries with graffiti. More than a hundred such Greek inscriptions have been discovered, including some dedications to Diomedes. One, of the end of the fourth or early third century BC, reads ΤΡΙΤΟΣ ΔΙΟΜ[ΕΔΙ] ('Tritos (offers to) Diomedes', fig. 2.19), perhaps a dedication made by an Illyrian seaman to Diomedes. Another interesting graffito scratched on a bowl of fine grey clay reads ΔΙΟΜΕΔΙ ΔΟΡΟΝ ('a gift to Diomedes') and is dated to the late third or early second century BC. Such bowls have also been found on other sites in Dalmatia at Issa, Pharos, Lastovo and Nakovana.

Most of the pottery seems to have been produced at Issa, and it looks as though the Issaeans occupied a dominant position on this site on the border between the Illyrian communities of the Hilli and Bullinoi on the one side and the powerful Liburnians on the other. These were an Illyrian community that inhabited the northern part of Dalmatia up to Istria, to whom the Issaeans exported wine, as is attested by the numerous amphorae found on many sites in Liburnia.

LUMBARDA ON THE ISLAND OF KORČULA

The famous foundation inscription, the 'Lumbarda *psephisma*', was found on top of the hill called Koludrt on the eastern side on the island at the end of the nineteenth century. A recent proposal to date it to the first half of the third century BC corresponds well with the offerings from several poorly excavated tombs in the valley some 100 metres to the south of where the inscription was found. No remains of this Issaean settlement are visible. On the Koludrt hill a large cistern measuring 17 x 10 x 1.9 metres was partially excavated some fifty years ago, and seems to have been in use in Hellenistic and Roman times.

Recent field surveys have not detected any traces of the land division mentioned in the *psephisma*, according to which some 200 colonists received 4.5 plethra of cultivated land each (five times less than the Pharians received on Hvar, see above), as well as land for a house within the city wall. The fertile area around Lumbarda is not more than fifty hectares, which is not really enough land for a Greek colony, although it might have been sufficient for a military settlement, as has been suggested. The graves discussed above are all individual, rather than the family graves that are characteristic in Issa (although the grave goods are the same). The straits between Korčula and the Pelješac peninsula were always an important trade route on the way to the mouth of the Neretva river, the ancient Naron, the longest river that runs into the east Adriatic coast, where the Greek *emporion* (trading post) Narona existed, but

2.18 Aerial view of the Cape Ploča site. Photo: Siniša Bilić Dujmušić.

concerning which we know little, except that it stood on the site where the Roman colony of Narona was founded. One rare and extraordinary work of art from this site is the Hellenistic marble relief with dancing girls that could have been part of a mausoleum (fig. 2.20). All the goods from present-day Bosnia-Hercegovina (such as *Iris Illyrica*, a medicinal plant) had to go down this river, which was navigable for more than ten miles inland.

The significance of the western Pelješac peninsula can be accounted for by the presence of an impressive native hill fort at Grad near the village of Nakovana, above which a cave sanctuary of Hellenistic date was discovered just recently (see below).

TROGIR, STOBREČ AND SOLIN

The vast and lucrative production of wine caused Vis to be overpopulated, and from the third century BC the Issaeans created new settlements at Trogir (Tragurion), Stobreč (Epetion) and very likely at Solin (Salona), all on the mainland near Split, the most fertile part of central Dalmatia. Not only is this area fertile but it has the only natural pass through to the mountainous hinterland at Klis between the high Kozjak and Mosor mountains. The northern edge of this area is dotted with more Bronze and Iron Age hill forts than any other region in Dalmatia. Contact with the Greeks started in the sixth century BC, but it seems that the Greek settlements, the Issaean cities in league with them, Epetion and Tragurion, were not founded before the end of the third century BC, when the Illyrian kings Skerdilaid and Pleurat (217–181 BC) were, like Issa, in alliance with Rome. It is hard to believe that Epetion and Tragurion could have been founded earlier or later, since Rome

2.19 Wine jug (skyphos) of Gnathia style with an inscribed dedication to Diomedes, third century BC. Photo: Siniša Bilić Dujmušić.

was at war with the Illyrians and Issa was an ally of Rome.

Tragurion is located on a small flat island between the mainland and the island of Čiovo (ancient Boa), at the west end of the Salonitan gulf. The presence of an Illyrian settlement is suggested by recent finds of local Iron Age pottery beneath the foundations of a Hellenistic house. Hellenistic fortifications are known from several places on the east side of the island and enclose an area of 3,000 or 4,000 square metres. On the mainland, there is a fertile plain with traces of a land division that could have been incorporated later into the early Roman 'Ager Salonitanus' (the territory of Salona). Recently, different kinds of Greek and Hellenistic fine-ware pottery were excavated inside Tragurion, but little has been published and the excavations were not carried out in a stratigraphic (contextual) manner. A public inscription mentioning a board of *logistai* and a *grammateus*, a relief of a seated woman at work, and a votive altar dedicated to Hera (fig. 2.21) are finds from Tragurion that have long been known.

The site of Epetion is situated on the north slope of a small rocky peninsula facing the fertile Žrnovica Bay. Traces of a fortification wall with a gate have been excavated, together with Hellenistic fine-ware pottery and amphorae of the Issaean type. The fortifications enclose an area measuring 250 x 170 metres. Not much has been done in the way of excavation at this site, which is not built over like Trogir.

A fragmentary Greek inscription found at Salona and dated to 56 BC suggests that the settlement was established from Issa. Prior to this, in the late second century BC Salona was a port (*epineion*) of the Illyrian community of the Delmati, according to Strabo. Some fragments of 'Megarian' bowls and lamps, along with several vases of Issaean production, are known from the late Hellenistic period. An archaic or classical Corinthian pyxis is known from Salona (fig. 2.22), as well as a small marble altar depicting a procession of Greek gods (fig. 2.23) that was found in the late nineteenth century, but the context of these finds remains obscure.

Whatever the details, it very much looks as though in the Hellenistic period Issa controlled the region from Tragurion and

2.20 Marble relief with dancing girls from Narona, mid-second century BC. Photo: Živko Bačić.

2.21 Lyso Sosia's small votive stone altar dedicated to Hera, from Tragurion, third/second century BC. Photo: Frane Beusan.

Cape Ploča to the west as far as the island of Korčula to the east. In fact, the cities in league with Issa formed a real Hellenistic state, the first and only one in the Adriatic. Pharos was surrounded by this state, but we do not know the precise role it played.

NAKOVANA CAVE ON THE PELJEŠAC PENINSULA

The mouth of the Neretva river and the island of Korčula have long attracted the attention of archaeologists, and much has been written about them. But the region between those two areas, namely the Pelješac peninsula, especially its western part, is poorly known and explored. The geographical position of western Pelješac is of extreme importance, since it offers control of the exit to the open sea to anyone coming from the Neretva river and to anyone wishing to approach it. According to a recent analysis, the bay of the Neretva has been identified as the bay of the Manioi mentioned by Pseudo-Skylax in the fourth century BC. Earlier, the bay of the Manioi was thought to cover either the whole central Dalmatian area or the bay of Salona alone, what is today called Kaštila Bay. The ancient name for Pelješac is not preserved (unlike places in the neighbourhood such as Korčula, Hvar or Neretva). It was presumably the case that the Illyrian tribe of the Manioi controlled this area in the Iron Age. There were attempts

2.23 Marble altar depicting a procession of Greek gods, fifth/fourth century BC. Photo: Živko Bačić.

to identify Pelješac with Scheria (see above), but there is very little in the way of evidence to support this hypothesis.

Recent excavations in the cave called Spila above the village of Nakovana in the western part of Pelješac produced some extraordinary results. We had been working on prehistoric layers containing material from the early Neolithic and later when, somewhat unexpectedly, we found an unknown gallery. This part of the cave contained a sealed archaeological layer of Hellenistic material that had remained undisturbed since its abandonment at the turn of the Christian era. The evidence unambiguously testifies to ritual activities that were carried out within the cave over a period of three centuries, roughly between the fourth and middle to late first centuries BC. The bulk of the material comes from the third or second century BC (similar in date to that found on Cape Ploča but in smaller quantities).

The finds included large quantities of pottery (around 8,000 sherds). Comparatively few were fragments of pots that had been imported from Greek colonies in southern and northern Italy or from Greece proper; most came from Issa. Drinking vessels (*skyphoi* and *kantharoi*), vessels for serving food (plates and bowls with or without decoration) and amphorae dominate the assemblage. Local native pottery occurred much less frequently, constituting around 25 per cent of the whole.

2.22 Corinthian pyxis from Salona, sixth/fifth century BC. Photo: Živko Bačić.

2.24 Gallery in the Spila cave at Nakovana with the phallic stalagmite at its centre. Photo: S. Forenbaher.

All the finds, apart from the majority of the amphorae, were concentrated around a prominent stalagmite sixty centimetres high in a position that dominated a wide segment of the main cave opening (fig. 2.24). There can be little doubt that ritual feasts were staged at the cave, and that votive offerings were placed at the foot of the phallic stalagmite. In view of the fact that the site is located in the immediate vicinity of the major *grad* (town) hill fort, at that time occupied by a native population, the participants in this ritual presumably belonged to a local Illyrian tribe. This can be confirmed by the lack of coins at this site (in contrast with Palagruža and Cape Ploča discussed above). There were graffiti at this site, too, but in rather fewer numbers than at Palagruža and Cape Ploča: only six or seven. One bears the name of Eukle(ides or similar) in Greek, and another Ammato and Heraclides in Latin. This may mean that the sanctuary was not intended for locals alone.

Another special feature among the fine ware found in Spila is that many sherds have fine drilled holes for mending. However, some show that the holes were made for hanging the vessel or for use as a censer. In some cases even handles were drilled. This is a unique feature if we compare it with pottery found on other cult sites. These holes may show that the imported pottery was not used in everyday life and that it was considered as having a special value. At a certain moment local people would take it to the shrine.

The site of the naturally fortified hill fort of Grad, situated below the cave, was a location that easily controlled the Korčula channel and the bay of the Neretva, and therefore must have been of great importance to the local community, contributing to its influence in the region. Future research may shed more light on the reasons the Issaeans founded a settlement at Lumbarda on the island of Korčula, and why it was so short-lived.

Next to the excavations at Spila, a two-week survey has shown that in the wider area of Grad there are some eighty barrows (fig. 2.25). Some of them, situated near the hill fort, have an unusual shape like a kind of ziggurat – a shape that is unknown among the barrows on the Dalmatian islands, but seems to be similar to the barrows in Hercegovina. The barrows at Nakovana (in most cases plundered) yielded surface finds of Hellenistic fine-ware sherds similar to the ones found at the cave. This kind of pottery was also found at the lower part of the Neretva river, on Illyrian sites in Hercegovina and especially at Ošanići hill fort, the central hill fort of the Daorsi community that has fortification walls clearly made under Greek influence.

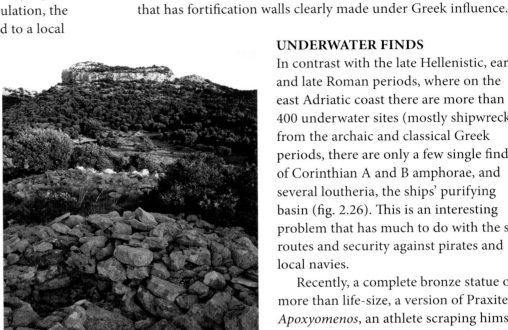

2.25 View of the Grad hill fort at Nakovana with two barrow tombs in front. Photo: S. Forenbaher.

2.26 Clay louterion, ship's purifying basin, fourth/second century BC, found near Palagruža. Photo: B. Kirigin.

UNDERWATER FINDS

In contrast with the late Hellenistic, early and late Roman periods, where on the east Adriatic coast there are more than 400 underwater sites (mostly shipwrecks) from the archaic and classical Greek periods, there are only a few single finds of Corinthian A and B amphorae, and several loutheria, the ships' purifying basin (fig. 2.26). This is an interesting problem that has much to do with the sea routes and security against pirates and local navies.

Recently, a complete bronze statue of more than life-size, a version of Praxiteles' *Apoxyomenos*, an athlete scraping himself with a strigil after exercise, was found by chance in the sea near the island of Mali Lošinj (see Chapter 12, fig. 12.13). It is a Hellenistic copy of an original from around 350 BC. It was probably thrown into the sea during a storm as the remains of the ship have not been found. Now in Zagreb, this remarkable piece of art will be exhibited in the museum in Mali Lošinj.

The existence of independent Greek settlements and sanctuaries came to an end when the Romans incorporated the area into the province of Dalmatia at the end of the first century BC. This brought about major changes in social, economic and religious life. Although today nothing at all remains of the life of the ancient Greeks, it was they who laid down the foundations of western civilisation in Croatia. The Iron Age in Croatia is, however, little surveyed and even less excavated, so it is evident that future research will reveal more details of interaction between the native population and the Greeks.

ROMAN ART IN CROATIAN DALMATIA FIRST TO THIRD CENTURIES AD

J. J. Wilkes

INTRODUCTION

The familiar artistic media of the Greco-Roman world are fully represented in Croatian Dalmatia, though the degree of record and preservation varies for the different categories. These include architecture and architectural ornament, bronze and stone sculpture in the round, relief carving in stone, wall painting and mosaic floors, and the so-called 'minor arts' in metal, glass and minerals. A significant proportion of the material was imported from elsewhere in the Roman world. These obviously include coin and medallion portraits and sculpture in imported marble, some of which may have been finished in local workshops. It is reasonably certain that many portable objects – including ceramic, metal and glass vessels, intaglios, etc. – were imported, yet production in local workshops is still likely for the numerous objects fashioned in amber – jewellery, dress ornaments, etc. – found in the area.

Dalmatia exhibits a changing balance between imports and local production similar to that observed in other Latin-speaking provinces. An early dominance of imports, in the case of Dalmatia clearly demonstrable in ceramic tableware, bricks and stamped tiles, gradually gives way to local production where the raw materials are available. This accompanied the large number of settlers, military and civil, who came into the area during the first century AD, although it is significant that later locally produced work adhered closely to the version of the canon of classical art currently in fashion in the Roman world. Native Illyrian influence is not significant, except in the area of religious art, which reflects the enduring belief in the Roman versions of indigenous deities.

The outstanding natural resource of Dalmatia is an abundance of limestone of such quality that there was little need for the import of architectural marble on the scale that took place in other provinces. The famous quarries on the island of Brač (ancient Brattia) lay conveniently close to the coast, and their products were employed extensively not only in ancient times but also from the Renaissance in Italy and later in the wider world. As a result, Dalmatia has a rich legacy from ancient architects and sculptors working in the local stone. Here a selection of the outstanding examples of Roman art in the province may include some exotic items, but pride of place is taken by the works of local craftsmen. These include not only official portraits of the ruling

3.1 Statue of Augustus from Aenona, Archaeological Museum, Zadar. Photo: Živko Bačić.

emperors, their families and high officials, but also many private portraits of individuals and their families depicted on funeral stelae and other memorials and identified by epitaphs. It seems clear that funeral stelae with portraits in relief were not the preserve of the wealthier office-holding class, but were also available to those of lesser status. In the later period many funeral monuments, both with and without portraits, were evidently produced to a standard design for members of the urban craft guilds (*collegia*) and trade associations.

The Roman art in Croatian Dalmatia was a product of its political and social condition. As a province of the Roman Empire, Dalmatia was administered by a Roman governor appointed by the emperor in Rome. At the provincial level Roman authority was based on the local cities, in which local administration and social and economic life were centred. A powerful professional army of two legions and numerous ethnically recruited auxiliary units that had played a major role in the conquest of the interior had been transferred out of the area before the end of the first century AD, leaving only two or three of the latter as a permanent garrison. The art of Roman Dalmatia can be labelled provincial also in the sense that its forms and styles had originated elsewhere and long before the Roman occupation. Existing native traditions in ornament gradually became visible through newly introduced Roman media, notably stone-carving, and these can be observed in votive sculpture. In addition, more exotic influences, including those from the non-Greek East and Egypt, also flowed into the region along the many channels of cultural influence that grew up during the centuries of the Roman Empire.

The material selected here is presented under four headings:

1. imperial portraits in stone and other materials;
2. portrait sculpture and funerary reliefs of private individuals, including serving and former soldiers;
3. expressions of religious belief in various media;
4. architecture and architectural ornament in the public and private domain, along with interior decor, notably mosaic floors.

(Numbers in parentheses refer to the 'Catalogue of objects' in the Appendix.)

THE IMAGE OF AUTHORITY: IMPERIAL PORTRAITS FROM AUGUSTUS TO THE SEVERI

The often forbidding 'veristic' portrayal of human features was adopted by the Romans of the late republic from the Hellenistic world to convey in visual form the Roman qualities of gravitas and unflinching discipline. Following its reception by the Roman nobility, it was adopted also by those of lower, even humble class who aspired to a Roman identity. It was this adoption that produced the striking funeral portraits of prosperous artisans, many former slaves or their descendants. Though these can now be recognised as stereotypes rather than authentic individual portraits, they present the ravages of time on human features following a lifetime of accumulating wealth through hard work. By the time of the Second Triumvirate (43–33 BC), leading figures at Rome had already returned to Hellenistic models for an image more expressive of emotions and inner tension that derived ultimately from the official portraits of Alexander the Great (d. 323 BC).

The larger than life-size head in white marble (1) recovered from the sea near the island of Apsorus (modern Osor) can, despite its damaged state, be identified as belonging to the early 'Actium type' and depicts Caesar's heir in the role of priest with covered head (*velatio capitis*). The image in the Hellenistic tradition is not a common one and dates from Augustus' early years (30–20 BC); it was soon to be displaced by the more familiar 'Prima Porta' type. The Hellenistic tradition is still visible in the portrait of M. Agrippa (2), Augustus' closest colleague and son-in-law until his death in 12 BC (once in Zadar, now in Copenhagen). The features exhibit through facial detail an intensity of emotion, while military achievement is indicated by the mural crown. No Dalmatian context is on record, while Greek parallels suggest it may have been produced in Athens. During his middle years Augustus adopted an image that

was destined to be the basis of the imperial dynastic portrait, both male and female, adult and child, for most of the Julio-Claudian era, and was also to have a significant influence on those of all classes of society. The characteristics of this 'Prima Porta' type were devised to suit the new era of peace following decades of civil war and exhibits what is termed 'a calm classicistic expression'. The prolonged repetition of this successful image into the reign of Augustus' successor Tiberius (AD 14–37) resulted in a measure of artistic paralysis, with the earlier careful rendering of the detail of facial muscles and hairstyle becoming simplified through repetition. One of the most imposing Julio-Claudian dynastic groups was erected in the temple at Aenona (Nin). The remains of at least ten statues were recovered, four of which remain in Zadar. Two are headless, one cloaked around the lower body suggesting the nakedness of divinity. Two wear togas, as also do the two complete statues. The first represents Augustus in a version of the 'Prima Porta' type (fig. 3.1), with only the lower body covered in the fashion of a Jupiter statue (3). The second togate statue portrays Tiberius (4) with veiled head in the role of priest (an earlier identification with Claudius can now be discounted) (fig. 3.2). The entire Aenona group appears to have been created at the same time, and perhaps represents a tribute to Tiberius, his family and ancestors, in a province where he had achieved some of his most hard-earned military successes.

3.2 Statue of Tiberius from Aenona, Archaeological Museum, Zadar. Photo: Živko Bačić.

Another group may have been erected at Oneum (Omiš) on the coast south of Salona (Solin), from where comes a fine head of the same emperor in white marble, unfortunately damaged (5). Another head possibly from the Aenona group (once in the Danieli collection in Zadar but now in Aquileia) portrays Tiberius' nephew Claudius (6) before his unexpected ascent to the throne in AD 41. The hair and facial expression differ from the head of Tiberius, and there must be some doubt that it belongs to the Aenona group.

A head of Livia Drusilla (fig. 3.3), consort of Augustus and mother of Tiberius, later deified as Diva Augusta in the reign of her grandson Claudius, belongs to the recently excavated group of Julio-Claudian statues at Narona (7). The portrait in white marble (now in Oxford), which conveys all the qualities of the formidable empress, may have been veiled and has been dated to the reign of her son. The difficulties in identifying images of the many minor members of the Julio-Claudian dynasty are an intended consequence of the thinking behind their portraits. Thus, two heads from Salona that appear to portray young princes (one in Split museum, the other in Zagreb) seem likely to belong to a Julio-Claudian ensemble of the late Augustan period. Idealised features and standard details in the hairstyles indicate Julio-Claudians, but individual identifications are near impossible (8). If they are brothers, the sons of Germanicus, Nero and Drusus Caesar are possibilities, although one cannot exclude Augustus' own grandsons Gaius and Lucius Caesar. A small head, from Kijevo near Sinj (now in the Franciscan Collection at Sinj), may represent Nero Caesar, one of the sons of Germanicus, a suggestion based on some similarities to one of the Salona heads described above (9). Yet another Julio-Claudian candidate is the marble head of a six- or seven-year-old boy (now in Pula museum) that resembles in some details the portraits of Augustus and Tiberius (10). The military connection of Tiberius with the region, already noted, brought the imperial image to a new medium, a glass disc (*phalera*) recovered from the legionary base at Burnum (now in Zadar museum) (11). A similar disc (unpublished, now in the Franciscan Collection at Sinj) that depicts either Germanicus or Drusus, the son of Tiberius, may come from the nearby legionary fortress at Tilurium (Gardun). The latter may be the subject of another head recovered from the sea off Apsorus along with that of Octavian (12). The identification is based on coin portraits and can plausibly be linked with the periods he spent in Dalmatia in AD 17–18 and 18–20 acting on behalf of his father.

Beginning with that of Caligula, the official image of the later Julio-Claudians appears to revert to an earlier age, with increased facial detail, furrowed brows and thoughtful looks suggesting an inner anxiety, but is not so far known in Dalmatia. A bust of Caligula (now in Trieste museum but once in the Zadar collection), later reworked, may have belonged to the Aenona group (13). It has been suggested that the absence of later Julio-Claudian portraits from the area may be attributed to local unrest in the aftermath of the unsuccessful rebellion by a provincial governor early in the reign of Claudius that was suppressed by the provincial garrison. Several more heads have reasonably been

3.3 Head of Livia Drusilla from Narona, Ashmolean Museum, Oxford. Photo: © Archaeological Museum, Split.

3.4 Head of Vespasian from Narona, Vid collection. Photo: Vidoslav Barac, Ministry of Culture of the Republic of Croatia.

3.5 Head of Domitian reworked as Trajan from Issa, Archaeological Museum, Split. Photo: Tonći Seser.

assigned to other members of the Julio-Claudian dynasty. The damaged head in limestone from Istria (now in Pula museum) may be the Elder Agrippina, widow of Germanicus and mother of Caligula, whose image continued to appear on coins during the reigns of her son and of her brother Claudius (14). A large female head in marble (now in Pula museum) seems likely to have been part of a statue in a public place somewhere in the city and has a Tiberian hairstyle, but there is no probable identification (15). Another female head in white marble from the forum of the same city almost certainly depicts a Julio-Claudian princess, possibly the Younger Aprippina, second empress of Claudius and mother of Nero (16). A third head in white marble recovered from the sea off Apsorus is badly damaged like the rest, but seems likely to have represented a Julio-Claudian princess (17). Finally, the small female head in marble from Aenona appears to depict another member of the Julio-Claudian dynasty and may belong to the main Aenona group (18).

The Flavian dynasty of Vespasian and his sons Titus and Domitian (AD 69–96) employed their images to advertise and sustain the hereditary transmission of power, a principle that some vehemently opposed. Flavian statues were erected in several areas of Dalmatia, and these show a return to the older Roman severe portrait discarded by Augustus. The image of Vespasian on a head from Issa (now in Vienna), possibly belonging to a statue from the same context, is that of wisdom gained through a lifetime's experience (19). A more refined portrait than that from Issa is presented by the over life-size head in white marble at Narona (fig. 3.4), on which some of the facial marks of old age are suppressed (20). Despite epigraphic evidence for a cult of the deified Titus (Divus Titus), established after his premature death in AD 81, no image of the reputedly popular elder son of Vespasian has survived from Dalmatia. Given the extent to which his images were destroyed and his name erased from inscriptions, it is surprising that any image of Vespasian's deeply unpopular younger son Domitian (AD 81–96) survived.

The fine head in white marble (now in Kotor museum, Montenegro) once belonged to a resident of Salona and very likely came from there (21). The facial image is a development of the Narona Vespasian, while the hair is rendered in red-brown colouring. One of the ladies of the Flavian dynasty, Vespasian's wife Domitia or Titus' daughter Julia, may be portrayed in a head of white marble (Zadar museum, formerly in the Danieli collection) that exhibits the distinctive, artificially bulked hairstyle of the period, though this was possibly likely to have been a private portrait rather than one intended for a public place (22). While the vengeance taken on the memory of Domitian might consist of a frenzied assault on his image, a more pragmatic instinct was to rework some of his images to portray his elderly successor Nerva (AD 96–8). A head intended for public display in the Aenona forum was reworked to transform the round features of Domitian into the slimmer features of his successor below his distinctive hairstyle (23). It is suggested that the work was done while the head remained in place, a prompt reaction to the sudden change of ruler.

Direct hereditary succession of emperors disappeared for nearly a century after the murder of Domitian, though more by accident than design, and the result was that a succession of long-serving emperors were portrayed as individuals rather than being assimilated within dynastic groups. The image of Trajan (AD 98–117) discarded Flavian realism in favour of the heroised classical portrait. A monumental head in white marble from Issa is another example of the reworking of a portrait of Domitian (fig. 3.5), done probably at the start of the reign (24). It seems that the reworking was not completed, but enough had been done on the hair to establish the identification with Trajan, while traces of a laurel wreath also confirm its imperial identity. The more familiar image of the emperor appears in a fine bust from Salona (now in Vienna) and is linked with the coin portrait celebrating his tenth anniversary (*decennalia*) (25). The element of unflattering realism makes it one of the most striking of all imperial portraits, officially sanctioned after a decade of military victories by the Optimus Princeps. Sadly, the fine head recovered from the sea off the island of Crexa (Cres) is badly damaged, but enough remains of the facial details and hairstyle to make the identification certain (26). Though dynastic groups have disappeared, individual portraits of imperial ladies in the court of Trajan were produced. One of these may be the female head from Salona (now in Zadar museum) for which possible identifications include the emperor's sister Marciana, her daughter Matidia and the latter's daughter Sabina, Hadrian's empress (27). Such was the popularity of the Trajanic female hairstyle that the portrait could equally well be a private image in the provincial capital.

The bearded features of Hadrian (AD 117–38) are the most widespread in the Roman world after those of Augustus but are absent from Dalmatia. At the same time, its influence on contemporary private portraits in the province was considerable. A headless statue in armour certainly represents an emperor and has been identified with Hadrian, as has also the fragment of a leg and a kneeling barbarian. The same is the case with Hadrian's successor Antoninus Pius (AD 138–61), though his image is less widespread than those of his predecessor. A possible portrait is a head in white marble originally in the Danieli collection at Zadar, judged to have been an import from the Greek world (28). A large head in white marble from Flanona on the east coast of Istria has been identified with the Younger Faustina (29), daughter of Antoninus Pius and wife of Marcus Aurelius (AD 161–80), from the evidence of a coin portrait. It could equally be a private portrait based on the features of Faustina during the reign of her father before the accession of her husband. Similar arguments can be applied to the head of an elderly woman dated to the early Antonine period (formerly in the Danieli collection, now in the Zadar museum), whose elaborate coiffure derives from that of Sabina, Hadrian's empress, or from that of the Elder Faustina, the empress of Antoninus Pius (30). The relative scarcity of Hadrianic and Antonine imperial portraits in Dalmatia, particularly of the latter, is also reflected in the smaller number of surviving private portraits directly influenced by those of emperors and the ladies of the imperial court. The memory and images of the third Antonine emperor Commodus (AD 180–92), the first instance of hereditary succession since Domitian, suffered a similar fate to those of the latter following his assassination. While still in power, Commodus and his empress Crispina appeared to have enjoyed a measure of popularity among the provincial population, from the evidence of two gem portraits (one in Zadar museum, unpublished, the other from Shkodra in Albania, now in New York) (31).

The dynasty of the Severi, Septimius Severus (AD 193–211), his empress Julia Domna, and sons Caracalla (AD 211–17) and Geta, has left more memorials of their rule around the empire than any other, and their images are significantly more familiar than those of their Antonine predecessors. Dalmatia appears an exception to this state of affairs, and the only surviving portraits

3.6 Heads of Plautilla from Salona, courtesy of the Archaeological Museum, Zagreb.

of their rule are two heads from Salona (fig. 3.6), identified as Plautilla, the ill-starred wife of Caracalla (32). She was exiled to the Lipari islands following the downfall of her father Fulvius Plautianus, the praetorian prefect, in AD 205 and executed after the accession to power of her husband in AD 211. The first of the heads, both in white marble, has the distinctive 'melon' hairstyle and matches closely the images of Plautilla on coins issued in AD 202. Some significant discrepancies in the rendering of the hair appear now to have put the identification in doubt, although we cannot rule it out altogether. Whether or not it is the ill-fated princess, the portrait, with eyes of glass paste that once filled the now empty sockets, remains a powerful image of high technical quality. The identification of the other head also rests on the evidence of a coin portrait but differs in some details from that described above. The 'melon' coiffure is arranged diagonally, in the manner found on other portraits attributed to Plautilla. The first head has been judged by N. Cambi to display 'safety, pride and beauty', while the other seems to convey the 'sorrow and anxiety' characteristic of later eras, with a 'cheerless emotion' enhanced by the inclination of the head towards the right shoulder. The Severan period also reflects the entry of the imperial image into the private sphere, as the image of Septimius Severus on a gemstone (private collection) derives from that on coins and medallions, while a pearl of jet (now in Split museum) bears the image of Severus' formidable empress Julia Domna (33). Confronting images of the brothers Caracalla and Geta appear on a gilded ring of cast bronze from Salona (34), a common feature of Severan imagery, while other rings portray either the entire family of four or Severus surrounded by his sons. A more stylised portrait of Caracalla alone is depicted on a glass cameo (once in a Split collection, now lost).

The portraits of Roman rulers and their families in Croatian Dalmatia belong mostly to the dynastic groups of the Julio-Claudians, Flavians and Severans. The association of images of current rulers with those of a younger generation destined for the succession was directly responsible for the proliferation of images in those periods. Before the end of the third century the empire had passed under a new political order, where the imperial image remained important but the features of individuals were suppressed to sustain collective rather than dynastic rule.

THE PROVINCIAL IMAGE: SCULPTURE, FUNERAL RELIEF AND PRIVATE ART

There are around twenty heads known to have been found in Dalmatia (though some were likely to have been made elsewhere) that appear to portray private individuals who lived in the area. In most cases no archaeological context is on record, while no associated inscriptions furnish evidence of identity. In each case dating depends on the perceived influence of imperial portraits and hairstyles. Three heads in white marble, an elderly man from Pula in Istria, a male head from the Zadar area (now in

Copenhagen) and a male head from the Zadar area (now in Zadar museum), portray their subjects in the severe late republican style with high quality technique (35). They can be dated to the last decades of the first century BC, and the likelihood is that they are not local products, although they may represent local dignitaries. More significant is the large head of an elderly male (36) in local limestone from the Lollius mausoleum in the western cemetery of Salona, and thus the product of a local workshop (fig. 3.7). The severe portrait, which can also be dated to the last decades of the first century BC, has a furrowed complexion, though the lines are not deeply incised, and appears to belong to a statue of a figure dressed in toga or palium. The move to a bland and expressionless image adopted by the early Julio-Claudians is reflected in two female heads in Zadar, both with the distinctive 'melon-slice' of the late Augustan-Tiberian era and carved in imported white marble. A veiled female head (37) from Salona in the local limestone of the same period matches in quality those produced in imported marble. A second female head from Salona (38) in the local limestone and also dated by hairstyle to the same period has more individual features, as local workshops displayed an ability to create a portrait in the prevailing fashion, but without the stifling blandness that resulted from the slavish reproduction of the official image. Thus, a male head from Pula (39) in local Istrian limestone reproduces in detail the features of Tiberius, as is also the case with numerous funeral portraits. A more relaxed imitation is evident under the later Julio-Claudians, reflecting the apparent return to a measure of individuality in the imperial prototypes. The fine head of an elderly male in local limestone from Salona (40) modelled on the features of Claudius, with a wrinkled forehead and hair arrangement, but with a degree of realism that echoes the realism of the late republic. A male head in local limestone from Salona (41) modelled on the image of Nero was evidently produced in the same workshop as the two female portraits described above. The last of the Julio-Claudian heads produced in Salona (42) is another Neronian type, a young male with traces of a beard.

While there are several examples of Flavian and Trajanic portraits in funeral relief sculpture (see below), there are so far no surviving examples of free-standing images based on the distinctive imperial portraits of those eras. The head of a young male in white marble (43) from Flanona on the east coast of Istria has the characteristic features of Hadrian: long curled hair, short beard and moustache. The imperial influence on the portrayal of males and females continued into the Antonine and Severan eras. A massive head in white marble from Salona (44), apparently unfinished, can be dated from its similarity in several details, including the eyes, the oval face and feathery base, to the image of the young Marcus Aurelius. It may be an imperial portrait, but a private subject seems more likely in a period when the fashion for larger than life-size heads was widespread. The bearded male head from Zadar (45) is unusual because it was found during excavations within the city and the context is certain. There is a general resemblance to the well-known image of Lucius Verus with his forked beard, but the head has a number of individual features to indicate that it was a monumental statue of some local dignitary in the Roman colony. Similarly, the female head in white marble from Salona (46) has the distinctive Antonine hairstyle, long wavy hair falling sideways. Despite the features being much abraded, the eyes are expressive, and while the image has a resemblance to that of the Younger Faustina, it is most likely to be a private portrait. A male head in white marble (47) once in the Zadar collection (now in Copenhagen) depicts a youth with unruly long hair but is generally assigned to the Antonine era. However, the thick mane of hair is not the usual Antonine style and appears to be an evocation of the famous image of Alexander, an indication that the head is probably not a local find. The same workshop seems also likely to be responsible for the head of a young male in white marble (48), once part of the same Zadar collection as the Copenhagen head. The influence of Severan portraiture is evident in the large female head in white marble (49) that has the distinctive hairstyle of Julia Domna, the formidable consort of Septimius Severus. Another head from the Zadar collection (50), and thus with no record of provenance, is dated by style to the second decade of the third century, with deeply drilled long hair. The double ring on the head may indicate a priest of Demeter, perhaps an indication that it was created in an eastern workshop.

During the second century AD the taste of the educated Roman classes to adorn their public places and private houses with images from the remote past became widespread in the provinces. There was evidently a demand for copies of Greek originals created in the fourth century BC, when a repertoire of portraits of Greek poets, philosophers and statesman, some patently imaginative, were created. Many of the statues and busts of such figures were mass produced in high-quality white marble in Greek or Italian workshops for the Roman market. Most of the subjects are shown in venerable old age and can usually be identified. An exception is the head in white marble (51) from Salona (now in Zagreb) which has the long beard and bald pate of a philosopher, dated by style to the period of Trajan or Hadrian. The fine head in white marble (52) now in Zadar is a copy of the well-known Hellenistic image of Socrates (fig. 3.8). Another philosopher's head from Salona (53), in the local limestone and thus likely to be a local product, cannot be matched with any individual, although it matches a type known from elsewhere in the Roman world. A fine head in white marble from Salona (54), dated by technique to the early third century, is a portrait of Aeschylus (fig. 3.9), derived ultimately from an original that stood in the theatre of Dionysus below the Acropolis in Athens. The most intriguing evocation of images from the past are two brackets from the facade of the Porta Caesarea at Salona on which the images of Alexander the Great and an unidentified Ptolemaic ruler are carved as telamones (55). That of Alexander is based on the official portrait created by Lysippus during the lifetime of the king, while both portraits are dated by style to the era of Hadrian.

The many portraits that have survived from the private sphere include carved gems from signet rings, metal rings with portraits, and images on other materials such as bone, amber or jet. Some are identifiable as imperial portraits, perhaps to indicate some association, such as civil or military service, or some other connection with the ruling dynasty. Images from the past are also found in the private sphere: a gem at Salona has the familiar portrait of the tragedian Euripides (56) widespread in the Roman

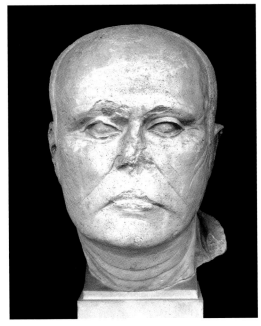

3.7 Head of elderly male from Salona, Archaeological Museum, Split. Photo: Tonći Seser.

3.8 Head of Socrates, Archaeological Museum, Zadar. Photo: Dražen Maršić.

3.9 Head of Aeschylus from Salona, Archaeological Museum, Split. Photo: Tonći Seser.

3.10 G. Utius stele from Salona,
Archaeological Museum, Split.
Photo: Tonći Seser.

3.11 C. Publicius Romanus stele from
Narona, Archaeological Museum, Split.
Photo: Tonći Seser.

many of these memorials, mostly upright tombstones (stelai), of such interest is that the portraits were accompanied by epitaphs that identify by name and specify the relationships of those commemorated. The nuclear family was the social unit responsible for these monuments, most of which place the portraits, often down to waist level, within an architectural frame of a triangular gable supported by flanking columns or pilasters, a classic combination of Greek and Italian traditions that spread through the Roman world.

A small number of portraits appear to reflect the persisting influence of the republican severe image in funeral monuments. One of the finest monuments from the region is the large stele that portrayed the seafarer G. Utius (fig. 3.10), his brother P. Utius and his concubine Clodia Fausta (61). Unfortunately, the relief of Utius himself is badly damaged, but those of Clodia and his brother remain intact. Both figures have a fixed stare, while all the details of their physiognomies are conveyed with the utmost realism: rough skin, deep furrows, unruly curly hair and veins on arms. While the date is likely to be Augustan, the monument exhibits a tenacious adherence to the traditional Roman image from the time of the late republic. That the Utius monument is not an exception in this regard is indicated by a male head on the fragment of a funeral stele from Salona (62) that exhibits the same degree of republican realism. The tradition of realism in local workshops eventually gave way to the more bland 'classical' image of the late Augustan-Tiberian era. This can be seen in the male and female relief portraits on the surviving upper part of a stele from Salona (63). The faces of both are without expression, frozen into a fixed stare with eyes wide open. The same characteristics are visible on the surviving fragment of another stele, now at Vranjic near Salona (64). Two of the three male figures are badly damaged, but that on the left has a similar appearance, although the expression is less fixed than on the preceding example and appears to convey a degree of sadness. The stele erected in northern Istria by Q. Labienus Mollio (65) in accordance with his will to his wife Aquilia Tertia and other members of the family commemorates a family of local Istrian origin. The images of Labienus and his wife have an engaging naivety that appears to be the result of a local sculptor attempting to reproduce the hairstyles of the Julio-Claudian era.

Figured stelae of the Flavian-Trajanic era can be identified from the influence of the changing imperial image, but are also instructive for the adoption of Roman memorials by the native communities of Liburnia in the hinterland of Zadar. The

world, while a gem in carnelian (57) portrays Socrates in the form of a satyr, but another of the same subject in glass paste is modelled on the traditional Hellenistic portrait. Finally, the portrait of Alexander the Great on a carnelian gem from Salona (58) with the horns of Zeus Ammon is based on the official miniature created during the king's lifetime by Pyrgoteles. Not all images on objects in the private sphere are identifiable as emperors or deities, and some may be generalised images not intended to represent individuals. That seems to be the case with the bust figure of the Flavian-Trajanic era depicted on an amber ring from a grave (59) in a cemetery near Scardona (Skradin) or the female image on a bone pin from Aenona. A gem in red carnelian from Salona with male and female heads may be a betrothal image of real individuals. The former is shown with head and beard reminiscent of Antoninus Pius, while the latter has the hairstyle of the Younger Faustina (60). Some of these gems and rings may have been produced in local workshops, but the presumption is that in most instances such easily portable items were produced elsewhere in specialist workshops, notably Aquileia, which is known to have been a major centre of production from the first to the third centuries AD.

❊❊❊

Few areas of the Roman world can match in quality or quantity the figured funeral monuments of the early empire from Salona and its area. Executed by local workshops, they include a range of expressive individual portraits produced in the fashions stemming from imperial images that prevailed at the time. What makes

monument of Prostinia Procula, for a long time built into a house in Split (66), portrays two females with the fashions of Trajan's court. She set up the stone for herself while still living and for her 'darling child' (*delicata*) Faventina, who died aged ten. Both mother and daughter have Trajanic hairstyles but do not convey the expression of sadness that is typical of portraits of Trajan's empress Plotina, which would certainly not have been out of place on this monument. A fine single portrait in the Trajanic style appears on the monument of C. Publicius Romanus (fig. 3.11), member of a city council (*decurio*), presumably of Narona where the stone was found (67). The epitaph records that the tombstone was set up by a grieving mother and aged father, neither of whom is named, to their son Romanus, who died aged thirty, C. Licinius Expectatus, and their granddaughter Publicia Ilurica, who died at the age of five. The lack of names, filiation and Roman voting tribes is unusual at this date for a person of this status. On the other hand, the known character of Narona's population suggests that freedmen played a major role in this commercial city, and a freedman or servile origin is suggested by both the names Publicius (often taken by former municipal slaves) and the cognomen Romanus, and also the name of his daughter Ilurica (Illyrica), used for slaves of native origin. Two monuments in the Roman style and the fragment of a third testify to the adoption of Roman memorials by indigenous groups in the area of Asseria (near Benkovac), a Claudian muncipium in southern Liburnia, including some yet to become Roman citizens. A fine stele from Ostrovica (68) was set up by G. Veronius Aetor while still living for himself, his wife Veturia Aia and their sons Ce[u]nus and C. Julius Nepos. The enfranchised Liburnian family (Aetor, Aia and Ceunus are common local names) are portrayed in two registers, parents above and children below. All three males hold scrolls (*volumina*) in their left hands, an assertion of Roman identity rather than social rank, while Veturia Aia, in the fashion of Roman ladies, holds what appears to be a jewel box. The portraits have Flavian hairstyles, but individual features are not consistent. The elder male has the sober realism of Vespasian, with the wrinkles of passing years, while his wife wears a scarf beneath a veil, evidently a form of local dress. The lower portraits of the younger males are modelled on that of Domitian, as it were following the younger Flavian generation. Another stele from Asseria (69) was set up by Vadica Titua, daughter of Aplus, while still living for herself and her mother

3.12 Vadicus Titua stele from Scardona (Ostrovica), Archaeological Museum, Zadar. Photo: Dražen Maršić.

3.13 Stele fragment with male and female portraits from Salona, Archaeological Museum, Split. Photo: Tonći Seser.

Pasina Voltisa, daughter of Quintus, with the assistance of Vadicus Aetor and Vadicus Ceunus, the entire family apparently yet to acquire Roman citizenship, but commemorated on a fine monument in a flawless Latin epitaph (fig. 3.12). The veiled images of Vadica and her mother appear within a semicircular niche. The lower part of the stele is presented as the 'Door to the Underworld' (Porta Inferi) familiar on the tombstones produced for soldiers by the workshops of the legionary fortresses at Tilurium (until *c.* AD 50) and Burnum (until *c.* AD 85). The fragment of a third monument from Asseria (70) carries a fine female portrait with a degree of facial realism recalling pre-Augustan types though lacking any expression of emotion. Though the epitaph is lost, there seems little doubt that the fragment adds to the impression of the adoption of Roman monuments by native groups in southern Liburnia. The rate at which the newest imperial fashions were adopted in provincial communities appears to have slowed or at least become more eclectic after the end of the first century AD. Thus, the portrait of a young male within a circular niche appears to be modelled on the decennial image of Trajan from the evidence of the hairstyle, but other details, the cut pupils and irises, would indicate that the portrait belongs to a later era. Three fragmentary stelae have portraits that place them in the late Antonine era. The male and female portraits on the upper half of a stele from Rupotina in the area of Salona (71) are images of the deceased that equal any from the region (fig. 3.13). The woman has the parted hairstyle of the Younger Faustina or of Lucilla, and there is a facial resemblance to the former. The male portrait has long hair, a moustache and a pointed beard that resemble the features of Antoninus Pius rather than Marcus Aurelius. Unlike the expressionless gaze of the woman, the face of the male is judged to reveal a measure of tension or anxiety. The recently discovered stele set up by P. Urgulanius Ursus for his mother Sempronia Quarta (72) shows the deceased with a late Antonine or Severan hairstyle. The image is now relegated to a small figure confined by the round gable that crowns this plain monument, and is characteristic of the many monuments of the early third century at Salona. Finally, the female head on a stele fragment from Salona

3.14 Titus Fuficius stele from Salona, Archaeological Museum, Split. Photo: Tonći Seser.

(73) has a remarkable individuality unusual for this era. The hair has a central parting with a narrow braid separating front from back. The ears are exposed, and a striking feature is the four hooked curls on the forehead. The expression lacks emotion, but the effect of ageing is conveyed by careful attention to facial detail.

With the organisation by Augustus of a professional army based on the citizen legions and the ethnically titled units of auxilia, soldiers served for a set term, eventually fixed at twenty-five years, after which as veterans all could look forward to various forms of rewards and privileges. Before the end of Augustus, permanent memorials were provided for serving soldiers who died through a burial fund to which all contributed. Soon the bases of individual legions around the empire began to be surrounded by soldiers' memorials produced to a high quality by the legionary workshops, which were able to procure stone of a high quality even from a long distance. In the case of the legions stationed in Dalmatia during the first century AD, at Tilurium (Gardun) inland from Salona and Burnum (near Kistanje) on the river Krka inland from Scardona, stone of the highest quality in ample quantity was available in the vicinity of both camps. Most of the monuments set up in the vicinity of the camps record serving soldiers, and name only the deceased, rank, unit, age and years of service, along with fellow soldiers or servants as heirs. Those who had completed their term of service preferred to move to a more agreeable life in the nearby cities, where they appear on their memorials with family and household. These were evidently produced in the local workshops, and for that reason show a greater variety in design than is the case with the more standardised monuments of serving soldiers created in the military workshops.

The imposing monument of Titus Fuficius at Salona (74) portrays the family and household of a veteran of the Twentieth Legion, stationed at Burnum until it departed for Germany in AD 9 (fig. 3.14). The epitaph, part of which is lost, evidently furnished no further details of his military service, nor does it appear to record his age at death, which might provide a more precise date for the monument. Seven figures are portrayed in two superimposed registers; the upper has Fuficius and three members of his family, the lower three freedmen members of his household. The hairstyles of the male figures are those of the late Augustan fashion, except that of Fuficius which follows the Claudian model. The features of the boy (his son) in the upper register and of the freedman in the lower exhibit an Augustan calm, but those of Fuficius appear to display an inner tension. The hairstyles of the four women are similarly inconsistent; three follow the late Augustan-Tiberian style, but that of the wife of Fuficius, like that of her husband, follows a later style. This unusual state of affairs brings into question the value of a precise dating by an imperial model of hairstyle. The absence of any visual reference to military service suggests that Fuficius may have survived for many years following his discharge, which must have taken place some years before his unit left the area in AD 9, since release is most unlikely to have been granted during the crisis years of AD 6–9, when even Salona was threatened during the Pannonian uprising. The monument of a serving soldier of the Seventh Legion, stationed at Tilurium from c. AD 6 until c. AD 50, is typified by that of Quintus Mettius Valens (fig. 3.15), discovered in the eastern cemetery at Salona (75). He died aged thirty-eight after eighteen years' service. No other name appears in the epitaph, which simply records that the stone was erected under the terms of his will (testamento fieri iussit). The date must be after AD 42, since the legion has the epithets 'Claudia pia fidelis', conferred in that year by a grateful Claudius on both legions in the province following the failure of a local rebellion. The stele has four elements of decoration: an upper gable with a frieze of weapons below the image of a veiled female in the field of the gable; the figure of the deceased within the aedicule flanked by columns with spiral fluting, with features and hairstyle modelled on those of Tiberius; the Latin epitaph in monumental lettering centred and carved by a skilful stonecutter; and the 'door to the underworld' in relief with handles on the two upper panels and thunderbolts on the two lower. The last element was evidently adopted by the legion's workshop during its years in Asia Minor before AD 6, and was also a feature of tombstones produced in the workshop of the Eleventh Legion stationed at Burnum.

Alongside the heavily armed infantry of the legions, the large number of auxiliary units stationed in the province provided light infantry, cavalry and mounted archers. Like the legions, serving soldiers in auxiliary units were also commemorated with fine monuments with details of their origins and years of service. Many were yet to acquire Roman citizenship, normally a reward on completion of twenty-five years' service, but grants of that status were made before completion of service to reward distinguished conduct in the field. The cavalryman Melvadius, son of Macer, was born a Cugernus, a German people on the lower Rhine north of Cologne, and died aged thirty after twelve years' service in the Ala Claudia Nova, a new formation named after the emperor Claudius. His fine monument, set up near the legionary base at Tilurium in accordance with his will by a fellow soldier Tiberius Claudius Aurelius, who had already been granted Roman citizenship, portrays the deceased not, as is often the case, mounted on his horse but standing in civil dress in a round niche (76). Below the epitaph a relief depicts the trooper's horse held by a servant. From the other extremity of the Roman world was a unit of mounted archers from the region of Cyrrhus in northern Syria that left several monuments to its serving members in the area. Marcus Pytha, son of Segnus, came from the city of Beroea and may have been a serving member of the unit when he died aged sixty after thirty-five years' service (77). The epitaph also mentions his freedman Felix, and it seems that both the soldier and his servant are depicted standing within a shell niche reminiscent of Palmyrene monuments. Despite the fact that the figures portrayed appear to date to the late Julio-Claudian or even Flavian era, the exceptionally long term of service is characteristic of the later years of Augustus, when there was a severe shortage of military manpower that caused postponement of discharges. The main imperial fleets were stationed at Misenum and Ravenna on the west and east coasts of Italy. There were also substations of these units, including one at Salona. Both fleets drew large numbers of recruits from the peoples dwelling east of the Adriatic, some remote from the coast and thus likely to have been used more as marines than sailors. The latter probably came from the traditional seafaring communities on the coast and islands of Liburnia and Dalmatia. Liccaeus, son of Veius, was a centurion on the warship (liburna) Lucusta from the island of Apsorus (Osor) who died aged thirty; his monument was erected in accordance with his will to his friend by his heir Dabalus, the son of Tritus, on land granted by the local community (78). The portrait appears to be modelled on that of the emperor Claudius, and shows Liccaeus holding what appears to be a coiled rope, perhaps a symbol of his rank comparable to the vine stick (*vitis*) of the infantry centurion.

The monument of Gaius Laberius at Tilurium is unusual in several respects. The deceased male is portrayed within a circular frame with features clearly modelled on those of Trajan (79). The epitaph records that he died aged seven, but the portrait, though it shows Laberius holding a ball in his right hand, depicts a much older individual. No family appears to be recorded, either in the main epitaph or in the five lines of verse that implies no member

of his family was available to set up the memorial. The findspot and the character of the monument suggest a military connection, but there is no hint of what this may have been. The stele of Servius Ennius Fuscus (fig. 3.16) belongs to the period following the departure of the legions and the drastic reduction of the auxiliary garrison to two or three units under the Flavians (80). Ennius was serving in the Eighth Cohort of Volunteers, one of several units raised in Italy under Augustus, stationed first at Andetrium (Muć) where the monument was set up and later at the old legionary base at Tilurium. Ennius, who came from Cemenelum (near Nice) in the Maritime Alps, is portrayed on the monument alongside his wife Fulvia Vitalis, while the epitaph records that he died aged thirty-eight after eighteen years' service. The figure of Ennius, clad in body armour with a sword and holding a volume in his left land, is an imposing one and seems to belie his modest status of a simple serving soldier. His features and hairstyle are Trajanic, but Fulvia has the artificially bulked Flavian hairstyle.

By the late second century the fashion for ornate stelae appears to have passed. The wealthy now began to opt for stone coffins with increasingly elaborate external decoration, while the tradition of military epitaphs appears to have ceased altogether. Most monuments consisted of simple slabs, much smaller than the earlier memorials, with the epitaph contained within an

3.15 Quintus Mettius Valens stele from Salona, Archaeological Museum, Split. Photo: Tonći Seser.

3.16 Servius Ennius Fuscus stele from Andetrium, Archaeological Museum, Split. Photo: Tonći Seser.

3.17 Tyche relief on Porta Caesarea from Salona. Photo: Tonći Seser.

incised border taking up the entire surface except for a small triangular or curved gable that might contain a floral design or a human image, but rarely does the latter appear to be a portrait of the deceased. The memorials recording members of the detachment from the First Italica Legion based on the lower Danube were produced in the local workshops at Salona where the soldiers were stationed. Most of the deceased were of local Thracian origin, and their epitaphs show an imperfect command of Latin and the conventions of recording military service. The monument of Aurelius Pontianus, a soldier who died aged fifty after sixteen years' service, was erected by his son Quintianus, and has a small relief portrait cut into the head of the tombstone showing the deceased in a military cloak with a heavy belt (*cingulum*) to which a dagger was attached (81).

THE REPRESENTATION OF RELIGIOUS BELIEF AND RITUAL IN SCULPTURE AND RELIEF

The expression of religious belief and its associated ritual in concrete form appear with remarkable consistency in the surviving monuments throughout the Latin-speaking provinces of the Roman Empire. Many free-standing sculptures, reliefs, altars, temples and shrines are testimony to the widespread reception of the Greco-Roman pantheon of individual deities with human attributes, mythological figures along with the personification of all types of forces that impacted on the human experience for the purpose of protection or appeasement. Several currents can be identified in this process of religious observance: the collective and individual worship of the gods of Rome, notably Jupiter, Juno and Minerva, as an expression of loyalty to the prevailing order that included deified rulers of the past and an explicit cult of the ruler in the guise of 'Roma et Augustus'; the familiar Greco-Roman Olympian deities in the various guises willingly accepted into both the public and private life of settler and indigenous communities; the identification of some of these deities with established local cults for which little or no written evidence survives, easily recognised in the case of Silvanus and his associated deities but hard to define for its origins and meaning; the reception of several cults of eastern and Egyptian origin in a

Greco-Roman version, notably Magna Mater/Cybele from Asia Minor, Isis from Egypt, Jupiter of Doliche in northern Syria and Mithras from Persia, whose elaborate ritual involving personal initiation appears to have had an increasing appeal to several classes during the early Roman Empire.

According to tradition, the bearded figure of Jupiter, lord of the gods, had been the deity of the Romans from earliest times. His image seated in majesty appears at Salona and in relief at Iader, while his consort Juno was portrayed in a fine statue of white marble at Aenona (once in the Danieli collection at Zadar, now in Copenhagen) (82). Within the general area of the imperial cult, it was a practice to assimilate the image of an individual dynastic figure with that of a popular divinity: thus one of the imperial ladies of the late Julio-Claudian court was portrayed in the forum at Pula with a statue in the guise of Fortuna. Similarly, the religious element at the local level of civic organisation is represented by the Fortuna or Tyche that served as the personification of the city (83). At Aequum, the Claudian veteran colony inland from Salona has Fortuna in the form of a statue, and at Salona she appears in a relief of the Olympian gods that included the image of Fortuna or Tyche wearing the turreted mural crown (84). The most vivid expression of the civic deity is the Tyche of Salona (fig. 3.17), a keystone in one of the arches of the Porta Caesarea as reconstructed in the early fourth century (85). She is personified as a young woman with loose hair and wearing a mural crown. She holds upright in her right hand a banner (*labarum*) and leans with her left arm on a corn measure (*modius*) full of sheaves of grain. On the flag are the initial letters usually interpreted to read: M(artia) J(ulia) V(aleria) S(alona) F(elix), the ancient titles of the colony with the added Valeria from an association with Diocletian, a native of the city. Tyche's large eyes with incised pupils and irises partly concealed beneath the upper eyelids are believed to indicate a Tetrarchic or Constantinian date. At Aequum, the forum was also embellished with a relief of Victoria, a relief on the keystone of an arch portraying Dea Roma, and a free-standing statue of the same deity (86).

The reception of the Olympian deities, some with imperial dynastic connections, into the private life of provincial communities is demonstrated at Salona by a number of high-quality images in white marble, many modelled on known classical and Hellenistic prototypes, likely to have been produced by workshops in Rome or in the Greek world. An unfinished image of Venus may have been imported in an unfinished state for reworking (87). Others include copies of the classical Apollo or Dionysus, with spiral locks on the chest and raised arms; a naked youth in a chlamys based on a Pheidian original, more likely Hermes or Diomedes than Apollo; a small statue of a boy based on an original of Polycleitus; a female head based on a type of Pheidias; the head of a female cult statue with a hairstyle based on types of the second century BC, a notch for a diadem, open mouth with pathetic expression in the tradition of Scopas and the small head of a divinity; also another with diadem and unfinished hair with some traces of colouring, with calm expression and brooding eyes modelled on a prototype of Praxiteles (88). These are dated to the Julio-Claudian era, but the practice of importing high-quality copies of famous prototypes continued under the Flavians and later. Later imports include a spirally poised female torso, a popular Hellenistic type, the equally famous aged fisherman from Alexandria, and the head of Flora or Persephone, with centrally parted hair drawn to a bun at the rear and a diadem of flowers based on a Praxitelean original (89). None of the above has any recorded context, being collected over the centuries from the site of Salona and the area. On the other hand, a fine marble relief from a monumental fountain (*nymphaeum*) close to the main city gate portrays Neptune or some other water deity (90). Not all images of the classical deities were imported. From the amphitheatre at Salona come two herms, each with a pair of bearded heads, produced in local limestone in the Antonine period (91–2). On one the better preserved head has strong individual features, with wide face, warm eyes and slightly furrowed brow. The other (once walled into a local house) is almost certainly from the amphitheatre. The better preserved head has a thoughtful expression and furrowed brow. The features are distinctive, with stretched skin and short sparse hair, and are modelled on some Hellenistic literary or philosophical original of the third to second centuries. The enduring appeal of the healing deity Asclepius is indicated by a small statue produced in the Antonine period. The god Dionysus, a deity with several identities who brought the liberating products of the vine to all peoples, is prominent among the surviving sculptures. A fine bearded head with long hair and ribbons, modelled on the transition from the severe to the classical style, is assigned to the Julio-Claudian period. A seated Jupiter in the same white marble appears to belong to the same group, and depicts the god with the upper body naked but the lower part covered, a modest variant of the Pheidian Zeus. The most common image of Dionysus in the area was based on the prototype of Polycleitus: a small unfinished marble statue of the late Flavian or Trajanic era was likely to have been an import, but was evidently discarded since it was found in a pithos. An image of the god with a bunch of grapes and a panther seems to be

a local variant of a common type (93). The labouring hero Heracles was also a popular figure, in one instance weary, craving peace and rest, with empty hands on his back, portrayed at Salona in a white marble image likely to have been imported under Hadrian, as was also a piece of inferior quality portraying the hero with the apples of the Hesperides (94). His image persisted into a later era when his labours became a popular theme for the relief decoration of stone coffins (*sarcophagi*).

In Istria and northern Liburnia several local deities are identified through votive inscriptions (Sentona, Iria, a local identity of Venus, Iutossica, Ica/Ika). All are female, but as yet no iconographic images appear to have survived. In southern Liburnia the well-known images from a shrine near Aenona are dated to the early Flavian period, and provide one of the most striking images of a local cult assimilated to a classical deity. The Hellenistic figure of Aphrodite Pudica is depicted with a small Priapus in the cult image of Venus Anzotica (fig. 3.18), and is identified as such by an inscription on the base (95). Despite the fact that it appears to have been an import, the sculpture was evidently judged to be a suitable figure for a local cult.

3.18 Venus Anzotica and Priapus relief from Aenona, Archaeological Museum, Split. Photo: Tonći Seser.

Some interesting questions of identity arise from the portrayal of Silvanus, the most common cult in central Dalmatia. His image appears in the following groups: Silvanus alone; Diana alone; Silvanus and Diana; Silvanus with nymphs; Silvanus and Diana with nymphs; Silvanus and Diana with nymphs and other deities. The god is generally depicted with the attributes of the Greek Pan rather than in the more anthropomorphic Italic version. It may well be that along with Diana he represents an Illyrian cult (some have suggested an equation with the Illyrian Vidasus and Thana, identified by name on an altar but without any images). Both Silvanus and Diana were deities of vegetation, pastures, herds and breeding. How the cult came to become widespread in a region dominated by settlers such as the Salona area and adjacent islands remains a mystery. Presumably an Illyrian version of the Pan cult was translated into that of Silvanus. Dating of the reliefs remains a problem, but the cult seems to have been established by the middle of the first century AD. A relief from the Salona area (Peruča near Klis) is dated by the hairstyle to the Julio-Claudian period, but most of the reliefs of the deity were not created with any reference to

3.19 Silvanus and nymphs plaque from Tilurium.
Photo: Tonći Seser.

classical models in regard to details. In this instance some of the traditional features can be recognised: the heap of stones on which the god is seated, a snail, a worm, trimmed olives, fruit, etc. Another less refined relief from Salona still allows some of the traditional details to be recognised. One of the most striking reliefs of Silvanus with the nymphs was dedicated by the bugler (*bucinator*) of the local auxiliary unit stationed at Tilurium (fig. 3.19). The arrangement of figures, their attributes and hairstyles follow local traditions, although the beardless Silvanus has an unusually youthful appearance. This local identify of Silvanus appears also on the island of Pharia (Hvar), site of the ancient Greek settlement Pharos, where it is reported that on one occasion a relief of the god in the guise of Pan was destroyed in the belief that it was the image of the Devil. On the other hand, a recent find from near Scardona (Ćulišić) has the more traditional version of a bearded elderly Silvanus with tree, syrinx, pedum and dog (96). The local production of votive sculptures modelled on imported originals is visible in the small relief of Diana the Huntress from Proložac near Salona, on which the sculptor Maximinus has signed his name (fig. 3.20). He is the only one known to have done this, and his signature appears also on the relief of the girl Lupa from Sovići. While Maximinus succeeds in conveying the essence of his model, the execution of proportion and detail is not judged to be successful, while the inscribing of his name ('Maximinus sculptet') disfigures the work somewhat (97).

The spread of the worship of several cults from the eastern provinces has recently been demonstrated by a survey of the evidence from the Roman province of Dalmatia, which also includes a comprehensive catalogue of the remains of each of the imported cults. Inevitably, most of the material comes from the larger coastal cities to which the cults spread through their frequent overseas contacts. That appears to have been the case with the Magna Mater or Cybele cult that originated in Asia Minor, the Egyptian cults (Isis and Serapis) that spread widely in a Hellenised form in the western provinces, as well as the Syrian cult of Jupiter of Doliche that has a special link with metal-working. Study of their remains has been one of the main currents in the discussions of social change and cultural interaction within the empire as a whole. In northern Dalmatia the small harbour settlement at Senia (Senj) probably relied for its prosperity on the route that led inland across the towering range of the Velebit Mountains. The remains of a well-appointed religious precinct have produced seated figures of Cybele, a fine marble group of the Dionysiac cult of Liber, and also a statuette of the Egyptian deity Serapis (98). Perhaps the most distinctive and intriguing cult to spread from the East is that of Mithras, which may for some time have rivalled Christianity in its appeal to those seeking a deeper spiritual experience than was offered by the traditional Roman gods. In origin the deity portrayed as a young male was the Persian god of light, whose victory over the forces of darkness was symbolised by the slaying of the bull (tauroctony), whose blood released the fertility of the earth. Many hundreds of reliefs depicting the bull-slaying, showing the god in eastern dress and with his two attendants Cautes (with torch raised) and Cautopates (with torch lowered), have been found in the small cave-like shrines, not only in the larger cities but also in the military camps and towns around the frontiers and even in some more remote rural settlements, where the cult scene was carved in a rock face. A recent study has demonstrated that local variations in tauroctony reliefs appear to be linked with fashions in funeral sculptures, notably the use of a circular frame for the scene that appears to derive from the circular wreath or medallion with leaves common on funeral stelae in the Danube lands (fig. 3.21). In some areas they enclose portraits of the deceased, but other places have simple plant motifs in the place of a portrait. In the

Mithraic reliefs from Dalmatia, it is possible to identify high-quality imported reliefs in marble and, mainly in the smaller centres, locally produced examples seeking to reproduce replicas of the more expensive imports. An interesting third group displays the influence of older pre-Roman traditions in decoration that results in a rustic appearance found on other local versions of imported Roman cults. There are a few examples of double-sided reliefs, with on one side the tauroctony and on the other a depiction of

3.20 Diana relief by Maximinus from Prolozac. Photo: Tonći Seser.

3.21 Circular plaque of Mithras from Salona (*Proceedings of the 8th International Colloquium on Problems of Roman Provincial Art*, p. 271, fig. 2). Photo: Tonći Seser.

3.22 Aerial view of amphitheatre at Salona, Archaeological Museum, Split. Photo: Tonći Seser.

the meal that formed a part of the ritual showing the different grades among initiates to the cult. Recently, there has been some debate that has given rise to a suggestion that the Mithraic cult which spread so widely in the Roman world owed little or nothing to any Persian origins, but was largely a Roman creation that evolved during the early empire.

ART AND ARCHITECTURE IN THE PUBLIC AND PRIVATE BUILDINGS OF CROATIAN DALMATIA

(For references to individual sites, see the 'Catalogue of sites' in the Appendix.) Despite the fact that the most famous relic of antiquity, the palatial residence of the emperor Diocletian that today forms the historic nucleus of the city of Split, lies outside the scope of this chapter, enough has survived of the public and private architecture of Croatian Dalmatia to indicate its high quality and diversity. Much less is currently known of private residences than of public buildings, but enough has come to light to indicate that there are many remains yet to be excavated in many places.

Around half of the cities reveal their planned origin through the distinctive feature of a regular street plan. Like the early Greek settlements of Pharos (Stari Grad on Hvar) and Issa (on Vis), both of which had regular street plans and were enclosed by regular perimeters of defences, the Roman colonial settlements generally followed a similar pattern. Thus, the Augustan colony at Iader (Zadar) had a regular street grid, although the walls were constructed to follow the limits of the peninsula it occupied, except for a straight section on the landward side that contained the monumental entrance to the colony. Similarly, the Claudian veteran colony at Aequum (Čitluk near Sinj) shows all the signs of having been a planned city despite the fact that the walls do not enclose an entirely regular perimeter. The plan of Salona, by far the most important city of the area, had a conjoined double-walled enclosure, neither a regular perimeter. The eastern of the two was the later and was possibly constructed in AD 170 during

the Marcomannic emergency under Marcus Aurelius. A monumental gate (the Porta Caesarea) in the east wall of the earlier western enclosure was first constructed under Augustus, and was evidently still in use in the early fourth century following a major reconstruction. The Roman colony was established by Julius Caesar, evidently to acknowledge the vigorous support he received from the settlement of Romans already established there during the recent civil conflict with Pompey. The new foundation may have occupied the site of a native Dalmatian settlement. Whether or not the new city was ever a planned settlement based on a regular grid of streets, it seems clear that all trace of this was eradicated during the several centuries of prosperous existence that followed. The major Roman settlement at Narona (Vid) in the Narenta (Neretva) valley lay on an ancient passage between the Adriatic and the interior, and was already flourishing as the principal Roman centre in the area before it became the site of a Roman colony under Caesar or Augustus. Despite the recent investigations of the site and the spectacular find of several imperial Julio-Claudian statues, there is as yet no certain indication that a regular grid of streets was imposed on the existing settlement; it appears to have grown up piecemeal enclosed by a perimeter of defences that date from the pre-colonial era. In the fertile plain of southern Liburnia south of Zadar, the conversion of existing Liburnian settlements into cities organised on the Roman model (*municipia*) during the first half of the first century AD resulted in an exceptional combination of native and Roman urban planning. The most notable examples of this transformation are Asseria (Podgradje near Benkovac) and Varvaria (Bribir). Both retained more or less intact their imposing circuits of walls whose irregular perimeter was dictated by the contours of the hill, while a regular Roman urban plan was laid out in the interior. In addition to the forum and other public buildings at Asseria, a monumental entrance was inserted into the perimeter wall aligned not with the wall but with the axial street of the Roman city.

3.23 Mosaic with portrait of Triton with unkempt hair and sea creatures. The spaces between intersecting squares are occupied by birds and heads representing Seasons, with the outer borders occupied by leafy vases and acanthus. Split. Photo: Zoran Osrečak.

Any settlement of any significance on or near the Dalmatian coast had to make provision for an adequate and reliable supply of water. In some cases the larger cities were able to construct aqueducts that conveyed water from some distance and on a scale sufficient to support baths and monumental fountains, both distinctive features of the Roman city. Among the several known examples, none appears to have used the closed pressure system by which the water could flow up and down using the inverted siphon described by Vitruvius, and it seems that a gravity feed with the channel following the natural contours was sufficient. Salona was fortunate to draw its supply from the river Iadro that emerges in full flow from the foot of Mount Mosor, though a part of this was later diverted to supply the great residence of Diocletian. Remains of the channel crossing low ground on a series of arches are still visible on the outskirts of the city, until recently in working order following a comprehensive restoration in the nineteenth century. The aqueduct for the Roman colony of Epidaurum (Cavtat near Dubrovnik) passed along the fertile valley of Konavle, a part of the city's territory. While mainland cities such as Iader could draw their water from deep in the interior, the cities on the islands faced greater difficulties. At Curicum (Omišalj on Krk) a new supply was proudly titled the Aqua Flavia Augusta, while on the island of Arba (Rab) it is recorded that in the second century AD the agent of a prominent local citizen managed to locate a source of water that had long been forgotten.

In the planned Roman city two or three street blocks (*insulae*) would be earmarked for the forum, a complex of buildings enclosing a large open space that served as its political and social centre. In its most elaborate form, the forum could be an axially planned double precinct that would also include the temple of the Roman state gods (Capitolium) within its own precinct, in addition to the forum itself enclosed on two or three sides with shops (*tabernae*) and an aisled hall (*basilica*) and council chamber (*curia*) for the conduct of formal public business. At Iader the great temple and forum complex dominated the city, but it is the only example so far known of the double-precinct type in Dalmatia. At Salona the outlines of the forum block and of the temple within it have been traced in the south of the earlier (western) city, but with no indication of any unified axial planning. Many cities, both planned and unplanned, had a single-precinct forum, an open space with shops and aisled hall, often in an arrangement that resembled the headquarters building (*principia*) of a Roman military camp of the early empire. Fora of this type are known at Aenona, Asseria, Aequum and Burnum. At the last of these, the headquarters of the earlier legionary camp was evidently adapted to serve as the forum of a new city established on the site early in the second century AD, and whose standing arches remain a prominent relic. Even modest cities created at a later date, such as Delminium in the plain of Duvno, were equipped with a central public building of this design, including open space, shops and aisled hall, and a small council chamber.

Among public amenities, an abundance of water in some of the larger cities supported large civic baths, a prominent element in the city that also served as a social and cultural centre. Such baths are known at Salona, and they are known to have existed in smaller centres such as Epidaurum in the south and Senia (Senj) in the north. An inscription records that the colony of Narona had a set of baths designed specifically for use in winter (*thermae hiemales*). Most cities managed to acquire some form of provision for its citizens to enjoy games and similar spectacles, but only a minority were able to afford purpose-built arenas for the games and theatres for staged productions, both of which might involve elaborate constructions based on concrete vaulting enclosed within decorative facades. Salona had both, where the remains of the arena are second in the region only to the great arena of Pola (Pula) in Istria (fig. 3.22). Gladiatorial combats were evidently very popular, and a professional troop appears to have been maintained there with its own organisation and burial ground. The arena was also the scene of public execution, including those of Christians whose suffering was recorded not only in writing but also by the conversion of the Nemesis shrine at the side of the arena to a chapel dedicated to their memory and whose portraits decorated the walls.

As has already been noted, only a few remains of private houses have been fully excavated, either town houses or villas in the country, although enough has been recorded to indicate that many existed and fortunately remain to be explored. At Iader the remains of a house have been excavated and those of a villa in the area of Rider (Danilo) near Šibenik. Older excavations record the existence of several fine villas in the area of Narona, but these are yet to be fully examined. In the many places where Roman remains have been located, the visible sample is often too small to determine plan or function, but many have produced sections of mosaic floors, both black and white and polychrome and with geometric and figured decoration. Much less is known of wall decoration, although again fragments are sufficiently common to indicate that many houses did have an elaborate interior decor to accompany mosaic floors. Mosaics are also found in the public domain, notably in baths, while many of the finest examples known from the area occur in basilicas of the early Christian era. The recently published catalogue of Roman floor mosaics in Croatia by Jagoda Meder (see Appendix) reveals that the majority of domestic mosaic floors of the early empire had geometric patterns of varying complexity executed in black and white tesserae. Most of these are found in the coastal cities and as a whole follow the traditions of the Hellenistic world. Recent studies have suggested that the immediate inspiration and the artistic influences on local workshops arrived from north-east Italy, but these also included styles and motifs of both African and Asia Minor origin. The majority of mosaics in the region are dated by style and context to the late first or second centuries, and a selection of the better preserved examples will serve as representative of the whole.

The flourishing state of the ancient settlement of Pharos on the island of Pharia (Stari Grad on Hvar) is indicated by the well-appointed urban residence excavated in 1990, with some fine

3.24 Mosaic of Orpheus and Tritons from Salona, late second or early third century AD. Archaeological Museum, Split. Photo: Zoran Osrečak.

mosaic floors dated to the second century AD. Two of these have complex geometric designs executed in polychrome: one has a central roundel framed by four semicircles and four quadrants within an enclosing square frame, while the central motif has a hexafoil pattern of knotted circles, and the central ornament has acanthus in the semicircles and geometric motifs in the quadrants. The second has a circle of rosette triangles defined by a frame of consols in perspective enclosed by a black border, and with alternating shields (*peltae*) and roses filling the corners. At Zadar the remains of a town house excavated in 1975 included four mosaic floors. Three of these were well preserved and had geometric patterns in black and white dated to the first century AD: one with an arrangement of meander bands, the second a pattern of diagonal fields more commonly found on painted ceilings, and the third an elaborate arrangement of scallop shells in semicircles around a central medallion. A few miles to the north the excavation of a villa rustica near Aenona (Nin) during the Second World War was subsequently reburied. A mosaic floor was divided into square and circular panels defined by guilloche borders. Within the panels there appear elephants, ibex, zodiac symbols and pairs of gladiators in combat. The latter are rendered in black and white, and depict combats between the heavily armed fighter (*hoplomachos*) and a net fighter (*retiarius*) and are dated stylistically to the second century AD. At the island settlement of Curicum (Krk) there is a fine version of a type of mosaic, familiar at several places in Italy and often in bath houses, where several marine figures are rendered in black and white, a Triton and dolphins in the wake of Poseidon. In one scene a sea horse (hippocamp) and dolphins are shown circling a Triton. The baths excavated in 1963 on the island of Issa (Vis) contained a mosaic with a pattern of linked squares in black and white, fringed along one side by a panel of dolphins, that is dated to the first century AD.

Polychrome mosaics of high quality with figures are known only at Salona, although not in any great number. Beneath a later Christian basilica in the north-west corner of the eastern city, a mosaic dated to the late second or early third century with a fine portrait of Sappho was discovered during excavation in 1902. The poetess occupies a central roundel within an outer circle radially divided into nine segments, each containing the image of one of the Muses identified in Greek (some of the names were later erased). Others at Salona from the same era include one with Apollo with his lyre as a central figure enclosed by four concentric circles. The hair of the god is wreathed with laurel, while the corner quadrants were once occupied by animal figures (now erased). Another has the bust of Triton within an eight-pointed star formed by intersecting squares, with vases and acanthus occupying the corners (fig. 3.23). In another the familiar figure of Orpheus is at the centre, taming with his song the wild beasts who occupy surrounding semicircles and quadrants (fig. 3.24).

THE PALACE OF DIOCLETIAN AT SPLIT

Sheila McNally

The city of Split lies on a shallow bay between the mountains and the sea. Along its harbour front a wide expanse of Roman wall still stands (fig. 4.1). The city has grown up in and around a building complex called the Palace of Diocletian after the Roman emperor who built it in the late third and early fourth centuries AD. The palace appears in all introductory art history textbooks because of its grandeur and high state of preservation. It shapes our ideas about Roman architecture but in some ways remains an enigma. Although much of the original has been destroyed or absorbed into later building, much stands clear and more emerges year by year, manifesting the range of its builders' creativity.

BACKGROUND

Architects and workers were facing new challenges. Construction took place during a time of radical transition within the Roman world, and had to fulfil an unprecedented need: a residence for an emperor in retirement. During his twenty-year reign (284–305 AD), Diocletian had restored stability to the Roman Empire after many years of disorder.

Ancient writers and modern scholars differ about his intentions and the depth of his accomplishments, but some characteristics seem both clear and pertinent to the work he instigated at Split. He respected Rome's past but had no hesitation in preserving it through radical innovation; he was, from both personal conviction and political policy, devoted to traditional polytheism; he saw himself as closely connected to Jupiter and requiring increased courtly homage as a result.[1]

Having put things, he hoped, in order, Diocletian celebrated the twentieth anniversary of his accession to power in 304 and in the following year did something unheard of for a Roman emperor: he renounced power voluntarily, abdicated, and came to this quiet, south-facing little bay halfway down the eastern Adriatic coast, within an hour's walk of the flourishing Roman port of Salona, where he may have been born.[2]

The palace must have been under construction for some years before Diocletian came there, although work may have continued during his retirement.[3] The basic building materials were fine local stone and locally made bricks, supplemented by decorative materials from Italy, Africa and the East. Some of the workers may have been local, but many came from the East, as attested by Greek masons' marks and by details of the architectural decoration. Wide variations in workmanship suggest the recruitment of craftsmen who had not trained or even worked together before. Who was in charge of the whole undertaking cannot be known, but it was probably someone whom Diocletian trusted because he had seen him or them at work in the East, in fort building among other activities.[4]

Fig. 4.1 Split from the south; the sea wall of Diocletian's Palace runs from an arch at the left to a tower on the right. Photo: Sheila McNally.

Fig. 4.2 Diocletian's Palace, reconstruction by E. Hébrard and J. Zeiller, *Spalato, le palais de Dioclétien*, Paris 1912.

Fig. 4.3 Sea facade, view to east: reconstructed west loggia; arcades framed by engaged columns. Photo: Sheila McNally.

His retirement home has been called a palace for many centuries, but what does that mean? Should we rather call it a villa, the common Latin word for a country house? Compared with earlier Roman palaces or villas, this structure is clearly unusual, but it comes from a time of far-reaching change, commissioned by a prime mover in those changes and providing him with a kind of structure no emperor had needed before.

His residence places traditional elements in an unprecedented combination, giving a particular prominence to sacral constituents. In many ways it is a rearrangement of the past and a bridge to the future, if not the future Diocletian may have intended.

Centres of power were shifting throughout the Roman Empire. Relations between city and country, civil and military, were in flux. The builders drew flexibly on traditional notions of what suited a fine country home (villa) or a palace, or even a city or a military camp. They reshaped relationships between public and private and even between the living and the dead. They inserted references to the empire's ancient centre, the city of Rome, into an architectural organisation to which the empire's peripheries also contributed.

Their product is a many-faceted structure that eludes easy classification. It has also proved remarkably adaptable. In 1979 UNESCO placed 'the historical complex of Split, with the Palace of Diocletian' on its World Heritage List according to several criteria, which include 'exhibit[ing] an important interchange of human values, over a span of time'. I am concentrating on the original palace in this essay, while also mentioning its evolving relationships. The later life of the city has not merely added new structures, but also enriched the original Diocletianic accomplishment by reuse and incorporation in new contexts. Some parts disappeared; others survived because of their welcome strength or reassuring grandeur.

BASIC COMPONENTS

In 1912 Ernest Hébrard and Jacques Zeiller published a reconstruction showing what was then known and filling in the missing portions by similar shapes (fig. 4.2). The result clearly conveys much of the original character of the complex while suggesting a misleading uniformity. The seaside wall still presents its high arcade framed by columns (figs 4.1 and 4.3). Two of the land walls also survive with arcades, gates and corner towers, as do the basic alignments of the main east–west and north–south thoroughfares (fig. 4.4), and two sacred buildings (figs 4.5 and 4.6) on either side of the Peristyle (fig. 4.7), a colonnaded court that culminates in a porch before the onetime residential block.[5]

The massive perimeter walls guaranteed the continuance and transformation of the palace as refugees from Slavic invasions crowded into their security and turned the complex into a city. The sacred buildings became a cathedral and a baptistery for the surrounding area, fostering the city's importance as an ecclesiastical and therefore political centre.[6] Inside these walls and around these buildings, new inhabitants gradually created a typically medieval town plan with narrow, winding streets (see fig. 4.4) and closely pressed houses.[7] Later construction has incorporated Roman foundations and Roman walls, continually changing what is concealed and what is laid bare, reshaping the way the original structure works in its current context.

In his book on *Art Forms and Civic Life in the Late Roman Empire*, L'Orange linked characteristics seen in Hébrard's reconstruction drawing to the spirit of the times: he thought the complex expressed the loss of freedom and gain in law and order that he found in Diocletian's military, economic and religious policies.

'Diocletian's Palace is a closed stereometric block of mathematical regularity, with a ground plan of rectangles arranged according to a strict coordinate system. It is fixed in each part, unchangeably stipulated on a geometric formula, thus without possibility of further growth and development. Here is the same contrast between free grouping and mechanical coordination, between organic growth from within and symmetrical stabilization imposed from above [that characterizes] all relations between the principate and the dominate ...'[8]

L'Orange here follows those historians who see Diocletian as breaking decisively with tradition, and so distinguish the imperial system from Augustus to the late third century, called the principate, from a new system instituted by Diocletian and followed by his successors, called the dominate. Others deny such a dramatic change.[9] This building, like the whole of Diocletian's reign, is less a radical break with the past than a supple reinterpretation.

Over the last sixty years much more of the original structure has emerged. Looking at the overall plan as we know it today (figs 4.8 and 4.9) both reinforces the truths of Hébrard's reconstruction and draws attention to its simplifications. Limited irregularity exists. Use of rectangles is not formulaic but a means to an end, or rather to two quite different ends in the northern and southern halves of the palace. In the north, repetitive rectangles dominate, while in the south differently sized rectangles frame a variety of shapes. The way the framing separates and occasionally links areas shows the planners knew they were packing a remarkable range of functions together.

CURRENT STATE OF KNOWLEDGE

Our increased knowledge comes from work Cvito Fisković began in 1947,[10] which Jerko Marasović and others continue to the present day, removing later accretions to reveal Roman construction and often to create new relationships. Typical of both accomplishments was the clearance of the street inside the eastern gate, together with the once colonnaded walkway to its south, allowing some sense of the original sweep of these thoroughfares while also creating a view across the Mausoleum to the Peristyle, one of the most picturesque sights in today's Split, and one that could never have been imagined by the original builders (see fig. 4.5). Diocletian's builders segregated functions both visually and physically where modern users often prefer to see them superimposed.

Fig. 4.4 Route of Roman street from North Gate to Peristyle (visible in centre distance). Photo: Sheila McNally.

At the south, many well-preserved vaulted rooms re-emerged (e.g. fig. 4.10). Later building had destroyed or hidden almost the entire main floor of Diocletian's seaside residential block, but the ground, sloping roughly eight metres from the north, necessitated substantial basements at the south that had remained invisible but almost intact for centuries, gradually filling with rubbish and sewage from houses above. Today almost all those basement rooms stand clear, with massive walls and piers designed to support

Fig. 4.5 Mausoleum (cathedral of Split), an octagon between medieval additions; view to south across Roman east–west street and adjacent walkway (under awnings). Photo: Sheila McNally.

Fig. 4.6 Temple, view from south-east. The original columnar porch has been demolished. Photo: Živko Bačić.

elements above, so they establish the basic plan of the residence.

Even in the comparatively well-known areas of the Mausoleum, Temple and Peristyle, unexpected elements emerged. Investigation in the Peristyle led to lowering its floor level and opening the original stairway to the basements. Marasović explored remains of a small round building in the Temple sanctuary and correctly predicted the existence of a second, symmetrically placed structure there.[11]

Greater surprises occurred in the areas between the well-defined edges of the residential block, the Mausoleum and Temple enclosures and the perimeter walls. On the west, Marasović uncovered a small but elegant bath complex filling much of that space.[12] During the late 1960s two new structures came to light in the east, a courtyard surrounded by mosaics lying just south of the east–west street, and the hot room or caldarium of a second bath close to the residence.[13] The mosaic courtyard may have served as the palaestra, or outdoor exercise area of this bath. We can tentatively suggest that there was a large bath accessible both to people who entered the East Gate and also to those using the dining area (see below) in the residence.[14]

These two baths and the mosaic courtyard introduce irregularities to the plan, contradicting its supposedly 'mechanical coordination' (L'Orange, above). Routes through these areas are not clear. Hébrard's restoration shows a set of streets going around the inner perimeter a short distance from the circuit walls. In the northern half of the palace, evidence of those streets survives in numerous places. In the south, they did not exist (see fig. 4.8); the line of piers stops abruptly on both east and west. On the east, building levels change abruptly. Do these irregularities all belong to the original programme? The palace cannot have been planned without baths, but changes may have occurred. At present, it seems most likely that the eastern bath was part of the original plan, while the mosaics in the courtyard, if not the courtyard itself, may be later. The western bath also may be later.[15]

Although less well documented, the northern half of the palace appears simpler in both plan and execution. Each section between the central street and the perimeter streets seems to contain building blocks on central open spaces: details remain unclear. Small square rooms along the perimeter walls have parallels in Roman forts, and the whole area has generally been consigned to Diocletian's bodyguard and servants. So far, the only decoration found behind the central street consists of two simple mosaic floors.[16] The contrast with the south suggests utilitarian functions, not necessarily military ones.[17] Our lack of knowledge has been underlined by two recent suggestions: that the palace was in fact a city, in which case private residences would have existed, presumably in this area; or that a factory known to have been in the palace at a later date might be an original component, so that the northern spaces might have housed industrial activity, as seems to have been true later and on a much smaller scale at nearby Mogorjelo.[18]

Fig. 4.7 Peristyle, view south towards residential block. Photo: Sheila McNally.

At present, neither suggestion seems likely, but obtaining a clearer picture may be difficult. This part of the palace sits on higher ground than the southern part. It lacks extensive substructures, so later construction has eliminated much more not only of Roman architecture but also of any debris levels. For now, interpretations of the whole complex can draw little support from this half.[19] Such interpretations have involved Latin words, modern scholars' terms, and the status of Diocletian. They tend to focus on specific, well-defined areas. There is indeed a hierarchy of importance in palace spaces, but all parts of the hierarchy entered into its life. The existence of irregularity in the south and simple regularity in the north emphasises the distinctiveness of the complex and regular areas.

RECENT DISCUSSIONS: LATIN TERMS

One debate has concerned the appropriateness of two Latin words, 'villa' and 'palatium' (palace). St Jerome tells us that Diocletian 'in villae suae palatio moritur' (died in the palace of his villa). Zeiller, finding this a senseless phrase, preferred a different reading, but both the manuscript tradition and the grammar support this version. Zawadski has demonstrated that both words were used with changing meanings in late antiquity.

Villa, he argues, had come to mean land, an estate, more often than it meant a building. Furthermore, as emperors' lives changed, palatium, a word once linked to the Palatine in Rome, or at least to the city residence of a reigning emperor, had acquired looser meanings, used for permanent or impermanent residences in town or country, from Tivoli to Panopolis to Pfalzel.[20]

Contemporaries would, therefore, have called this a palace because that word was no longer linked to specific functions. They could also have called it a villa, with some ambiguity as to whether they meant the building or its estate. Examination of contemporary word usage helps us grasp the breadth and instability of concepts in the minds of the original patron, users and observers of this complex. Mistakes arise from giving either word a sharply limiting meaning. Changing nomenclature goes with adaptable functions.

Duval, considering neither ancient term appropriate, has proposed 'chateau'. The word has the advantage of avoiding the usual scholarly associations, however outdated by late antiquity, with villa and palatium. The term carries its own baggage. It suggests a fundamental difference from earlier villas or palaces, and a similarity with medieval and later fortified residences. Like other grand late antique country residences, Diocletian's Palace is, however, very much a part of Roman tradition, preserving what we may paradoxically call urbanity in its baths and in the reception areas discussed below (*urbs in rure*).[21] The most unusual features of Split are those that relate to Diocletian's unprecedented situation rather than to any broader break with previous standards.

RECENT DISCUSSIONS: SCHOLARS' GROUPINGS

In addition to words the Romans employed, scholars have introduced modern terms by which to group Roman residences. Those sometimes applied to this building (or some part of it) have included the winged corridor villa, the fortified villa, aulic (perhaps better apsed) architecture and 'axis of ceremony'. Each selects parts to define the whole. With the possible exception of the first, each has validity as contributing to a more complex achievement. Winged corridor villas, common in Britain and northern Gaul but found occasionally in this area, had a frontal corridor providing main and subsidiary entrances between projecting wings. Examples slightly later in date than Split are Konz near Trier, which belonged to an emperor, and Mogorjelo, a short distance to the south of Split. The corner towers at Split do not resemble wings. The corridor runs along the back of the block, completely changing the possibilities for movement. The main (and so far, the only known) entrance to the main storey was through the protruding porch and Vestibule at the north, highly unusual features.[22]

FORTIFIED VILLAS

Scholars use this term for a broad category rather than a narrow type. Examples come from both mosaic representations and architectural remains. Criteria include rectangular shape, prominent towers, and porticos high above the ground.[23] Several North African mosaics of the fourth to fifth centuries show a facade with an arcaded upper storey and two corner towers. Architectural remains range from Nadir in North Africa, with two corner towers at the ends of one wall, to Pfalzel, another imperial villa near Trier (named palatiolum or little palace), with three rectangular projections on each wall and no corner towers. Examples more similar to Split include Mogorjelo and Gamzigrad in Serbia.[24]

Military elements at Split come from different sources. The arrangement of square towers found here, at Mogorjelo and in the first (inner) stage at Gamzigrad arose in simple forts on the southern and eastern frontiers, a late development, pre-Diocletianic in origin but continued by him.[25] The gateways and internal arrangements build on more elaborate constructions.

Corner towers flank the seaside wall (see figs 4.1 and 4.2). Along its upper storey runs an arcade framed by engaged columns and an entablature broken by five accents, three tripartite porches at the ends and centre, and two arches in the entablatures roughly midway between them. The horizontal band of arched openings continues, undecorated, along the land walls. Stretches of a

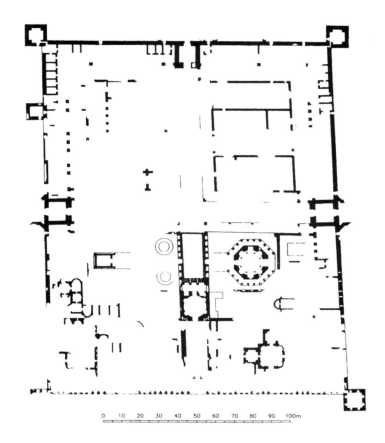

Fig. 4.8 Plan of remaining walls of main storey, *c.* 1996. Drawing: Jerko Marasović, by permission.

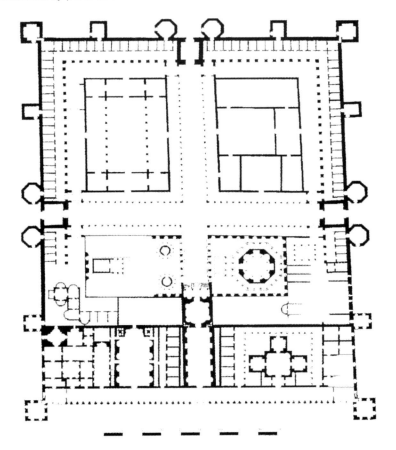

Fig. 4.9 Proposed plan of main storey, *c.* 2002. Drawing: Jerko Marasović, by permission.

Fig. 4.10 Basement under reception hall of palace, view north towards apse. Photo: Sheila McNally.

Fig. 4.11 Light well and foundations for triclinium (extensive reconstruction). Photo: Sheila McNally.

Fig. 4.12 North Gate after recent cleaning and stabilisation. Photo: Sheila McNally.

walkway survive inside these arcades.[26] These walls differed from the sea wall, first, in the number of towers and, second, in the concentration of decoration at their central gates, designed for closer viewing. Each gate had a lintel under a relieving arch, niches for free-standing sculpture on either side and ornamented mouldings. The main North Gate had more niches above the arch, pedestals above those, and richer ornamentation throughout (fig. 4.12).[27]

Did this impressive perimeter really serve as a fortification? Two considerations raise doubts, one historical and one structural. The building lies far from the frontier that Diocletian had spent much of his lifetime securing. Can he have anticipated a military attack? Certainly, he did not retire in the expectation that civil war would break out, although in time it did.

Structurally, the arcades cause problems for defensibility. Large archways occur on other Roman towers and gates as places for ballistae (defensive weapons), but never along a whole circuit. Walkways behind them would be a dangerous way for soldiers under attack to move from place to place. The Younger Pliny describes in detail what writers as late as the fifth-century Sidonius Apollinarus echo, namely the importance of views to leisured country life, differing views for different seasons, different weather, and different times of day. Pliny talks of long covered walkways that ran across his grounds. Here we find such walkways in straight lines and right angles. The arcaded corridor along the sea certainly provided a promenade for Diocletian, and so probably did the corridors behind the land arcades, looking out over vineyards and olive groves, the fruitful landscapes Romans extolled.

The militaristic effect would have been strong, but expressive rather than practical. Later inhabitants had to fill in these arches, as they did the seaside arcade, to make a defensible city. The great gates were also narrowed or completely closed. Those gates reinforce the perimeter's expressive function. They distinguish the palace from other fortified villas.[28] They may follow military precedent, but only because Roman forts themselves took on such functions at the expense of defensibility: 'By the late third century, the Roman fort with its city gates symbolized the seat of power and Roman civilization along its frontiers.'[29] These gateways seemingly exceeded any military source, incorporating embellishments unparalleled in surviving forts.

Statues at the gates, as in other empty niches around the palace, would have conveyed messages now lost. The only surviving figures are the bull-man heads at the North Gate (fig. 4.13), which I have identified as satyrs marking the entrance into a Dionysiac Paradise while Verzár-Bass has recently revived L'Orange's identification as river gods relating to the agricultural fertility praised in panegyrics. Either reference would stress the fruits of peace that are both an imperial accomplishment and the hoped-for accompaniment to a quiet retirement: the second reference would echo a theme traditional on triumphal arches and an iconography from city gates of this region.[30]

Fig. 4.13 North Gate, detail: heads on consoles over gate.
Photo: Sheila McNally.

AULIC (OR APSED) ARCHITECTURE:
RECEPTION AND DINING SPACES

A second development in late antique domestic architecture, both urban and rural, is the proliferation of reception and dining spaces: large halls with apses at one end (aulae) and multiple apses in triconch or multi-conch formation.[31] Both allow flexible reception of different numbers and kinds of visitors. To receive visitors, the owner, the dominus, might stand in the apse. For dining, small groups might gather in one or more apsed spaces: a single apse for an intimate group, multiple apses for more extensive entertainment.[32]

Such rooms become common in important residences, but are far from universal. They are often missing (or do not survive) in fortified villas. Both imperial Pfalzel and the relatively humble Mogorjelo lack them. Imperial Konz had a single prominent apsed hall (smaller apses formed part of the bath, not dining areas).[33] The grand, unfortified private villa at Piazza Armerina in Sicily, on the other hand, had a great apsed hall, a smaller one nearby, and a large triconch area at a greater distance. The residential block at Split has the same three spaces with unusual features.

Inside this rectangular block, areas of large simple spaces alternate with smaller, more intricately shaped ones, the whole punctuated by light wells. From the northern porch visitors entered a grand circular space, the Vestibule. Its walls survive with their niches for statues or urns and with small, high windows. Above them a partially restored dome still exists, once completely closed and covered with mosaics.[34] Only minor traces survive of the hall behind the Vestibule and its decorated doorframe on the corridor side. That southern doorway once gave a broad view of the bay through the porch opposite. The relatively small rows of piers under this hall may have supported columns or, more likely, only the floor above.

To reach the reception hall, visitors turned right into the long portico, passed a series of small rooms, probably for servants or guards, and an airshaft, then turned right again into an apsed hall. Part of the apse still survives, hidden in later building. Its basement (see fig. 4.10) shows this hall was wider than the central one. Marasović restores both halls convincingly with high roofs allowing clerestory lighting. Heavy piers under this hall may have supported columns above. In the most recent plan (see fig. 4.9), however, Marasović has eliminated the columns and introduced wall niches, because the walls have the same thickness as those of the niched Vestibule and central hall. Stairways on either side of the apse, partially preserved, connected it with the basement.

This room is neither dominant in the plan, like the central hall at Konz, nor particularly large. The indirect approach traversed impressive spaces. In the slightly later private villa at Piazza Armerina, a visitor followed an equally indirect route to reach the reception or audience hall. The halls of Piazza Armerina and Split are both 14 metres long; the hall at Konz was 14.5 metres. A second, narrower apsed room lay on the other side of an airshaft followed by a group of small, intricately varied rooms, known mainly from their basements and assumed to be the emperor's private quarters. Fragments of upper walls survive embedded in later housing.

The third area accented by a large opening in the corridor arcade is the dining suite on the east. An entry flanked by small (supply?) rooms led to a central room with three others opening from it. The small entryway kept light from the corridor from penetrating the dining area itself, which was set in a large open court allowing windows on all sides (see fig. 4.11, showing court and foundations). This suite forms a unique variant of the triconch. The central room and its three appendages are notable for their complicated shapes and separation from each other. Within square outlines, corner projections break up the side rooms into cruciform shapes. On the upper level, walls across the corners of the central space turned it into an octagon with niches. Narrow doorways connected the rooms.

In the 1990s the western room was fully rebuilt with large windows in two walls, similar to the doorways in two others, and the outline of the other rooms was reconstructed to a height of several metres (fig. 4.14).[35] Comparison with the slightly later triconch of the Piazza Armerina shows how easy movement from centre to individual dining area would have been in the latter, and how groups dining in separate curved spaces would continue to be aware of each other and of possible entertainment in the central square. The arrangement at Split not only segregates each group of diners, but also constricts space for service and for entertainment.[36]

Servants may have entered each dining area from the rear, using bridges from surrounding corridors (see reconstructed plan, fig. 4.9), a cumbersome proceeding since diners on couches require service from the front, as shown in all contemporary images. These peculiarities seem uncomfortable enough that I

Fig. 4.14 Triclinium, reconstructed: view north through entry into central room and dining area beyond; at left, reconstructed western dining area; octagonal Mausoleum in background. Photo: Sheila McNally.

resisted considering this a dining area before the discovery of a typical late antique dining tabletop in the basement hall nearby.[37]

Although both impressive and odd, these rooms have no specifically imperial qualities. They resemble those at (private) Piazza Armerina and are outdone by the spaces at (imperial) Gamzigrad, which, shortly after the building of the palace, acquired both a more conventional combination of apsidal hall with a multiple apsed space (as well as a free-standing structure like the dining area at Split).[38] In contrast to all three of these complexes, neither of the imperial villas near Trier provides obvious space for ceremonious hospitality. Konz has a central apsed hall, Pfalzel does not, and neither provides obvious space for multiple groups of diners. For reigning emperors near their capital cities, such provisions were apparently less important and not a precondition for calling a residence a palatiolum.

AXIS OF CEREMONY

A final term used to link this complex with others, and intended to emphasise imperial activity, is Dyggve's 'axis of ceremony'. Ejnar Dyggve saw the palace as a possible source for symbols of power repeated in later Byzantine palaces and in Christian churches. He invoked the outer walls, especially the sea facade, but his main interest centred on places inside the walls where he believed that

court ceremonies occurred.[39] From time to time, he and others identified various rooms in the residential block itself as settings for such activities, but also emphasised the central axis leading from the open outer court or Peristyle through the porch into that block.

Fig. 4.15 Peristyle, porch of residential block with seventeenth-century additions between columns. Photo: Ivan Sikavica.

DIOCLETIAN'S STATUS

Such talk of power and ceremony led Duval to emphasise a third factor in interpreting the palace: historical context. He has objected effectively to much interpretation of the architecture, but his major contribution is his focus on Diocletian's position.[40] He pointed out that Split was never the home of a reigning emperor and denied that imperial ceremonies would have occurred here. Keeping the name palace, with its newer, looser meanings, does not eliminate that contention. Archaeology has shown that apsed halls and triconches began in private buildings. Aristocrats were increasingly shaping country estates such as Piazza Armerina or Montmaurin in southern Gaul (France) to convey their power, while an imperial country residence such as Pfalzel might have no interior features that are strikingly ceremonial. Whether in its walls or its residential area, we can identify elements at Split designed to display power without invoking a specifically imperial mystique. It does not seem to me, however, that we should do so. Neither the historical nor the architectural evidence is so clear-cut.

Certainly, Dyggve elided the difference between Split and the homes of active rulers, but equally certainly Diocletian did not abandon all status and authority. In 305, he dramatically bestowed his purple garb on his successor and resumed his pre-imperial name, Diocles. No one seems to have taken much notice. He appears as Diocletian together with Maximian as *invicti seniores augusti* in the subsequent dedicatory inscriptions of the Baths of Diocletian in Rome, and with the same name and title on coins until 309. Later, he would be buried in a purple (porphyry) sarcophagus veiled in purple.[41] In 308, his deadlocked successors persuaded him to meet them at Carnuntum and exert his authority. Asked to return to active office, he refused, famously inviting Maximian to come to Split and see the vegetables he had planted with his own hands. This 'Lust am Gemüse'[42] provides a convincingly Diocletianic variation on the otium proper to country life: leisure spent not in literary or philosophical musings but in practical gardening.[43]

Additional material evidence of Diocletian's continued status comes from Gamzigrad, and perhaps also from Luxor. At Gamzigrad pilasters represent three pairs of tetrarchs, identified as Diocletian and Maximian as well as the members of the second tetrarchy. Paintings in the cult room at Luxor (see below) show Diocletian and Maximian in the central places of honour: Kolb, however, thinks that their clothing differentiates them from the four figures beside them and on the adjacent wall, so he dates the paintings to either the second or third tetrarchy, assuming later rulers included their predecessors in cult.[44] After 309, Diocletian seems to have slipped into an obscurity he probably did not expect – an obscurity great enough so that we can have four different accounts of his death.[45]

The tetrarchic system created a new status that led to a new task: the housing of *augusti* who had retired while retaining their special status. The imperial villas at Konz and Pfalzel, used by

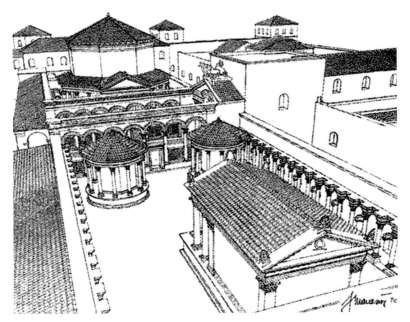

Fig. 4.16 Reconstruction drawing of Mausoleum, Peristyle, Vestibule and Temple with round buildings. Drawing: Jerko Marasović, 2002, by permission.

reigning emperors, are identified by historical evidence, not by any particular qualities in their plans. Many more oddities appear in the plans of Split and Gamzigrad, and although I cannot accept Srejović's point-by-point comparison of the two, I agree that both represent conscious efforts not only to incorporate indications of present power but also to establish a legacy.[46]

NEXUS OF POWER?

Prominent elements set this design apart from contemporary residences. The gates are one, as are the entrance porch of the residence and the two sacred enclosures, all tied together by the colonnaded streets. The placement of the elements indicates not only that they are important, but also that their importance depends on their relationships.

The entrance porch formed a visual culmination to dominant paths through the palace, a place where Diocletian might meet his guests or observe ceremonies.[47] Four columns of red granite from Aswan support a triangular pediment like a temple facade (see fig. 4.15). The lintel above the columns curves up in the centre, forming an arcuated pediment. Behind the columns a roughly five-metre deep porch once extended to the rectangular door of the Vestibule. Dyggve thought these shapes were specifically imperial, citing similar architecture on a later fourth-century silver plate, the Missorium of Theodosius, and an early sixth-century mosaic from Ravenna. Without adopting Dyggve's precise theories, Bolognesi Recchi-Franceschini has recently emphasised these similarities.[48]

As it did for the land gates, expressive military architecture may have prepared the way for this porch. Diocletian's most elaborate and impractical castrum resulted when the temple of Amon Re at Luxor became the central corridor of a military camp,

Fig. 4.17 Temple interior: crown moulding and coffered ceiling vault. Photo: Zvonko Buljević.

Fig. 4.18 Mausoleum interior: reconstructed colonnades, original frieze and later church furnishings. Photo: Sheila McNally.

leading to a shrine where columns and arch framed a niche depicting the tetrarchs, creating a permanent meeting between the emperors and their subjects. The architects of the palace may have had this experiment in mind when creating a more developed aedicula at the south porch. A concentration of column shafts and sphinxes brought from Egypt in this area of the palace testifies to Diocletian's responsiveness to Egyptian monuments.[49]

More Egyptian column shafts, together with others of cipollino, form the abutting colonnades. What we call the Peristyle is the carefully planned meeting place of three distinct constructions: the temple-like porch and the enclosures on either side. These enclosures are unusual. Roman temples on city streets or villa grounds often stood alone. Here walls around three sides of the sacral buildings isolate them from their environment, then give way to open arcades at the Peristyle.

Modern visitors to the Peristyle (see fig. 4.7) see the historical layering of Split at its best, and have to make an effort to imagine the very different situation of Roman viewers. On the east, we can look through the colonnade to the complex bulk of the Mausoleum/cathedral with its original porch and decorated doorway as well as its prominent medieval additions. Disappearance of enclosure walls, however, inserts the building into a wider totality unthinkable for its original visitors. On the other sides, still more imagination is required because later architects have skilfully filled in the colonnades. On the west, instead of small circular buildings flanking a rectangular one in a boxed space, we now see a screen of fine later palazzos, leaving only a narrow opening towards the Temple. On the south, the baroque central arch and side chapels now close what would have been an open view back to the Vestibule, and perhaps even through the linear axis to the sea (fig. 4.15).[50]

IDENTIFICATION OF SACRAL BUILDINGS
What are the buildings the original approach would have so suddenly and forcefully revealed? Two are well preserved, with some restoration and later embellishment. I have called them the Mausoleum and the Temple, and I think these conventional names are accurate, but they can be contested.

In the eastern enclosure an octagonal structure stands on a high podium that also supports a colonnaded porch about half the height of the building (see fig. 4.5). Inside, niches (six of the original seven), a much restored double-storeyed colonnade and a figural frieze still form a dramatic backdrop for medieval and baroque church furnishings (fig. 4.16). The western enclosure has almost completely vanished, as have the small circular buildings mentioned above, but a rectangular building survives, also on a high podium that once also supported a porch usually restored with four columns across and one on each side between those and the wall antae. Much external and internal decoration survives. This is one of the best-preserved Roman temples, and perhaps the last.

Medieval writers and architectural comparisons provide evidence for identifying these buildings. The written evidence is contradictory and often discussed.[51] It provides good evidence that the octagonal building, now the cathedral of Split, was Diocletian's Mausoleum, and weaker evidence that there was a temple somewhere dedicated to Jupiter. Reappraisals were prompted first by the discovery of the two small buildings, not yet firmly identified, and increased by the excavation at Gamzigrad of two mausolea, together with signs of cremation, on a ridge outside Galerius' residence.[52] If the practices at Gamzigrad can be applied to Split, then we have to ask whether Diocletian was not cremated and buried outside the palace.

Building activities at the two sites differed greatly. Split was built to one design, a daring and many purposed one. Gamzigrad evolved. Galerius began its construction to honour his mother rather than himself. The ultimate funerary practices reflect her religious preferences.[53]

Constantine Porphyrogenitus' identification of the cathedral as Diocletian's tomb is supported by its shape, its interior frieze and porphyry fragments found nearby. The plan allies it with other late antique mausolea.[54] The figural frieze in the interior guarantees its funerary function. Wreathed images of Diocletian and his wife echo a familiar sarcophagus theme that could be prepared for a tomb, but not for a temple, during their lifetimes. More evidence comes from the fragment identified as part of a porphyry sarcophagus.[55]

The building on the west is certainly a temple, but not necessarily a temple dedicated to Jupiter. Jupiter is the obvious deity for Diocletian, the Jovius, to honour, but the literary evidence is flawed (see note 51). An obvious alternative is a temple of the imperial cult (as distinct from a temple for the deified Diocletian, which he would not have built). Lavish decoration expresses emphatic values but nothing identifying a specific cult. External friezes recall the Forum of Trajan, and the interior ceiling has a layout taken from triumphal arches (fig. 4.17).[56]

The Mausoleum, based on the Pantheon, provides a third reference to structures in the city of Rome that had become icons of imperial power. Perhaps the most surprising element of its rich decoration is its internal frieze, placed in an unusual but prominent position, presenting generic funerary themes that could be found on the sarcophagus of any ordinary Roman (fig. 4.18).[57] Diocletian tried to restore traditional values. In retirement, he combined continued authority with simple private activities. The sacred buildings invoke the continuing tradition of imperial authority. At their heart the Mausoleum frieze presents humble private hopes (fig. 4.19). The palace is rich in such layers of meaning.

If it is a mistake to doubt the basic identifications of tomb and temple, it is certainly not a mistake to note their oddity. What are these sacred buildings and their surroundings doing in front of the residential block? Tombs and temples are not uncommon in villa grounds, but always in their own spaces as at Gamzigrad, not as here, flanking the grand entrance to the residence, a truly surprising arrangement and one made insistently visible by the design.

We see how carefully the builders reveal or conceal. Many Romans saw only the outer frame of the palace, militarism lightened by arcades and enriched by gates. Those who entered found themselves framed by broad colonnaded streets that masked what lay behind. So far as we can now tell, all the areas for everyday private life lay concealed: both humbler housing and workspaces in the north, and provisions for bathing, dining, taking one's ease in the south. The only open lines for sight or movement led along the thoroughfares towards the Peristyle. In that place, energies suddenly intersected. The visitor stood between colonnades opening onto walled spaces, tight boxes filled with a variety of elaborate buildings – an octagon, two cylinders, a cube – all encrusted in ornament. It would have been impossible not to feel the impact of all three sides at once. Living and dead, human and divine, could not be more emphatically connected. We do not know what set ceremonies or improvised rituals were envisaged or occurred over time, but the plan clearly shows the combination of powers involved.[58]

Whatever combination of expectations prompted Diocletian to build this structure how and when he did, he knew it would remain an imperial possession. Future uses would occur in the context of a powerfully evident past, and despite the obvious dislocation of so much he believed in, that remains true.[59]

Taken together, recent scholarly promotions of alternative names and functions emphasise the multiple sources and meanings – urbane, military, private, imperial, and above all richly religious – combined in the complex. In the 1960s, argument began over a supposition that certain characteristics peculiar to imperial residences remained fixed over a long period and extensive space, conveying meaning in themselves and correlating with set ceremonies. That thesis has vanished not because of problems with its details but because of its rigidity. It cannot be replaced with another equally simplistic one. There is much still that we do not know about this complex, but we can see that the builders were negotiating multiple relationships. Long after the work in the north and comfortable leisure in the south had given way to other ways of working and living, a part of these relationships survived and still survives, while the meanings of the surviving parts change with their physical boundaries. The original strength of the complex lay in its multiple uses; its continuing legacy stems from the grandeur of its experiments.

Fig. 4.19 Frieze inside Mausoleum, detail: cupids hold wreath containing bust of Diocletian. Photo: Ivan Sikavica.

ILLUMINATED MANUSCRIPTS IN CROATIA

Christopher de Hamel

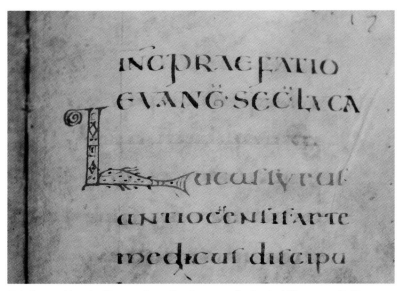

5.1 Gospel book, *Evangelium Spalatense*, Cathedral Treasury, Split. Photo: Živko Bačić.

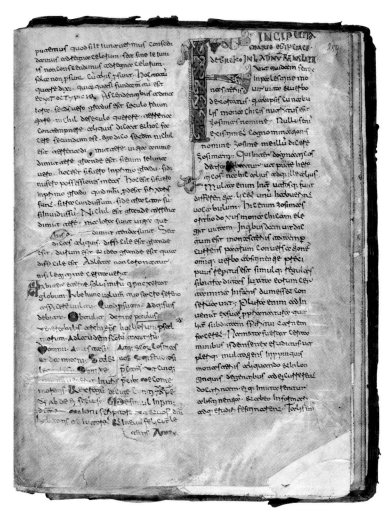

5.2 Passionale in Beneventan script, MR 164, fol. 259r, State Archives, Zagreb. Photo: courtesy of the Croatian State Archives and the Metropolitan Library

Unlike many countries of Europe, Croatia has possessed books continuously since ancient times. There has been uninterrupted access to literacy and some kind of written culture there for about 3,000 years. However, throughout all its history Croatia has been torn apart and re-formed, invaded and reconstructed, and its medieval books, like its people, seem to have been on the move forever. This beautiful and brave little country, facing out over the blue Adriatic towards Italy on one side and up into the dark forests of southern Hungary on the other, has never stood still. Its medieval illuminated manuscripts are like a microcosm of Croatian history: they have been imported and lost again, sold and rebought, sometimes preserved against all odds and often ruthlessly scattered. Many of the finest manuscripts used in medieval Croatia were originally brought in from other countries far away, and some of the most important books actually made and illuminated in Croatia itself have now long since been exported. This is a tale of endless journeys and chance survivals.

At one level, Croatia is curiously bare of medieval books. The finest examples of Croatian illuminated manuscripts are now in Istanbul, London, New York and elsewhere. The Croatian libraries often exhibit what are little more than fragments and scraps of

salvage. At another level, however, to visit Croatia in pursuit of manuscripts is like stepping back into the distant European past, for the manuscripts are not at all well known and many are still in the possession of monasteries or medieval churches, preserving a way of life which has hardly changed since the Middle Ages. There is a lot of knocking on doors and peering through grilles; one meets nuns, monks, friars and priests; and conversations are slow, in German, French or, if all else fails, in Latin. This is the old way of antiquarianism, and it is a precious survival.[1]

Archaeological inscriptions apart, the oldest manuscript now in Croatia is a Latin Gospel book (fig. 5.1), probably written in Italy in the seventh century.[2] It still belongs to the cathedral in Split, itself constructed around the converted mausoleum of the emperor Diocletian (d. 313). The city of Split, or Spalato, was from Roman times one of the most Italianate corners of Croatia, accessible by sea. The Gospel book is written in an elegant half-uncial script, with simple decorative initials in the shape of birds or fish, all appropriately maritime. It was clearly in Croatia by the tenth century, for it has additions of that time mentioning the districts of Split and Nin, near Zadar, the earliest Croatian diocese, suppressed in 928. The script of these extra texts is in the exotic hand known as Beneventan minuscule, one of the supreme oddities in the history of writing and an unexpected feature in early Croatian books. Very briefly, the ancient Romans had employed two classes of handwriting – capital letters and informal cursive. The capitals gradually evolved over the centuries into uncial, half-uncial and ultimately into the European alphabet we use today. The cursive, however, was the script of Roman administration. Its principal descendants were finally suppressed during the reforms of Charlemagne in the early ninth century, and they rapidly became extinct in all but the most inaccessible outposts of the old Roman Empire. The version which survived in the far south of Italy, like a living fossil cut off from the rest of the world, is named Beneventan minuscule, after the town of Benevento, near Naples. It was common at Monte Cassino. It is an entirely cursive script formed of curves and ligatures. The fact that Beneventan minuscule was clearly also in use right up the Adriatic coast of Croatia tells us two things. It suggests a nostalgic adherence to the ancient world, and it shows that early learning and literature came there from southern Italy.

MR 164 in the Croatian State Archives in Zagreb is a vast two-volume Passionale written in Italy (in normal script) in the mid- to late eleventh century. Once it reached Croatia, however, additions were made in Beneventan minuscule (fig. 5.2), fols 258r–266r. There is a long inscription on fol. 259r in which the Beneventan scribe identifies himself as Maion the deacon, and he says he supplied the text for the venerable Paul, archbishop of Split 1015–20. Even as late as the thirteenth century, Beneventan minuscule was still being expertly written on the Adriatic coast of Croatia. Culturally, southern Italy was not far away. Split is only about 110 miles by sea from the Italian coast, and even Naples 160 miles away was probably more accessible than Zagreb. A late thirteenth-century Gospel lectionary owned by the cathedral of Trogir, a few miles west of Split, has spectacular illuminated miniatures in a style which we will see later as characteristically Croatian, but the script is in a beautiful Beneventan hand (fig. 5.3). By the late Middle Ages, however, Beneventan minuscule had died out in Croatia and had probably become illegible to most people. Single leaves and recycled parchment scraps of old

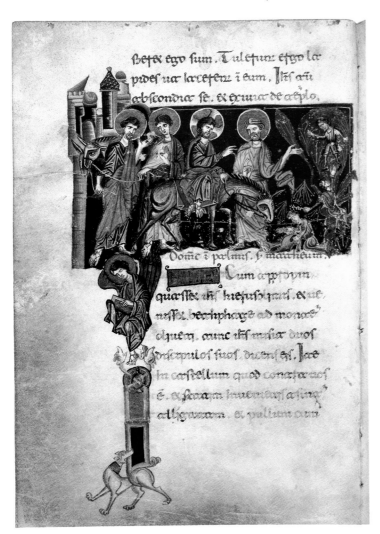

5.3 Gospel lectionary in Beneventan script, fol. 30v, Cathedral Treasury, Trogir. Photo: Živko Bačić.

5.4 Bible, MS 58 (*sub vitro*), Dominican convent, Dubrovnik. Photo: Vlaho Pustić, courtesy of the Croatian Conservation Institute.

Beneventan manuscripts are still to be found in Croatia, such as the discarded leaves of Jeremiah used to line the fifteenth-century binding of a martyrology in the Franciscan convent in Dubrovnik (RKP 189).

Other early books arrived by sea from Italy. There is an enormous two-volume Latin Bible exhibited in the Dominican convent in Dubrovnik, MS 58 (*sub vitro*). It must have been made in Rome in the third quarter of the eleventh century (fig. 5.4). It measures about 612 x 392 millimetres. It is extremely similar to a giant Bible presented to Geneva Cathedral before 1083 (Geneva, Bibliothèque publique et universitaire, ms Lat. 1), and it is one of a group of very similar Bibles associated with the papal reforms of Hildebrand, chancellor of the apostolic see 1061–73, and Cardinal Desiderius, abbot of Monte Cassino 1058–87, later Popes Gregory VII and Victor III respectively.[3] The Dubrovnik Bible's presence in Croatia suggests close contact with the latest developments of the papacy. It cannot have been made for the Dominicans, of course, for the order was not founded until the thirteenth century, and the friars did not reach Dubrovnik until 1225–8 at the earliest. The manuscript is marked up for public reading,

described twice as being 'in refectorio' (fols 76r and 85v), and the alphabetical symbols in its margins are those of Carthusian use. It was certainly not the only giant Italian Bible in Croatia. There is a defective volume of another almost identical Bible of similar date in the Franciscan convent in Šibenik, with the text from Psalms to the Pauline Epistles, inscribed in 1387 by Friar Paulus of Šibenik, warden of the Franciscan custody of Zadar. R 4040 in the National Library in Zagreb is a collection of fragments recovered from Croatian bookbindings. The first item is a portion of Genesis 7–8, written in Italy in the tenth century.

Christianity in Croatia, like much else there, was never simple. When the Roman Empire was divided into two parts in 395, the dividing line had been just to the east and south of the modern Croatian border. Therefore, while the ninth- to eleventh-century settlements along the Adriatic were looking westwards to Italy, even to papal Rome itself, the people in what are now Bosnia and Serbia turned to Byzantium. The missionaries Cyril (d. 869) and his brother Methodius (d. 885) are credited with the introduction of a version of eastern Orthodoxy. In an extremely unusual assertion of cultural independence (the kind of unhelpful gesture

5.5 Glagolitic missal, MR 180, fols 24v–25r, State Archives, Zagreb. Photo: courtesy of the Croatian State Archives and the Metropolitan Library.

that makes this such an interesting part of Europe), the brothers and their colleagues defiantly invented new scripts for their manuscripts, so that the different strands of the Christian faith and language would never be able to mingle. These scripts were Cyrillic (named after Cyril and still used in Russia) and Glagolitic. This second script is important. If Beneventan minuscule is strange, Glagolitic is the weirdest and most distinctive writing of all. It was intended for writing Slavic languages phonetically. It uses an entirely invented alphabet of about forty letters, quite unlike anything known anywhere else. Glagolitic manuscripts were mostly written in the south or east of the country or even beyond the boundaries of modern Croatia, but the script was clearly readable by many Croatians. It was as if it were a secret code only accessible to the initiated. It was sometimes regarded as the most Christian of scripts, for this was the only alphabet actually invented for use by the Church, while other scripts were taken or adapted from pre-Christian traditions. By the mid-thirteenth century it did, in fact, cross the cultural barrier with the western Catholic Church, for it was being used for liturgical books translated into the Old Slavonic language. Examples include a fifteenth-century missal (Zagreb, State Archives, MR 180, fig. 5.5) and a breviary written in 1460 for Mavar, priest of Vrbnik, on the island of Krk in the Adriatic, signed by the scribe Blaž Baromić, deacon and later a printer in Senj of books in Glagolitic type (Zagreb, National Library, R 7822). There is one unexpected example of Glagolitic in a Western European context. MS 95 in the Bibliothèque municipale de Tours in France is a fifteenth-century miscellany of theological texts in Latin from the chapter library in Tours. It clearly came into the hands of a medieval Croatian, doubtless Juraj of Slavonia, who had studied in Paris and became a canon of the cathedral of Tours in 1404. He has added notes about his home country, including, for example, lists of bishops from Split, Trogir, Šibenik and Zadar (fol. 77r) and on fol. 75v a Glagolitic alphabet, with the names of each of the letters in Latin script, 'ars, az, bouki, vidi, glagoule, dobro, iest, siwite …', and so on, with the heading, 'Istud alphabetum est chrawaticum …' (This is the Croatian alphabet …), and he wrote out the Lord's Prayer in Old Slavonic, 'Otse nas ise iesse na nebessech ssweto sse ime twoye …', which must have astonished the canons of Tours.[4]

Then there was another Christian frontier to the north-east. The Hungarians were already encroaching downwards by the 1080s. King Ladislaus of Hungary invaded Croatia after the death of Stjepan II in 1091 had brought the native Trpimirović dynasty to an end. The diocese of Zagreb was founded in 1094. One can see a new style of manuscript appearing in northern Croatia almost immediately. The books provide graphic evidence of a rapid cultural transformation, as churches adopted the customs and liturgy of the Holy Roman Empire from the north. A good example is the very late eleventh-century benedictional in the Croatian State Archives, MR 89 (fig. 5.6). It is a small upright manuscript, easily portable. Unlike the vast volumes shipped from

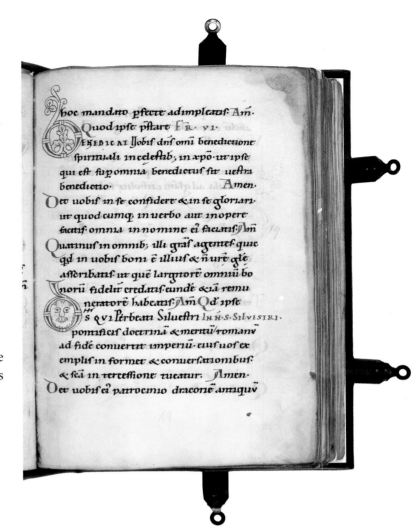

5.6 Benedictional, MR 89, fol. 19r, State Archives, Zagreb. Photo: courtesy of the Croatian State Archives and the Metropolitan Library.

Italy by sea, this volume doubtless travelled by horse. At far as fol. 34r, it is beautifully written in a thoroughly Germanic style, with red flourished initials including animals and sometimes faces. The second half of the volume is more quickly written. Maybe the book was sent unfinished and hastily completed on arrival, and these added parts include invocations of the patron saints of the new cathedral in Zagreb, SS. Stephen, Adalbert and George (fol. 83v). They also include a heavily used and corrected section for the ordination of new bishops (fol. 75r) and the office for the dedication of churches (fol. 98r). It is easy to see this as one of the first books needed for the new diocese. Another is MR 165 in the same library, a pontifical, or service book for bishops, written in a slightly sloping Germanic hand of the very early twelfth century. The infusion of religion from the north clearly brought manuscripts into Croatia along the old trading routes of the entire empire. A fine example is MR 153 in Zagreb, a volume which apparently once contained all four Gospels with an abbreviated psalter sandwiched between Mark and Luke, an unusual omnibus combination, compressed, like the benedictional, into a narrow and portable volume, suitable for a saddle-bag. The manuscript is French, *c.* 1100, almost certainly (to judge from its style) written in Normandy. The two surviving evangelist portraits, those for Luke and John, show the Gospel writers as scribes with wings and the heads of the animals which were their symbols in art, an ox for Luke (fol. 17r, fig. 5.7) and an eagle for John (fol. 68v). This bizarre imagery, which ultimately descended from Irish Gospel books, was used in Brittany in the ninth and tenth centuries and reappeared in Normandy around 1100, as in Rouen, Bibliothèque municipale, ms 31, from St-Evroul.[5]

One would expect that the establishment of churches and monasteries from northern Europe would have brought the monastic traditions of book production and scriptoria into Croatia. There are a few (but only a very few) Latin manuscripts which may have been written in Croatia itself in the twelfth century. One is a copy of Origen's commentary on Genesis, about 1180, in the chapter library at Split, MS 626, decorated with initials showing engaging little men with big heads and wild eyes. This seems to be almost the only volume of quality which

has any likelihood of having been made locally at this period. The twelfth century was the greatest age for the foundation of religious houses, both of the old Benedictine order and of the new orders of Cluniacs, Cistercians, Augustinians and others, and in other countries of Europe monks were busily copying books and stocking their libraries systematically. It is difficult to know how much weight to give to the absence of extant twelfth-century manuscripts in Croatia. Chances of survival are necessarily random in a region constantly buffeted by warfare and invasion (including the Mongols in the thirteenth century), but there really do not appear to be in Croatian collections today those great sets of homogenous Romanesque monastic books which obviously occupied so much of the labour and resources of monks elsewhere in Europe. The Cistercian house of Stična in Slovenia, by contrast, only about fifty-five miles from Zagreb, evidently had a notable scriptorium in the twelfth century, with a line of supply through to the Rhineland, and some thirty-three of its Romanesque

5.7 Gospels of Luke and John, MR 153, fol. 17r, State Archives, Zagreb. Photo: courtesy of the Croatian State Archives and the Metropolitan Library.

5.8 Bible, MR 159, fol. 4r, State Archives, Zagreb. Photo: courtesy of the Croatian State Archives and the Metropolitan Library.

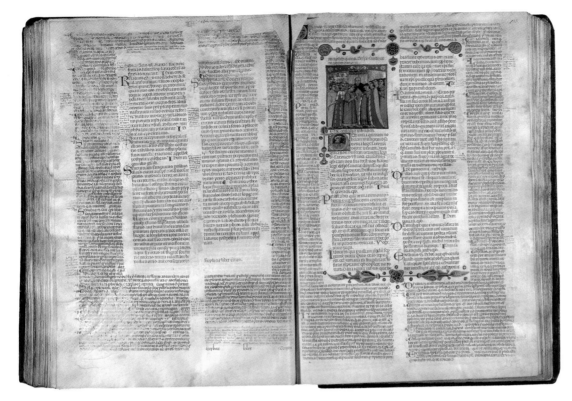

5.9 Decretals of Gregory IX, MR 49, fol. 186r, State Archives, Zagreb. Photo: courtesy of the Croatian State Archives and the Metropolitan Library.

one-time students. The Dominican, Augustin Kazotić (*c.* 1260–1323), was born in Trogir and studied in the University of Paris. He was later bishop of Zagreb (1303–17), and was a major benefactor of the cathedral library. He is a likely source for former textbooks such as MR 12, Hugh of St-Cher's commentary on Maccabees and Chronicles, written in Paris around 1280. Two Parisian manuscripts now in the Dominican convent in Dubrovnik include *pecia* notes. These are numerical calculations in the margins which reveal that the books were copied from the separate quires, or *peciae* in Latin, which were held by licensed university stationers and were rented out to scribes to act as their exemplars. One is Thomas Aquinas, *Sententia libri ethicorum*, MS 15, and the other is Mauritius de Pruvinis, *Disticiones*, MS 25, both typical

manuscripts still survive together with fragments of five others.[6] There is no apparent indication of anything remotely comparable in Croatia, and this was evidently a lean time for Croatian manuscript production.

By the thirteenth century, even in the most resourceful monasteries in Europe, domestic book production was falling away. Professional scribes and illuminators were settling in the big commercial cities and especially around the universities, of which the two most important were Paris and Bologna. Students or visitors there from abroad would acquire manuscripts during their studies or travels, and would commonly bring them back to their home countries or religious communities. MS 54 in the Dominican library in Dubrovnik is a volume of sermons written in France. It has the ownership inscription of Friar Peter of Ragusa (Dubrovnik), who bequeathed it to his convent so that they might pray for his soul. Friar Peter's studies and journey abroad had been sponsored by his convent in 1343, and the book was one result of that trip.[7] A later but precise example of a purchase occurs in Zagreb (Croatian State Archives, MS 147), a copy of the *Mamotrectus* with a contemporary note recording that it belonged to Master Andreas of Poland, archdeacon of Dubica and canon of Zagreb, who had bought it in Tendeta for two ducats in the currency of Buda and finally in 1478 bequeathed it to the monastery of St Nicholas in Zagreb. The term 'Master' there (*Magister*) suggests an academic qualification. There are a good number of manuscripts from the medieval library of Zagreb Cathedral which must have arrived as personal bequests from

student books. The use of *peciae* is securely documented only in Paris and Bologna. The Aquinas text was available in Paris in thirty-eight *peciae* and the Mauritius in eighty-four.[8] It is absolute proof of a Parisian origin.

Another bishop of Zagreb, Jakop de Placentia (Jacques de Plaisance, bishop 1343–8), had been medical doctor to the kings of France and chaplain to the popes in Avignon. He was the donor of a pontifical, now MR 163 in the Croatian State Archives in Zagreb, which has a long inscription recording that it was completed by an Italian scribe in the bishop's own house in Avignon in 1339. He was the presumed donor, too, of a pontifical illuminated for John XXII himself (pope 1316–34), now MR 32, and a number of French medical texts in Zagreb were probably brought back by him. It is likely that one of the most spectacular fourteenth-century manuscripts in Zagreb was also acquired by Bishop Jakob. This is MR 159, known as the *Biblia Solemnis Ecclesiae Cathedralis Zagrabiensis*, a very large Latin Bible, about 372 x 246 millimetres (fig. 5.8). It, too, was almost certainly illuminated in Avignon. It shows a mixture of two styles, French and Italian. The first part, as far as fol. 404r, closely resembles that of a missal illuminated in Avignon in 1331, now Toulouse, Bibliothèque municipale, ms 90.[9] From fols 404v to 513v, however, the decoration looks Italian. That combination of styles is characteristic of the exiled papal court in Avignon.

Italy itself was predictably a prolific overseas source of manuscripts which found their way to Croatia in the late Middle Ages. Bologna was by far the most famous centre in Europe for legal studies, and the university book trade there operated a *pecia* system similar to that in Paris. It specialised in texts of civil and canon law. There is a Bolognese manuscript of the decretals of Gregory IX in Zagreb (fig. 5.9, Croatian State Archives, MR 49), illuminated about 1320. It, too, contains *pecia* notes, this time in the Bolognese form, such as 'fi. xx pe. secundi partis' (end of the twentieth piece of the second part, fol. 201v). The manuscript is annotated in the same contemporary hand as MR 49, a Bolognese copy of Gratian's encyclopaedia of church law, which has the late medieval ownership inscription of Zagreb Cathedral. The books must have been a pair, probably acquired together from a stationer or bookseller in Bologna. We gain a rare glimpse of the operation of this trade from MS 1 in the library of the Dominicans in Dubrovnik, a late thirteenth-century Bolognese manuscript of Justinian. It includes at least one *pecia* note (fol. 5v), but, more importantly, someone entered on the flyleaf a list of twenty-five exemplars of civil and canon law texts held by an unnamed bookseller, certainly in Bologna, with the number of *peciae* for each text, from two to forty-two. The list can be dated

from accompanying verses to 1296–7.[10] Such records of medieval stationers' stocks are almost unknown.

There are two further interesting records of values, both in texts by the great Dominican master, Thomas Aquinas. MS 2 in the Dominican convent in Dubrovnik is the first part of the *Summa* of Aquinas, inscribed by Friar Alexius of Ragusa, prior of the convent there in 1386–8, who asserts that for the sake of Christ the volume is worth five and a half florins in gold. Another book, Aquinas on the Epistles of St Paul (MS 11 there), has a note dated 1372 recording that it was presented to the convent in Ragusa by Ser Gine de Faczotin in exchange for three Masses on the condition that, if ever he should pay three ducats to the friars, they would give him his book back, and he would then be permitted to retain it for as long as he wished. It sounds like some kind of amicable pledge, which was presumably never redeemed. Soon afterwards, to judge from holes in the binding, it was chained in the convent's library.

The route of manuscripts from Italy into Croatia seems well established by the late fourteenth century. There are two

5.10 Gratian, *Decretum*, MS 22 (36-VII-3), fol. 215v, Dominican convent, Dubrovnik. Photo: Photo: Vlaho Pustić, courtesy of the Croatian Conservation Institute.

5.11 Peter Lombard, *Sententiae* (Sentences), MR 11, fol. 217v, State Archives, Zagreb. Photo: courtesy of the Croatian State Archives and the Metropolitan Library.

points which we should bear in mind. One is that scribes and illuminators could travel too, and doubtless often did, and so a book which appears from its style to have been executed in one location could, in theory, have been made somewhere else by craftsmen working far from home. The second point is that manuscripts were sometimes written in one place and illuminated elsewhere, which adds to the problem of trying to localise a volume by style alone. Let us look at examples of each.

Some Croatians made their own books while abroad. We can document a law student's university life from MR 17–18 in the State Archives in Zagreb, a two-volume commentary on the decretals by the Italian author Angelo de Castro. It was copied by Blasius (Blaž) de Marowcha, canon of Zagreb. He described himself as a student of canon law in Padua, signing MR 17 there on 16 October 1463 (fol. 310v) and two and a half years later at the third hour of the night on New Year's Eve 1465 (fol. 150r). He was still working on his manuscript in 1466 (MR 18, fol. 234r), but eventually handed the task to a colleague from home, Martin de Gragena, another canon of Zagreb and also a student in Padua, who finished it on 2 January 1467 (fol. 324r). In the meantime, Blaž de Marowcha had undertaken the copying of another commentary on the decretals, which he completed at the fourteenth hour on 3 April 1467 (MR 60, fol. 241r). In a marginal note in MR 18, fol. 212v, Blaž tells us of his Italian journey. He recounts that he had crossed to Italy in October 1462 and initially spent nearly three months in Ferrara. On 1 January 1463 he came to Padua, where he studied canon law and eventually had his doctorate conferred on him by the sacred college of Padua on 28 March 1467. He could not depart immediately, as he was still transcribing MR 60. He finally left Padua for Venice on 4 May 1467 and celebrated Ascension Day there (it was on 7 May that year), and at last he arrived home in Zagreb on 17 May, doubtless carrying his three new manuscripts with him.

Blaž was a competent scribe but he was not an illuminator. He left a large blank space at the top of the first page of MR 17, evidently in the confident expectation that someone, perhaps in Zagreb, would one day be able to fill in an appropriate miniature. This is logical, if unfounded. A new text, not available locally in Croatia, would have to have been written somewhere where an exemplar was available, but any decoration could, in theory, be added at any stage, even after the volume had reached its new home. MR 19 is a mid-thirteenth-century Italian manuscript of Peter Lombard's commentary on the Psalms from Zagreb Cathedral library. The scribe left space for illumination, which was never added. Similarly, R 3001 in the National Library in Zagreb is an Italian gradual of the first half of the fourteenth century: it has a large space left for a three-quarter page initial 'A' on the opening leaf. It is not that the manuscript was abandoned unfinished, for it was still in use in the eighteenth century, to judge from additions on fols 150v–152v and elsewhere; it is simply that the particular destination, presumably in Croatia, had no facilities or expertise

in book illumination even in the early fourteenth century.

In fact, a distinctive style of Croatian illumination was already beginning to emerge by about 1300. One of the initials in the Bolognese decretals (Zagreb, MR 49, mentioned above) was accidentally left blank and was supplied in a more Germanic hand (the initial 'D' on fol. 17r). MS 22 in the Dubrovnik Dominican library is an early fourteenth-century copy of Gratian's *Decretum* with the gloss of Bartholomew of Brescia, a typically Bolognese law text in a script which seems likely to have been written in Bologna itself. All its main initials were probably left blank. They were inserted in a style which is utterly unlike anything from mainstream Italy (fig. 5.10). They show narrative scenes peopled with serious little men with dark eyes and pronounced (almost Byzantine) draperies. What is so remarkable is that their immediate exemplar was quite clearly a French copy of Gratian of around 1180, illuminated in Sens or more likely Paris, with exaggeratedly sinewy nude figures and clumps of petalled foliage characteristic of French Romanesque copies of Gratian and Peter Lombard.[11] One such earlier manuscript must have been in Croatia, and it was used to furnish the unfamiliar imagery for a Gratian newly bought unfinished in about 1320. Another manuscript may show a similar local illumination of an imported book: a copy of Peter Lombard's *Sentences* from the beginning of the fourteenth century (Zagreb, Croatian national archives, MR 11). The script looks French, but the illumination, which is of high quality, is quite unlike anything from France, although it has elements of German or Bohemian art and the same busy, serious little figures in the pictures (fig. 5.11). Compare the Beneventan Gospel lectionary from Trogir (fig. 5.3 above), and we may begin to form a sense of an early Croatian style.

It is evident that not every city in Croatia had professional manuscript illuminators, even in the late Middle Ages. One city which certainly did was Dubrovnik. We know this not only from extant manuscripts but also from a group of contracts for the making of books there between 1405 and 1453.[12] This is precious information, for actual medieval scribal contracts of any kind are extraordinarily rare. Two concern a scribe Marinus Kovačić, evidently a priest in Dubrovnik. A pair of Dominican friars from Šibenik took the opportunity of an extended visit to their order's convent in Dubrovnik in July 1405 to commission a missal from Marinus on behalf of their own house in Šibenik. Marinus was to write the book himself and it was to be appropriately decorated. The agreed price was thirty-four gold ducats, of which Marinus received fifteen ducats as a down payment and promised to complete the volume within one year. Human nature being what it is, the book was not remotely ready within the agreed time. The prior of Šibenik wrote to his colleagues, still in Dubrovnik, frustrated by the scribe's apparent excuses, 'per verba dilatoria fabulationes et tardationes', asking them to extract a financial pledge from Marinus and a promise that he really would get to work. Šibenik was too far away to enforce the contract's penalty

clauses, the prior admitted, but the friars were to withhold all further payment in the meantime. He listed again exactly what they should insist on, which included red painted initials and fifteen very large initials in fine quality gold and blue for each of the main feasts of the year, which are listed. The missal was finally completed nearly two years late on 20 April 1408.

Marinus Kovačić appears again in a contract of 26 June 1412. This time a 'beautiful, correct and solemn missal' was commissioned by Ser Jacopo de Ugodonis, notary and chancellor of Dubrovnik. It was to be copied from the missal which had been given to Dubrovnik Cathedral by the executors of Anne de Mense. It was to be written on regular and large leaves with wide margins, with illuminated borders throughout and all appropriate large and small initials in red and blue, to be executed in cinnabar (vermilion) and the finest ultramarine. The text was to conform to the Use (or local custom) of Ragusa (Dubrovnik), subject to

inspection and approval by two canons of the cathedral, Matteo de Georgio and Matteo de Ragnina. The price was thirty-five ducats, and the manuscript was to be completed within eight months.

Dubrovnik had been a possession of Venice from the beginning of the thirteenth century to the mid-fourteenth century, and although it then became an independent republic, its art and architecture remained strikingly Venetian for centuries to follow. Zadar was sold to Venice in 1409, and the Venetians dominated the Dalmatian coastline. Fifteenth-century illuminated manuscripts from the Croatian seaports are often so Italianate in style that we might well wonder whether they were actually made in Italy or by scribes and artists from the Veneto working abroad. There are two very fine volumes which, to judge from their municipal texts, must have been local productions, and both are datable. One is the matricola or guild statutes of the Fraternity of the Holy Ghost in Trogir, begun in 1428 and still in use as late as the nineteenth century, now in Trogir Cathedral library (fig. 5.12). It opens with a beautiful full-page frontispiece, like a tiny panel painting, of the members of the fraternity kneeling in

5.13 Matricola of the Fraternity of St Anthony, fol. 15v, Historical Archives, Dubrovnik. Photo: Vlaho Pustić, courtesy of the Croatian Conservation Institute.

5.14 Gradual, Franciscan convent, Dubrovnik. Photo: Vlaho Pustić, courtesy of the Croatian Conservation Institute.

prayer below a banner showing the Venetian lion of St Mark. It is, however, Croatian work, ascribed to the illuminator Blaž Jurjev. Another matricola is in the historical archives in Dubrovnik. It comprises the statutes of the town's Fraternity of St Anthony. The manuscript was begun in 1348. It was updated in 1432 with a monumental half-page miniature of St Peter with his keys and St Anthony with his pig standing on either side of the throne of Christ (fol. 15v, fig. 5.13). In a typically Italian whorl of foliage at the foot of the page is a little face peering out, of the kind sometimes associated with manuscript artists' self-portraits.[13]

The liturgical manuscripts in the Franciscan convent of Dubrovnik mostly date from the late fifteenth and early sixteenth centuries. Were it not for their current location and the likelihood that they have never moved, one might easily have taken them for Venetian productions. One is the Franciscan martyrology, RKP 189, which is of Franciscan and clearly local use, as the calendar singles out in red the patronal feast of St Blaise, 'Festum ragusinorum'. The huge manuscript choir books of the convent include a gradual with superb illumination in the monumental classical style of north-eastern Italy, festooned with vases and fruit dangling against backgrounds flecked in blue (fig. 5.14). This illusion was pioneered by Mantegna and others, and became characteristic of manuscripts from Mantua, Padua and eventually Venice. This is the work of an artist of extraordinary skill, and it would be very pleasing to hope that he worked in Dubrovnik itself.

The ultimate symbol of the partnership between Croatia and book illumination of the Italian Renaissance lies in the supreme figure of Giulio Clovio (1498–1578) (fig. 5.15). He was one of the few manuscript artists eulogised without moderation by Vasari in his *Lives of the Painters*, where he was equated with Michelangelo: 'There has never been, nor perhaps will there ever be for many centuries, a rarer or more excellent miniaturist,' Vasari wrote.[14] Clovio's most famous manuscripts include the Hours of Cardinal Alessandro Farnese, dated 1546, now in the Morgan Library and Museum in New York (M 69), and the Towneley Lectionary in the New York Public Library (MS 91). His portrait was painted by El Greco. What is perhaps less well known is that Giulio Clovio was Croatian. He was apparently born Juraj Glovičić in the town of Grižane on the northern Adriatic coast. He moved to Italy about

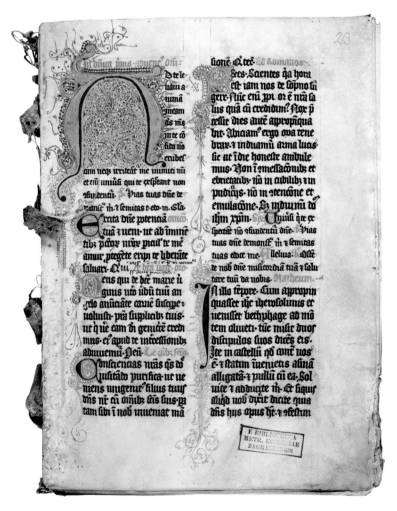

5.16 Missal, MR 13, fol. 23r, State Archives, Zagreb. Photo: courtesy of the Croatian State Archives and the Metropolitan Library.

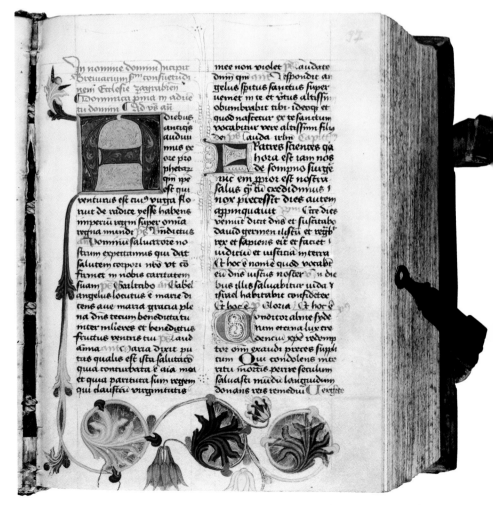

5.17 Breviary, MR 103, fol. 97r, State Archives, Zagreb. Photo: courtesy of the Croatian State Archives and the Metropolitan Library.

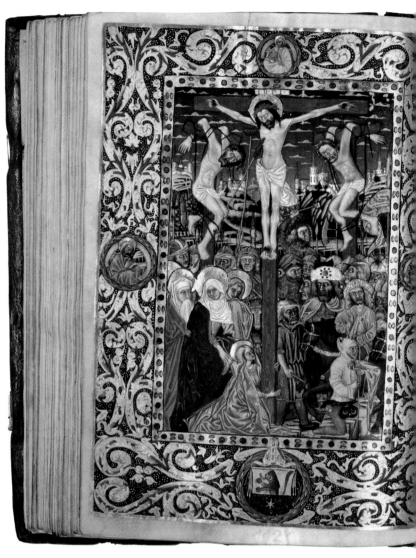

5.18 Missal of Dominic Kálmáncsehi, BR 355.1, fol. 7r, Cathedral Treasury, Zagreb. Photo: Mario Braun, courtesy of the Croatian Conservation Institute.

5.19 Missal of Dominic Kálmáncsehi, BR 355.1, fols 112v–113r, Cathedral Treasury, Zagreb. Photo: Mario Braun, courtesy of the Croatian Conservation Institute.

1516. There he adopted the name Guilio, apparently in honour of Giulio Romano; his usual surname is an Italianisation of 'Crovatus', the Croatian. He was the favourite illuminator for the Sistine Chapel. There is no evidence whatsoever that Clovio ever worked in or for patrons in his homeland, despite some credulous or patriotic claims in the past. Nonetheless, the baroque putti of the gradual from the Dubrovnik Franciscans, just cited, have uncannily close parallels with similar frolicking putti executed some years later by Clovio in Rome.[15] The Dubrovnik volume must show us something of the cultural climate which produced the greatest Renaissance illuminator, as clearly as the icons of Giorgios Klontzas in Crete teach us about the genesis of El Greco.

Let us now return to the north. While most churches and monasteries of Croatia accepted the liturgical reforms of Italy from the late thirteenth century onwards and used more or less the same church rites as similar institutions in Western Europe, the diocese of Zagreb doggedly held on to its own liturgical use. Later it ignored the standardisation promoted by the Council of

Trent and maintained its own distinctive rite until 1788. This had various effects on manuscript production. It meant that, unlike religious houses in Dubrovnik, for example, which could import and use manuscripts originally made in Italy or elsewhere, the churches of Zagreb were obliged to make their own. It meant, too, that when printing became common in the later fifteenth century and general liturgical books could be bought on the open market, patrons from Zagreb were still obliged to use texts which were not normally available in print. Manuscripts, therefore, continued to be copied by hand in Zagreb long after many other places had abandoned the practice.

A reasonable number of surviving liturgical books survive from Zagreb Cathedral. One from the mid-fourteenth century is MR 13 in the Croatian State Archives, corresponding with an entry in the cathedral's contemporary inventory where it is described as a new missal bequeathed by a dominus Blasius for the use of the prebendary of Saints Cosmas and Damian. While the script is Germanic and rough, doubtless made locally, the

5.20 Missal of George of Topusko, BR 354, fol. 168v, Cathedral Treasury, Zagreb. Photo: Mario Braun, courtesy of the Croatian Conservation Institute.

penwork initials are much more Italian in style and are perhaps from the fifteenth century (fig. 5.16). Probably this, too, was an unfinished book, completed later by someone such as Canon Blaž de Marowcha, who had worked in Italy. Another, from the second quarter of the fifteenth century, is much more Austrian or Bohemian in style. This is MR 103 in the same library, a breviary explicitly described as 'secundum consuetudinem Ecclesie zagrabiensis' (according to the Use of the Church of Zagreb, fig. 5.17). At the end is a list of items on the altar of Saints Cosmas and Damian in the cathedral in 1478, including a breviary on parchment, doubtless this volume.

There are two very grand and late missals still kept in the treasury of Zagreb Cathedral itself. It is appropriate to end with these, for they are manuscripts of great splendour. Their origins, however, are not yet fully unravelled. The first, BR 355 (figs 5.18–5.19), contains the arms of two contemporary bishops, those of Dominic Kálmáncsehi (fols 7r, 16r and 112v) and those of Osvald Thuz (fols 131r, 136v, 183v, etc.). Kálmáncsehi was a Hungarian, ambassador to Matthias Corvinus, king of Hungary 1458–90. He took part in the wars against the Turks in Moldavia in 1475, in

1485 was governor of the defences on the Adriatic coast, and in 1495 was appointed bishop of Nagy-Várad in Hungary. At least three other manuscripts are known elsewhere with the same arms. One is a Book of Hours dated 1492, showing that by that year Kálmáncsehi was already using a mitre over his arms, as in the Zagreb book, even though he was not yet technically a bishop.[16] The missal has marvellous illumination, including a full-page miniature of the Crucifixion. It has a curious feature, for there is a court jester kneeling in the right-hand corner of the picture. On the face of it, the manuscript is likely to be Hungarian, and the very fine contemporary red morocco binding with painted and gilt borders was surely made in Buda.[17] Osvald Thuz was bishop of Zagreb from 1466 to 1499. In his time northern Croatia became closely allied to the Hungarian court. Osvald Thuz actually crowned László II, king of Hungary (1490–1515). If BR 355 had survived alone, we would not doubt for a moment that it was made in Hungary and presented by Kálmáncsehi to Bishop Thuz for use in Zagreb Cathedral between about 1490 and 1499.

5.21 Missal of George of Topusko, BR 354, fol. 210r, Cathedral Treasury, Zagreb. Photo: Mario Braun, courtesy of the Croatian Conservation Institute.

5.22 Missal of George of Topusko, BR 354, fol. 27r, Cathedral Treasury, Zagreb. Photo: Mario Braun, courtesy of the Croatian Conservation Institute.

The second missal in the cathedral treasury is BR 354. It is even larger and more opulent. It is known as the Missal of George of Topusko. It is in two distinct styles. The first of these (fols 2–16, 37–267 and 286–97) is late fifteenth century, executed by a wonderfully eccentric artist, with frenzied borders crammed with people and animals in exuberant and comic combinations (figs 5.20–5.21). Many of these are copied from images in printed engravings by the Master of the Playing Cards (*c.* 1430–50), the Master of the Berlin Passion (perhaps *c.* 1450–60), the Master E.S. (*c.* 1460–7), and Israel van Meckenem (d. 1503). In 1942, during the Nazi occupation of Zagreb, it was declared that the manuscript's art was of such quality that it could only have been executed by a German, and it was proposed that he was Hans Alemanus, a painter recorded in Zagreb from 1503 to 1526.[18] The dates do not entirely match, and the only documented commission from Alemanus (in July 1503) was a panel and not a book. For the moment, let us call the illuminator the Master of George of Topusko. His work in the missal includes a coat of arms which is uncannily similar to that of Dominic Kálmáncsehi, with

the slight variant that the lower compartment now shows a half star instead of a full star. These half-star arms are said to be those of George (Juraj) of Topusko, provost of Čazma, east of Zagreb, abbot of Topusko and suffragan of Bishop Osvald Thuz of Zagreb. He had died by 1518. The second style in BR 354 occurs on fols 17–35 and 268–85. This later artist worked in a much more Italian manner, and the work dates from the early sixteenth century (fig. 5.22). The second artist sometimes completed work of the first (as on fol. 54v) but not the other way round. Their two campaigns of work were quite distinct. The work by the second artist includes the arms of Simon Erdödy-Bakócz, bishop of Zagreb *c.* 1518–43.[19]

Yet another missal with a close variant of the Kálmáncsehi/Topusko arms is now in the Croatian State Archives (MR 170, fig. 5.23). Its colophon is dated 1495, and it is signed by the scribe Matheus of Milethencz, parish priest of St Paul in Otnja. This village is apparently in Hungary, but the scribe could have worked anywhere. It, too, is illuminated by the Master of George of Topusko, but only as far as fol. 104r; thereafter, it was completed by a much later artist, probably in the late sixteenth century. The importance of MR 170 is that it contains an inscription inside the upper cover recording that in 1518 the missal was delivered to the cathedral by the executor of George of Topusko, prebendary of the church of Zagreb.

These three missals, one certainly for Kálmáncsehi, two probably for Topusko, are evidently intimately connected to each other, but in a relationship which is not entirely clear. Some writers simply assume that the arms are within the range of acceptable variation and that all three were made for Kálmáncsehi, which would mean that they are Hungarian.[20] However, the script of BR 354 is extremely like that of a prayer added on fol. 71v of MR 62, an earlier Zagreb missal which cannot reasonably have been in Buda. More importantly, the hand of the Master of George of Topusko also occurs in MR 10, an antiphoner 'pro alma cathedrali ecclesiae Zagrabiensis' (as its title describes it), with the arms of Bishop Osvald Thuz. Although the illumination of the choir book is more restrained, even the smallest ornamental details are identical, and this must be the work of the same painter (fig. 5.24). If the antiphoner was illuminated in Zagreb, so too were the missals.

One explanation is that the Missal of Dominic Kálmáncsehi arrived first, given to Osvald Thuz in Zagreb around 1490–5. Bishop Osvald's suffragan, George of Topusko, saw it, admired it, devised his own arms by only slightly modifying those of Kálmáncsehi, and commissioned two more missals locally. Alternatively, he may have been the agent for Kálmáncsehi and undertook the supervision or completion of all three for the Hungarian prelate, and the arms may all be Kálmáncsehi's, increasingly degenerating into hybrids as they were copied and recopied away from Hungary. Two of the books were only partly finished and still unbound when Osvald Thuz died in 1499. After Topusko's own death, the incomplete books were finally delivered by his estate to the cathedral in 1518, where the arms were mistakenly assumed to be his own. In either case, the Master of George of Topusko is most likely to have been working not in Hungary but in Zagreb.

The missals' style is a kaleidoscopic confection of boisterous good humour and piety, of German, Netherlandish and Hungarian art, and of Italianate script and local liturgy. Their joyful and utterly beguiling mix of cultures and artistic enterprise is characteristic of the making of manuscripts for use in medieval Croatia. They aptly symbolise that country's altogether unique and complicated civilisation of the Middle Ages, which was to be shattered again when the Muslim armies of Suleiman the Magnificent defeated Hungary at the battle of Mohács in 1526.

5.23 Missal of George of Topusko, MR 170, fol. 95v, State Archives, Zagreb. Photo: courtesy of the Croatian State Archives and the Metropolitan Library.

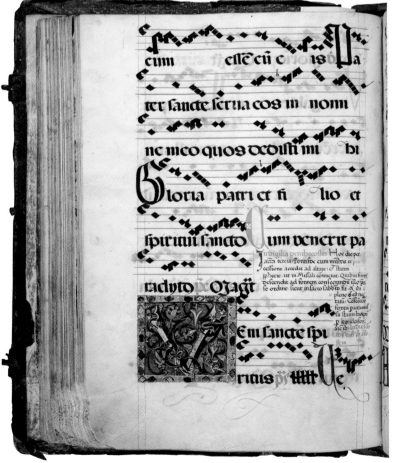

5.24 Antiphoner, MR 10, fol. 82v, State Archives, Zagreb. Photo: courtesy of the Croatian State Archives and the Metropolitan Library.

GOTHIC ART & THE FRIARS IN LATE MEDIEVAL CROATIA
1212–1460

Donal Cooper

The 'coming of the friars' – the rise of the mendicant orders in the thirteenth century – transformed the social and artistic face of medieval Christendom. Within decades every European town of any size had a clutch of significant mendicant foundations firmly embedded within its expanding urban fabric. Led by university-educated preachers, fired to varying degrees by the zeal of apostolic poverty, and committed to the pastoral care of merchants and the urban poor alike, the friars quickly became the most dynamic spiritual force in the towns and cities of late medieval Europe. Their architectural and artistic patronage, funded by an eager and engaged laity, was on an unprecedented range and scale, while the pan-European organisation of the orders facilitated the rapid transmission of visual ideas and models.

Physical trace of the mendicant orders has, however, been largely erased from much of Europe. Their convents in England and Germany were easy targets for Protestant reformers; in France they were secularised by the state during the Revolutionary period.

6.2 Seal of the Dalmatian province of the Franciscan order, *c.* 1397, British Museum, London. Photo: Bet McCleod, © Trustees of the British Museum.

Yet the numerous mendicant foundations of coastal Croatia were to some degree spared these depredations. Even the Napoleonic suppressions of the early nineteenth century were not so thorough here compared to elsewhere in Europe. This is not, of course, to claim that mendicant monuments on the eastern Adriatic littoral have not suffered damage and destruction down the centuries – from Ottoman raiders in the sixteenth century (who burned the Franciscan convent in Hvar town in 1571), from the great earthquake that struck Dubrovnik in 1667 (the subsequent fire that engulfed that city's Franciscan convent probably represents the greatest single loss to Croatia's mendicant heritage), and more recently from the bombardments of 1944–5 and 1991–2. Nevertheless, it can be asserted with reasonable confidence that modern-day Croatia has the best-preserved patrimony of mendicant art and architecture from the late Middle Ages and Renaissance of any European country after Italy. Of the 'excessive abundance of churches, convents and ecclesiastics' that Thomas Graham Jackson encountered on his travels in Dalmatia during the 1880s, a very large proportion were Franciscan and Dominican foundations.[1]

It is, therefore, surprising that this patrimony is not better known or better published in the Anglophone art historical literature. For the Middle Ages as for other periods, Croatian material has tended to be marginalised for a variety of linguistic and political reasons, a bias that I hope to redress in some small measure here. This essay is intended as an introduction to the art commissioned by the Dominican and Franciscan orders in Croatia from their first arrival on the eastern shores of the Adriatic at the start of the thirteenth century until *c.* 1460 – the point at which the organisations of both orders began to be complicated by the internal splits between traditionalist Conventuals and reforming Observants, and also the moment when mendicant artistic patronage in the region began to lose its wholeheartedly Gothic vocabulary. It presents the most significant surviving buildings, paintings and sculptures, as well as other artefacts, including ecclesiastical plate and pieces of church furniture like choir stalls. Where appropriate, this material is related to, and supplemented by, the copious contemporary documentation preserved in local archives (another resource too little known to scholars of late medieval art and mendicant patronage outside Croatia).

6.1 St Francis, St Timotheus (?) and St Dominic below an unidentified bishop saint, late thirteenth-century fresco, sacristy of Zagreb Cathedral. Photo: Mario Braun, Croatian Conservation Institute.

Very little of what follows is new research, but it will likely be unfamiliar to those without a reasonable reading knowledge of Croatian. Indeed, one of the essay's principal aims is to reference and synthesise the extremely rich Yugoslav/Croatian literature in this field from recent decades, together with the main contributions in Italian and German. Perhaps predictably, the focus is largely on the Adriatic regions of Dalmatia, the Kvarner, and to a lesser degree Istria to the north. While the friars settled in continental Croatia from an early date, most of their convents there were later remodelled in the baroque style.[2] A rare but telling indicator of the early prominence of the Franciscans and Dominicans in Zagreb is provided by the late thirteenth-century programme of frescoes in the cathedral sacristy, where Francis and Dominic are conspicuously portrayed to either side of a bearded saint holding a scroll, who may be St Timotheus, a New Testament follower of St Paul and onomastic patron for one of Zagreb's most dynamic medieval bishops (fig. 6.1).[3]

Both orders claim an ancient heritage in Croatia. St Francis's early biographies record that his first attempt to reach the Holy Land in 1212 from Ancona got no further than the shores of Dalmatia ('in partibus Sclavoniae').[4] Francis's return from the Fifth Crusade in 1220 may also have entailed landfalls in Dalmatia as he sailed up the Adriatic to Venice, although Franciscan legend is not explicit on this point.[5] Local tradition certainly held that Francis had personally founded several communities of friars along the coast, the most persistent account relating to the Franciscans in Zadar. By 1232 the Franciscan convents in the region had been consolidated into the order's province of Sclavonia. According to the oldest list of Franciscan convents compiled by Paulinus of Venice around 1334, this administrative unit comprised thirty houses divided into four custodies (Dubrovnik, Split-Zadar, Rab and Istria).[6] In 1397 the province was renamed after St Jerome, reflecting the Illyrian origins of this Doctor of the Church as well as the parallels that the friars drew between Jerome's penitence in the wilderness and St Francis's own eremitism. As a result, Jerome often appears as the titular provincial saint on Franciscan altarpieces after this date. The renaming was marked by a new silver seal matrix for the provincial minister, now in the British Museum in London, which depicts St Jerome picking the thorn from the lion's paw with a friar kneeling in prayer below (fig. 6.2).[7]

St Dominic never travelled to the region, but the Dominican province of Hungary, which included both Dalmatia and inland Croatia, was instituted as early as 1221.[8] The Preaching Friars had established themselves in Dubrovnik by 1225, Nin by 1228, and Split and Zadar by the 1240s at the latest. Dalmatia's geographic remoteness from Hungary meant that the convents on the coast answered to a separate vicar, and in 1380 Dalmatia was finally recognised as a separate province within the Dominican order, extending from Udine and Koper in the north to Durrës on the Albanian coast in the south. As was the case elsewhere in Europe, the Dominicans were concentrated in fewer houses than the Franciscans, with only fifteen convents documented by 1378.

❊ ❊ ❊

The natural starting point for a consideration of the mendicants in Dalmatia is the Franciscan church in Zadar (fig. 6.3).[9] The foundation claimed a history dating back to St Francis himself, as local tradition held that the saint had landed at Zadar in 1212 when his first voyage to the Holy Land was frustrated by contrary winds.[10] An inscription on one of the pilasters of the present choir, originally the high altar chapel of the church, gives a dedication date of 13 October 1280, and the church has a reasonable claim to be the first Gothic building in Croatia.[11] Even were it not for these early beginnings, a remarkable sequence of artistic commissions would still make the church an excellent initial case study, as the Zadar Franciscans gradually assembled what must have been one of the most impressive ensembles of Gothic art in Dalmatia by the mid-fifteenth century.

Today the interior is dominated by a polychrome marble high altar erected in 1672 after designs by Baldassare Longhena, but the medieval church remains intact behind the baroque veneer, and its plan is very close to a number of Franciscan churches constructed around the same time in central Italy. It had a single nave with a beam roof culminating in three apsidal chapels, which

6.3 Church of St Francis, Zadar, consecrated 1280, exterior.
Photo: Živko Bačić.

were the only areas of the church to be vaulted (in accordance with early Franciscan architectural legislation). Today, the three apsidal chapels have been merged into a single chamber which now houses the choir, while the high altar has been moved forward from its original location below the vault of the central chapel. The nave is lit by the original single lancet windows, four on the north side and three on the south, and by a bifore lancet on the facade with a small oculus above.[12]

6.4 Anonymous Venetian miniaturist, *St Francis Receiving the Stigmata*, 'F' illumination from Antiphonary E, fol. 38v, *c.* 1292–1317, Museum of the Franciscan convent, Zadar. Photo: © Zadarska Nadbiskupija.

Among the early treasures held in the convent museum is a group of five beautifully illuminated antiphonaries dating from the very end of the thirteenth century.[13] The Zadar antiphonaries are the most complete set of choir books from medieval Croatia and are thought to be the work of Venetian miniaturists. The illuminated 'F' initial of the *Stigmatisation*, where St Francis tumbles backwards below the seraph, is one of the most original early interpretations of the subject in any medium (fig. 6.4). A painted panel crucifix which shows Christ alive on the cross may well predate the Franciscans' arrival in Zadar, and it is tempting to think of the Friars Minor perceiving an echo of the miraculous speaking crucifix of San Damiano in this effigy, which is probably the work of a local master of the late twelfth century.[14] The church's bell, cast in 1328 with images of Saints Anthony and Francis and signed by 'Magister Belo' and his assistant 'Vivencius', represents a remarkable survival for this category of object.[15] By the early fourteenth century the church and convent must have been complete, and the sacristy provided a sufficiently impressive setting to be chosen for the signing of the Peace of Zadar in 1358 between Venice and King Louis of Hungary, by which the Serenissima ceded its claims on Dalmatia to the Angevin monarch.[16] Shortly afterwards, Louis's queen, Elizabeth Kotromanić, seems to have presented the friars with an elaborately enamelled silver processional cross to commemorate this historic victory.[17]

In the latter half of the fourteenth century and the early decades of the fifteenth, the Zadar Franciscans undertook a staged but comprehensive renewal of their church. We first learn of this indirectly from an order placed in 1374 by two citizens of the nearby town of Nin with the Zadar painter Nikola Cipriani de Blondis for two crucifixes, which were to be identical to a crucifix earlier painted by the same artist for the Franciscan church in Zadar.[18] None of these images survive, but Nikola had trained in Venice with Paolo Veneziano, and it is tempting to envisage the documented crosses as painted panels similar to that painted by Nikola's master for the Dominicans in Dubrovnik roughly twenty-five years before.[19]

In the final years of the fourteenth century, the friars turned their attention to their choir, and commissioned Giovanni da Sansepolcro in May 1394 to produce an elaborate set of wooden stalls, for which the Tuscan master was paid 436 gold ducats.[20] In August of the following year, Giovanni's brother Jacopo was given a further 55 ducats for additional lecterns and intarsia panels for the choir, meaning that altogether the Franciscans disbursed nearly 500 ducats on this commission. Giovanni's choir survives to this day and is one of the best-preserved sets of medieval stalls in any Franciscan church in Europe.[21] The precinct, now located behind the high altar, was situated in front of the altar in the upper nave of the church until the seventeenth century, according to the prevailing norms for liturgical arrangements before the Council of Trent. The present cornice covering the stalls is also a later addition, but Ivo Petricioli, in his fundamental publication on Gothic woodwork in Zadar, has reconstructed the original appearance of the upper stalls from fragments now divided between the sacristy and the local Archaeological Museum. The decoration of the stalls is still characterised by a preference for carved relief over intarsia work: the latter is limited to simple geometric bands. Gothic leaf and tendril forms proliferate, and three stalls incorporate the coat of the arms of the prominent local Matafaris family, doubtless a record of the 200 ducats that Juraj Matafaris had bequeathed for the construction of the choir.[22]

The most remarkable aspect of the Zadar choir is the figurative decoration of the two outermost stalls. These incorporate 'cut-out' images carved front and back of *St Francis Receiving the Stigmata* (fig. 6.5) and the local patron St Chrysogonus on horseback. The St Francis scene includes the rocky form of La Verna and the church and cloister on the mountainside, as well as the saint and the apparition of Christ crucified as a seraph, their wounds linked by rays carved in relief. Subsidiary quatrefoils below depict St Louis of Toulouse and a kneeling friar in prayer, identified by the inscription 'FR[ATER] B[E]N[E]DICTUS', who must be the 'fratre Benedicto', custodian of the convent, cited in the 1394 contract with Giovanni da Sansepolcro. Giovanni himself is described as a Venetian citizen, and he was absent in Venice when the supplementary notarial act of August 1395 was drawn up, but as his name indicates he hailed from the Tuscan town of Sansepolcro. Recently discovered documents in Florence indicate that his family ran an important workshop, specialising in the production of choir precincts for the Franciscans and other mendicant orders in Tuscany and the Marches, but the Zadar choir is their only surviving work.[23]

In 1408 the church was further embellished with a pair of polychrome wood statues of the Virgin Annunciate and the Angel Gabriel.[24] The local chronicler Paulus de Paulo recorded the donation of these sculptures by one 'Francolum a Portornario filium Anzeli de Galgano', an Italian merchant from San Gimignano, and described the ceremony that accompanied their installation in the church. This occurred on 22 April (that is, the

6.5 Choir precinct of the church of St Francis, Zadar, carved by Giovanni da Sansepolcro, *c.* 1394–5, detail of *St Francis Receiving the Stigmata*. Photo: Donal Cooper.

Sunday preceding the feast of the Annunciation), when the figures were taken to the church of St Francis where they were duly consecrated by the bishop of Zadar accompanied by the city's clergy, magistrates, nobles and a great number of the populace.[25] We do not know where these sculptures were mounted within the church, but they are likely to have framed the high altar in some way. The two statues have been identified as central Italian works imported into Dalmatia, a hypothesis rendered more plausible by the Tuscan origins of the documented patron.[26]

The high altar itself soon benefited from a major commission of its own. In 1433 the Franciscans ordered an elaborate carved relief altarpiece from the Milanese woodworker Pietro de Riboldis.[27] Only fragments of this retable survive, among them a relief of *St Francis Receiving the Stigmata*, originally the central image from the third tier of this multi-storeyed polyptych (fig. 6.6). But the original appearance of the altarpiece can be reconstructed from the lengthy and detailed contract that the

6.6 *St Francis Receiving the Stigmata*, wooden relief carved by Pietro de Riboldis *c.* 1433, painted and gilded by Dujam Vučković *c.* 1452, Museum of the Franciscan convent, Zadar. Photo: Živko Bačić.

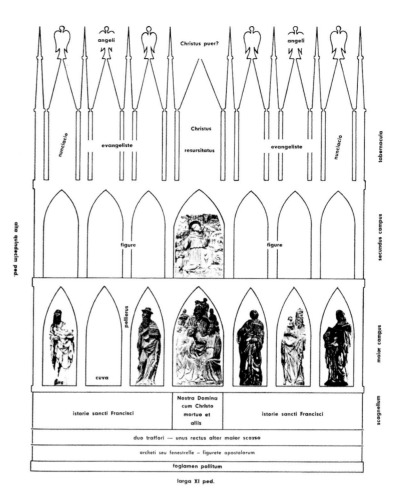

6.7 Reconstruction by Ivo Petricioli of Pietro de Riboldis's polyptych for the high altar of the church of St Francis, Zadar.

friars signed with Riboldis on 9 January 1433, published in full by Petricioli (fig. 6.7).[28] This specified a polyptych with five distinct registers of images, which had already been outlined by Riboldis in a drawing that he had submitted 'in una carta pergamena'. The lowest register comprised a gallery of apostles; above them narratives of the life of St Francis with a *Pietà* at their centre were to constitute an upper predella; the third register had a *Coronation of the Virgin* at its centrepiece – this scene still survives in the convent's collection; the fourth register was arranged around the *Stigmatisation* relief; the fifth had a *Resurrection of Christ* in the centre, with the four Evangelists in the pinnacles to either side and an Archangel Gabriel and Virgin Annunciate at the outer corners. As if this were not enough, the friars asked for the soul of the Christ Child ('in forma pueri') to be included in a tabernacle above the *Resurrection* together with the dove of the holy spirit ('in forma columbe') emanating from it. The figures to either side of the *Coronation*, *Stigmatisation* and *Resurrection* are not specified, but five standing saints can be connected with the altarpiece.[29] These statues represent a Franciscan saint (probably Anthony of Padua), St Clare, the Prophet Simeon (another of Zadar's patron saints), St Jerome and St John the Baptist. The first

two figures were later reused as part of a baroque altar in the church of St Mary in Pag old town; the other three are still in Zadar in the convent's collection. In his reconstruction, Petricioli placed these figures to either side of the *Coronation of the Virgin*. It is not clear how long Riboldis worked on the polyptych, but it appears to have been complete by 1452, when the Franciscans contracted the painter Dujam Marinov Vučković from Split to gild and polychrome Riboldis's carved reliefs for the sum of 200 gold ducats.[30] Despite its present fragmentary nature, Riboldis's polyptych must be reckoned among the most ambitious and complex high altarpieces produced for the Franciscan order in the fifteenth century.

The renewal of the Zadar church was completed in the middle of the century with the construction of a new choir screen. This structure does not survive, but local notarial documents record how in 1444 the friars commissioned Juraj Matejev Dalmatinac (better known in Italy as Giorgio da Sebenico), a native of Zadar who had trained in Venice with the Buon workshop, to construct a 'podium' of three chapels in the middle of the church ('in medio ecclesiae') complete with capitals and foliate ornament.[31] This 'podium' was surely the main choir screen of the church, dividing the building into two between the lower nave, open to the laity, and the upper nave, where the friars' choir stalls were arranged in front of the high altar.[32] The chapels would have faced the laity, and the friars themselves undertook to construct the screen wall at the back of the chapels. Juraj Dalmatinac is remembered today as the principal architect of Šibenik Cathedral from 1441 onwards. Although the Zadar chapels were destroyed in the seventeenth century, the quality and significance of the Franciscan choir screen is indicated by the high cost of the work (280 gold ducats). Furthermore, in 1452 Juraj asked his assistant Andrija Aleši to

prepare the capitals for the Loggia dei Mercanti in Ancona after the examples they had created together for the Franciscan convent in Zadar.[33] Their work for the friars in Zadar had evidently been completed by this date. The Zadar screen may also have incorporated an organ loft, as was the case in the city's Dominican church (see below). If so, it was no coincidence that the Franciscans had commissioned a new instrument for their church in 1443.[34] Shortly afterwards, in 1445, the Trogir painter Blaž Jurjev (of whom more shortly) was paid for painting beams in the church, and in his testament of 1448, Blaž asked to be buried in the church

6.8 Giovanni di Pietro or Dujam Vučković, the Ugljan polyptych, mid-fifteenth century, from the church of St Jerome, Ugljan, now Museum of the Franciscan convent, Zadar. Photo: Živko Bačić.

of St Francis in Zadar wearing the habit of the Friars Minor.[35]

The Franciscan movement was always torn between its urban mission and the solitude of hermitages, and the friars in northern Dalmatia were no exception. While their church in the centre of Zadar thrived, the rocky spines of the neighbouring islands offered relief from the pressures of city life, and the Zadar archipelago supported a number of isolated but important Franciscan foundations. A convent dedicated to St Domnius was founded by the powerful Grisogono family from Zadar at Kraj on the island of Pašman in 1392 for Franciscans who had been expelled from Bosnia.[36] A fragmentary altarpiece in the church depicting the *Virgin and Child Enthroned with St John the Baptist* is attributed to the 'Master of the Tkon Crucifix', an anonymous artist whom Emil Hilje has identified as Meneghello di Giovanni de' Canali, a prolific Venetian painter documented in Zadar for some forty years from 1385 onwards.[37] On the adjacent island of Ugljan, the Franciscan church of St Jerome was built between 1430 and 1452, and from around the middle of the century its high altar was decorated with one of the most important altarpieces painted in Dalmatia in this period (fig. 6.8).[38] The attribution of the Ugljan polyptych is still the subject of debate: several scholars give it to the Split painter Dujam Vučković (first proposed by Davor Domančić in 1959, and supported by Gamulin, Prijatelj and Belamarić), but Emil Hilje has instead identified the altarpiece as a work by the Milanese artist Giovanni di Pietro, documented in Zadar between 1431 and 1448.[39] The issue is complicated by the close relationship between the two painters, who are known to have collaborated in 1429 when together they painted and gilded the chapel of St Domnius in Split Cathedral.[40] Whoever the artist, the Ugljan polyptych (now displayed in the sacristy of the Franciscan church in Zadar) is one of the most ambitious and best preserved altar retables in Dalmatia, and perhaps the single most significant example of the 'International Gothic' style in the region. In the predella arcade, Christ is flanked by the twelve apostles (with St Matthew in place of St Paul), who hold books and scrolls citing sections of the creed.[41] In the main register, the enthroned Madonna and Child form the centre of a heptaptych. St Peter Martyr, St Nicholas and St Francis are depicted to the left; St Jerome (prominent here as the titular of the church and patron of the Dalmatian province of the Franciscan order), the Prophet Simeon, and St James the Greater with his pilgrim's staff (the same saint is also present in the predella) to the right. Each of these saints stands on a wooden pedestal, as though the artist conceived them as fictive polychrome statues. In the pinnacles above, a triptych of *Christ as the Man of Sorrows* flanked by the Virgin and St John the Evangelist surmounts the Virgin and Child. St Chrysogonus, St Stephen and St John the Baptist populate the pinnacles to the left. To the right are St Demetrius, a bishop saint (perhaps St Donatus, Zadar's early episcopal patron) and a mysterious lay saint holding a rosary who has not been satisfactorily identified.[42]

Such remote locations held little appeal for the Dominicans, who invariably focused their efforts on the major urban centres. The Preaching Friars founded several houses in northern Dalmatia, but only their church of St Platon in Zadar itself remains standing.[43] The Dominicans had arrived in Zadar by 1228, and around the middle of the century were given the small Benedictine monastery of St Platon, named for a ninth-century Byzantine ascetic, by Archbishop Lovro Periandro. In Zadar, as was often the case in cities across Europe, the Dominicans and Franciscans settled at opposite ends of the urban centre. The Benedictine complex proved insufficient for the Dominicans' needs, and in 1267 they began the existing church on the site, which was consecrated in 1280. Its building history was, therefore, contemporaneous with that of the church of St Francis, and it shares some of the Franciscan church's Gothic features. St Platon has a single nave lit by simple lancet windows concluding in a high altar chapel with a ribbed groin vault. The apse itself was illuminated by a large eastern window, recently restored. The convent was suppressed by the French in 1806, converted into a barracks by the Austrians, and badly damaged by aerial bombing in 1944, but documentary sources allow the reconstruction of some key aspects of its decoration. More specifically, Dominican patronage in Zadar can shed a good deal of light on the role played by Venetian artists and craftsmen in the decoration of mendicant churches in northern Dalmatia.

The interior is now stripped of its artworks, but the Dominican scholar Stjepan Krasić has identified a number of surviving artworks in the convent's pre-suppression inventories, the most significant of which is the signed and dated panel of the *Virgin and Child Enthroned* painted by the Venetian artist Nicolò di Pietro in 1394 and now in the Gallerie dell'Accademia in Venice (fig. 6.9).[44] The panel includes a kneeling donor figure from Zadar, one Vučina Belgarzone, but it had long been thought to come from a church in Venice. Krasić established its Zadar provenance via a description of the painting in an eighteenth-century inventory of the convent, where the donor inscription is reproduced precisely.[45] The painting is described as having many saints with the Virgin and Child at the centre, so the 'Belgarzone Madonna' must be only the central section of a large polyptych, and one hopes that in time other fragments of this important altarpiece will come to light. By then the picture was hanging in the sacristy of St Platon, but it may have been the 'palam veterem' recorded over the altar of the small chapter house during the apostolic visitation of 1579.[46] One highly unusual aspect of the inscription is the manner in which Nicolò di Pietro included his address in Venice: 'Nicolaus filius magistri Petri pictoris de Venetiis, pinxit hoc opus, qui moratur capite Pontis Paradixi' ('Nicolò son of master Pietro, painter of Venice, painted this work, who resides at the head of the Ponte del Paradiso' – a bridge in the parish of Santa Maria Formosa in Venice). Nicolò evidently perceived an opportunity in this Zadar commission to extend his

6.9 Nicolò di Pietro, *Virgin and Child Enthroned* (the 'Belgarzone Madonna'), 1394, from the church of St Dominic, Zadar, now Gallerie dell'Accademia, Venice. Photo: © Ministero per i Beni e la Attività Culturali.

networks of patronage through some none too subtle publicity. Any citizen of Zadar who desired a similar work would not only know that Nicolò had painted it, but also know where to find him in Venice.

Another major commission for St Platon in the late fourteenth century was the crucifix painted by the Venetian artist Catarino. A notarial act from 1386 records the Dominicans' desire to take possession of a crucifix and two altarpieces that they had commissioned from Catarino and his Venetian compatriots, the painters Donato and Pietro di Nicolò (Nicolò di Pietro's father) and the woodworker Andrea Moranzon.[47] Ivo Petricioli first connected this document with the large cross (measuring 353 x 249 centimetres) now in the Permanent Display of Ecclesiastical Art in Zadar.[48] Taken together, the 1386 and 1394 commissions for St Platon illustrate how artistic networks could be transposed

from Venice to Dalmatia. Catarino is known to have collaborated with two generations of the same workshop, Pietro di Nicolò and Nicolò di Pietro.[49] For his part, Nicolò di Pietro had – as Andrea De Marchi suggests – probably inherited the commission for the 'Belgarzone Madonna' from his father, who had worked for the Zadar Dominicans eight years earlier. The location of Catarino's cross within St Platon is unclear, but it may well have been mounted on the church's choir screen, which was rebuilt or at least restored around 1396.[50] The patronage of the Dominicans in this period extended to the furnishing of their sacristy, for which they commissioned elaborate cupboards and benches in 1399 from the local woodworker Nikola Arbuzjanić for the sum of 100 ducats.[51] St Platon's importance was reflected in it being chosen as the seat of the city council while the commune's own palace was taken over in 1366 by the court of the Angevin prince Charles of Durazzo, King Louis of Hungary's chosen heir.[52] Taken together with the Franciscan patronage discussed above, the case of the Dominican church of St Platon indicates that Zadar's mendicant convents flourished in the period of Hungarian rule that followed the Peace of Zadar in 1358, and in particular after the end of the destructive Chioggia War in 1381. It is also instructive that the friars gave several significant commissions to Venetian artists, given the tense relations between the two cities at the close of the fourteenth century.

Although it is not as early in date as the two Zadar churches, the Franciscan church in Pula in Istria is a better preserved example of thirteenth-century mendicant architecture (fig. 6.10). The Friars Minor are thought to have arrived in Pula in 1227, perhaps during St Anthony of Padua's preaching tour of Istria in that year.[53] They were given a small church dedicated to St John the Baptist within the medieval walls on the slopes of the ancient capitol, and the early community was led by Brother Ottone, who would be venerated as a blessed after his death in 1241.[54] Recent analysis of the church indicates that the building had been completed by the early years of the fourteenth century, with most of the construction taking place in the second half of the thirteenth.[55] The church has a single nave with a beam roof concluding in three vaulted apsidal chapels, the central high altar chapel being lit by twin lancet windows (figs 6.12 and 6.13). An external pulpit, reconstructed in the 1920s, was set halfway along the south side of the nave (fig. 6.11). Attilio Krizmanić has argued that this was originally linked to the screen that would have bisected the interior of the nave, allowing the friars to access their internal and external pulpits by means of a single staircase.[56] The exterior of the church is very plain, but the facade is embellished with an impressive Gothic portal, while the back wall of the main apse has a cross motif picked out in red tiles (fig. 6.12). A well-preserved chapter house entrance, following a common Franciscan typology of twin windows flanking a central door, is still visible in the adjacent convent (fig. 6.14).

The friars, however, did not always have to build their own

6.10 Church of St Francis, Pula, exterior. Photo: Nataša Nefat.

6.11 Church of St Francis, Pula, external pulpit. Photo: Donal Cooper.

6.12 Church of St Francis, Pula, exterior of apsidal chapel. Photo: Donal Cooper.

churches: sometimes they inherited existing buildings. In Rab town in the Kvarner, the Franciscans were given the large church of St John the Evangelist, previously a Benedictine nunnery, in 1278 by the local bishop, Juraj Hermolais I (fig. 6.15).[57] This was a long-established monastery in the old town, and the church was a large Romanesque structure with a three-nave basilica plan culminating in a round apse incorporating a shallow ambulatory. The present church was probably constructed in the eleventh century, replacing a much earlier fifth-century building of similar plan, while the large bell-tower was added in the twelfth. The Franciscans retained possession of the convent until 1783, after which, following a brief occupation by the local bishops, the church gradually fell into ruin. By the 1880s Thomas Jackson found the nave columns doing 'duty as posts on the quay for mooring vessels'.[58] Only the bell-tower survived the process of decay and spoliation, although the ambulatory has recently been reconstructed on the basis of surviving fragments and old photographs. The church's original artworks have been completely dispersed, and several are now displayed nearby in the church of St Justina. These include a polyptych attributed to Paolo Veneziano with a central *Crucifixion* flanked by six standing saints, which Miljenko Domijan has traced back to St John the Evangelist.[59] The total absence of Franciscan saints, however, makes it doubtful that this image was originally made for the church. Indeed, the inclusion of the otherwise obscure St Ermolaus is probably a reference to Bishop Juraj Hermolais III (1329–63), the fourth member of that family to occupy the see of Rab in the later Middle Ages, and Paolo's retable is likely to be an episcopal rather than Franciscan commission.[60]

In central Dalmatia, the Franciscans and Dominicans were

6.13 Church of St Francis, Pula, interior towards high altar. Photo: Nataša Nefat.

present in all the major cities from an early date. The Friars Minor are recorded in Šibenik and Split from 1229 and arrived in Trogir as early as 1214, making this the earliest securely documented Franciscan settlement in Dalmatia.[61] Despite the precocious history of the Minorites in Trogir, they were never able – unlike their Dominican rivals – to acquire permanently a convent on the main island of Trogir town. Milan Ivanišević has shown that they moved eight times between 1214 and 1538. Although the Franciscans made several attempts during this period to found a new house within the old town, their main convent – with its church dedicated to St Mary of the Angels – remained close to the site of their first primitive settlement in the city's mainland suburbs.[62] Following a catastrophic collapse in 1831, only a few ruinous outcrops of this church remain visible today. Ivanišević, however, has convincingly connected a venerated image of the *Virgin and Child with Angels* by Blaž Jurjev now displayed in the gallery of the local church of St John the Baptist with the Franciscan foundation (fig. 6.16). This is very likely the surviving central fragment of the high altarpiece that Blaž had been commissioned to paint for the friars' church in 1437.[63]

The Dominicans arrived in Trogir before 1230, and by the early fourteenth century had completed their church dedicated to St Dominic, a single nave building with a ship's-keel timber roof. In 1372 the Venetian sculptor Nicolò Dente signed and dated a carved lunette over the main portal (fig. 6.17).[64] The tympanum programme places the Virgin and Child at the centre with Mary Magdalen to the right, clothed in her own hair. To the left stands the Dominican Augustin Kažotić (d. 1325), a native of Trogir and bishop of Zagreb from 1303 to 1322, later venerated by his confrères as a blessed. Beside Augustin kneels the diminutive donor figure of his sister Bitkula Kažotić, identified by a donor inscription, and the family seems to have been the moving force behind the creation of the tympanum, as Augustin's nephew

Nikola was also bishop of Trogir in the early 1370s.[65] A fragmentary polyptych by Blaž Jurjev survives from the church with a polychrome wood statue of St Catherine of Alexandria set in a central tabernacle framed by six standing saints: the Magdalen, St Dominic and St Michael to the left; St Anthony Abbot, St James and the local civic patron, St John of Trogir, to the right.[66]

Blaž had earlier worked for the Franciscans in nearby Split, painting the wooden vault above the high altar of their church by the harbour in 1412.[67] A large painted panel crucifix in that church, now shorn of its terminals, is also attributed to him as an early work.[68] Measuring 202 x 144 centimetres in its present reduced state, this must have been the main rood cross of the church. Later in 1436, Blaž's woodworker collaborator Martin Petković, together with one Ivan of France, would be paid for providing twenty-eight intarsia designs for the stalls in the convent's chapter house.[69] For the church's high altar, Andrea De Marchi has convincingly established that a number of panels attributable to Dujam Vučković now in the Hermitage in St Petersburg are fragments of a large polyptych painted by that artist as a high altarpiece for the Split Franciscans around the

6.14 Franciscan convent, Pula, chapter house. Photo: Donal Cooper.

6.15 Basilica of St John the Evangelist, Rab town. Photo: Donal Cooper.

6.16 Blaž Jurjev, *Virgin and Child with Angels* (the 'Madonna of the Rose Garden'), *c.* 1437, Museum of the church of St John the Baptist, Trogir. Photo: Živko Bačić.

middle of the fifteenth century.[70] The five panels in St Petersburg combine the patron saints of Split, Domnius and Anastasius, with St Louis of Toulouse (a good indication of a Franciscan provenance), St John the Evangelist and St Mark (a reflection perhaps of Venetian suzerainty over Trogir).[71]

The Clarissan convent in Split possesses a much older relic of the Franciscan presence in the city, a large (253 x 196 centimetres) thirteenth-century panel crucifix (fig. 6.18). This cross is such a singular survival that it is stylistically difficult to place or attribute. Kruno Prijatelj argued that the panel should be understood in relation to Tuscan and Umbrian painting of the mid-thirteenth century, especially the work of Giunta Pisano, but Grgo Gamulin and more recent commentators have been more cautious, proposing instead that the Split cross reflects a mixture of Byzantine and Italian Romanesque influences specific to Dalmatia, a synthesis that Joško Belamarić has christened 'Adrio-Byzantinism'.[72] The Split panel differs from contemporary Italian crucifixes in eschewing the so-called 'Byzantine-curve' in the body of Christ. The Virgin and St John the Evangelist are, as usual, portrayed in the lateral arms of the cross, but are set within

circular medallions rather than the rectangular, icon-like fields prevalent in Italian painting. The other terminals are damaged, but the lower half of an angel is still visible at the very top of the cross. The bottom terminal has been cut down, but the roundel here depicts a bearded saint who has now been identified as St Francis, which would reflect the practice of portraying supplicant figures of the saint by the feet of Christ on Franciscan crucifixes in central Italy.[73] Irrespective of this identification, the Split crucifix remains a highly original rendering of the iconography of the suffering Christ (the *Christus patiens*) distinct from both Byzantine prototypes and contemporary Italian interpretations. Its quality is underlined by the fictive porphyry decoration of the panel's reverse, which suggests that it was originally visible from the back (as would have been the case had it originally hung in the nave of a church). The panel's provenance is unclear, as it certainly predates the foundation of the Clarissan monastery in Split in 1308.[74] It may well have been commissioned for the first Franciscan church in the city before being donated to the Poor Clares.

Continuing south we reach the Republic of Dubrovnik, and both mendicant orders established important convents in that city in the thirteenth century. The Dominicans had already arrived by 1225, and three years later were given a small church dedicated to the Assumption of the Virgin in the eastern suburb of Ploče, just outside the city walls.[75] In 1301 construction began on a new church to be dedicated to St Dominic. With the active support of the Ragusan Republic and archbishop of Dubrovnik, the new church, the largest in the city, was consecrated on 14 November 1314 (fig. 6.19). Together with almost all Dubrovnik's historic buildings, the Dominican convent was badly damaged in the devastating earthquake that struck the city on 6 April 1667, but the principal structure survived. The church is of fundamental importance for our understanding of medieval and Renaissance painting in Dalmatia thanks to the remarkable ensemble of altarpieces commissioned by the Dominicans that are now preserved in the convent's museum. The significance of this collection was reflected in the 2008 exhibition at the Galerija Klovićevi Dvori in Zagreb dedicated to the history of the Dominicans in Croatia, which gave a particular focus to the Dubrovnik foundation. Some of the convent's treasures – notably the magnificent trio of altarpieces by Nikola Božidarević – are too late in date to be included here, but the greatest panel commissioned by the Dominicans for their church is much earlier: Paolo Veneziano's mighty fourteenth-century crucifix (fig. 6.20).

This majestic image, which still dominates the interior of the church, was dated and attributed by Grgo Gamulin with the help of two notarial documents preserved in the Dubrovnik archives.[76] The first of these, Šimun Restić's testament of 1348, left money for a crucifix in the Dominican church.[77] The second, Nikola Lukarić's will of 1352, referred to 'Magister Polo' by name and specified that he make a 'superaltare' for the testator's chapel of St Nicholas in

6.17 Nicolò Dente, *Virgin and Child Enthroned with the Magdalen and Blessed Augustin Kažotić*, 1394, lunette over the main portal of the church of St Dominic, Trogir. Photo: Živko Bačić.

the same church.[78] The Dominican historian Seraphino Cerva, writing in the 1730s, stated that Paolo's cross was erected in 1358, and that it helped to stop the plague in that year.[79] Of the 'superaltare' nothing more is known, although it was surely a polyptych of some kind.[80] The Ragusan crucifix measures 500 x 407 centimetres, making it much larger than the only other surviving crucifix that can be connected to Paolo, the panel from San Samuele in Venice (163 x 108 centimetres but missing its original terminals).[81] Indeed, the Dubrovnik cross is one of the largest painted medieval crosses to survive anywhere in Europe.

Paolo's crucifix is today mounted high above the floor of the church just below the chancel arch. It rests on a painted and gilt wooden platform which appears to have been reconstructed after the 1667 earthquake. While this structure is obviously not the original support for the crucifix, the panel's dimensions seem to be well matched to the span of the chancel arch. The central crucifix is flanked by subsidiary panels of the Virgin and St John the Evangelist, which have been related to two different documents. Restić's 1348 testament referred to images of the Virgin and St John, but these were elements of an entirely separate 'anchona' intended for another altar in the local cathedral.[82] On the other hand, a much later document of 1456 tells us that the painter Lovro Dobričević was paid for two panels of the Virgin and the Evangelist to be placed to either side of a crucifix, or more specifically 'in the place where the women stand by the cross'.[83] The most satisfying resolution of these apparently contradictory notices is that by the fifteenth century the Dominican church had two crucifixes: the extant Paolo Veneziano cross and another image, possibly the large polychrome wood corpus now displayed in the sacristy (the 1456 document does not, after all, specify a painted panel cross). The notice of a crucifix 'ubi stant mulieres' probably refers to a cross set either on the rood screen or in the

lower nave: that is, the area of the church accessible to laywomen. By the sixteenth century there was a 'divotissimo crocifisso' over one of the twelve altars to the lay side of the choir screen.[84] Paolo Veneziano's cross was most likely always set within the chancel arch above the high altar, or 'aprovo al altar grande' in the words of Restić's testamentary bequest.[85] Stylistically, the side panels of the Virgin and St John should also be attributed to Paolo (an attribution to Dobričević is not credible) and were almost certainly coeval with the crucifix. For one thing, Paolo depicted the Evangelists' symbols in the terminals of the cross rather than the Virgin and St John, a less common choice that foresaw the presence of the two lateral images. Two comparable panels of the Virgin and St John now in the Galleria Sabauda in Turin and attributed to Paolo Veneziano indicate that the artist painted at least one other three-panel Crucifixion ensemble. Cristina Guarnieri has, moreover, now convincingly reattributed the lion of St Mark traditionally given to Michele di Giambono in the Museo Correr in Venice to Paolo Veneziano, identifying the panel as a terminal from a third cross of this type.[86]

The wording of the 1352 Lukarić bequest has been taken to suggest that Paolo was indeed present in Dubrovnik, rather than painting the panels in Venice and having them shipped to

6.18 Anonymous Dalmatian master, painted panel crucifix, second half of the thirteenth century, Convent of St Clare, Split. Photo: Živko Bačić.

6.19 Church of St Dominic, Dubrovnik, interior towards the high altar. Photo: Vlaho Pustić.

Dalmatia.[87] The sheer scale of the Ragusan crucifix reinforces the impression that it was painted on site. Art historians have speculated that Paolo may have travelled to Dalmatia to escape the ravages of the Black Death in Venice, and we should recall that Dubrovnik was nominally part of the Venetian Stato da Mar until 1358. Be this as it may, it is important to acknowledge that Paolo painted for the Ragusan Dominicans at the height of his career. In Venice, the painter had recently painted the tomb lunette of Doge Francesco Dandolo in the Frari (c. 1339), the *Pala Feriale* to cover the *Pala d'Oro* on the high altar of San Marco (1345), as well as the altarpiece for the doge's private chapel in the Palazzo Ducale (1346). By this date, Paolo was the pre-eminent painter in Venice, and his work for Dubrovnik is a marker of the Dalmatian city's significance by the early fourteenth century. It also reflects the importance of the mendicant orders and their networks of patronage for the leading artists of the day. Paolo's links with the Franciscans in Venice and Vicenza are well known, but he also painted a major altarpiece for the Dominican church at San Severino in the Marches on the other side of the Adriatic.[88]

The history of the decoration of the high altar of the Dominican church is somewhat complicated. It is likely that there was already a high altarpiece in the fourteenth century, if only because the side altars of the church were receiving expensive polyptychs of their own by mid-century. The 150 hyperperi (Dubrovnik continued to use this Byzantine unit of currency) bequeathed by Nikola Lukarić in 1352 to pay Paolo Veneziano for the 'superaltare' for his chapel of St Nicholas would have bought an impressive altarpiece. Whether or not there was an earlier high altarpiece, we know from the compendium of Dubrovnik notarial documents published by Jorjo Tadić that the Ragusan Dominicans commissioned an elaborate silver 'palla' for their high altar from the goldsmith Pietro di Panfano of Sermoneta in 1432.[89] Work on this metal altarpiece was still ongoing in 1443, when further goldsmiths were contracted to complete the altarpiece, Pietro

having evidently left Dubrovnik by this date.[90] In his history of Dubrovnik published in 1595, the Dominican humanist Serafino Razzi described the high altarpiece of his order's church as being 'all of silver with two rows of figures … in low relief. In the middle of the upper row, there is a resurrected Christ with four saints on the right side and as many on the left. In the middle of the lower row, there is a Virgin and Child and the same number of saints on both sides. Among these are the glorious apostles St Peter and St Paul, St John, St Dominic, St Peter Martyr, St Thomas Aquinas, St Blaise, Mary Magdalen and other saints, up to eighteen large figures and some smaller figures of angels and prophets. This altar is so beautiful that – they say – together with the other silver of the sacristy, it is worth 100,000 ducats.'[91]

Razzi judged the Dominican silver 'palla' superior to similar examples in the cathedral and the Franciscan church as it was made of silver mixed with gold, and added that 'it is exhibited only during important religious holidays; otherwise it is locked in a wooden cabinet that is decorated with fine paintings of the same number of figures. It is so well done that whoever did not know of the silver altar would think that the wooden cabinet is the main altar.'[92] Unfortunately, the altarpiece does not survive: having been damaged in 1667, its silver was then sold to pay for the subsequent restoration of the church. One can only guess its appearance from other silver altarpieces that survive elsewhere on the Adriatic littoral, particularly the example commissioned by Count Ivan VII Frankopan for the high altar of Krk Cathedral in 1477 (which also has a double tier of saints), or that over the high altar of Kotor Cathedral fashioned by the Swiss master John of Basel in collaboration with local Montenegrin goldsmiths in 1437.

Razzi's description of the Dominican silver altarpiece suggests that it was designed as a retable set on top of the altar *mensa*, and not as an altar frontal set on the front face of the altar block. In 1448 the friars commissioned a painted 'pala' with a predella ('cum scabello') for their high altar from Lovro Dobričević and Matej Junčić, two artists from Kotor who had settled in Dubrovnik.[93] The silver high altarpiece would have been completed a couple of years before, and the 1448 document should probably be associated with the ferial painted panel cover later described by Razzi at the end of the sixteenth century. The 1448 contract has often been linked to the surviving polyptych of the *Baptism of Christ* (240 x 249 centimetres) attributed to Dobričević in the convent's museum (See fig. 8.16 on p119). However, this connection seems improbable, if only because it is hard to see how this two-tier pentaptych could have functioned as a cover for the silver altarpiece (and in any case Razzi stated that the cover had the same number of fields as the silver altarpiece, nine not five). The central image of the *Baptism of Christ* would also have been an unprecedented iconographic focus for the high altar of a Dominican church, and would have been much more suited to a side altar dedicated to St John the Baptist.

Furthermore, the relatively low price (forty-five ducats) paid for the 1448 'pala' would be more appropriate for a painted shutter rather than a free-standing altarpiece. For example, Junčić was paid eighty ducats in 1450 for a polyptych destined for a side chapel in the city's Franciscan church.[94]

Aside from Paolo Veneziano's crucifix, almost all the medieval furniture of the Dominican church has been removed. As with the other churches we have examined, the nave was divided by a choir screen, which is still visible on seventeenth-century plans of Dubrovnik. Razzi gives a detailed description of this structure, which was supported on columns and incorporated a subsidiary choir on its upper storey for the friars to use for the canonical hours.[95] Igor Fisković has suggested that the curious trio of chapel vaults constructed on the counter facade of the church by Ludovik Maravić in 1538 in what was by then a deeply conservative florid Gothic style owe their design to the lost choir screen of the church.[96] A restored fifteenth-century marble pulpit with polychromed relief figures of Dominican saints can still be seen on the north side of the nave. There is also the worn gisant tomb figure of the Dominican friar Andrija of Durrës (d. 1393)

in his episcopal regalia together with the epitaph from his tomb monument, which records his successive offices as prior of the convent, minister of the Dalmatian province, and finally archbishop of Ragusa.[97]

The adjoining cloister, one of the most beautiful in Croatia, was built in the late 1450s after the designs of the Florentine architect, sculptor and engineer Maso di Bartolomeo (fig. 6.21). The surviving contract of 29 February 1456 stated that the cloister's carving was to be executed by local stonecutters according to Maso's design. The work of these local masons may account for some of the Gothic detailing in the cloister, but the expansive round arches within which the tracery is set seem to derive from Florentine examples, particularly – as Janez Höfler has suggested – from the novitiates' corridor in Santa Croce, dating from the 1440s and the work of Maso's associate Michelozzo, who arrived in Dubrovnik as Maso's replacement in 1461.[98] Maso himself did not live to oversee the construction of the Ragusan cloister, as a couple of months after he had signed the contract with the Dominicans he was killed when one of the canon he had cast for the republic exploded during a test firing.[99]

6.20 Paolo Veneziano, *Crucifixion with Symbols of the Four Evangelists Flanked by the Virgin and St John the Evangelist*, *c*. 1348–52, tempera and gold leaf on panel, church of St Dominic, Dubrovnik. Photo: Vlaho Pustić.

The Franciscan church in Dubrovnik was situated at the other end of the city's main axis, the Stradun, beside the western Pile Gate, and the Friars Minor enjoyed a similar prominence and prestige within Ragusan society to their Dominican rivals.[100] The Franciscans had settled first in the suburb of Pile outside the city walls, where they were given the monastery of St Thomas before 1230. As was the case elsewhere, the friars outgrew their first foundation, and its suburban location was also exposed to the military incursions of the Serbian King Stefan Uroš II. The decision to build a new convent within the city walls was endorsed by the Ragusan government in 1309 and backed by a bull from Pope John XXII in 1318. The new church, which came to be known as Male Braće (of the Lesser Brothers) was completed by mid-century, and specific altars are referred to in documents from 1329 onwards, suggesting that parts of the building were in use by that date. The convent was the largest on the Dalmatian coast, and became famous for its pharmacy, one of the oldest in the world. In his description of the city of 1440, the Lucchese magistrate and schoolmaster Filippo de Diversis was impressed by the wells and fountains of the convent and praised the olive and orange trees that grew in the friars' cloister (fig. 6.22).[101] This cloister was built contemporaneously with the church in the first decades of the fourteenth century by Mihoje Brajkov of Bar on the Montenegrin coast (d. 1348), whose authorship is confirmed by his tomb epitaph cut into the south-east angle pier.[102] The cloister is on a similar scale to the later Dominican precinct, but its ornament is considerably more complex. Here the spacious vaults of the cloister have six-light openings divided by pairs of slender octagonal columns. The double capitals of these columns are richly carved with an array of foliate designs, birds, mythical creatures and masks. Every capital is different, 'fantastic and capricious in the highest degree', in T. G. Jackson's judgement.[103]

Many Ragusan nobles elected to be buried in the Franciscans' cloister, and the best-preserved tomb is the fourteenth-century wall sarcophagus on the eastern side of the quadrangle commemorating Marin Gučetić (d. 1370), a senior Ragusan diplomat and member of one of Dubrovnik's leading families (fig. 6.23).[104] The sarcophagus has the Gučetić coats of arms carved on either end, while the long side of the tomb chest is decorated with reliefs of the *Ascension* at the centre and the *Stigmatisation* to the left (with St Francis's right hand superimposed over the corner column as if he is leaning out of the tomb towards the viewer). Balancing the *Stigmatisation* to the right is *St Dominic Supporting the Lateran*, an abbreviated version of Pope Innocent III's vision of a poor man supporting the Roman basilica of St John the Lateran from collapse. To my knowledge this is unique in an artwork produced for a Franciscan context, as the Friars Minor interpreted the poor man of Innocent's dream as St Francis, contrary to persistent Dominican claims that he was their founder, St Dominic. Selecting St Dominic for this scene would, therefore, go against the best iconographic efforts of the Franciscan order, but

the figure's heavy, flowing mantle and the absence of the Franciscan cord leave little doubt that he does indeed wear the Dominican habit. The combination of Franciscan and Dominican imagery on Gučetić's tomb probably reflects the institutional significance of both orders for the Ragusan state.

The Franciscan church was comprehensively gutted by the fires that followed in the wake of the 1667 earthquake. Its interior was then thoroughly renewed in the baroque style, but key aspects of its medieval decoration can be reconstructed on the basis of the rich documentation surviving in Dubrovnik's State Archives. For example, it is known that prior to 1667 the church had a large crucifix set on a beam above the high altar in similar style to Paolo Veneziano's cross in the Dominican church. The Franciscan cross, which was venerated as a miracle-working image, is known

6.21 Cloister, late 1450s, after designs by Maso di Bartolomeo, Dominican convent, Dubrovnik. Photo: Donal Cooper.

6.22 Cloister, before 1348, Franciscan convent, Dubrovnik. Photo: Donal Cooper.

through a drawing made as a basis for a print in 1614 (fig. 6.24); it seems that the copperplate etching was never realised.[105] The interpretation of this visual source has been controversial: Gamulin considered it to record a fifteenth-century image, but more recently at the Paolo Veneziano exhibition held in Rimini and Zagreb in 2002–3, a panel of St John the Evangelist from the Museum of Applied Arts in Zagreb was advanced as a surviving fragment of the Franciscan crucifix from Dubrovnik with an attribution to the workshop of Paolo Veneziano.[106] Technical analysis confirms that this panel was originally the right terminal of a large painted cross, but the attribution to the Venetian master is problematic, and the provenance of the image does not extend back beyond its presence in the Solomon Berger collection in Zagreb between the two world wars. Furthermore, the commentary that accompanied the 1614 drawing described the Franciscan cross as at least partially sculpted ('questa divotissima imagine fatta di rilievo'), and the design does indeed seem to show a sculpted corpus mounted on a panel cross, admittedly with painted terminals.[107] The same text also claimed that the crucifix had been mounted above the high altar in the mid-fifteenth century – not the fourteenth – on the initiative of the charismatic Franciscan preacher St James of the Marches during one of his stays in Dubrovnik in 1431-2 or 1464.[108]

Documents and contemporary descriptions confirm that the Franciscans in Dubrovnik possessed an elaborate silver high altarpiece similar to that in the Dominican church, but even earlier in date. De Diversis praised the 'anchona, seu palla argentea' on the high altar of the Franciscan church, at the same time noting that the Dominicans would shortly install a silver 'palla' of their own that would rival that of the Friars Minor.[109] The Franciscan silver altarpiece lauded by De Diversis is probably the same silver-gilt 'palla' later described in greater detail by the Milanese priest and pilgrim Pietro Casola in 1494 as having 'two rows of large figures with twelve figures in each row. In the upper row, in the centre, is a God the Father; in the centre of the lower row there is Our Lady with her Son in her arms, and, as I said, everything is of silver. For greater ornament there are jewels of every colour, and they are so large that I doubt that they can be genuine, because if they were, there would be a great treasure there, little guarded.' The fastidious Milanese cleric was evidently perplexed by this trusting attitude towards the laity – 'I did not find anyone who could remove that doubt from my mind', he concluded.[110]

This silver altarpiece had been commissioned in 1388 from Bartolomeo de Domno, 'aurifex de Venetiis', and a series of documents allow us to follow the progress of the work in some detail. The initial contract with Bartolomeo described twenty-six figures, corresponding to Casola's description of two registers of twelve figures with images of God the Father and the Virgin and Child at their centre.[111] Twenty-one figures had already been completed by other, unnamed goldsmiths ('pro manus aliorum

magistorum'), leaving five to be made by Bartolomeo, who was also to fashion the smaller figures between the larger ones and to decorate the altarpiece with enamels, crowns and other appropriate ornaments. The first clause suggests that work had already started on the altarpiece, and the first bequest of money 'pro laborerio anchone' can in fact be traced back to 1358. By 1394 Bartolomeo had been paid 1,572 hyperperi, and had provided 1,301 hyperperi worth of work in the form of crafted silver, stones, enamels and a carved wooden 'anchona' brought from Venice, perhaps the wooden form for the silver altarpiece, which was eventually finished in 1401.

In addition to Bartolomeo's silver 'palla' on the high altar, Canon Pietro Casola described another silver gilt 'Maestà' in the Franciscan church and noted the impressive choir stalls of the friars. He also commented on the beautiful cloister and the spacious chapter house, 'which contains three very ornate altars'.[112] The church itself had numerous altars, and the State Archives record a number of altarpiece commissions. In 1455 the Franciscans paid Lovro Dobričević 105 hyperperi to paint a retable for their church (the intended altar is not specified) according to the drawn design that he had already submitted.[113] Several art historians (Gamulin, Miklòs Boskovits) have connected this document to a fragmentary altarpiece by Lovro now divided between the Národní Galerie in Prague (lateral saints, fig. 6.25) and the Wernher collection in London (central panel, fig. 6.26).[114] The selection of saints on what was originally a seven-field polyptych with at least two registers firmly indicates a Franciscan provenance. The main register includes St Francis, St Louis of Toulouse, St Anthony of Padua and St Bernardino of Siena – all Franciscan saints – together with St Jerome, who, as we have seen, had a particular resonance for the Dalmatian Franciscans. The sixth saint was replaced at some later date by an unrelated panel of St Nicholas which appears to be a product of the Vivarini shop. The Prague panels are now mounted in a nineteenth-century frame, and it may be that the original saint was damaged or missing, and so was replaced by another Venetian panel of similar shape and size.[115] The original saint is unlikely to have been St Nicholas, who is also present in the upper register of half-length saints.

The affinities between the Wernher Collection *Annunciation* and the saints in Prague were first noted by Federico Zeri, who christened the artist the Master of the Ludlow Annunciation after that painting's former owner, Lady Ludlow.[116] Soon afterwards, Dobričević's authorship was convincingly established by Boskovits.[117] These panels were, however, unlikely to have been painted for the main Franciscan church in Dubrovnik. Dobričević is known to have received numerous commissions for the city and the surrounding area, and the 1455 contract probably refers to another altarpiece which does not survive.[118] Zeri was surely correct to observe that the heavy concentration of Franciscan saints on the main register indicates a high altarpiece

6.23 Tomb of Marin Gučetić, *c.* 1370, cloister of the Franciscan convent, Dubrovnik. Photo: Vlaho Pustić.

commission for one of the Order's churches. But the high altar of the Dubrovnik church was already decorated with the fourteenth-century silver retable discussed above, for which Nikola Božidarević was later commissioned in 1501 to paint a hinged 'inchona' to act as a ferial cover.[119]

Instead, the selection of saints on the Prague panels suggests an alternative provenance for the altarpiece. St Elisabeth, mother of John the Baptist, appears at the far right of the upper register of saints.[120] She is an unusual choice for a Franciscan altarpiece, and it can scarcely be a coincidence that the only Franciscan church in Dalmatia dedicated to the Visitation of the Virgin and St Elisabeth was located just to the north of Dubrovnik, at the village of Rožat on the inlet of the river Ombla known today as Rijeka Dubrovačka.[121] This convent had been founded in 1393 and was soon ceded to the Franciscans of the Vicariate of Bosnia, a body of friars based in Dalmatia but dedicated to preaching in the Balkan interior. Already in 1440 De Diversis described a beautiful and richly decorated convent on the Ombla river belonging to the Bosnian friars.[122] The Ottoman conquest of Bosnia in 1463 plunged the Vicariate into crisis, and the convent of Rožat was transferred in 1464-5 to a new grouping of Observant convents based around Dubrovnik and autonomous from the rest of Dalmatia.[123]

It is tempting to associate the London and Prague panels with another of Dobričević's documented projects, a commission for two altarpieces from the Vicariate of Bosnia in 1459-61.[124] The larger of these was to measure five Ragusan *braccia* across, i.e. 256 cm.[125] Allowing for framing elements, this would accord with the dimensions of the altarpiece split between London and Prague (together the surviving fragments have a total width of approximately 230 cm).[126] Dobričević certainly completed these altarpieces, as he received the fee for his work, from which he in turn paid his assistants.[127] However, the surviving documents state that the two altarpieces were to be sent to an unspecified convent in Bosnia, which may exclude the Rožat church, located only five miles from Dubrovnik.[128] It is of course possible that the Turkish conquest and reorganisation of the Franciscan convents in the region may have complicated the Bosnian commission, or that the convent at Rožat may have ordered another altarpiece of similar dimensions. A tantalizing notice from 1469 records that Dobričević had painted an 'anchona' for the church of the Virgin at Rožat, but this seems to refer to the parish church on the hill overlooking the Franciscan convent.[129] In 1461 Dobričević had also contracted to paint a high altarpiece for Rožat's sister convent further up the coast at Slano.[130] The Franciscan church at Slano, founded in 1399, was dedicated to St Jerome, the new patron of the Dalmatian province, who is prominently portrayed on the main register of Dobričević's altarpiece. Like the Rožat convent, the Slano foundation was swiftly given to the Bosnian Franciscans before being integrated into the new Vicariate of Dubrovnik in the 1460s. It is almost certain that the London and Prague panels are fragments of a high altarpiece from one of these two Franciscan churches, with Rožat the more likely candidate given the presence of St Elisabeth.[131]

The Wernher Collection *Annunciation* is an image of considerable sophistication which deploys a remarkable range of iconography alluding to Mary's virginity and the Incarnation. The Virgin stands behind an unusually complex lectern, incorporating a cage in its lower tier which holds three quails feeding from a water bowl. The birds stand for souls awaiting redemption through the grace of the Incarnation and the intercession of the Virgin.[132] Above the cage Dobričević painted a clear glass vase filled with lilies and roses standing in water. This motif, developed in Florence in the 1440s by Filippo Lippi in his images of the Annunciation, draws an analogy between the flowers being nourished within the glass vessel and the virgin birth.[133] Light passes through the glass without breaking it as the holy spirit enters the Virgin's womb. The Virgin's mantle is woven with a repeat design of unicorns, a common emblem of the Incarnation, and the motto 'AVE M[ARIA]'.

There are further iconographic messages in the Virgin's chamber where Dobričević included a bowl beside the bed containing a walnut, another emblem of the Incarnation (St Augustine had interpreted the shell of the walnut as the wood of the cross, enclosing a sweet kernel, symbolising

6.24 Design for an engraving, dated 1614, depicting the miracle-working crucifix over the high altar of the Franciscan church in Dubrovnik, library of the Franciscan convent, Dubrovnik.

the body of Christ). A pair of doves, a common allusion to the Virgin's chastity, is perched on a beam above. Behind the figure of Gabriel is a walled garden, the *hortus conclusus* of the Song of Songs, commonly linked to the Virgin's womb in medieval exegesis. Dobričević populated the garden with hares and a peacock and planted it with a variety of flowers and shrubs including an orange tree to the left. Between the Virgin and Gabriel there is a column surmounted by a statue of a warrior with a spear and shield. For now it remains unclear who this figure is intended to represent. David Ekserdjian has suggested a derivation from the *Belvedere Antinöus*, but the combination of swaggering pose, left hand poised on hip/shield, overt nudity, and fashionable boots may just reflect an awareness of Donatello's bronze *David* in Florence.[134] A number of Florentine masters working in Dubrovnik in these very years would have been familiar with the latest innovations in their native city, particularly Michelozzo, the architect of the Palazzo Medici, who arrived in 1461.[135] As we have seen, the glass vase on the Virgin's lectern also depends on the most recent Florentine models. Beyond the column and garden Dobričević painted a distant city that provides the setting for tiny grisaille narratives, which seem to depict the legend of the Virgin's parents, Joachim and Anna.[136]

The Franciscans and Dominicans were often integrated into the civic rituals of medieval cities, but the example of Dubrovnik seems to be especially pronounced. The two principal mendicant convents were amongst the most favoured ecclesiastical bodies in the city, receiving regular alms from the state.[137] Moreover, the Dubrovnik authorities, ever mindful of Venetian influence, worked assiduously to separate the local houses from their sister convents elsewhere in Dalmatia. This aim was achieved for the Dominicans in 1486, when the houses in Dubrovnik, Gruž and Lopud were organised into a discrete administrative

6.25 Lovro Dobričević, saints from a polyptych, c. 1465 (now mounted in a nineteenth-century frame), Národní Galerie, Prague. Photo: © National Gallery in Prague 2008.

congregation, following the stricter Observant rule. Generally, the reformed Observant branches of the mendicant orders chose to (or were obliged to) build new convents, often in suburban locations, while the friars who continued to live as before in unreformed communities (known as Conventuals) retained control of existing foundations. Dubrovnik is notable in not following this pattern, principally because the Ragusan state encouraged the Observant takeovers of both the main urban convents.

The Observant reform movements of both orders, originating in Italy at the end of the fourteenth century, had a profound impact on the religious landscape of Dalmatia. The fifteenth century was marked by a wave of new Franciscan and Dominican Observant foundations along the length of the coast. For the Dominicans, the most significant of these were the suburban convents on Čiovo opposite Trogir (1432) and at Gruž outside Dubrovnik (1437), both dedicated to the Holy Cross.[138] Later in the century, further Observant Dominican convents were established at Stari Grad on Hvar in 1481 and on Lopud in 1482. For the Franciscans, Observant houses in Dalmatia outnumbered Conventual foundations by the end of the century.[139] These included the church of St Jerome on Ugljan in the Zadar archipelago discussed above. In Zadar itself, the main Franciscan convent was taken over by the Observants in 1453, thereby following the precedent set in Dubrovnik.[140] But many of these Observant convents were founded in remote locations removed from the main urban centres. The Ugljan convent is one example; another is the convent of Košljun on Krk island, founded in 1447 in the bay of Punat several miles from Krk town with the financial backing of the local Frankopan rulers.[141]

One of the earliest and best preserved Franciscan Observant houses on the Adriatic coast is the convent of St Euphemia on Rab, overlooking the cove of Kampor two miles west along the shore from Rab town.[142] In 1446 the small church of St Euphemia was given over to the Observants as the core for a new convent, to be funded by the Rab nobleman Petar Car. This charter was also commemorated by an inscription that can still be seen in the cloister today, which records that the church was to be dedicated jointly to St Francis and St Euphemia.[143] However, the 1466 consecration stone inside the new church confirms that it was instead consecrated to St Bernardino of Siena, the greatest saint of the Franciscan Observant movement who had been swiftly canonised in the interim (in 1450, only six years after his death).[144] The new dedication was reflected in the polyptych that the Observants commissioned from the brothers Antonio and Bartolomeo Vivarini, whose workshop was the most important in Venice after that of Jacopo Bellini (fig. 27). The Vivarini altarpiece, signed by both brothers and dated 1458, survives in excellent condition over the high altar of the church.[145] St Bernardino faces the congregation at the centre of the main register, holding his attribute of the name of Jesus, the 'IHS' monogram that the Vivarini picked out in silver which has tarnished over the centuries. The altarpiece also depicts St Christopher as patron saint of Rab, St Jerome again, the Franciscan Saints Francis, Anthony and Louis of Toulouse, and St Peter, doubtless to underline the orthodoxy of the Observant movement and their obedience to Rome. Miljenko Domijan has plausibly connected the superbly preserved frame with the Venetian woodworker Francesco Moranzon, whose father Matteo had earlier carved the choir stalls of Zadar Cathedral.[146]

The adjacent convent conserves a number of illuminated manuscripts and a beautiful silver-gilt processional crucifix dating from the mid-fifteenth-century, which formed part of Petar Car's original donation (fig. 6.28).[147] On the corpus side Christ crucified is surrounded by the symbols of the Evangelists in the terminals in conventional fashion, but on the reverse an extraordinary swaying figure of St Francis is placed at the centre, his arms ecstatically raised to receive the stigmata. A raised sarcophagus in the cloister is traditionally identified as the tomb of Modruša

Budrišić, a local noblewoman who died in 1532, but the carvings on the coffin are certainly much older (fig. 6.29).[148] The long side of the chest bears reliefs of St Francis, the Virgin and Child and an unidentified female saint holding a cross, which should be dated to the early fifteenth century (if not somewhat earlier). The carving combines a Gothic arcade of trilobe arches with more classicising dentils above.

With new Observant foundations like that at Kampor, the Franciscan and Dominican orders entered a new era. Up and down the Adriatic, the number of mendicant convents multiplied, with Observants taking over some of the principal existing Conventual houses in urban centres, while *ex novo* foundations proliferated in the hinterland and on the islands. The new convents in time provided patronage networks for artists like Juraj Ćulinović (Giorgio Schiavone) and above all the Venetian Santacroce family of painters, but this remarkable institutional expansion and artistic renewal lies beyond the scope of this essay.

6.26 Lovro Dobričević, *Annunciation*, c. 1465 (now mounted in a nineteenth-century frame), Wernher collection, Ranger's House, London. Photo: © English Heritage.

6.27 Antonio and Bartolomeo Vivarini, *St Bernadino and Saints*, painted panel polyptych, signed and dated 1458, church of St Bernardino, convent of St Euphemia, Kampor, Rab. Photo: Jovan Kliska.

By the mid-fifteenth century, the Franciscan and Dominican orders had already transformed the artistic landscape of Croatia. Their churches on the Adriatic coast were architecturally simple affairs, with aisle-less, beam-roofed naves concluding in simple, square-plan and groin vaulted apsidal chapels. In Dalmatia the mendicants rejected the vaulted naves, side aisles and polygonal apses favoured by their confrères in both the Veneto and continental Croatia.[149] The closest parallels are instead to be found in central Italy. Jackson, an accomplished architect, found the mendicant churches of Dalmatia a disappointment in this respect, considering the Dominican church in Dubrovnik 'so simple as to have hardly any architectural character'.[150] But within these plain interiors, the friars and the growing merchant classes of the Adriatic cities commissioned a wealth of art. By the end of the period under discussion, impressive altarpieces (either

6.29 Detail of raised sarcophagus chest, early fifteenth century (?), cloister of St Euphemia, Kampor, Rab. Photo: Donal Cooper.

surviving or documented) can be associated with almost all the major urban convents. Indeed, the available archival evidence suggests that the larger churches possessed numerous polyptychs, such that Lovro Dobričević's *Baptism of Christ* for the Dominican convent in Dubrovnik, often considered to have been painted for that church's high altar, was probably commissioned instead for one of its many side altars. The now lost but amply documented silver high altarpieces in both the Dubrovnik churches are unique in mendicant art of the Middle Ages, and reflect what might be called a 'silver aesthetic' on the Adriatic coast born of the plentiful supply of the precious metal from the Bosnian and Serbian mines, a trade that the Ragusans had been careful to nurture and monopolise.

As well as altarpieces, the churches of the friars were provided with painted crucifixes, elaborately carved choir stalls, a vast array of liturgical plate, imposing tombs for the laity, and elegant cloisters. A wide range of artists and artisans benefited from this demand. Many were local, but the regional and international links of the Franciscans and Dominicans provided access to the best Venetian workshops, artists from other Italian centres like Florence and Milan, and also other centres within Dalmatia. Blaž Jurjev, the most important Dalmatian artist of the fifteenth century, worked for the friars in Trogir, Split and Zadar, and seems (to judge from his testament) to have been especially close to the Franciscans. These artistic networks often transcended the prevailing political currents of the day. The Zadar convents, for example, seem to have thrived during the period of Hungarian rule after 1358, but both orders actively patronised Venetian art at the same time. In this sense, the artistic patronage of the Franciscans and Dominicans reflected not only the wealth and sophistication of the Adriatic cities in the later Middle Ages, but also their international horizons.

6.28 Unknown Venetian goldsmith, silver-gilt processional cross commissioned by Petar Car, mid-fifteenth century, convent of St Euphemia, Kampor, Rab. Photo: Goran Vranić.

THE RENAISSANCE IN CROATIA & ITALY: THE CHAPEL OF THE BLESSED GIOVANNI ORSINI

David Ekserdjian

The subject of this essay is the chapel of the Blessed Giovanni Orsini in the cathedral of St Lawrence at Trogir (Traù in Italian), an ensemble whose sheer artistic quality and virtual completeness make it one of the most remarkable sculptural decorations of the entire Renaissance (fig. 7.1). Yet it seems safe to assert that almost no non-Croatian reader of this essay – and that includes specialists in Renaissance sculpture – is likely to be familiar with the work in question. Moreover, the three principal sculptors involved in its creation – Niccolò di Giovanni Fiorentino, Andrea Alessi and Giovanni Dalmata – are not exactly household names. The reasons for this state of affairs have nothing to do with merit and everything to do with geography and hierarchy, and above all with the way in which the periphery suffers at the expense of the centre in such contexts. It seems important to begin by explaining why this is so, and to sketch in the rich networks which bound the visual arts in Croatia and Italy to one another in the Renaissance.

The major focus of my professional activity as an art historian has been on painting in Parma in the sixteenth century, and above all on two great artists, Correggio and Parmigianino, about both of whom I have written monographs.[1] Anyone who has worked off-centre – as one might say – on the art of the period will on occasion have experienced a sense of exhaustion and even oppression at the extent to which the vast majority of art historians, not to mention interested amateurs, unreflectively assume that the Italian Renaissance only really took place in Florence, Rome, Venice and their dependencies. It goes without saying that the fate of art in Croatia – and the art of Croatians in Italy – is incomparably more likely to suffer from entirely undeserved neglect. It is my intention here – through concentrating on a particularly remarkable monument which involved a combination of Croatian and Italian forces – to go some way towards setting the record a bit straighter.

The first point to be made in this connection is that the links between Italy and Croatia were of very long standing, as the extraordinary remains of Diocletian's megalomaniacally grandiose palace in Split (Spalato) eloquently testify. It is no less vital to recognise that the coast of Croatia – or Dalmatia, as it was then known – was eminently accessible from the ports on Italy's Adriatic coast during the Renaissance. Travel by road over long distances was almost invariably something of a nightmare, but sea routes – and indeed navigable rivers and canals – were comparatively easily negotiated. That is the reason a number of significant works of art created in Venice made their way down the eastern shore of Italy during the fifteenth and sixteenth centuries. Examples comprise various paintings, including altarpieces, by the Vivarini family of painters from Murano,[2] not to mention masterpieces by Giovanni Bellini. Giovanni's great *Coronation of the Virgin* altarpiece was destined for the high altar of the church of San Francesco at Pesaro, and has never left the city (it is now in the Museo Civico there).[3] It followed in the footsteps, so to speak, of the high altarpiece of the church of San Giovanni Battista in the same city (now in the Gemäldegalerie, Berlin) of strikingly comparable dimensions, representing the *Virgin and Child Enthroned with Saints*, by Marco Zoppo. Zoppo, who was born in Cento, near Bologna, and trained under Francesco Squarcione in Padua, signed and dated the work 1471, and added that it had been executed in Venice.[4] Bellini's *St Peter Martyr* went considerably farther afield, since it came from the church of San Domenico at Monopoli before ending up in the nearby Pinacoteca Provinciale in Bari.[5] Generally dated to the 1480s, the *St Peter Martyr* is painted on panel and measures 194 x 84 centimetres, and is therefore a substantial piece of work. For all that workshop intervention has sometimes been posited,[6] it is a painting of great refinement and beauty, whose existence underlines the fact that such long-range commissions were not disdained by even the most illustrious of artists at the height of their powers.

In view of the fact that large-scale panel paintings could travel to the very heel of Italy, there was nothing to stop them ending up on the other side of the Adriatic. In the case of such works as the *Virgin and Child Enthroned* of 1489 by Alvise Vivarini and the polyptych of 1513 painted by Giovanni Bellini's near contemporary, Giovanni Battista Cima da Conegliano, both for Koper (Capodistria) or environs, they actually had considerably less far to go.[7] The latter's dimensions are impressively imposing: it measures well over two metres high by two metres wide.

Alongside what might be dubbed the export trade in works of art and especially paintings, artists could naturally also move around. They did so in both directions, with Italians transferring to Dalmatia quite as enthusiastically as Dalmatians moved to Italy. (Carpaccio's enchanting canvases in the Scuola degli Schiavoni were painted for the Dalmatian expatriate community in Venice, and underline their muscle as patrons in the Serenissima.) One of the most celebrated in the former category was Carlo Crivelli, originally from Venice but like Zoppo almost certainly a pupil of Squarcione's, who is documented as a 'citizen and resident' of Zadar (Zara) in 1465, which indicates that he must have been there for some time by that date. Carlo was back in Italy by 1468, when he signed and dated his altarpiece in Massa Fermana, and – as it happens – not a single surviving work from his sojourn on the 'other' side of the Adriatic is known.[8] For at least some of the time he was there, he was accompanied by his less talented brother Vittore, who stayed on after Carlo's return to Italy. The influence of both brothers on local developments is readily apparent in the work of the painter Pietro Jordanic of Zadar, who signed a *Virgin and Child* 'Opus presbiterj Petrj Jurdanici de Jadra'.[9]

Before moving to Dalmatia, it is generally agreed – as stated above – that Carlo Crivelli must have studied in the workshop-cum-academy of Francesco Squarcione in Padua. Squarcione's most celebrated pupil was Andrea Mantegna, but a number of remarkable painters – not least among them the aforementioned Marco Zoppo – passed through his hands. One of the most gifted was Juraj Ćulinović, invariably known in Italy as Giorgio Schiavone, which simply means 'the Slav'. He was evidently not a novice when he entered Squarcione's establishment in 1456, and instead appears to have had a senior role, as is suggested by such works as the polyptych he executed for the Frigimelica Chapel in San Nicolò, Padua (now National Gallery, London), which is probably a work of the late 1450s. It and a now dismembered triptych for San Francesco, Padua (Gemäldegalerie, Berlin, and Duomo, Padua) must in any event both have been completed before his return to his native Dalmatia, where he is documented in 1461 at Zadar. Although he did not die until 1504, little is known concerning the works of his last four decades, and one of the few pieces of information we have about him is that in 1463 he married Elena, the daughter of the sculptor and architect Giorgio da Sebenico (Šibenik), who will be discussed more fully in due course.[10]

Another fifteenth-century Dalmatian painter of real distinction whose art was profoundly influenced by Italy

7.1 Chapel of the Blessed Giovanni Orsini, general view, Cathedral of St Lawrence, Trogir. Photo: Živko Bačić. Unless otherwise stated, all images are of the Chapel of the Blessed Giovanni Orsini

was known until comparatively recently by one of those *noms de guerre* of which art historians are so inordinately fond, and called the Master of the Ludlow Annunciation, because his most distinguished and distinctive work is part of the Wernher collection, formerly at Luton Hoo, Bedfordshire, and now in the Ranger's House in London, and because the first Lady Wernher became Lady Ludlow after her remarriage. The artist in question has now been convincingly identified as one Lorenzo Marini da Cattaro (he is known as Lovro Dobričević in Croatia), who contracted to execute the high altarpiece of the church of San Domenico at Dubrovnik (Ragusa) in 1448, and died in 1478.[11] In this instance, however, for all the Italianate flavour of his art, I am not aware of any documentary proof of Dobričević having visited Italy.

Conversely, the fact that Dalmatian painters continued to make the journey to Italy in the sixteenth century, and indeed to settle there, is not hard to demonstrate. The two examples who spring to mind are Andrea Schiavone and Giulio Clovio, both of whom have been almost as shamelessly adopted into the great tradition of Italian artists as ever Hans Holbein or Anthony van Dyck have been press-ganged into service as honorary Brits.

Andrea Schiavone, otherwise known as Andrea Meldolla or Andrija Medulić, appears to have been established in Venice by the late 1530s, and it remained his base until his death in 1563. Although he was an energetic and dramatic painter, a master of somewhat gloomy religious scenes rendered with a loaded brush, it is without question his prints that have ensured his immortality. The supreme influence upon them was the work of Francesco Mazzola, known as Parmigianino, who was also an eminent printmaker and the first Italian wholeheartedly to embrace the technique of etching. It therefore comes as no surprise if a number of Schiavone's prints are based upon those of his bold precursor from Parma, but in a select few instances it appears to be demonstrably the case that he must also have had access to original drawings by Parmigianino.[12] Vasari records that various such sheets were stolen from Parmigianino by a printmaker collaborator of his called Antonio da Trento around 1530.

7.2 Niccolò di Giovanni and workshop, *Putto*, Trogir. Photo: Živko Bačić.

7.3 Niccolò di Giovanni, *Putto*, Trogir. Photo: Živko Bačić.

What is more, the sculptor Alessandro Vittoria (of whom more in another context below) owned a substantial collection of Parmigianino drawings by the end of his life, and is known to have acquired them in two tranches, respectively in 1558 and 1581.[13] It is also worth noting that Schiavone was far from unaware of the art of Raphael and Michelangelo, for all that this has tended to be underplayed. His Prague *Holy Family* is obviously based upon Raphael's *Madonna della Tenda*, now in Munich, while – entirely fittingly – his grisaille *David* in the church of San Giacomo dell'Orio in Venice is equally blatantly adapted from some record of Michelangelo's lost bronze statue of *David*, whose appearance is known through an autograph drawing.[14]

Moving on to Don Giulio Clovio (he was born Juraj Klović, but took the name Giulio when he became a Benedictine, and retained it when he left the monastery to become a priest), there is much the same pattern of early departure from Croatia and dependence on such masters of the high Renaissance as Michelangelo and Raphael. The fundamental difference is that Clovio worked almost exclusively as an illuminator, and that he spent three years or so away from Italy at the court of Louis II and Mary of Austria, who were the rulers of Bohemia and Hungary. It is also the case that even in his late works, such as the *Passion of Christ* in the Galleria Sabauda, Turin, he could still reveal a dependence on Albrecht Dürer, whose works he had first encountered in the Grimani collection before 1523, when he was a young man. Here the *Agony in the Garden* is an amalgamation of motifs from the corresponding scenes in Dürer's *Small* and *Engraved Passions*.[15] In 1540, Clovio had entered the service of Cardinal Alessandro Farnese, who was the 'nipote' (grandson) of Pope Paul III, and the connection only came to an end with the artist's death in 1578. This placed him at the heart of artistic life in Rome, and one of the most memorable testimonials to his pivotal position is the *Portrait of Clovio* (Museo e Gallerie Nazionali di Capodimonte, Naples) by another painter who was close to the Farnese, El Greco, in which Clovio is represented holding his masterpiece, the *Farnese Book of Hours* (Pierpont Morgan

Fig. 7.4 Niccolò di Giovanni and workshop, *Coronation of the Virgin*, Trogir. Photo: Živko Bačić, courtesy Venetian Heritage Inc.

Library, New York).[16] It need hardly be added that El Greco, whose real name was Domenikos Theotokopoulos, was for a period another honorary Italian before ending up as an honorary Spaniard.

Thus far, all the examples of cross-fertilisation I have explored have been concerned with painting, but the same spirit of mutual regard is at least as apparent when it comes to sculpture. The principal sculptural medium in Croatia during the Renaissance was stone or marble, with the necessary consequence that it was not as a rule practicable for sculptors to send their works from afar in the way painters could. The result is that virtually all Italian sculpture in Croatia was effectively carved *in situ*, and contrariwise this may well have served as something of an encouragement to any Croatian sculptors who wanted to work in Italy. Unarguably, the most distinguished of these was Francesco Laurana (Franjo Vranjanin, *c.* 1420–1502) from Zadar: his apprentice years were spent with Pietro da Milano in Dubrovnik, but after moving to Italy with his master, he never returned to Croatia, and his illustrious subsequent career was mainly spent in Naples, Sicily and the south of France.[17]

The existence of a great sculptural tradition in Croatia stretching back to long before the Renaissance is thrillingly demonstrated by the recently restored portal of Radovan on the west front of Trogir Cathedral, which – as is proved by the inscription with the artist's name it bears – was begun in 1240.[18] No less impressive are the even earlier monumental wooden doors – they are 530 centimetres high by 360 centimetres wide – of the cathedral of St Domnius in Split, which are the work of Andrija Buvina and date from 1214. That there was a notable revival in the early Renaissance is plain to anyone who has visited the interior of Split Cathedral, where the altar-tomb of St Domnius by Bonino da Milano of 1427 and the altar-tomb of St Anastasius by Giorgio da Sebenico of 1448 may be admired in close proximity.[19] Both look more like tombs than altars, since they are topped by reclining effigies of their respective saints being unveiled by angels, and have sarcophagus-style arrangements below, but what really brings one up short, especially in the case of the latter, is the formidable energy of the carving. Giorgio's relief is carved from stone from Brač, which has then been painted, and is often compared with the work of Donatello, but this has more to do

Fig. 7.5 Left wall, Chapel of the Blessed Giovanni Orsini, Trogir. Photo: courtesy Venetian Heritage, Inc.

with its tragic dynamism and sheer brilliance than with actual stylistic links.[20] (For an illustration, see p. 126, fig. 9.6) In any event, since Giorgio's summons to return to Croatia from Venice or the Veneto to become master of the works of Šibenik Cathedral dates from 22 June 1441, and Donatello only left Florence for Padua in 1443, the former is most unlikely to have been acquainted with the latter's art.

This is not the place to attempt a survey of Giorgio da Sebenico's distinguished career as a sculptor, far less as an architect, but it does seem essential to observe that he was extremely active in the decades up to his death in 1473.[21] At Šibenik, he was responsible for the overall appearance of the cathedral of St James, which was completed by Niccolò di Giovanni Fiorentino and is a considerably larger cousin of the church of Santa Maria dei Miracoli in Venice. He also oversaw various sculptural projects, the most notable of which is arguably the baptistery.[22] Another major sculptor is documented as working on the cathedral in 1445: this was Andrea Alessi, who was born in Albania but spent almost his entire career in Dalmatia.[23] Giorgio da Sebenico also worked in other Dalmatian centres such as Split and Dubrovnik, but was equally in demand

in Ancona on Italy's Adriatic coast in the 1450s, where his facade for the Loggia dei Mercanti again brought Andrea Alessi into contact with him. As stated at the outset, both Niccolò di Giovanni and Alessi were responsible for the chapel of the Blessed Giovanni Orsini in Trogir Cathedral, and interestingly enough their collaborator Giovanni Dalmata also worked in Ancona.

It was the commission to work on the chapel that brought Niccolò to Dalmatia. He is first named in the Trogir documents on 19 December 1467, when he was present and entrusted Coriolano Cippico, the noted humanist, with authority to sign the contract for the construction and decoration of the chapel in collaboration with Andrea Alessi. That contract was drawn up in his absence on 4 January 1468, with one ser Nicolò, the son of the late ser Cipriano, the administrator of the cathedral works, and envisaged the very considerable expenditure of 2,300 ducats on the project. It was further noted that the design drawings for the chapel, whose authorship was not specified, were to be stored in a box in the chancellery of the *comune*. The fact that these drawings must have been extremely detailed would appear to be confirmed by the painstaking specificity of the contract, which can only be summarised here.[24] The contract envisaged the destruction of the external wall of the cathedral, and the construction of a chapel which would measure twenty-four Venetian feet long by twenty-four feet wide on the exterior, and twenty feet long by fifteen feet wide by seventeen feet high on the interior. It also specified that the floor should be constructed of red and white Verona marble slabs, each one foot or so square, and gave detailed instructions concerning the design of the altar (allowing for an alternative option to the one detailed in the drawing) and the placement and appearance of the Blessed Giovanni's shrine. As will become apparent, not all of the provisions outlined in the contract were followed to the letter.

The most crucial part of the contract in the present context, however, concerns its specifications for the sculptural embellishment of the chapel. This was to comprise three tiers of decoration. Proceeding from bottom to top, the first was to be placed above a continuous stone bench at a height of three feet, modelled on the one in the cathedral baptistery (which had just

been completed by Alessi), and was to consist of reliefs of three-foot tall putti with flaming torches – seventeen in all – emerging from small doors, to a height of two and a half feet. Above them were to be sixteen niches large enough to accommodate standing figures carved in the round measuring five feet in height. The plan was for there to be six niches along both the longer side walls, and four additional niches in the corners of the shorter entrance and altar walls. Since the contract requires that the sixteen figures should represent the twelve apostles and four unspecified additional figures, it seems logical to suppose that the apostles were intended to go along the side walls and the four remaining figures in the corners of the end walls. That is basically what happened, but neither the way Christ was flanked by the Virgin and St John the Baptist to create a kind of Deesis arrangement, nor indeed the generally hierarchic ordering of the apostles to place such figures as Peter and Paul, and James and John, at the altar end, is actually detailed in the contract. In addition, there

Fig. 7.6 Andrea Alessi or Niccolò di Giovanni, *St Jerome*, Trogir. Photo: Živko Bačić.

Fig. 7.7 Right wall, Chapel of the Blessed Giovanni Orsini, Trogir. Photo: courtesy Venetian Heritage, Inc.

Fig. 7.8 Giovanni Dalmata, *St Thomas*, Trogir. Photo: Živko Bačić, courtesy Venetian Heritage Inc.

Fig. 7.9 Giovanni Dalmata, *St John the Evangelist*, Trogir. Photo: Živko Bačić.

was to be what is described as a seven-foot square 'casamento', which was to house a figure of Christ to a height of five and a quarter feet, flanked by pairs of angels respectively measuring three and two feet in height. This was to go between the apostles, by which is evidently meant in the otherwise vacant space behind the altar. The figures in their niches were to be flanked by twelve columns to a height of five and a half feet, half of them fluted and half with a spiral decoration, each one of which was to be crowned by a two-foot high seated putto. Next, on the altar wall above the cornice, there was to be a representation of the *Coronation of the Virgin* with a choir of angels in more than half relief within a lunette. The width of this opening was to be thirteen feet, and the – by implication and as was customary – seated figures of God the

Father and the Virgin were to be on a scale such that, if standing, they would measure five and a half feet. Finally, the ceiling was to be in the form of a barrel vault, each of whose coffers was to house a seraph, with a central roundel containing a half-length figure of God the Father. In order to comply with the requirements of decorum, the proportions, gestures, movements and faces of the figures were to befit their respective ages.

Before discussing the relationship between this meticulous battle plan and what actually happened, it seems important to address the question of whom the sculptural protagonists were and to speculate concerning why they came to be chosen for the job in hand. In the case of Alessi, he is first documented in 1435 at Zadar, where he was a pupil of Marco di Pietro da Troia, and –

Fig. 7.10 Niccolò di Giovanni, *St James Major*, Trogir. Photo: Živko Bačić.

Fig. 7.11 Niccolò di Giovanni, *St Paul*, Trogir. Photo: Živko Bačić.

as stated – was subsequently in Šibenik in 1445. Between 1448 and 1460, he was in charge of his own workshop in Split and on the island of Rab, before moving to Trogir in 1466 to work on the baptistery of the cathedral. The baptistery is a barrel-vaulted structure to the left of the entrance porch, which is attached to the main body of the church but is not accessible from it. Its main sculptural adornments, which had been completed by the following year, are a relief of the *Baptism of Christ* over the entrance door, and inside another relief of *St Jerome in the Wilderness*, a subject that appears to have been a particular favourite of Alessi's, to judge by the number of small-scale variations on the theme he was to execute over the years.[25] These works are highly proficient exercises in a distinctive if more

tranquil version of the manner of Giorgio da Sebenico, and the cathedral authorities were doubtless impressed by Alessi's combination of accomplishment with expeditiousness.

The situation with Niccolò di Giovanni is less obvious, but he may have seemed an even more desirable catch. There is no absolute certainty concerning his career prior to his arrival in Trogir, but it seems reasonable to suppose that – regardless of his Florentine origins – he had been active in Venice. In her 1978 monograph on the artist, Anne Markham Schulz argued with passionate conviction that he was responsible for a number of major sculptural projects in Venice, notably the tombs of Francesco Foscari (Santa Maria Gloriosa dei Frari), Orsato Giustinian (originally Sant'Andrea della Certosa) and Vittore

Capello (Sant'Elena). This thesis has not been widely accepted by other scholars of Venetian sculpture, but much more recently Markham Schulz has in effect demonstrated that an impressively well-connected 'lapicida' (which can mean sculptor as well as stonemason) called Niccolò di Giovanni, who may have come from near Florence, made his will in Venice on 10 July 1462. The witnesses to the will were two Venetian noblemen, while this Niccolò named Francesco Trevisan and Alvise di Marino Landi as his executors. The former was in charge of the monastery which contained the Giustinian tomb, attributed to Niccolò by Markham Schulz, while the latter is known to have been a patron of his, and subsequently held the office of count (i.e. governor) of Trogir between 19 April 1470 and 16 November 1472.[26] Whether he was responsible for some or all of the works ascribed to him by Markham Schulz or not, Niccolò di Giovanni can plausibly be supposed to be the sort of person a man like Coriolano Cippico might have been recommended to employ by his Venetian contacts. What is more, Venice is a much more likely place than Florence for the powers that were in Trogir to have gone in search of a sculptor, in view of the fact that the city, and indeed Dalmatia more generally, had been under Venetian dominion since 1420.

If the cathedral authorities at Trogir were hoping for their immensely ambitious project to be relatively swiftly completed, they were in for a grave disappointment. It is far from straightforward to reconstruct exactly how matters proceeded, not least since the documentation we possess is incomplete and there were certainly at least some changes of plan, but it is best to begin with the factual information we do have at our disposal. The first point to be made is that the only parts of the sculptural decoration for which we have dated payments are the free-standing statues, which means we have no documentary evidence concerning the authorship or sequence of execution of the vault, the *Coronation of the Virgin*, or the two tiers of putti. In the event, almost all these elements seem to be the work of Niccolò di Giovanni and his workshop, unevennesses of quality being a reflection of the sheer volume of carving required. Predictably enough, the most impressive carving is on the *Coronation* relief (fig. 7.4), although there are also charmingly inventive conceits among the upper and lower ranks of putti. In inspired contravention of the original contract, the former are standing, not seated, and at least one of them has turned his back on us, while another has pulled up his shift, seemingly with the dangerous intention of peeing from on high (fig. 7.2). For any of the figures other than the

Fig. 7.12 Niccolò di Giovanni and workshop, *Putto*, Trogir. Photo: Živko Bačić.

putti, this would naturally have been a scandalous breach of decorum. Down below, there is again considerable variety (fig 7.12), but there is no question that the finest of all the putti is the one puffing out his cheeks to blow on his torch (fig. 7.3).[27]

Turning to the statues, it is vital to begin by explaining that – in addition to the figure of Christ and two rather than four angels – there are now four apostles along each of the side walls (figs 7.5 and 7.7) and that three of the four corner niches are filled, which gives a total of twelve full-size figures, comprising eleven saints and Christ. Four additional apostles by Alessandro Vittoria were added in 1559 to make sixteen, but were subsequently removed to make way for windows; they were placed high up at the corners of the pinnacle of the campanile, and are now exhibited in the church of San Giovanni Battista in Trogir.[28] In 1482, there was a payment of 186 lire, 4 soldi – presumably to Niccolò, although he is not actually named – for a *St John the Evangelist*: the figure in question, who is instantly identifiable by virtue of his accompanying eagle, occupies the antepenultimate niche on the right side wall. Then, in 1487, Niccolò received payment of 673 lire, 16 soldi for statues of *Christ*, the *Virgin Mary* and *St Peter*. This is usually assumed to represent 224 lire, 12 soldi per statue, but it is at least worth asking whether the statues of the *Virgin* and *St Peter* may not have been costed at much the same rate as the *St John*, with the larger *Christ* – with the two attendant angels perhaps thrown in for good measure – representing around 300 lire of the total. In 1488, Niccolò was paid 155 lire for the *St John the Baptist*, and received the same fee for four further statues the next year. It seems reasonable to assume that these must be the *St James Major* (fig. 7.10), *St Paul* (fig. 7.11), the *St Philip* and the final figure, which presumably represents *St Andrew*. The next payment is one of 1494, not explicitly stated to be to Niccolò, but said to be for a figure of *Christ*, again at the by now standard rate of 155 lire. Since another figure of *Christ* had been paid for in 1487, it has not unreasonably been assumed that the statue now in the chapel must have replaced the group of *Christ with Two Angels* formerly in the cemetery at Trogir and now in the Town Museum there.[29] The fact that this second statue was so much cheaper than the inferior one it replaced, and that the documents give no indication that Niccolò incurred any financial penalty for his original work being deemed unsatisfactory, makes it tempting to propose an alternative hypothesis. If the reference to Christ were a scribal error, then this could be the first of Giovanni Dalmata's two statues for the chapel.

Confusingly enough, this figure gives every indication of being a second *St John the Evangelist*, and is thus identified by an

7.13 Giovanni Dalmata, *Virgin and Child*, marble, 54 x 38 cm, Town Museum, Trogir. Photo: Daniel Katz Ltd, London.

inscription on the front of its base ('S . IOANNES . EVANGELISTA.'), which is complemented by one ('IOANNIS . DA[L]MATAE . F[ECIT].') on its reverse, which is effectively invisible *in situ* (fig. 7.9). There is no reason to doubt the fact that the statue in question is indeed by Giovanni Dalmata, but it is possible that the inscription on the front – and possibly even the one on the back – are both later additions. This could explain the considerable anomaly of a chapel with two statues of *St John the Evangelist*, one of them entirely lacking the usual attributes, and is certainly more plausible than the suggestion that a statue by Giovanni Dalmata of exactly the right height but originally intended for a different location was subsequently transferred to the chapel. A date of around 1494 would work reasonably well both in terms of Giovanni Dalmata's biography (his Hungarian patron Matthias Corvinus died in 1490, and he is next documented in Trogir in 1497) and in terms of his stylistic development as it is generally understood.[30] It would suggest that the kinship between Niccolò's *St Philip* and Giovanni's *St John* revealed the influence of the former upon the latter, as opposed to

vice versa, and would not allow for the possibility that the latter statue was a disguised portrait of Coriolano Cippico's son, Alvise, dating from the early 1480s.[31]

In that case, the final payment of 155 lire for an unidentified figure dating from 1508 to 'Magistro Joanne lapicida' (presumably Giovanni Dalmata) would be for his *St Thomas* (fig. 7.8), as is anyway generally assumed.[32] We therefore potentially have payments for eleven of the twelve statues still in the chapel, which might support the idea that the single undocumented statue is the *St Jerome* (fig. 7.6), which is commonly but not invariably attributed to Andrea Alessi (the only other possibility would be Niccolò di Giovanni). If not, then he would appear to have made no contribution to its decoration whatsoever before the dissolution of his and Niccolò's partnership in 1479–80, unless he was responsible for one or both figures of the *Angel* and the *Virgin* of the *Annunciation* group flanking the chapel's entrance arch.[33]

Such an interpretation of the documents would indicate that the securely documented statues by Niccolò were executed over a comparatively brief span of time from 1482 to 1489, and is supported by the fact that they are indeed stylistically broadly speaking of a piece. Thereafter, Giovanni Dalmata may have taken over, although documentation concerning Niccolò's work on Šibenik Cathedral dating from 1497 suggests that he was still notionally involved with the chapel in Trogir Cathedral at that time.[34]

In the final analysis and regardless of all these attributional, iconographic and chronological problems, it is the quality of the best of the individual sculptures and of the ensemble that makes the chapel so memorable. At his best, as with *St John the Evangelist* and *St Paul*, Niccolò is capable of endowing his figures with a rare combination of dignity and fluidity, which contrasts delightfully with the unruly energy and playfulness of the putti both above and below. The *St John the Evangelist* of Giovanni Dalmata is arguably even more impressive as a work of art, and underlines the classical poise and sheer elegance of which he was capable, and which are also splendidly apparent in his marble relief of the *Virgin and Child* (fig. 7.13), recently acquired by the Town Museum in Trogir.

Vittoria's additional statues may well have disrupted the calm and near uniformity of this unusually coherent and complete monument, which at one stage may therefore only have lacked one niche figure (was it supposed to have portrayed St Lawrence, in honour of the cathedral's patron?). Perhaps happily, they are long departed, and the only other distraction results from the translation of Giovanni Orsini's body and his effigy in 1681 (when another Cippico was still involved),[35] the introduction of baroque angels, and the transformation of the pavement. For the rest, the combined forces of church and state, whose respective coats of arms adorn the chapel's entrance, would have had every right to feel proud of their accomplishment as patrons. The main phase of the project took four decades from the signing of the contract to the payment for Giovanni Dalmata's *St Thomas*, but it was worth the wait.[36]

NIKOLA BOŽIDAREVIĆ

Joško Belamarić

Translated by Graham McMaster

The Dubrovnik archives record seventeen works by Nikola Božidarević, but only four have survived. He signed himself in brush strokes only twice, as 'Nicolaus Rhagusinus' and 'Nicolo Raguseo' – Nikola of Dubrovnik. The first occasion was in a marble medallion under the arm of Gabriel in the middle of the *Annunciation*, which he painted in 1513 for the Đorđić family; the second was for his last work (1517) at the foot of the Virgin's throne on the main altar retable in the church of Our Lady of Dánče. Until the archival discovery of his Croatian family name,

this name fired the imagination of those researching Dubrovnik Renaissance art and even became a kind of myth.[1]

The fact that twenty years after his return home Nikola Božidarević took the name of the city in which he lived may mean that following his travels in Italy between 1477 and 1494 he had carried back in his bags not only brushes but a certain element of fame, which perhaps later allowed him to place his works abroad from Dubrovnik. With this signature he probably wished to convey what art historians say today: his painting was at that time more or less a synonym for Dubrovnik painting. To call himself 'Rhagusinus' in the middle of Dubrovnik was undoubtedly a self-confident declaration vis-à-vis his artistic contemporaries – especially Mihajlo Hamzić and Vicko, the son of Lovro Dobričević – and even perhaps in relation to his own father, whose workshop he had recently left. Finally, to call himself 'Rhagusinus' within the city itself was perhaps for him a sign that he had finally shaken off the village dust from the shoes brought by the Božidarević family from little Kručica on the Slano coast, where he and his father had given up their land and become full citizens of the famous city.[2]

In the imagination of his contemporaries Dubrovnik was like a

8.1 Nikola Božidarević, Madonna and Saints, triptych from the Dominican church in Dubrovnik. Photo: Živko Bačić.

8.2 Nikola Božidarević, model of Dubrovnik in the hands of St Blaise, detail of fig. 8.1.

precise demands of the patron, inherited style and themes, stylistic conventions and, above all, the working ambience in which he had to operate that lacked great innovative impulses. Immediately after Nikola's return from Italy, he and his father Božidar Vlatković received a very large commission. In 1495 they agreed a contract for the retable of the main altar of the Franciscan church in Cavtat.[5] The church authorities required that the central composition and figures on the left side should be composed according to the pattern of a polyptych executed almost half a century earlier by Matko Junčić in the church of the Minorite Friars in Dubrovnik, while figures on the right side were to be done according to the pattern of another altar in the same church. The saints in the upper part of the polyptych, shown down to the waist, were to be done after Junčić also, and only the central Pietà according to an earlier painting by Božidarević.

When we stand today in front of polyptychs of this kind (which, when preserved in full, amaze us by the perfect balance of their general composition), we rarely think that they were created as *bricolage* from the elements of existing works. The same is true of their style. Experts have very easily 'stripped down' Božidarević's work into the style and themes found in the Crivelli brothers and Vittore Carpaccio.[6] But Božidarević obviously, as Kruno Prijatelj observes, also knew the fresco paintings of Perugino and Pinturichio in the Vatican palace (Appartamento Borgia) and elsewhere in Rome where his brush may, according to Vladimir Marković, have indeed been involved, as can be seen in his triptych executed for the Dominican church in Dubrovnik (fig. 8.1).[7]

By 1500 the form of the polyptych which the 'Dubrovnik School of Painting' retained until its end had become a Procrustean bed. It did not allow figures to be shown in a natural context, to be enlivened by being shown with real objects, nor for drawing breath or relaxing posture. Thus, in Božidarević's paintings, the representation of real life and the movement of the real world are only found in miniatures, on the borders of polyptychs, in 'footnotes' on individual articles or when we study details microscopically. We will consider in such a context the model of Dubrovnik held on the palm of the hands of the city's patron saint, Blaise, as it stands between Blaise's crosier and the drawn sword of St Paul (fig. 8.2). Nikola was painting Dubrovnik

treasure chest. It was not then what it has become today: an archetypal stone model, a stereotyped symbolic picture conceived according to one single view, a perhaps over-idealised identity. It was then a living ambience, carved, gilded and polished. But let us turn to the statistics: the bishop's visitation of 1573 registered 150 polyptychs above the altars of Dubrovnik churches. Today there are no more than ten. 'Rivers of gold and silver flowed' in the fire that for twenty days raged in Dubrovnik after those few seconds of the great earthquake of 1667 in the dawn watches of Maundy Thursday.[3] The copious newsprint reporting the calamity shows to what extent it excited the whole of Europe, as do also the verses of the Croatian poet Palmotić. Over the church threshold – he wrote – down the steps of the Minorite Brothers into Placa flowed rivers of molten gold.

Božidarević's paintings of Renaissance Dubrovnik tell us more about the city than about him. We have some indirect details about his schooling and his travels in Italy, but about the man we know only that he was a bachelor and that he emancipated himself from his father very late in life, probably not until he was fifty years old. From September 1514 he began to build up his own fortune, which by the end of his life was considerable. He gathered his own collection of medals. He contracted for work on his own, nurturing his own workshop. That he could also be tempestuous can be seen from the three-month prison sentence passed on him for 'singing ribald songs and upsetting Marin Petrić and his maid' during Carnival 1509.[4]

But what does any of this mean for an understanding of his surviving works? Very little. The painter of his day in Dubrovnik was confined within tight concentric circles comprised of the very

8.3 Nikola Božidarević, altarpiece of the *Annunciation* from the Dominican church in Dubrovnik. Photo: Živko Bačić.

at its apogee. It was the city that his contemporary Machiavelli at the beginning of his *Discorsi sopra la prima Deca di Tito Livio* (*Discourses on Livy*, 1513–21) compared with ancient Rome, Athens, Alexandria, Venice and Florence, and whose legendary founders, along with those of Rome and Venice, he placed beside such heroic figures as Theseus, Alexander of Macedonia, Aeneus and Moses. Even when Dubrovnik was portrayed by lesser artists than Božidarević, and when it was beaten out in metal by Renaissance goldsmiths, it could not be shown without its harbour full of shipping. St Blaise holds the city like Gulliver. From the patron's cope through the city gates by the Minčeta Tower, an embroidered St Gregory peeps out, and we see the harbour full of boats. Dubrovnik's painters never took greater care than when depicting the model of their city. Božidarević reveals valuable facts concerning Dubrovnik which, even after so many changes, retains its crystalline harmony. With a sensitivity for volume and a precision of geometry not found elsewhere, he draws all the plans of the city walls where guards are busily walking and horses trotting.

The form of a polyptych (like the form of a sonnet) does, however, help the artist to construct a rationally and symmetrically balanced figural composition. It equalises lighting, concentrates gaze and attention: even when its constructional elements are removed, it continues to have an invisible effect for a long time. Like the gilded background to the figures (where the impression is not of earthly but heavenly things), the polyptych form also serves to underline the particular religious subject matter. When the polyptych is used by the painters of the sixteenth century, as Panofsky remarked, it is like Verdi

composing in the Gregorian mode when writing church music. But, then, in Dubrovnik even Titian used the polyptych. The continued use of this traditional form does not, however, indicate date or stylistic backwardness.

The four surviving paintings by Božidarević are typologically different. This only shows how impoverished we are not to have his entire opus. The oldest painting is the triptych for the Bundić family chapel in the Dominican church (*c*. 1500, see fig. 8.1), the first completely Venetian Renaissance painting in Dubrovnik art. It is characterised by a forced symmetry of composition: two bearded bishops (Blaise and Augustine) in golden copes on the outside, and two bald saints (Paul and Thomas Aquinas) beside them, with the Virgin on the central panel. The lyrical *Annunciation* which he painted as an *ex voto* for Captain Marko Kolendić from Lopud (fig. 8.3) and the *Sacra Conversazione* for the Đorđić family (fig. 8.4), both 1513, are often considered his most outstanding artistic creations since they are both typical Renaissance compositions. It is Božidarević's last work – the altar retable for the church of Our Lady at Dance from 1517 – which probably radiates the greatest internal energy of the painter (fig. 8.5). His *Sacra Conversazione* (a term not coined until the late nineteenth century) only seemingly presages the dissolution of the polyptych. The compactness of the figures of the saints and the tiny portrait of the rector of Dubrovnik (from the Đorđić family, painted in old-fashioned 'iconic' perspective in which the size of figures indicates their importance) transmit less life than in the Dance retable, where each figure is identified by a restless gesture or position, although the nocturnal *Lamentation* scene, composed in the lunette, evinces a strict symmetry which almost neutralises expressiveness. It is of some interest that the gesture of lamentation is given not to any of the saints that make up the quartet of women, but to John.

The bodies of Božidarević's saints, in spite of everything, are still cut from Gothic cloth. The beggar beside St Martin has no blood in his veins, but the little angels are truly plump and greedy Renaissance figures. Although each of the figures seems to expand beyond the enclosing frame, any space which we might acquire by removal of the triptych frame is not specifically indicated. The eyes of the phlegmatic St Martin on his horse and those of the beggar are not in discourse. The beggar becomes a protagonist of the scene with the flash of his features on the saint's sword. It has been thought that it could portray a reflection of Christ's face (who would be behind the beggar and invisible to us,[8] iconographically a rarity without precedent) or Božidarević's self-portrait.[9]

There is another important and unusual pictorial element: the beggar has a halo. The beggar's complexion, the horse's neck and Martin's gloves are not painted naturalistically. Yet Božidarević's brush, which reveals a man of spirit but without the gift of penetrating observation of the material world around him or of the secret places of human character, allows decoration to prevail:

8.4 Nikola Božidarević, altarpiece of the Đorđić family from the Dominican church in Dubrovnik. Photo: Živko Bačić.

8.5 Nikola Božidarević, *Madonna and Saints*, polyptych from the church of St Mary in Danče, Dubrovnik. Photo: K. Tadić.

the strange *contrapposto* of the horse, the plaits between the horse's ears, the clothing.

In fact, it is drapery which is the most convincing, arresting and almost tactile element of Božidarević's painting. Just as we perceive the bustle of the harbour on the model of Dubrovnik held by St Blaise, so too Božidarević was fully aware of the richness of the materials produced at this time in Dubrovnik. It is enough to remember the fame of Dubrovnik's cloth manufacture (especially that of the Pantella brothers, who introduced it on a large scale). Its importance was singled out by the then *rector scholarum*, the early Renaissance Tuscan humanist Philip de Diversis. (The enterprise of the brothers from Lombardy certainly promoted Dubrovnik's interests and gave rise to ideas about constructing the famous aquaduct and even mills in the harbour.) 'It would be fitting to raise a marble statue to Petar Pantella in the middle of the city in lasting gratitude … It was never before recorded that cloth was made in Illyria from the wool of sheep from Valencia and Tortosa, which is now done in Dubrovnik thanks to him.'[10] Cloth was as important as salt for the trade of Dubrovnik and was a very tangible element in the consciousness of the city.[11] Bosnian musicians accepted pay in linen, which they found difficult to obtain at home, while in the state warehouses there was always plenty. It may be paradoxical but it is accurate to say that Božidarević did not paint portraits of saints (using patterns of characters); rather, he portrayed materials in which his saints were clothed. It is significant in this context that the most outstanding assistant in his workshop (for which in 1507 he rented a whole floor in one of the mansions on Placa, suitable because of its good light) was Marin Kriješić, who is recorded in one of the archives as 'pictor sive coltrarius', painter of pictures, curtains, coverlets and cloth.[12]

All four of Božidarević's surviving paintings were private votive offerings. Their subject must, therefore, be read according to the wishes of the person who ordered them, as may be seen from the contract for a lost triptych for the patrician Gradić family for the chapel of St Jerome in the Dominican church. Nikola had to portray the saints of the namedays of the Gradić brothers, Jerome in the desert between Stephen and Matthew. In fact, the reasons for chosing a particular saint were varied. They were often an indication of the class or occupation of the person ordering the painting, or were selected to ward off disease. St Julian with a hawk on his wrist (sometimes the saint holds a book in the other hand: he chooses between the worldly and spiritual) on the Đorđić *Sacra Conversazione* (where the rector of Dubrovnik is kneeling at the foot of Matthew, his beard making him resemble the saint) makes a logical pair to St James. Similarly, in Lovro Dobričević's polyptych (1465) in the church of Our Lady of Danče, he makes a pair with St Nicholas. St Julian the Hospitaller, that Christian Oedipus with the melancholy face of a maiden, is shown here with a typical Pinturichio cap on his head. He was the protector of travellers and traders, as were St James

and St Nicholas.[13] As penance for killing his parents, Julian rowed travellers across a dangerous river and beside it built a hospital for the poor. For this reason churches beside water are often dedicated to him, as for example on Pantan and Blato near Trogir. St Thomas (with the iron square in his hand used when he built a magnificent palace in India), depicted beside the *Lamentation*, was also a great traveller. It was the Dubrovnik merchants who were the main patrons of the arts. As Philip de Diversis, their great admirer, said, the mercantile oligarchy 'could not have existed – because of the infertility of the land and the large number of inhabitants – had not they been much richer than the rest … [and] fathers brought up their children to be merchants as soon as their nails began to grow'.

It is usually considered, taking into account their formal superiority, that the *Sacra Conversazione* of the Đorđić painting and the *Annunciation* done for Captain Marko Kolendić provide the measure of Božidarević's ambitions as an artist.[14] If the former is the first example of a particularly popular Renaissance composition in Croatian art, the second is its first independent central altar painting.

In Croatian art history of the fifteenth and sixteenth centuries there are two categories: 'the Dalmatian' and 'the Dubrovnik School of Painting'. But we may say that they resemble each other more than they differ. The specific characteristics of individual Zadar, Šibenik, Trogir and Split painters do not differ so much from their Kotor and Dubrovnik contemporaries. The work of all was connected, as Kruno Prijatelj would say, by the same discreet retardation and by influences of common stylistic denominators which came from the western shores of the Adriatic, especially from Venice and the Marches of Ancona. During the second half of the fourteenth century, the whole coast from Kotor to Zadar and the Kvarner was integrated into a monumental political Angevin project. Divisions between Venetian Dalmatia and the free Dubrovnik Republic in the first half of the fifteenth century were easily bridged by painters such as Blaž Jurjev of Trogir and by sculptors and architects such as Juraj Matijev.

Abundant written material and detailed art historical analysis of the works preserved show us the way Božidarević's *bottegha* was organised and the humanistic milieu for which his paintings were executed. Private orders in Dubrovnik of the time continued to demand the traditional religious, especially votive, themes. But in the wider sphere new, more secular, opportunities presented themselves. A study by Vladimir Marković shows this programme to have risen out of the unity of the political intentions and the moral principles of the patrician oligarchy, which coincided and were identified with the Renaissance view of Christianity and especially with classical Roman *exempla*.[15]

We understand art most often by comparison of pairs – not only through Heinrich Wolfflin's stylistic pairs, but through pairs of equally important artists. In the Dubrovnik of that time, such a pair was Lovro Dobričević and Nikola Božidarević. Nikola's great

8.6 Nikola Božidarević, left predella, detail of fig. 8.5. Photo: K. Tadić.

predecessor returned to Dubrovnik bringing with him the late Gothic inspiration of the Venetian painters Michele Giambono and Antonio Vivarini. The work of Dobričević has been critically reconstructed in an almost dramatic way by the efforts of Croatian and Italian art historians during the last ten years, although some of their hypotheses are still being debated.[16] I am afraid, however, that in spite of his sensitivity to the early currents of the Renaissance, we must be cautious in seeking its stylistic signs in Lovro's Virgins, the Christ Child, and his angels playing musical instruments. We shall look in vain in Dobričević for any signs of living landscape. The Baptism on the polyptych of the Dubrovnik Dominicans shows a Byzantine ambience with no real topographical interest. The horizon is high above the heads. The landscape which rises steeply is in fact two-dimensional, blocking in gold background the place where we should expect to see the sky. It is not a geographical landscape but an attributional one (fig. 8.10).[17] In the entire opus of Lovro Dobričević, we cannot find a single tree. But when we consider Božidarević's landscapes, we also notice a paradox: the endless journeys of the globe-trotting men of Dubrovnik did not give rise to the desire to extend the pictures they commissioned to include realistic landscapes.

However, it would have been unrealistic to expect Nikola Božidarević to show the *Annunciation* against Kolendić's Lopud landscape. Instead, he presents the stereotypical picture of the humanists' idea of Arcadia, but omitting Bellini's ploughmen and donkeys. This is no bucolic Virgilian landscape as created in the circle surrounding Giorgione – no mundane utopia in which we might like to live. Behind Gabriel the landscape is wild and rough, while behind the Virgin it is cultivated; these are symbolic rather than any true *mise-en-scène*. In off-centre focus the hexagonal pavilion behind the Virgin floats rather than standing on any architectural foundations. This is a clearly pictorial quotation

framed in the deep perspective of the Visitation, above which we see a *tempietto*. Mary and the Archangel Gabriel, in exalted elegance with butterfly wings and carefully arranged folds and ribbons, almost face each other to strengthen the decorative effect. On this painting colourism and luminism are almost equally present. And below in the centre of the predella, as a kind of personification of Kolendić himself, is a 'portrait' of his carack protected by St Blaise and St Nicholas within medallions.

The spatial positioning of the architecture, the architectural furnishings and the tiles beneath the representations of these

8.7 Nikola Božidarević, centre predella, detail of fig. 8.5. Photo: K. Tadić.

saintly statues are uncompromisingly Renaissance. But even more Renaissance are the relief frames of Božidarević's altarpieces and polyptychs, populated by harpies, masks of the ocean, acanthus, lacework, all suffused in gold. He luxuriates in the gold embroidery of dresses, in cascades of velvet. This is even more explicit in the miniatures on predellas (especially in the Danče painting). They are composed more like moves in ballet than liturgical acts. I do not know if the faces of Božidarević's saints tell us anything about any Dubrovnik ideals of beauty, but they could not have been very different from those of his time. Fair curling hair, a dark brown thoughtful look from below eyebrows almost too highly raised, Virgins with foreheads in pointed arches, complexions of a highly rosy glow, noses always with nostrils dilated, mouths always closed – this is the recognisable typology of his characters. If they did not have elaborate and individualised clothing, they would lack sufficient expression of character.

Božidarević was the contemporary of the poets Džore Držić, Šiško Menčetić and Mavro Vetranović. Marin Držić, the most successful writer of Dubrovnik's 'Golden Age', was born when Nikola was in prison for the ribald songs already mentioned. However, we cannot but feel that the painter's temper remains hidden behind the porcelain surface and perfect outer symmetry of his compositions. The Dubrovnik context did not provide opportunities for the expression of strong passions. The summons to caution and order were unremitting. There might be considerable personal pride, but there must never be bragging. It was a setting not for great philosophy or poetry, nor for tragedy, but for the natural sciences, economics and – along with them

– comedies. The city which had come into being as an answer to the challenge of the open sea before it and the stony desert behind it demanded continual alertness.

The state of Dubrovnik was, as Jacob Burckhardt would have said, a work of art with clearly calculated foundations and a finely gauged balance in relationship to neighbouring states. Dubrovnik capital was scattered throughout the whole of the Mediterranean and woven together through a web of sea routes, trading points and diplomatic legations. We may ask why the Ottomans spared this gilded miniature, when they so easily trampled over and crumpled up the map of the Balkans which was its hinterland. It may have been because it was through Dubrovnik that they contacted their trading partners. It was in Dubrovnik that they came down to the coast to buy and exchange luxury materials and other high quality goods. In the midst of the conflict of Ottoman and Catholic interests in the Mediterranean, Dubrovnik, the middleman, was protected from both sides. It is difficult to grasp that in the middle of the sixteenth century the Dubrovnik merchant fleet was almost as large as that of Venice. Thus, the ships painted by Božidarević on the model of the city held by St Blaise are as much a tangible attribute of the city as is the Minčeta Tower. All the other towns on the shores of Croatia are settled on a kind of lake, protected by an archipelago in front of them. Horace's *plumbeus auster*, the southern sirocco wind from the open sea, pounded the walls of Dubrovnik (and the sirocco is a universal wind, as the north-easterly bora is always local), calling sailors to ocean voyages (figs 8.6–8.8).

When we first come to Božidarević's paintings, we may be surprised by the fact that in spite of the concrete circumstances

8.8 Nikola Božidarević, right predella, detail of fig. 8.5. Photo: K. Tadić.

within which they developed, there is a lack of any penetrating observation of either inner or outer worlds. Where details appear, they largely represent a sanctified aspect of reality: 'spiritualia sub metaphoris corporalium' (spiritual things under physical appearances), as Thomas Aquinus would say. The political, diplomatic and commercial realism of the people of Dubrovnik came, surprisingly enough, to be reflected very late in an art which served symbolic ends. Thus, in Božidarević and his predecessors we find no dark allegory, by the standards of today's art critics, but a clear and balanced representation of the votive message. These polyptychs provide an unearthly view of many kinds of fear (of heaven, of the sea, of plague, of Turks of all kinds, of oneself), and also of much hope.

Unfortunately, Dubrovnik painting was fated to disappear almost unnoticed, with no fanfares or real climax, to be drowned in the import of baroque art from the other side of the Adriatic. When we talk about Dubrovnik, the Renaissance is our first association, for to Croatian culture Dubrovnik is more Florence than Athens, as the expression goes. Yet the Renaissance in Croatian painting never managed entirely to develop. Indeed, Gothic was never fully relinquished but rather gradually disintegrated. Its place was taken by the Counter-Reformation, together with a whole range of ready-made solutions, before the Renaissance had achieved its full definition. The Renaissance was in general far more fragile and temporally thinner than we usually suppose. Neighbouring Kotor, from where Lovro Dobričević came

and where Božidarević was born – a milieu no less humanistic – would see its highly charged medieval mysteries directly transformed into a suffocating Counter-Reformation exaltation of the baroque.

We cannot experience Nikola's paintings as Renaissance building blocks cut out from the reality of their own day. We may rather consider them as tables bearing rich fabric. His saints, enveloped in brocade, standing before an azure sky, are sunk in timeless melancholy. They are depicted in an indeterminate context as they appeared to the eye of the painter – without any later addition of colour. They did not attain the position of an academic standard for the Dubrovnik painting of the period that followed. Božidarević went *ad patriam paradisi* at the same time

as Mihajlo Hamzić (fig. 8.9), son of the German immigrant Hans, a 'bombardiere' from Cologne, and as Vicko Lovrin, son of Dobričević. The sudden and complete change of generations coincided with a fundamental change in the taste of the rich commercial class when it began to turn to the artists of the Bellini and Titian circle.

The colours of Božidarević's painting are the most harmonious chords of Dubrovnik's Golden Age. In old cities such as this, colour, like everything else except the stone, is recessive. What Bozidarevic has left us is a rationalised and at the same time idealised impression of past reality. His paintings provide, as it were, a rendering in colour of old Dubrovnik's genetic make-up.

8.9 Mihajlo Hamzić, triptych from the Dominican church in Dubrovnik. Photo: K. Tadić.

8.10 Lovro Dobričević, polyptych from the Dominican church in Dubrovnik. Photo: Živko Bačić.

ITALY & DALMATIA: ARCHITECTURE, SCULPTURE, PAINTING & THE DECORATIVE ARTS, *c.* 1400–1800

Timothy Clifford

Geographically Dalmatia is bordered to the south by Montenegro, to the east by Bosnia and Hercegovina, and to the north by the shield-shaped peninsula of Istria. This long strip of rocky barren land is eccentrically formed by bays, isthmuses, islands and archipelagos, with many deep sheltered harbours on the Adriatic coast which are bounded by the jagged range of the Dinaric Alps to the north-east. The Dalmatian peoples began by cultivating olives, figs, citrus fruits and vines. Goats provided milk and flesh to eat, while donkeys were the most common beast of burden. The people fished, were sailors and pirates. Later they panned for salt and quarried the excellent calcareous local stone, building up a substantial trade in hewn rock and finely carved masonry to mainland Italy. Their ports were ideally positioned for a wide variety of trade on the direct shipping lanes between Venice, the Levant and Constantinople.[1]

The history of what now constitutes Croatia – or what indeed constituted, after the Habsburg Empire's fall in 1918, the old kingdom, the so-called Regnum Croatiae, Dalmatiae et Sclavoniae, which consisted of Serbs, Croats and Slovenes – is varied, and much of its detail is of little concern here. Briefly, the land was fought over by the Hungarians and the Venetians from the twelfth to the fifteenth centuries. With the threat of the encroaching and expansive Ottoman Empire, most of Dalmatia was acquired in 1420 by Venice by a complex process of sale, conquest and protectorate, and remained a colonial possession of Venice, part of the Venetian Stato del Mar, until the Serenissima fell to Napoleon in 1797. Most was then ceded by treaty to the Austrians.

The sovereign Republic of Dubrovnik (Ragusa in Italian) was always the odd one out. It is situated to the extreme south of Dalmatia, and throughout the Middle Ages, until 1358, remained either under the suzerainty of the Byzantine Empire or under a Venetian protectorate. The state itself, since 1272, operated intermittently under the enlightened oligarchic rule of the Ragusan aristocracy and even had carefully regulated building statutes. Dubrovnik, as a republic, paid a massive annual tribute (*harač*) to the sultan which gave it protection from aggression and, above all, exclusive trading privileges with the Ottomans. From the late thirteenth century until Dubrovnik fell in 1808, this republic operated as a rich entrepôt between Venice and the East. Here the Renaissance became part of official culture, and republican values were consciously modelled after antique patterns. Humanists were invited from Italy specifically to reinvent Dubrovnik's classical past. The republic embarked on a large-scale programme of providing public buildings with classicising sculptures and inscriptions *all'antica*. Into Dubrovnik, in particular, and the rest of Christian Dalmatia came rich cargoes of grain, silks, spices, ceramics, glass and, notably, a knowledge of the sophisticated science of the Orient.

As it operated for so long as an independent republic and is still so rich in art and artefacts, Dubrovnik requires separate treatment, which follows on from this as Chapter 10. The rest of Dalmatia, which was regularly threatened by a sequence of Saracens, Tartars and Turks, had to develop their buildings in an ad hoc manner directly relating to the threats to the security of their territory. Their monies were certainly lavished on beautifying churches and palaces or on proud civic monuments, but such expenditure always had to be subservient to the exigencies of defence. This meant that for centuries the fortifications of Dalmatia were exceptionally well designed.

Fundamental to the many domestic buildings, monuments and sculptures of Dalmatia was the ever present memory of antiquity. Whether it was the classical remains of Pula (Pola) in Istria or Split (Spalato), Zadar (Zara) and Salona (Solin), artists had before them the stylistic remains of a great Roman civilisation and, before this, substantial traces of Greek colonisation. This ancient region of Illyria, having been conquered by the Romans, provided no fewer than six emperors of Illyrian origin: Aurelian, Claudius II, Probus, Diocletian, Valens and Valentinian. Emperor Diocletian's own mausoleum was to form the nucleus of the medieval city of Split as its cathedral. Much of the city of Zadar is built upon the ruins, or from the ruins, of the Roman *municipium*, in particular the foundations of the church of St Donatus. After the fall of the Roman Empire, the story of Dalmatia was that of various semi-autonomous or separate communes, which were often riven by the internal strife of nobles, merchants and the proletariat. These interest groups then allied themselves for support and protection to the great powers of Hungary or Venice. It was this classical past that particularly fascinated native Renaissance humanists like Marko Marulić, Dmine and Jerolim Papalić and Coriolan Čipiko.

By the end of the fourteenth century, the great mendicant preaching orders of Franciscans and Dominicans – as well as the Benedictines – had penetrated all the major towns and cities of Dalmatia, building fine churches that often mirrored stylistically their own mother churches, and that were usually situated close to the principal gates of the towns. The Roman Catholic Church, feudal nobles, merchants and communes all proved lively and generous patrons for the Italian and Italianate art that was created in Dalmatia from *c*. 1400. Indeed, the period *c*. 1400–40 was when the Dalmatian coastal towns reached their economic and artistic zenith. Communes built fine town halls, while the most successful merchants built for themselves handsome houses, just like many in the Veneto, even following similar plans, equipped with shops or counting houses on the ground floor and a *portego* on the first floor. The architecture of Dalmatian town houses from *c*. 1410 was conservative, with Venetian Gothic-style fenestration and doorways continuing until after 1600. In fact, the Dalmatian house resembled the Venetian house in most respects, but usually on a much more modest scale. The smaller scale was summarised by the well-known rather pejorative Venetian saying: 'Quattro stanze un salon é la casa d'un Schiavon' (Four small rooms and a living room is the house of a Slav).

What we consider as typically Italian in Croatian art is often difficult to disentangle from the native Croatian. For example, one of the most celebrated examples of the goldsmiths' art is the silver-gilt shrine of St Simeon (1377–80) (fig. 9.1), in the eponymous church of St Simeon (Sv. Šime in Croatian), Zadar. The effigy of the saint lies on a tomb chest/reliquary, which was constructed using a timber core covered with embossed silver-gilt plates. It was commissioned by Queen Elizabeth of Hungary, daughter of Ban Kotromanić, ruler of Bosnia, and wife of Louis of Anjou. Although designed and made by Francesco di Antonio of Milan, he was assisted by two local craftsmen, Andrija Markov of Zagreb and Stipan Pribčev. One of the repoussé images is of the *Presentation of Christ in the Temple*, which follows closely Giotto's fresco of the same subject in the Scrovegni Chapel, Padua. The whole glittering ensemble is supported on later bronze angels (not visible in this photograph), cast from canons captured from the Turks in the War of Candia by Francesco Cavrioli of Venice (1644–7), so the shrine is partly Croatian but mostly Italian.[2]

It appears that few Italian artists actually set up their studios and workshops or spent much time in Dalmatia. On the other hand, Croatian artists who had successful careers in Italy spent most, or sometimes all, their working lives in Italy. Giorgio Schiavone (Juraj Ćulinović, *c*. 1433/6–1504), the most famous Croatian painter of the fifteenth century, was born at Scardona near Šibenik (Sebenico).[3] His early training was in Sebenico, where he is said to have studied Italian stucco reliefs, medals and drawings, before moving to Venice in 1456, where he signed a

9.1 Francesco di Antonio of Milan and others, *Shrine of St Simeon* (with the lid raised), *c*.1377–80, silver-gilt plates fixed to a timber frame, church of St Simeon, Zadar. Photo: Živko Bačić.

contract on 28 March to assist Francesco Squarcione. He worked in Squarcione's studio in Padua, probably replacing Marco Zoppo. Schiavone's exquisite paintings in Squarcione's manner, betraying the strong influence of Donatello and Mantegna, proved highly successful in Padua, where his pictures influenced the young Carlo Crivelli; indeed, he may have been Crivelli's master. In late 1461, his contract having expired with Squarcione, Giorgio returned to Zadar in Dalmatia, perhaps even accompanied by Carlo Crivelli, who is known to have been working at Zadar 1465–7, along with his brother Vittore. In 1463 Schiavone was living at Sebenico and married Elena, daughter of the sculptor/architect Giorgio da Sebenico. It is said, with good reason, that his paintings influenced his father-in-law's style of sculpture. We are familiar with his works in Padua, including the *Virgin and Child with Saints* (National Gallery, London) painted *c.* 1458 for the Frigimelica Chapel of San Nicolò, Padua. His Dalmatian works are all lost, save perhaps for the *Virgin and Child Enthroned* in S. Lorenzo (Sv. Lovro), Sebenico, an unusually stiff and hieratic painting which many believe to be a late work.

Another artist and no relation, Andrea Schiavone (Andrija Medulić, *c.* 1510–63), came from Zadar, but his family had earlier hailed from Meldola in the Romagna. He was trained in the workshop of the Luzzo family, a studio operating in both Zadar and Venice.[4] As a youth he saw drawings and etchings by Parmigianino which greatly influenced his graphic style and composition. Schiavone's paintings show that he admired aspects of Giulio Romano (1499–1546), while his virtuoso technique in oil with open brushwork and dematerialised form was clearly influenced by the mature works of Titian. His paintings still exist *in situ* in many European, British and American collections. There are handsome examples, for instance, in the collection of HM the Queen at Hampton Court. Andrea Schiavone never returned to his native Dalmatia, and these pictures, so revolutionary and exciting in technique, seem not to have found favour in Croatia.

Giulio Clovio (Juraj Klović, 1498–1578), described by Giorgio Vasari as 'the Michelangelo of small works', was the greatest illuminator working in sixteenth-century Italy.[5] He was born at Grižani (Grisone) in Istria, and at the age of eighteen went to Venice to learn to be an artist in the household of Cardinal Domenico Grimani. Assisted by the Grimani family, he not only became familiar with their great art collections, including classical sculptures and works by Dürer, but visited Rome where he studied under Giulio Romano. Clovio left Venice *c.* 1523 to work for the court of King Louis of Hungary and Bohemia and for his consort Mary of Austria (sister of Emperor Charles V). Here Clovio illustrated a celebrated missal in 1525 for Siméon Erdődy, bishop of Zagreb. Clovio returned to Rome in 1526 after the death of King Louis, and joined the service of Cardinal Lorenzo Campeggi. He resumed contact with Giulio Romano and also studied avidly the works of Raphael and Michelangelo in Rome. During the Sack of Rome (1527), he was imprisoned and, after various traumatic

experiences, became a priest, joining a monastery in Mantua. He then moved on to another monastery in Padua and, becoming reacquainted with the Grimani family, received papal dispensation to leave the monastic life but remain a priest. Between 1540 and his death in 1578, Clovio joined the household in Rome of Cardinal Alessandro Farnese, grandson of Pope Paul III. He worked for other members of the Farnese family in Parma and Piacenza, producing exquisite Mannerist miniatures much influenced by Michelangelo, Raphael and especially Francesco Salviati. Salviati was a favourite of Cardinal Alessandro. While Clovio, befriended by Michelangelo and Vasari, was protector of the young El Greco, who painted a fine portrait of him. Clovio never returned to his native Croatia, dying in Rome, and was buried in S. Pietro in Vincoli.

How did Italian art, which is still so widespread in Dalmatia, find its way there? We know from Carlo Ridolfi's *Le meraviglie dell'arte …* (1648) that the prolific and competent Venetian artist Jacopo Negretti, called 'Palma il Giovane' (*c.* 1548–1628), painted works 'for Venice and other cities of Italy and abroad, and still more are dispersed in Dalmatia' (in particular, a *Lord's Supper* preserved in the cathedral of Poreč), yet Palma never visited

9.2 Girolamo da Santacroce, detail of altarpiece showing model of the Renaissance city of Split, oil on canvas, church of Our Lady of Grace, Poljud. Photo: Živko Bačić.

9.3 Lorenzo Lotto, *Bishop Tommaso Nigris*, 1527, oil on canvas, church of Our Lady of Grace, Poljud. Photo: Croatian Conservation Institute.

Croatia. It was, indeed, usual from the sixteenth to the eighteenth centuries for Italian painters, sculptors and craftsmen, in spite of receiving commissions in Dalmatia, to work in Italy and then ship their finished product back across the Adriatic. So, were one to provide a sequential history of Italian art in Dalmatia, it would be illogical. Many of the Italian artists never worked in Croatia. Italian works in Croatia are better understood in the context of the cities and buildings for which they were executed. Places in Dalmatia have their own particular intrinsic history and character, so connections between history, patron and artefact are discussed here by geographical location, for these works of art demand to be considered within their own socio-cultural surroundings. My narrative starts with Split, the major city of the region, which has its own international airport and is, moreover, where most visitors begin their tour of Dalmatia.

SPLIT (SPALATO)

This busy port has grown out of the very substantial ruins of Diocletian's Palace built by the architects Filotas and Zotikos around the turn of the fourth century AD. A medieval city grew up with many merchants' houses, shops and churches within Diocletian's massive turreted structure with a vast open loggia looking out to sea.[6] It is still dominated by the emperor's octagonal mausoleum, which was converted in the seventh century into the cathedral dedicated to St Domnius, while Diocletian's temple of Jupiter performs a new function as the baptistery. It is ironic that a pagan emperor, who did so much to persecute Christians, is memorialised by these monuments all now dedicated to Christian worship. Split benefited from close trading links with Constantinople during the Byzantine era and then in 1409 became part of the Venetian Empire. Under the

9.4 After a model by Giovanni da Bologna, probably cast by Antonio Susini, *Crucified Christ*, silver-gilt, Treasury Museum of Split Cathedral. Photo: Živko Bačić.

(fig. 9.2) in the Franciscan monastic church of Our Lady of Grace at Poljud, a suburb of Split. Incidentally, pictures by Girolamo Santacroce, who was born in Bergamo and was a pupil of Gentile Bellini, are numerous in Dalmatia and force one to reassess both Girolamo and his son Francesco (1516–84).[8] They were capable of painting far better than one would imagine from the generality of their works remaining in Venice and the Veneto. Their admiration for Cima da Conegliano (1459–1518) is manifest, and although neither artist was particularly imaginative, their competent draughtsmanship and elegant figures painted in a bright palette set against clear cerulean skies are attractive. Also at Poljud but of an altogether greater beauty, indeed sublimity, is the portrait of *Bishop Tommaso Nigris* (Toma Niger) by Lorenzo Lotto (1480–1557) (fig. 9.3). Painted in 1527, when this distinguished diplomat and reformer was visiting Venice and where Lotto had been living since December 1520, it portrays a venerable, bearded bishop. He wears a grey watered silk almuce over a white linen alb and cradles a crucifix under his left arm. The prelate's gnarled hands are clasped fervently in prayer, and his tired blue eyes are fixed on the hereafter. This picture is one of the most profound and serene images of holiness in the Italian Renaissance.[9] Lotto coincidentally painted it the same year as his opulent portrait of the collector *Andrea Odoni*, in HM the Queen's collection, at a time when Lotto was at the height of his inventive power.[10] What a contrast these two portraits provide! They both follow the same format, half-lengths within horizontal compositions. One, in an almost monochrome palette, is meditative and introspective; the other, richly chromatic, is full of bombast and theatricality. Incidentally, it does not appear to have been noticed that the panel of Bishop Nigris's portrait is in its original walnut frame and that the frame once incorporated a sliding cover, just like those one finds in Germany on little pictures by Lucas Cranach. This suggests that the cover would originally have been painted with a sacred image of similar dimensions by Lotto, which is now lost.

The treasury museum of Split Cathedral contains two handsome, but likely to be overlooked, crucifixes with silver *corpora* of the dead Christ (*Cristo morto*). These refined sculpted images are, I suggest, Florentine dating from soon after 1600 and depend on prototypes by Giovanni da Bologna (known as Giambologna, 1529–1608). They were probably cast in his workshop in Borgo Pinti by Antonio Susini (1580–1624). The larger processional cross is double-sided and richly embossed with exuberant foliage (fig. 9.4), with a standing group (which is clearly *not* after Giambologna) of the *Virgin and Child* on the reverse, while the second crucifix, ebony with silver appliqués, is supported on a tripod silver base.[11] Giovanni da Bologna holds a crucial position in cinquecento Italy as the most distinguished sculptor after Michelangelo and before the advent of the baroque. The museum also contains a much damaged predella panel of the *Nativity* (fig. 9.5). The kneeling Virgin, to the left sheltered beneath a primitive barn, adores the Christ Child, who is watched

Venetians the great defensive walls were restored, the Gripe Fort was built, and the arts flourished. The city was administered by a rector appointed by Venice, who served a two-year term of office, so that 177 rectors or so-called *conti-capitani* were appointed between 1420 and 1795. In 1579 Venice declared that Split was to be, from now on, a free export harbour in the Balkans; the city flourished exceedingly and in 1592 even founded its first bank.

Architecture in the Venetian style exists in much of the old city with the familiar carved and elaborately balustraded balconies, with *bifora* and *quadrifora* flamboyant-headed windows, and with richly carved heraldic well-heads in abundance. All these features can be seen to advantage in the Papalić Palace and are much in evidence especially in the old town square (Pjaca), with the Rector's Palace built by the Venetian governor but partly demolished in 1821. An excellent idea of what this Renaissance city looked like is provided by the model held by St Domnius in the altarpiece by Girolamo da Santacroce (c. 1480/5–after 1556)

over by two angels clad in long gowns with sickle-shaped pink and blue wings. The humble St Joseph stands leaning on his staff to the right. The figures are set in a barren rocky landscape still reminiscent of so much of Dalmatia. With its echoes of Uccello and Ghiberti, this predella probably emanates from the studio of the Florentine artist Bicci di Lorenzo (1375–1452).[12] Such a spare but distinguished Tuscan image as this predella may well have influenced local Croatian artists: for example, Mihajlo Hamzić's much larger *Baptism of Christ in the Jordan* now hanging in the museum of the Rector's Palace, Dubrovnik. It is diverting to think of some merchant or prelate from Split buying in Florence all these quintessentially Tuscan objects and returning home, triumphantly, to present them to his native cathedral.

Most of Split Cathedral is contained within Diocletian's centrally planned hexagonal mausoleum, with a diminutive chancel tacked on to the east and a disproportionately grandiose Venetian-style fifteenth-century campanile attached to the north. Inside, the altar of St Rainerius (1427), within a richly crocketed and gabled shrine, was built by Bonino di Giacomo of Milan. Bonino, who learnt his art among a host of talented mason/carvers trained at Milan Cathedral, also carved the main portal of Korčula Cathedral. The companion altar of St Anastasius (1448), which was commissioned to match it, is the work of Giorgio da Sebenico

(Juraj Matejev, fl. 1441–73).[13] The St Anastasius shrine contains a justly celebrated high relief of the *Flagellation* (fig. 9.6) carved in Brač stone that forms the small door of St Anastasius' sarcophagus. Giorgio da Sebenico worked with equal virtuosity as architect, sculptor and mason, and is celebrated for his masterpiece of Šibenik Cathedral, to be discussed later. It has been suggested that the *Flagellation*, powerfully Florentine in flavour, may depend upon a lost relief by Donatello, and predates two similar compositions from Donatello's studio in Berlin and London.

The other notable Italian work in the cathedral is the much later, lavish marble tomb of St Domnius (Sv. Duje) by that distinguished and prolific Venetian sculptor Giovanni Maria Morlaiter (1699–1781). Commissioned in Rome by the citizens of Split, it was begun in 1767 and consecrated in 1770.[14] The tomb chest below is embellished with a handsome low relief of St Domnius' martyrdom and supports, above, the reliquary urn of the saint held by female allegorical figures of Religion and Constancy; the reliquary's lid is surmounted by putti displaying the saint's processional cross and crozier. The monument's *gravitas* derives from Roman seventeenth-century prototypes. Sadly lacking in the rococo grace and flutter of Venetian art of its era, it surely reflects the tastes of a committee of particularly conservative Croatian churchmen.

9.5 Attributed to Bicci di Lorenzo, *Nativity*, tempera on panel, Treasury Museum of Split Cathedral. Photo: Živko Bačić.

9.6 Giorgio da Sebenico, *Flagellation* relief, Brač stone, Split Cathedral. Photo: Živko Bačić.

Another eighteenth-century sculpture, and rather neglected by scholars, is the serene marble of the *Madonna of the Rosary* (fig. 9.7) in the church of St Dominic outside the Silver Gate. It is now attributed to the Venetian Alvise Tagliapietra (1670–1747), but may be by an even better hand.[15] Certainly, Tagliapietra provided between 1717 and 1728 four statues of saints for the Benedictine monastery of St Chrysogonus (Sv. Krševan) at Zadar, but they are by no means as good as this Madonna.

TROGIR (TRAÙ)

The city of Trogir is to the west of Split as one travels along the coast passing Split airport and the remains of the Roman city of Salona.[16] This architectural jewel is, in fact, an island linked by a bridge to the Dalmatian mainland. As early as 1322, it put itself under the protection of the Serenissima but continued to respect and support the Hungaro-Croatian kings. In 1409 King Ladislas of Naples sold Trogir to Venice. This was a most unpopular move, and the populace resisted their new overlords until the city was captured by Pietro Loredano of Venice in 1420. Relations between Trogir and Venice remained uneasy, many of Trogir's inhabitants believing, with reason, that their ancient city was being exploited. It was then administered by the so-called Venetian 'duke' who, the

9.7 Attributed to Alvise Tagliapietra, *Madonna of the Rosary*, marble, church of St Dominic, Split. Photo: Živko Bačić.

locals felt somewhat ignominiously, was responsible to the Venetian governor-general (*providitor*) at Zadar. But culturally Trogir accepted with some misgivings their new masters and became, essentially, loyal and proud Venetians. Croatian scholars and humanists like Coriolan Čipiko, Peter Lucić and Pavao Andreis built palaces and fine libraries. For example, the Čipiko Palace on the town square was lavishly built in the Venetian taste by Andrea Alessi with two storeys of flamboyant *trifora* and a rich balcony. Čipiko even wrote a laudatory account of the campaign in Asia of Pietro Mocenigo, a Venetian: *Petri Mocenici imperatoris gesta: De bello Asiatico* (Venice 1477).

The most venerated hero of the city was the Blessed John Orsini (Ivan Trogirski, d. 1111), who was sent from Rome to become bishop of Trogir in 1062. His chapel, attached to the north aisle of the cathedral of St Lawrence (Sv. Lovre), is one of the most Italianate glories of Dalmatia (see Chapter 7, fig. 7.1).[17] This Renaissance masterpiece was created by a team of mason/sculptors all trained in Italy: Niccolò di Giovanni Fiorentino (Nikola Firentinac, *c.* 1418–*c.* 1506), Andrea Alessi (Andrija Aleši, fl. 1456–80) and Giovanni Dalmata (Ivan Duknović, *c.* 1440–*c.* 1508). The contract for the chapel is dated 4 January 1468; the first statue was completed in 1482 and the last in 1509. The team created an exquisite coffered barrel-vaulted structure, ornamented with heads of seraphim, a lunette with a relief of the *Coronation of the Virgin* in the tympanum and an attic storey pierced with a range of laureated *oculi* windows. The walls are articulated by free-standing statues of Christ and the twelve apostles placed in scallop-shell-headed niches flanked by alternating writhed and plain columns supporting standing putti. The *basamento* consists of a galaxy of nineteen lively putti carrying flaming torches that run in and out of the simulated doors to the burial vault beneath. Although the chapel is well described in Chapter 7, it demands a brief mention in any overview of Italian art in Dalmatia. The chapel's appearance is distinctly Tuscan, especially the Michelozzo-like putti, but the free-standing figures in niches and the chapel's dense, decorative appearance are more reminiscent of Venice, recalling a wraparound version of, say, Antonio Rizzo's monument to Doge Nicola Tron (1476) in the Frari. In 1559 statues in Istrian stone of St Andrew, St Matthew, St Simeon (fig. 9.8) and (probably) St James by Alessandro Vittoria (1525–1608) were acquired in Venice for the remaining vacant niches in the chapel. They must have made discordant companions. However, two of them were mentioned most approvingly by Vasari in 1568, though they were removed from this location in the seventeenth century, certainly with good reason, to be placed on the corners of the parapet of the

9.8 Alessandro Vittoria, *St Simeon*, 1559, Istrian stone, museum of Trogir Cathedral.
Photo: Živko Bačić.

cathedral's campanile. Vittoria's venerably bearded and cloaked figures are endowed with all his characteristic haughty gestures and emphatic *contrapposto*. Now sadly weathered, they are displayed in the little church nearby of St Barbara.

The cathedral baptistery predates the chapel of the Blessed John Orsini and was the work of Andrea Alessi from *c.* 1460. Beneath a coffered barrel vault, the chamber is dominated by a rather *retardataire* but charming *Baptism* relief, redolent still of Ghiberti and Masaccio. The iconography and viewpoint follow quite closely Piero della Francesca's painted *Baptism* now in the National Gallery, London. On the opposite wall in the lunette is a low relief of the bearded St Jerome in his cave, leaning with his head on his left arm while studying the Vulgate. The saint is watched over faithfully by his lion, who rather casually ignores two fearsome dragons, which emerge from the rocks to the left. The subject of the irascible old St Jerome, born at Siridon in Dalmatia *c.* 342, must have been chosen as he was patron of Dalmatia, a cardinal and, moreover, a learned Doctor of the Church. He was the quintessential saint for the Dalmatian humanist patron. Alessi and his studio specialised in Jerome images, carving more than a dozen small stone reliefs of St Jerome with variations in the composition, intended for private devotion. A good example can be seen at the Walker Art Gallery, Liverpool. They evidently proved, like the many Madonnas painted by the Bellini studio, a good selling line.

Trogir abounds with delightful Renaissance sculptures by the talented team of mason/sculptors who worked for the baptistery and for the chapel of the Blessed John Orsini. They also embellished the cathedral, the clock tower and the municipal loggia with the retable of *Justice*, and their works are to be seen in the gallery of the (former) church of St John the Baptist.

Trogir Cathedral also boasts three typical oils by Palma il Giovane: *St Augustine and St Dominic* (dated 1599), the *Visit of St Anthony to St Paul the Hermit* (*c.* 1620) and the ambitious composition of the *Circumcision of Christ*. These are all pictures that remind one how competent an artist Palma was, with a solid sense of form and a fine sense of colour, but his repertoire of poses within his massive oeuvre can be tiresomely

9.9 After Galeazzo Mondella, called 'Moderno', pax with the *Dead Christ Supported by the Virgin Mary and St John the Divine*, before 1517, silver, Treasury of Trogir Cathedral. Photo: Živko Bačić.

repetitive. He and his studio clearly had regular recourse to a limited range of poses, and these are then arranged, and rearranged, like the 'identikit' images used nowadays for forensic identification.

The cathedral treasury boasts many precious liturgical objects. Especially fascinating is the silver pax with the *Dead Christ Supported by the Virgin Mary and St John the Divine* (fig. 9.9). It is after a well-known plaquette by the so-called Moderno (Galeazzo Mondella of Verona, 1467–1528), but if

the reading of the cathedral inventory of 1517 indeed refers to this piece, it does provide a fairly early *terminus ante quem* for the original undated relief. Croatian sources appear to have overlooked that another silver pax of the identical composition is in the treasury of Mantua Cathedral and dated even earlier, 1513, while yet another superb example, also formed as a pax, in silver, niello and gilt, is in the Hermitage, St Petersburg (dated 1521).[18] Also in the Trogir treasury is a superb silver and parcel-gilt crozier (fig. 9.10), the voluted head consisting of a rich acanthus scroll inhabited by lively seated figures of Bishop Giovanni Orsini and of St Lawrence. It is related to another similar crozier in the Bargello, Florence, dating from the second half of the sixteenth century, and to a drawing, almost certainly by Perino del Vaga's pupil, Luzio Romano (fl. 1528–73). Luzio is recorded as working in Rome from *c.* 1548, so this crozier may have been commissioned by a Trogir prelate in Rome, *c.* 1550–70.[19]

The gallery of the church of St John the Baptist (also the Town Museum) boasts two large paintings on canvas of *St John the Baptist* and *St Jerome* (fig. 9.11) painted in 1489 in the workshop of Jacopo Bellini (*c.* 1400–70/1), which have been variously attributed to Gentile Bellini and Vittorio Carpaccio.[20] They originally functioned as the inner shutters of the cathedral organ, an instrument built by Fra Urbano of Venice. This celebrated organ builder four years later supplied another organ for the basilica of St Mark's, Venice. In this gallery are paintings by the distinctive local artist Biagio di Giorgio (Blaž Jurjev, *c.* 1375–1450), who is represented here not only by his only signed work, a rather dull polyptych, but also by a delightful little *Madonna of the Rose Garden* (see Chapter 6, fig. 6.20).[21] The Madonna is painted as a homely local girl with bee-sting lips and healthy pink cheeks seated upon a scarlet tasselled cushion encircled by a bank of roses. The Christ Child stands on the Madonna's knee, with his right hand raised in benediction. Behind them both hover diminutive adoring angels, cloaked in scarlet and white. This provincial Italianate work of the International Gothic seems to fall somewhere stylistically between Stefano da Verona and Gentile da Fabriano. The gallery also contains a superb marble relief of the Virgin and Child seated on the throne of wisdom by Giovanni Dalmata (see Chapter 7, fig. 7.13), recently acquired in London, which is closely related to another relief in the Museo Civico, Padua. The most memorable sculpture, however, must be Niccolò Fiorentino's relief of the *Lamentation* (fig. 9.12) carved *c.* 1468–9 for the Čipiko altar in the suppressed Benedictine abbey of St John the Baptist and now in the picture gallery of the church of St John the Baptist.[22] This extraordinary work, riven with anguish and grief, is almost as affecting as Giotto's *Lamentation* in the Scrovegni Chapel, Padua.

Trogir is less richly endowed with seventeenth- and eighteeth-century Italian works, but not to be overlooked are the boldly carved, painted and gilded standing wooden figures of St Peter and St Paul flanking the high altar of the church of St Peter (Sv.

9.10 Design here attributed to Luzio Romano, crozier with figures of the Blessed Giovanni Orsini and St Lawrence, Roman, second half of the sixteenth century, silver-gilt, Treasury of Trogir Cathedral. Photo: Živko Bačić.

Petar). Their frenzied draperies and grandiloquent gestures are by a virtuoso carver who was probably trained in Venice, perhaps in the studio of a sculptor like Giusto le Court (1627–79).[23] The Benedictine convent of St Nicholas (Sv. Nikole) is blessed with a really handsome group of nine oval half-length images of saints by Nicola Grassi (1682–1748), all in their original frames. These luminous, fluidly painted essays are typical of this competent, stylish Venetian master, executed when he was travelling away from Venice in Augsburg and in Dalmatia *c.* 1724–5. Other similar works by him are to be found on the nearby island of Vis.

ŠIBENIK (SEBENICO)

Somewhat further up the Dalmatian coast to the north-west from Trogir is a magnificent deep water harbour dominated by the heavily fortified town of Šibenik.[24] The town, wealthy from the local salt industry, became highly desirable to the Turks both as a trading post and for its key strategic position. In the twelfth century Šibenik had formed part of Hungarian Croatia; then between 1412 and 1797 it was ruled by Venice. The Venetian architect Gian Girolamo Sanmicheli (1513–1559) built between 1540 and 1547 the great fort of St Nicholas (Tvrđava Sv. Nikole) (fig. 9.13), just at the mouth of Šibenik harbour. This sophisticated low-profile building is triangular in plan with a massive semicircular bastion at the apex facing north, looking from the air like a gigantic pair of dividers opened at 45 degrees. Furnished with a range of gun ports situated just above the waterline ideally suited for sinking galleys, it numbers among the finest and most

9.11 Workshop of Jacopo Bellini, *Organ shutter: St Jerome*, 1489, Museum of the church of St John the Baptist, Trogir. Photo: Živko Bačić.

9.12 Niccolò Fiorentino, *Lamentation* relief, 1468–9, Istrian stone, Museum of the church of St John the Baptist, Trogir. Photo: Živko Bačić.

9.13 Gian Girolamo Sanmicheli, fort of St Nicholas, aerial view, 1535–44, Šibenik. Photo: Živko Bačić.

impregnable examples of Renaissance Venetian military architecture in the Adriatic. Indeed, that great biographer Giorgio Vasari singled it out, describing it as 'la meravigliosa fortezza di San Niccolò sopra la bocca del porto di Sebenico'. The fort, so formidable in concept, is entered from the sea by a handsome rusticated Doric gateway, the cornice supported by banded columns and pilasters.[25]

Michele Sanmicheli (1484–1559) of Verona, the greatly distinguished uncle of G. G. Sanmicheli, is alleged to have been the designer in *c.* 1532–43 of the Loggia Comunale (Gradska vijećnica), the former seat of the town council. This two-storey structure of nine bays with round-headed arches is supported on composite columns, the upper floor with an open balustraded loggia. The Loggia Comunale, seriously damaged by bombing in December 1943, was rebuilt, and although admittedly elegant, demonstrates little of the imaginative energy and *gravitas* one expects from Sanmicheli senior. The attribution is unlikely, but we do know that Sanmicheli, as official military architect to Venice, did make visits to Dalmatia to advise on its defences 1534–1550. This building is more likely to have been designed by a Croatian artist working in the Italian tradition.[26]

The treasure of Šibenik, and indeed probably the greatest

Renaissance building in Croatia, is the cathedral of St James (Sv. Jakova) (fig. 9.14). This church, which was damaged by shelling in 1991, has been beautifully restored and is now being cleaned by a team of Croatian and international experts. Built in gleaming white local stone, the cathedral is a stupendous monument and, when analysed, is also a most extraordinary but satisfying synthesis of Gothic, Byzantine, Venetian and Florentine forms. It consists of a high Gothic nave of six bays lit by a clerestory, flanked by lower aisles lit by lancet windows. The crossing supports a hexagonal dome, and the east end is furnished with three richly ornamented apses. The west end is dominated by a handsome Gothic portal, flanked by lancet windows and surmounted by a large rose window with Gothic tracery. The Gothic appearance of the facade is transformed by segmental brackets pierced by *oculi* linking the lower aisles to the higher nave, while the great rose window in the attic is framed by Corinthian pilasters and surmounted by a lunette. The exterior resembles Venetian churches by Mauro Codussi (*c.* 1440–1504), like San Michele in Isola and San Giovanni Crisostomo.

The architectural project for the cathedral, slow in gestation, had the foundations laid in 1431 by Bishop Bogdan Pulsić. It was originally Gothic in conception, but the bishop died in 1436, to be succeeded by Bishop Juraj Šižgorić. Šižgorić, an enlightened patron and nephew of a celebrated humanist poet of the same name, breathed fresh and (moreover Renaissance) life into the building, employing Giorgio da Sebenico as the new 'capomaestro'. Giorgio, born in Zadar, was trained in Venice. He signed a new contract in 1441, and he was employed for six years not only as 'capomaestro' for the construction works but also to labour 'di propria mano quale scultore e scalpellino' (work with his own hands as sculptor and mason). Giorgio da Sebenico continued with this great undertaking until he died c. 1473–5. Since 1464 he had been assisted by Niccolò Fiorentino (Nikola Ivanov Firentinac, fl. 1464–1507), and Niccolò was then confirmed as 'capomaestro' in 1477. Niccolò is believed to have been a certain Nikola Kokarić (Coccari) originally from near Šibenik, who had been a pupil of Brunelleschi and collaborator of Donatello. Certainly, the superb design of the masonry of this church proclaims its Florentine artistic antecedents, like Brunelleschi's Pazzi Chapel, his Old Sacristy of San Lorenzo, and Donatello's Cantoria in the Duomo.

Šibenik Cathedral is embellished with an extraordinary *jeux d'esprit* of masonry, like the realistic ranges of portrait heads of local dignitaries, patrons and masons, carved on the exterior of the north apse, and the *gloria* of angels and putti carvings on the baptistery. Notable also is the shallow stone pavilion carved over the bishop's throne by Bartolomeo del Mestre, which, with its draped canopy, may be an echo of Piero della Francesca's fresco of the *Dream of Constantine* in San Francesco, Arezzo.

The art of Šibenik would be incomplete without any mention of that able goldsmith and engraver, a native of Šibenik, Orazio Fortezza (Horacije/Horatio, c. 1530–96).[28] His oeuvre is small and no vessels in precious metals are now known by him. There exist, however, an impressive group of most sophisticated

9.14 Giorgio da Sebenico and Niccolò Fiorentino, exterior of Šibenik Cathedral from the apse, 1431–1536. Photo: Živko Bačić.

9.15 Michele Sanmicheli, Land Gate, Zadar, 1534–43. Photo: Milan Pelc.

9.16 Michele Sanmicheli, study for the Land Gate, Zadar, pen and brown ink, Gabinetto Disegni e Stampe, Uffizi, Florence. Photo: courtesy of the Soprintendenza Speciale per il Patrimonio Storico, Artistico ed Etnoantropologico e per il Polo Museale della città di Firenze, Gabinetto Fotografico.

engraved brass ewers and basins and sets of silver mounts on covers of rule books (so-called *mariegola)* of the confraternities of the Holy Ghost, of St Andrew, of St John, and of St Barbara. Four signed, dated and engraved basins survive, and two of them are in British collections: one at the British Museum, his earliest known work, is signed: 'HORATIO.FORTEZZA. DISCIPOL.D.MASTRO.STEFANO.HAVRIFICE.IN. SEBENICO.F.1555'. It is engraved with scenes from Roman history. The second, an even more splendid affair, is again engraved with scenes of Roman history – the arms of the Dolfin family of Venice in the centre – and dated at Šibenik 1562. The third basin in the Bargello, Florence, is signed and dated 1557, and engraved with scenes from the Second Punic War. In the centre it has the arms of the Soppe family of Zadar. The fourth basin is in the City Museum, Šibenik, engraved with portraits of Roman emperors, generals and heroes, with three scenes from the battle of Kosovo Polje in 1389. It is signed but not dated, and bears the arms of the *providitor* in Zadar, Alvise Grimani. It was probably created *c.* 1570–3 during the period of the War of Cyprus when there was increased pressure by the Turks upon Dalmatia. These fine engraved basins, superficially reminiscent of engraved contemporary Veneto-Saracenic brass-work, differ from them in that they are covered not with minute arabesques but by Mannerist strap-work cartouches containing images from history and portraits of the heroes of antiquity. The basins with their companion ewers are, in fact, each conceived as *exempla virtutis* and are all entirely different. The images are taken from woodcuts and engravings after Andrea Mantegna, Nicoletto da Modena, Marcantonio Raimondi and Fortezza's contemporary, Phillipe Galle. Fortezza's work on the silver mounts to the confraternities' rule books demonstrates that, although he was a talented engraver, he was much less able at chiselling and embossing these silver appliqués.

Engraving on brass is technically very similar to engraving on copper. Indeed, were Fortezza's engraved basins covered with printers' ink and then wiped clean, the ink remaining within the engraved indentations should provide a perfect impression of the reversed image on a sheet of white paper. For this reason it seems possible that Fortezza trained two industrious and versatile Šibenik engravers on copper of the next generation, Natale Bonifacio (Natal Bonifačić, 1537–1591) and Martino Rota Kolunić (*c.* 1540–1583).[29] Rota was in Venice by 1565 while Bonifacio was in Venice by 1570. While Bonifacio moved on to Rome for the Holy Year celebrations and to live closer to his twin brother Francesco (Franjo), a surgeon, Rota went on first to Vienna and then to Prague, operating there as court portrait engraver. In Rome Bonifacio was particularly productive extolling the virtues of the Dalmatian Pope Sixtus V and producing a series of magnificent plates after Giovanni Guerra (fl. 1540–1618), recording the transporting and setting up of the Vatican Obelisk and some of the building ventures of Sixtus V.

ZADAR (ZARA)

Further to the north-west up the coast from Šibenik can be seen the fortress city of Zadar.[30] It is situated on an isthmus jutting out into the Adriatic, sheltered to the east by the Velebit Mountains. From as far back as the seventh century BC this was an important settlement of the Liburnians, an Illyrian tribe of expert sailors. They had strong ties with the peoples who lived across the Adriatic in eastern Italy. Conquered in the first century BC by the Romans, the city was refounded as Colonia Iulia Iadar in 48 BC, settled as an independent *municipium* by Julius Caesar for his veterans. The city's layout today follows closely that of the original *municipium* with the remains of fortified walls and gates, an extensive forum, temples, sculptures, inscriptions and mosaic floors. Many are now visible since the bombing in 1942–3. After the Roman period, the ruins were quarried by later inhabitants for building material. Zadar was occupied by the Ostragoths until 537 AD when they withdrew from Dalmatia, and then the city came under the dominion of Byzantium, becoming the metropolis of Byzantine Dalmatia, the main base of the Byzantine fleet and the major rival of Venice in the Adriatic. From the year 1000 onwards, the city was under attack by the Venetians. In 1202 crusaders on their way to the Holy Land were carried to Zadar by a Venetian fleet led by the blind Doge Enrico

9.17 Martin Filipović and Nikola Spanjić, facade of the church of St Mary the Less, Zadar, *c.* 1508–10. Photo: Jovan Kliska.

Bonifacio was also a senior member of the Croatian brotherhood of St Jerome in Rome, whose protector was the pope.

Natale Bonifacio executed the illustrations to Leslie's *De origine, moribus et rebus gestis Scotorum …* (Rome 1578), including heraldry, pedigrees and medallion portraits of the Scottish kings and queens and an important early map of Scotland, after drawings provided by Leslie, bishop of Ross (1526–96). Bonifacio worked mostly as a cartographer, and his maps were much admired by Ortellius, the great Dutch cartographer. Rota, however, was considerably more prolific, in Venice and Rome engraving always after Titian, Dürer, Battista Franco, Taddeo Zuccaro, Luca Penni and many images of sea battles against the Turks, culminating in Lepanto. In Vienna his oeuvre was largely confined to portrait engravings of the Habsburgs and their court.

Dandolo. The crusaders besieged and sacked the city with much brutality before relinquishing it to Venetian colonisation. In 1396 the Dominican friars of Zadar founded the first university in Dalmatia. The city was once again fought over by the Hungarians and the Venetians until, in 1409, King Ladislas of Naples sold it to Venice, with his other Dalmatian possessions, for 100,000 ducats. Zadar became the centre of Venetian administration in Dalmatia and the principal seat of the Venetian governor. It is consequently a treasure house of Venetian architecture, pictures, and sculptures.

For the next 300 years Zadar, heavily refortified, was regularly attacked by the Turks, who were equipped with powerful artillery. These hostilities were especially concentrated during the Cyprus War (1570–7), the War of Candia (1645–69) and the Morea War (1685–99), but the city of Zadar never surrendered, remaining Venetian territory until the Serenissima finally collapsed in 1797. Annexed by Italy in 1920, Zadar was bombed in the Second

9.18 Vittore Carpaccio, *St Martin Dividing his Cloak*, 1495–6, tempera on panel, Museo Permanente d'Arte Sacra, Zadar. Photo: Živko Bačić.

World War by the Allies, who sadly destroyed much of the surviving Medieval and Renaissance city.

Visitors usually enter the city by the Land Gate (Porta Terraferma/Kopnena Vrata) (fig. 9.15), which was designed by Michele Sanmicheli of Verona and completed in 1543 when Marc Antonio Diedo was *providitor* of Zadar.[31] This massive classical triumphal arch, with triple entrance, is built of rusticated masonry with engaged banded Doric columns supporting a rich frieze of alternating bucrania, shield bosses and florets set in the metopes. Carved on the keystone of the main entrance arch is a relief of St Chrysogonus, the warrior patron saint of Zadar. Above the main entrance arch stands the winged lion of St Mark, flanked above the two pedestrian entrances by the shields of arms, suspended from lion masks, of the city rector and the city captain who were in office when the gate was erected. The gateway is remarkably similar

to a drawing by Sanmicheli in the Print Room of the Uffizi, Florence (from the collection of Giorgio Vasari), there previously wrongly identified as for the gate of the fortress of San Andrea al Lido (fig. 9.16).[32] Michele Sanmicheli came to Zadar in May 1537 on the instructions of the Venetian state to provide a new system of fortifications, replacing those planned by Francesco Maria della Rovere, duke of Urbino (the Venetians' Generale Capitano della Terra). Sanmicheli left Zadar in the autumn of 1537, leaving his nephew Gian Girolamo Sanmicheli in control of the project. The suggestion that the gate was designed by the nephew rather than the uncle should be discounted, for such a bold and glorious conception was way beyond the imagination of his nephew. It shows Sanmicheli at a midway point of stylistic development between his Palazzo Pompei at Verona (1530), the quintessence of Vitruvian decorum, and the pared down, rugged simplicity of his Porta Palio at Verona (1557).

Despite Zadar's long and loyal history as part of Venice, it is surprisingly lacking in post-1400 Venetic architecture of note. The city is, however, rich in Italianate churches. St Donatus (Sv. Donat), of the early ninth century, is a magnificent centrally planned circular church reminiscent of the Palatinate Chapel at Aachen and the church of the Holy Sepulchre at Jerusalem and was built upon the salvaged spoils of Roman buildings. Then there is the cathedral of St Anastasia (Sv. Stošije), a handsome example of the twelfth- and thirteenth-century Pisan Romanesque with blind arcading and a mid-fifteenth-century Italianate campanile (incidentally, the upper section was constructed by the English architect Sir Thomas Graham Jackson, 1885–94), and the great monastic church of St Chrysogonus (Sv. Krševan), rebuilt in the Lombard Romanesque style of *c.* 1175. There is also the important church of the St Francis, founded 1270, with a plain exterior but, inside, magnificent choir stalls carved by Giovanni di Giacomo de Borgo San Sepolcro (1394) and a handsome polyptych from Ugljan, in the Zadar archipelago, by Giovanni di Pietro of Milan (see Chapter 6, fig. 6.5 and 6.8). Indeed, all these churches held, or formerly held, distinguished Italian pictures, sculptures and works of art.

The east front of St Mary the Less (Sv. Marija), the Benedictine convent, is the only surviving church in Zadar with a good Venetian Renaissance facade (fig. 9.17). It was designed by Martin Filipović of Zadar and Nikola Spanjić, the latter the principal assistant of the master mason of Korčula, Marko Andrijić. The church was built of Korčula stone in the style of the Venetian architect Mauro Codussi, following the prototypes of San Michele in Isola and San Giovanni Crisostomo, Venice. On the facade the east portal is confined within a Corinthian tabernacle (the female order being appropriate to the Virgin Mary) surmounted by a triangular head. The tall nave, pierced in the attic by a rose window, is flanked by narrow aisles to right and left lit by single lancet windows. The three bays of the facade are articulated by shallow pilasters that support a gable of trefoil form.

This Benedictine church, apart from the facade and campanile, and the ancient columns reused in the nave, was largely destroyed during the Second World War. It was rebuilt (1972) and the adjacent nunnery now contains a picture gallery, the Museo Permanente d'Arte Sacra, which provides a stylish and quite unexpected modern display of pictures and works of art. They either come from the nunnery's own historic collection or were salvaged, often by the nuns themselves, from Zadar's stricken places of worship.[33]

Undoubtedly the museum's greatest single Venetian treasure is Vittore Carpaccio's (c. 1465–1525/6) dismembered polyptych painted c. 1495–6 for the chapel of St Martin in the cathedral of Zadar.[34] It consists of a pair of semicircular-headed panels painted in tempera of *St Peter* and *St Paul*, both posed standing in landscapes lit by the setting sun. There is a panel of similar format of *St Jerome* naked to the waist, kneeling before a crucifix accompanied in prayer by Martin Mladošić, the patron who commissioned the altarpiece. There are three larger panels depicting *St Anastasia*, *St Simeon* and *St Martin*. The *St Martin* (fig. 9.18), the most ambitious and distinguished image, shows the saint dividing his cloak. He is the name saint of the patron and this panel is signed: 'Victoris carpatij venettj opus'. These separate panels originally formed a towering polyptych with, at the apex, a panel of the *Blessed Virgin Mary*, which, according to a visitation of the archbishop of Zadar, was still *in situ* in 1760 but is now lost. We also know that the patron, Martin Mladošić, had been a notary in Zadar and archpriest of Nin, and became a canon of the cathedral sometime before 1474. His tomb slab is in the cathedral, in the south aisle next to the altar of the Holy Sacrament. We learn from his will of 1496 that he wished the wood-carver Giovanni de Korčula to be paid thirty-two ducats for the frame of the altarpiece, which had already been begun. The Carpaccio polyptych, despite its sadly abraded and repainted state, remains a most distinguished work of art.

The museum contains a multitude of crosses, chalices, paxes, reliquaries and monstrances in precious metal, many of rarity and antiquity, but little of sophisticated design post-1450, save for a handsome reliquary bust of St Sixtus, which is identified by the inscription 'S[ANCT]I SIXTI' and dated 1596 (fig. 9.19).[35] It was probably made in Venice by a goldsmith influenced by Vittoria. This sensitive portrayal of a tired, bearded saint with profusely curling hair and beard is memorable. Although intended to represent Sixtus II, pope and martyr, who was executed on the Appian Way in AD 258, in reality the sitter has the features

9.19 Anonymous, reliquary bust of St Sixtus, 1596, silver, Museo Permanente d'Arte Sacra, Zadar. Photo: Živko Bačić.

of Pope Sixtus V (Felice Peretti, b. 1521, elected 1585, d. 1590). I suspect Pope Sixtus V would have been particularly admired by the clergy of Zadar, for the pope was no aristocrat and his family were Dalmatians who had fled to Italy from the Turkish menace. His father was a gardener, and in his youth he had kept pigs. The pope greatly enlarged the College of Cardinals, enforcing bishops to report in Rome regularly on the state of their dioceses, so it is likely that he would have known personally the bishop of Zadar. Of particular importance to Croatians and Venetians alike, Sixtus V was above all intent on annihilating the Turks. The companion reliquary bust of St Anastasia, dated 1622, is clearly not a portrait and is altogether inferior in conception and workmanship.

The nunnery's liturgical vestment collection, which is rich in stuffs and gold and silver thread, is not remarkable save for the superb altar frontal of crimson silk embroidered with gold showing the Virgin and Child enthroned flanked by standing figures of St John the Baptist and St John the Evangelist within Venetian Gothic arcading. It was almost certainly designed by Paolo Veneziano (fl. 1310–62) and commissioned by the priest Svećenik Radonja between 1337 and 1349 for St Mary's, Zadar.[36] The museum also contains a handsome, hieratic *Virgin and Child Enthroned* of c. 1350, attributed, with good reason, to Paolo Veneziano.[37]

Of special interest are the two oils, which are quite disparate in style, by Lorenzo Luzzo (called 'Morto da Feltre', 1480/5–1526). His father Bartolomeo moved from Feltre to Zadar soon after 1462, and subsequently both father and son seem to have moved back and forth between these two cities, maintaining studios in both countries. Lorenzo's first work here is a *Virgin and Child Enthroned*, a fragment presumably from a *sacra conversazione* painted for the church of the Madonna di Dubovice near Bozava on the Isola Lunga, which is said to resemble closely an altarpiece by him in San Giorgio at Villabruna (Feltre) in Italy. It is undeniably Bellinesque and resembles the Virgin and Child in Giovanni Bellini's San Zaccharia altarpiece of 1505, but the blessing Christ Child is standing, not seated. How different this is from the ambitious *Assumption of the Virgin* altarpiece at Zadar painted for St Mary's nunnery. It is signed 'Laurentis Lu[cius] Feltri[nus] fe[cit]' but undated.[38] The picture must surely date from after his San Stefano altarpiece of 1511 (now in the Bode Museum, Berlin) and stylistically now depends not on Venetian but on Marchigian prototypes, painters from Urbino like Genga and Timoteo Viti. The gallery also contains handsome altarpieces by Paolo Pagani, Giovanni Battista Pitteri, and Francesco Migliori.

The nunnery collection is not just confined to paintings and textiles, for it also boasts a marble statue of *St Chrysogonus* signed by Giuseppe Gropelli (1675–1735)[39] and an elegant companion statue of *St Anastasia* (fig. 9.20) signed by Antonio Corradini (1688–1752),[40] which were both formerly on the high altar of the church of St Donatus (after 1822 moved to the cathedral) and are thought to have been commissioned originally *c.* 1712–13 for St Donatus. This was according to the wish of the archbishop of Zadar, Antonio Priuli, who died in 1712. Little is documented of the two martyr saints Chrysogonus and Anastasia: St Chrysogonus, the patron of Zadar, appears to have been martyred in Aquileia in AD 304, and St Anastasia was martyred at Sirmium (Sremska Mitrovica, Serbia). She, poor saint, has had the misfortune of having her feast day rather eclipsed as it falls on Christmas Day. The written apocryphal *Passion of St Anastasia* attributes more than usually credible adventures to both these saints. The sculptor Gropelli, in this, his unique signed work, has made St Chrysogonus out to be a pretty boy in Roman armour, while Corradini's St Anastasia, an allegory of Faith, is the quintessence of grace and nobility. The willowy maiden, a stylish little scarf at her neck, is clad in a diaphanous shift, a cloak clutched around her waist, while gazing unconcernedly at her right hand, which happens to be on fire.

9.21 Ascribed to Gian Girolamo Sanmicheli, City Loggia, Zadar. Photo: Jovan Kliska.

9.20 Antonio Corradini, *St Anastasia, c.* 1712–13, marble, Museo Permanente d'Arte Sacra, Zadar. Photo: Živko Bačić.

Zadar is rich in eighteenth-century Venetian sculpture. Of special note is the high altar of the Benedictine church of St Chrysogonus, with standing marble figures of St Chrysogonus, St Simeon, St Zoilus and St Anastasia. I find their variations in height awkward, with St Zoilus dwarfed by the matronly St Anastasia. They were carved by Alvise Tagliapietra and his studio between 1705 and 1711. This was just before the sculptor was commissioned by Peter the Great and Count Menshikov to provide various statues for the gardens of Peterhof and Tsarkoye-Selo (now Pushkin).[41] The St Simeon would be an unusual

choice if we were not aware that his shrine (already mentioned) was in a nearby church. Zadar's remains of St Simeon, encased in their glorious silver-gilt coffin, were considered even more ancient and venerable than those of St Mark's in Venice. Tagliapietra shows the Jewish priest holding up the Christ Child and about to utter the words of the Evening Office, 'a light to lighten the Gentiles' (Luke 2:29–32), celebrated by the canticle of the *Nunc dimitis*. This figure's exaggerated *contrapposto* and exotic vestments make it a memorable statue.

Zadar's sculptures are often housed in fine Italianate buildings and these should not be overlooked. The Ghirardini Palace, on the corner of People's Square and Jurja Barakovića Street, boasts a fine flamboyant arched and cusped window frame of *c.* 1480. The window frame is supported by a pair of putti brackets that have suspended between them a heavy foliage festoon. This sort of ornament recurs in the pictures of Giorgio Schiavone and Carlo Crivelli. Close by is the rusticated city guardhouse of three bays of the Doric order perhaps by G. G. Sanmicheli (1562), a weak building, marred by the addition of a clock tower in the eighteenth century.[42] The City Loggia also attributed to G. G. Sanmicheli (1565), and also rusticated, has a single-storey facade of three round-headed arches enclosed by paired Tuscan Doric pilasters, with idiosyncratic capitals breaking forward to support a plain frieze and deep, balustraded parapet (fig. 9.21). The slender proportions are reminiscent of the main portal of the church of St Simeon (1572), which has a shallow fluted pediment enclosing a relief of the Virgin and Child within an oval strapwork cartouche. Most notable of this period is the exquisite but austere narrow three-bay Renaissance palazzo façade, which is part of the Palazzo del Governo (Kneževa palača) in St Simeon Square (Poljana Sv. Šime). It is modified from the designs by Sebastiano Serlio (1475–1553/5?), related to his design for the façade of a palace of *c.* 1540 reproduced in his *Tutte le opera d'architettura et prospetiva* (Venice

1619). His works, incidentally, also include images of Pula in Istria. A short distance from this little palazzo, on the Grimani bastion in the Queen Jelena Madio Park, are two magnificent marble herms of bearded satyrs that now form a gazebo, which is easily overlooked. Sadly, they currently suffer from a rash of graffiti. The style is reminiscent of Vittoria's decorative sculptures but a little coarser, and the musculature of their torsos is less richly modelled or understood. They may well be by a sculptor who worked prolifically in Vittoria's manner at Vicenza, Lorenzo Rubini (1541–74). Similar are the atlante supports for the grand chimneypiece in the Villa Caldogno, Vicenza, of 1569, and the telamons on the funeral monument to Ippolito da Porto in San Lorenzo, Vicenza, dated 1572.[43]

The museum of the city of Zadar (Muzej grada Zadra) contains a handsome and extensive collection of Italian maiolica all excavated in Zadar and inevitably in a rather fragmentary condition. The collection is well displayed so that one can examine the fronts and backs of all the jugs and dishes. At Split a rubbish pit in the south-eastern part of Diocletian's Palace was excavated in 1968 by a team of Yugoslavs and Americans, and this dig also uncovered large quantities of sherds of Italian maiolica, but the pieces were mostly small and of less status than the more substantial and handsome finds here at Zadar. Excavations in both cities demonstrate that, as there appears to have been no indigenous manufacture of maiolica in Dalmatia, so ceramics had to be imported mostly from Italy, although a little had come earlier from Syria, Byzantium, North Africa and Spain.[44] Sherds found in Split demonstrate that locals bought pottery from Venice, Rome, Florence, Montelupo, Castel Durante, Deruta, Castelli (in the Abruzzi), the Marches, Emilia Romagna and Apulia – which indeed constitutes nearly all of the centres of ceramic manufacture in Italy. That broad geographic spread is also reflected in the finds in Zadar, and helps document hypothetically the Italian geographical range of sources of so many other non-Venetian artefacts that were exported to Dalmatia. Notable in Zadar are the splendid group of graffito (or sgraffito) decorated pots, which are mostly from Reggio Emilia or the Veneto. One shallow bowl of the early sixteenth century shows a naked warrior holding the shield

of the Bentivoglio family of Bologna (fig. 9.22), while another small jug has a male profile portrait, possibly intended for the youthful Henry VIII of England c. 1520–5, flanked by heraldic roses (fig. 9.23). Graffito decorated earthenware had been made in Syria and later Byzantium from pre-Renaissance times and was even made in Korčula. There is also a rather larger jug, typical of Faenza c. 1480–1500, painted with the sacred *trigramma* associated with San Bernardino of Siena.

Two very distinguished artists often considered Italian were both, in fact, born at Vrana near Zadar. One was the sculptor Francesco Laurana (or de la Vrana, fl. 1453–1502). He apparently began his career in Dubrovnik working under Pietro di Martino di Milano (fl. 1431–52), but nothing can certainly be attributed to him while he was in Dalmatia. By 1453 he was with Pietro di Milano in Naples working on the Castel Nuovo, while in 1458 Francesco Laurana was employed completing the Triumphal Aragonese Arch at Castel Nuovo. For much of his career he was in the employ of René of Anjou: first in Provence (largely in Marseille) from 1461 to 1466 designing and casting medals, carving portrait busts and also a splendid fountain for Puy-Sainte-Réparade (1464). We know that from 1468 to 1471 he moved to Sicily, where he was working at Palermo, Noto , and Palazzo Acreide. Thence, at the Anjou court, he oscillated between Naples and southern France (Avignon, Marseille) from 1474 to 1481. Legal documents demonstrate that he was in Marseille in December 1492 and again in 1502. It has been suggested that he may also have worked at Genoa, Rimini, and Urbino, but there are apparently no documents to establish such putative visits. His distinctive portrait busts, like those of *Battista Sforza* (Florence, Bargello), *Beatrice of Aragon* (New York, Frick) and *Antonio Baressio* (Zagreb Museum) are typical of his most refined treatment of facial expression. He produced many lyrical images employing infinitely soft *sfumato* in the cutting and polishing of his portrayals of the *Madonna and Child* (Naples, Castel Nuovo and Capodimonte), while the *Christ Carrying the Cross* at St Didier, Avignon, despite certain infelicities, is moving and memorable.[45]

The second artist from the Zadar area was Luciano Laurana (or de la Vrana, fl. 1464–79), a celebrated architect. Nothing

9.22 Sgraffito (or graffito) earthenware dish incised with naked warrior holding the shield of Bentivoglio family of Bologna, *c.* 1500–10, City Museum of Zadar. Photo: Aleksandar Kotlar.

9.23 Sgraffito earthenware jug incised with possible portrait of King Henry VIII between roses, *c.* 1520–5, City Museum of Zadar. Photo: Aleksandar Kotlar.

is known of his early years in Dalmatia, but it is thought that he was the Slavonian who, according to Giorgio Vasari in his 'Life of Filippo Brunelleschi', worked as Brunelleschi's assistant in Florence and Venice. Certainly, Laurana's style seems influenced by Brunelleschi but also by Alberti and Piero della Francesca. Giovanni Santi (Raphael's father) in his manuscript *La vita e le geste di Federico da Montefeltro duca d'Urbino: cronaca* (1482–7) tells us that Laurana was the architect responsible for the Palazzo Ducale, Urbino, and this is repeated by Baldi in *Versi e prose* (Venice 1590). The first we hear of Laurana he was working in Fano in 1464 on the Porta Maggiore, and then he is mentioned in two letters both dated 8 May 1465, one from Ludovico II Gonzaga, second marquess of Mantua, to Alessandro Sforza, count of Pesaro, and the other from Ludovico's wife, Barbara of Brandenburg, asking him to come to Mantua.

Luciano Laurana probably designed the Palazzo Prefettizio on the main square in Pesaro and possibly the Church of the Osservanza, Pesaro (1465–9), demolished in the sixteenth century. We know that in 1467 Laurana had settled in Urbino as Ingegnero del Signore of Federigo da Montefeltro, and on 10 June Federigo issued a *patente* naming Laurana to supervise the erection of the Palazzo Ducale. He remained in Urbino for six years, where he built most of the palazzo including the magnificent cortile, grand double staircase and the facade with the *torricini* (small towers), while the Veglie wing seems more likely to have been by Francesco di Giorgio Martini. During Laurana's last years in Urbino, he seems to have supervised the foundations of the monastery of Santa Chiara, a building completed by Francesco di Giorgio. In 1472 he bought a house near Urbino, while between 1472 and 1474 he was in Naples as Master of Artillery. Later in 1474 Laurana was back in Pesaro and working on the Rocca Costanza. He died in 1479 at Pesaro after having started to build the bridge on the Adriatic side of the fortress of Senigallia.[46]

The working lives of the Lauranas show how fifteenth-century artists regularly moved considerable distances for work, nationally and internationally, following the demands of their powerful patrons. Although the Lauranas were apparently unrelated, they would surely have known each other. Such Croatian artists were entirely familiar with contemporary fashions and stylistic developments in the grandest Italian courts, and moreover were responsible sometimes for introducing the fashions themselves.

THE ISLAND OF HVAR (LESINA): HVAR TOWN

This slender island, about twenty-four miles long, is due south of Brač, an island famous for its stonemasons and quarries.[47] In the late fourth century BC, inhabitants from the island of Paros in the Aegean founded the town of Pharos (present-day Stari Grad or Cittavecchia) in north-west Hvar, where the island is at its widest. Hvar was subsequently ruled by the Romans, the Byzantines and then, in 1278, the Venetians, and remained their possession until 1797. After 1420 the Venetians rebuilt their defences and moved both the capital and the already ancient bishopric from Stari Grad to the town of Hvar, about five miles to the west. Hvar town flourished and provided a good sheltered harbour for the Venetian fleet.

Arriving nowadays at the harbour of Hvar, one sees a large paved piazza of a type familiar with minor variations throughout the former Venetian Empire: the west side consisting of the harbour, the north and south with rows of shops and private houses, the east dominated by the cathedral, its campanile and the Bishop's Palace and a large communal stone cistern (1520) in the centre. Beside, and indeed part of, the harbour to the south is the Arsenal (1530–59), a great plain barn of a building with a semicircular entrance to the sea built to house part of Venice's fleet during the winter, and then extended by the enlightened Venetian governor Pietro Semitecolo in 1612 to house, on the upper floor, the earliest communal theatre constructed, and still functioning, in Europe. The cathedral, which is dedicated to St Stephen (Sv. Stjepan), was built on this spot in the fourteenth and fifteenth centuries.[48] It was severely damaged by a Turkish raid under Uluz Ali, dey of Algiers, in August 1571, and rebuilt in the sixteenth and seventeenth centuries. Its three-bay facade follows the familiar Codussi type of elevation, with a trefoil gable and *oculus*, like the cathedral of Šibenik, St Mary's, Zadar, and the church of the Annunciation at Svetvinčenat, Istria. The interior of the church is unremarkable, although the marble frame of the high altar is by the architect Baldassare Longhena (of Santa Maria della Salute fame) enclosing a Palma il Giovane of the *Virgin and Child with St Stephen, St Jerome and St Charles Borromeo*.[49] This poor picture, unfinished at the time of Palma's death, is interesting as it is documented as having been completed by Palma's obscure pupil, Niccolò Reineri Mabuseo. Palma, at his best, is a follower of Titian and Tintoretto, and an able draughtsman who painted with brio. He was popular and prolific, but, sadly, his studio was capable of producing too much indifferent work, especially for the churches in Dalmatia. The remaining altarpieces in the cathedral are unexciting works by Andrea Celesti, Domenico Uberti, Antonio Grapinelli, Antonio Zanchi and Leonardo Negri. The cathedral, however, does contain a vigorous early variant of Giorgio da Sebenico's *Flagellation of Christ* from the sarcophagus of St Anastasius in Split Cathedral.

In the museum of the Bishop's Palace (Biskupski muzej) is a splendid Italian crimson velvet cope, the hood and orphreys richly embroidered in *or nué*, of *c.* 1495–1510. The fringed hood is embroidered with the Virgin and Child enthroned adored by flying angels, while the orphreys are embroidered, on the front, with the four doctors of the church and four apostles all enthroned within canopied tabernacles, with two demi-figures of saints behind the neck and above the hood.[50] It may have been made for Bishop Pritić, Francesco Patrizi (Patricius) (1509–22), who also commissioned a fine silver-gilt pastoral staff. The style of the embroidered figures is reminiscent of the Florentine

9.24 Jacopo Tintoretto, *Lamentation*, here dated *c.* 1550, oil on canvas, Dominican monastery, Stari Grad. Photo: Živko Bačić.

Raffaellino del Garbo (*c.* 1466–1524). Drawings by del Garbo for similar enthroned saints are in the Uffizi, Florence, and a double-sided drawing by del Garbo of an angel, like those on the hood, is at Rugby School, Warwickshire. From Vasari's 'Life' of Raffaelino we know that he made many such designs for embroidery, among the finest being the Bakocz chasuble in the cathedral treasury at Estergom in Hungary and sections of the Passerini vestments (in collaboration with Andrea del Sarto), now in the Museo Diocesano at Cortona.

Behind the Bishop's Palace are the remains of its original seventeenth/early eighteenth-century garden, and next to these traces of the sophisticated summer villa gardens (1532) of the great Renaissance poet and humanist of Hvar, Hannibal Lucić-Lucio (*c.* 1485–1553). Croatians were becoming increasingly aware of their ancient and distinguished independent nationhood, and it was Lucić-Lucio who wrote *Robinja* (or *La Schiava* – the Slave Woman), the first drama to be written in the Croatian language. His villa now hosts the Centre for the Cultural Patrimony of Hvar, which contains a small collection of Italian maiolica sherds and a rare but very damaged, and unpublished, polychrome group of *St Francis in Ecstasy Accompanied by Brother Leo*, probably made at Urbino in the mid-sixteenth century.

Walking back from the cathedral on the north side of the piazza, one has a good view of the unfinished Palazzo Užičić of 1463, with its elaborate late Gothic arcaded fenestration.

The Franciscan convent of the Madonna delle Grazie, just over five minutes' walk due south of the piazza on the promontory of Sridnji Rat, has a distinguished church and an interesting collection. It was built at the request of the admiral of the Venetian fleet, Piero Soranzo, with the financial support of various local families in 1465–71. The stone relief lunette over the main door by Niccolò Fiorentino, carved in three sections, shows half-length figures of the *Virgin and Child Adored by Angels* (1470). The interior of the church has a magnificent rood screen with accommodation for the choir in the gallery. The superstructure is painted with six *Scenes of the Passion* by a local, Martin Benetović (d. 1607), who was also the organist. The rood is supported by a concave bracketed frieze with, beneath and forming part of the integral structure, a triptych and a polyptych in matching frames by Francesco Santacroce (1516–84) in his best manner. The church also contains two fine altarpieces by Leandro Bassano (1557–1622) of *St Francis and St Anthony* and of the *Crucifixion*. The convent refectory boasts a magnificent and very large *Last Supper* looking to me like a good Palma il Giovane, but said to be the masterpiece of the young Dalmatian Matteo Ponzoni (fl. 1604–64).[51] A special treasure of the convent is the carved and gilded wooden *Winged Dragon*, which originally adorned the prow of the Lesina galley at the battle of Lepanto (1571). I also suspect that two unusual brackets in the form of dragons that, within the main church, spring from the rood and support silver sanctuary lamps may also have come from that galley.

STARI GRAD (CITTAVECCHIA DI LESINA)

This, the old capital, is situated about five miles east of Hvar, with a good harbour and next to a large and fertile plain.[52] The Dominican monastery of St Peter Martyr is its most important ecclesiastical building. In 1482 Fra Germanicus of Piacenza came to the island to work with the Venetian bishop of Hvar, Nikola de Crucibus, and started to build the monastery with the help of the townspeople. The monastery, along with much of the town, was attacked and burnt by the Turks on 19 August 1571. It was then rebuilt and fortified. In 1894 the old church was torn down and replaced, but the monastic collection remains intact. The collection includes oils: two set above the choir pews by Baldassare D'Anna (1560–1639), an altarpiece of *Our Lady of the Rosary with the Victors of Lepanto* by Andrea Vicentino (1539–1617) and yet another altar of the Rosary by Andrea Bruttapella of Bassano (1769), who came to live and work in Stari Grad. By far the most important painting in the monastery is the *Lamentation of Christ* by Jacopo Tintoretto (1518–94) (fig. 9.24). It was painted for the Hvar poet, patrician and humanist Petar Hektorović (1487–1572). There is a document to show that Hektorović received permission to build an altar of the Pietà in the Dominican church of St Peter Martyr in 1546. As that earlier church was burnt down by the Turks on 21 August 1571 and the Tintoretto altarpiece is first referred to in the 1579 visitation of Agostino Valier, apostolic vicar and bishop of Verona, it has been assumed that the picture dates from 1571–9. Professor Rodolfo Palluchini refines the dating more precisely to *c.* 1575–9. It would, however, seem a little odd that Hektorović, having received permission for building the altar in 1546, delayed commissioning the altarpiece for nearly thirty years. Stylistically, this Tintoretto could well date from the early 1550s, and I suspect that it does indeed date from this earlier period and at much the same time that Tintoretto was painting his altarpiece for the cathedral of Korčula. The patron perhaps managed to save it from the Turkish raid, bringing it to the safety of his own fortified villa nearby.[53]

Petar Hektorović's fortified villa, Tvrdalj, which still survives, is incidentally one of the most fascinating monuments of Croatian humanism, with all its explicit references to Pliny the Younger and Ovid – indeed, Hektorović translated Ovid into Croatian. Hektorović was the author of an extraordinary work of Croatian literature, the epic *Ribanje i Ribarsko prigovaranje* (Fishing and Fishermen's Conversations, 1556), which is a description in verse of a three-day fishing trip from the town of Stari Grad to the island of Šolta and back with two local fishermen, Paskoj and Nikola. Hektorović (1487–1572) was also the earliest Croatian to transcribe the music of folk songs and include the notation in a text. Tvrdalj, his extraordinary villa, was built as a refuge not just for himself and his family but for the local people as well. It was a carefully programmed structure, rich in classical inscriptions and allusions in Latin and Croat. Cosmic in conception, it has, on the side of the sea, a large inscription 'OMNIUM CONDITORI' (To the Creator of the World). In the atrium is a fishpond and around are lush gardens with flowers and trees. The tower also serves as a dovecote to harbour doves, sparrows and other creatures of the sky. Apartments on the eastern side were reserved for travellers and paupers, while under the loggia terrace was a cell in which lived a Beguine nun to care for Hektorović's body and soul. He also kept chickens and bees. Above the entrance to the fishpond (fig. 9.25) is carved in stone: 'PETRUS HECTOREUS MARINI FILIUS PROPRIO SUMPTU ET INDUSTRIA AD SUUM ET AMICORUM USUM CONSTRUXIT' (Built by Petrus Hectoreus, son of Marinus, by his own wealth and diligence to serve himself and his friends). Tvrdalj, the brain child of this eccentric Croatian patrician, would surely have delighted contemporary Italian humanists like Vicino Orsini at his monster garden, Bomarzo in Lazio, while today we can enjoy it as a recondite forerunner of the late Ian Hamilton Finlay's celebrated garden of Little Sparta in Scotland.[54]

The museum of the Dominican monastery contains a typical oil by Leandro Bassano of the *Vision of St Catherine of Siena*, a tabernacle decorated by Palma il Giovane, and a crucifix carved in boxwood (1703) by the Venetian Giacomo Piazzetta (*c.* 1641–1705).[55] This prolific wood-carver was the father of the celebrated

9.25 View of the fishpond of Hektorović's villa, Tvrdalj, Stari Grad. Photo: Milan Pelc.

Sebastiano ordered an altarpiece from Paolo Veronese, but this was destroyed by a fire in 1771.

The parish church of St Lawrence (Sv. Lovre) is a fifteenth-century foundation which was much enlarged during the seventeenth century. It now functions as the parish museum and art gallery. The museum houses a polyptych, original to this church, by Paolo Veronese (1528–88) and his studio, consisting of a central, tall rectangular canvas with semicircular head, depicting St Lawrence dressed in a dalmatic, holding his martyr's palm and gridiron, gazing up towards the Virgin and Child adored by music-making angels. St Lawrence is flanked to the left by St John the Baptist and to the right by St Nicholas of Bari. Below there are two predella panels in which St Lawrence appears. In the first is *St Lawrence Ordered by the Emperor Vespasian to Hand Over the Church's Treasures*. St Lawrence duly assembled the poor and the sick, presenting them to the emperor saying, 'Here is the Church's treasure.' The companion predella represents *St Lawrence Martyred on the Gridiron*. Detached from this same altarpiece, but on show within the museum, is a small painted tabernacle (or *custode*) for the host, a polygonal wooden structure, the central panel painted with a Pietà, the champfered side panels painted with angels swinging thurribles. These little paintings are from Veronese's studio. The high altar, which is now within in a much later and pretentious grey marble frame, is largely a workshop production probably by Benedetto, Paolo's brother, of *c.* 1576–8, but the handsome figures of *St Lawrence* and *St Nicholas* look substantially autograph (fig. 9.26).[58] Conveniently for us, Agostino Valier, bishop of Verona, on his visitation of 1579 mentioned 'the magnificent image of St Lawrence' on the high altar. The museum also contains a series of lesser pictures including *Our Lady of the Rosary* by Leandro Bassano, a *Madonna del Carmelo* (1659) by Stefano Caelesti (1637–1712) and a *Resurrection* by Giuseppe Allabardi (1590–1650). They are interesting in so much as they are documented works by rare minor but named Venetian artists. The treasury also contains a large silver processional cross ascribed, ambitiously, to the Paduan Tiziano Aspetti (1559–1606).

painter Gian Battista Piazzetta. The church of St Stephen (Sv. Stjepan) nearby contains a triptych of the *Virgin Mary Flanked by St John the Baptist and St Jerome* by the ubiquitous Francesco da Santacroce.

To the east of Stari Grad (the ancient Pharos), as one travels towards Vrboska, you pass through the *chora* of Pharos, a massive agricultural settlement laid out by the Greeks after 384 BC, when the new land was divided up into a grid system of more that seventy rectangular lots of 1 x 5 stadia (1 stadion = 181 metres), the ancient boundaries still being marked out in dry-stone walling. This remarkable Greek field system, which is now under threat from developers, is apparently the best preserved in the world.[56]

VRBOSKA (VERBOSCA)

The settlement grew up in the fifteenth century around a natural harbour near the village of Vrbanj.[57] It was destroyed when the Venetian fleet, under Providitor Sebastiano Giustiniani, put down a populist revolt led by Matija Ivanić, a local armourer, in 1512. In 1571 Vrboska was sacked again and destroyed by the Turkish fleet under Uluz Ali. The town is now a quiet, picturesque little port that specialises in pilchard fishing. Some of the old houses are still in ruins since the Turkish raid, but the most enduring memory of these unsettled times is the magnificent fortress church of St Mary of Charity (Sv. Marija od Milosrđa). It was started in 1535 and then had a powerful bastion added in 1573, just two years after the Turkish raid. In 1576 the Confraternità dei Santi Fabiano e

KORČULA (CURZOLA)

The Illyrian Greeks called this large island south of Hvar Kerkyra, 'the rock passage'. Livy tells us that the Romans first came here in 229 BC and later fought and defeated the Illyrians in 167 BC. The

Romans suffered continuing difficulties and so, in 35 BC, the exasperated Emperor Octavian invaded Illyria and, according to Appius, had all the young men of Korčula killed and the women and children sold into slavery. In 476 the island came under Byzantine administration, and over the succeeding centuries it was subject to constant raids and various attempts by others at colonisation. Doge Pietro Orseolo II of Venice (r. 991–1008) conquered the island in 1000, subjecting it to an annual tribute of timber for the Venetian fleet, but Korčula was to be no lasting Venetian colony. Marco Polo (d. 1324), the celebrated explorer, was a native of this island. He captained a Venetian galley, part of the fleet of Admiral Andrea Dandolo, that was soundly defeated in a sea battle by the Genoese off Korčula in 1299. Marco Polo was taken prisoner and then whiled away his time in a Genoese prison dictating to a fellow prisoner a report of his journeys in the East – a work later to be famous as the *Travels or Description of the World* by Marco Polo. It was only in 1420 that Korčula again became part of the Venetian Empire, and it remained so until the dissolution of the Serenissima in 1797. The island had forests of oak, cypresses and Aleppo pine. The plenteous local supplies of timber were used for ship building. There were also quarries which provided excellent building stone. On the lush pastures cattle were bred. All of these resources were exploited by the Venetians.[59]

Korčula town is on the extreme north-east of the island and encompasses a neat shield-shaped isthmus encircled by walls. It was founded *ex nihilo* in 1256 by a certain Marsilio Zorzi, son of the cardinal of San Gervasio, who was legate of Doge Jacopo Tiepolo, as a *castrum* or crucial fortified station in the Adriatic between Venice and the Levant. The town was massively strengthened by towers and bastions after 1410 by the Venetians. They also, for security, cut the town off from the rest of the island by a broad and deep canal, the Fossa. The most significant monument is the cathedral of San Marco (Katedrala Sv. Marka).[60] Started *c*. 1300, in its present form it dates largely from 1406, but was added to and modified by subsequent generations, limited resources always being spent on defence before cathedral building. The main Gothic doorway, which is by Bonino of Milan (1412), has an enthroned figure of St Mark in the lunette above the door flanked by richly carved brackets supporting lions couchant. Within the basilican structure is a monumental stone ciborium by Marko Andrijić (1486) enshrining the high altar, which encloses within an ornamental, shaped reserve a magnificent altarpiece by Jacopo Tintoretto of *St Mark Flanked by St Bartholomew and St Jerome* (fig. 9.27).[61] In 2002–3 this picture was very well conserved by Katarina Kusijanović of the Croatian Conservation Institute at Rijeka Dubrovačka. Under layers of grime, discoloured varnish and repaint, Tintoretto's original glowing colours were largely found to be in good shape. Also major *pentimenti* were found around the central figure of St Mark.

9.26 Paolo Veronese, *The Vision of St Lawrence*, 1576–8, oil on canvas, parish church of St Lawrence, Vrboska. Photo: Croatian Conservation Institute.

Research in the cathedral archives undertaken by the abbott, Don Ivo Matijaca, provided precious details of the circumstances of the original commission:

On February 9th 1550 'at the request of the noble gentleman Julije de Gabrielis procurator of the church of St Mark and of the vicar Master Klaudije Tolomei of the venerable bishop of Korčula, with the authority of Master Zakararije Salamon, headman of the same city, according to Demetrije and Nikola, heralds of the curia, the below named were called to the great room of the headman's court for the purchase and to determine the envoys to go to Venice to order a painting for the altar of the church of St Mark. At this meeting the councillors put forward many ideas, provisions and points of view of how the painting for the altar of St Mark should look, and at the end, unanimously and in concert,

9.27 Jacopo Tintoretto, *St Mark Flanked by St Bartholomew and St Jerome*, 1550, oil on canvas, Korčula Cathedral. Photo: Croatian Conservation Institute.

decided and concluded with full authority that a free hand be given to the noble master Julije Gabrijelis to travel to Venice and there according to the model and this order to have this picture made'. (my translation)

We learn from other sources that Julije Gabrijelis sailed to Venice to have the picture painted according to agreed specifications, taking with him a down payment of fifty ducats. We discover that he returned to Venice to see how the picture was progressing and to pay a further instalment. Having inspected the picture in the artist's studio, he then sought to have the draperies of the central figure of St Mark altered, providing him with a bishop's chasuble, and this reworking can now be confirmed by x-rays. We know that Tintoretto painted this altarpiece in 1550, and it was perhaps, as I have suggested here, its fame that induced Petar Hektorović to commission Tintoretto, at much the same time, to paint a *Lamentation* for him at Stari Grad.

Changes to the Korčula picture were made because the artist in Venice had thought that the central figure of St Mark was to follow the familiar Venetian iconography of the Evangelist wearing flowing robes over a tunic, often accompanied by a winged lion. The St Mark of Korčula, patron of the town and cathedral, had a different regional iconography and may even have been a different saint of the same name, a bishop of Alexandria who was martyred during the reign of Trajan. In Korčula the saint is shown wearing a bishop's mitre and chasuble as in Bonino di Milano's statue (1412) on the main portal of the cathedral. Tintoretto's composition with St Mark enthroned in the centre in full canonicals is boldly hieratic and strongly reminiscent, within its elaborate and eccentrically shaped proto-baroque frame, of Orthodox icons. These icon-like qualities are further theatrically enhanced by the painting being enshrined at the centre of the main apse above the high altar within a monumental stone ciborium.

The cathedral also contains a good *Trinity Adored by Saints with the Donor Bishop Teodoro Diedo* (1622) by the prolific Leandro Bassano. The island, incidentally, also boasts in Čara parish church an even more splendid Leandro Bassano of the *Incredulity of St Thomas* (1592–3).[62] Korčula Cathedral contains an altar of *Our Lady of Carmel* signed and dated 1642 by Carlo Ridolfi (1602–58), which is only notable because Ridofi was the great biographer of Venetian painters, celebrated for his *Le meraviglie dell'arte ovvero le vite degli illustri pittori veneti e dello stato*

9.28 Venetian foundry, perhaps workshop of Andrea Vittoria, *Neptune stilling the waves flanked by lions*, bronze door knocker, Civic Museum of Korčula. Photo: Ćiril Metod Iveković.

(1648).[63] Next to the door of the St Jacob's aisle is a trophy of spears and halberds, a votive display dedicated to the Virgin Mary, erected in gratitude for deliverance from the Turkish siege, invested by Uluz Ali on 15 August 1571, just before the battle of Lepanto. One hundred and fifty-four Korčulan men and women stoutly defended the town from land and sea attacks by over 2,000 Turks. The Korčulans were saved by their own brave feats of arms, apparently supported by a miraculous storm sent by the Blessed Virgin Mary.

Nearby the cathedral is the Renaissance palace of the Gabriellis family, which now houses the civic museum (Gradski Muzej). Among the many local portraits and archives, it boasts a handsome Venetian bronze door knocker of the late sixteenth century (fig. 9.28). The model, with variations, is not uncommon, growing out of the sculptural tradition of Andrea Vittoria (1524–1608), but this cast is unusual in that Neptune is more often shown flanked by seahorses, not lions as here.[64] The escutcheons at the top of the knocker can often be found with Venetian armorials, while a 'companion' knocker with a figure of Venus is recorded, which was probably made in a foundry associated with the Paduan Tiziano Aspetti (1565–1607).

Along the sea front is All Saints church (Svi Sveti), built in 1301 and then substantially remodelled in the baroque style. It contains a fine painted crucifix of the fourteenth century, reminiscent of Paolo Veneziano's in the Dominican monastery at Dubrovnik. Quite unexpected is the superb life-size sculpture of the *Pietà* in carved wood painted to resemble stone. It used to be attributed to the Austrian Georg Raphael Donner (1693–1741), but bought in Venice in 1801, it has recently been convincingly demonstrated stylistically to be a masterpiece by the Venetian Antonio Corradini (1688–1752) (fig. 9.29).[65] The little church of St Michael Archangel (Sv. Mihovila) contains an altarpiece by Francesco Maggiotto of Venice (1750–1808) of the *Madonna of the Girdle with St Augustine of Hippo, St Monica, St Charles Borromeo and St Agatha*, which, from a memorandum of the artist, was sent to 'Curzola' in 1785.[66]

Outside the walls of the city is the monastery and church of St Nicholas dating from the fifteenth century. It contains a *Madonna of the Rosary* by Matteo Ponzoni (1583–1675), which has an unusual iconography showing the Virgin Mary, centre, assisted by St Catherine of Alexandria and St Mary Magdalen, holding

9.29 Antonio Corradini, *Pietà*, wood painted to resemble stone, All Saints church, Korčula. Photo: Živko Bačić.

up a framed image of St Dominic, the whole composition adored by a kneeling Dominican patron.[67] The altarpiece is surrounded by eighteen smaller scenes illustrating the mysteries of the Rosary. This handsome altarpiece, still covered with grime and discoloured varnish, shows the artist at his mature and characteristic best, and seems quite unlike the *Last Supper* in the Franciscan convent at Hvar, now attributed to Ponzoni.

To the west of the island is the parish church of Blato. The high altar boasts a painting by Girolamo da Santa Croce (fl. 1480–1556) of *All Saints* (Svi Sveti), which is signed and dated 15 August 1540 with a long inscription on the steps in the foreground.[68] This extraordinary image, which has crammed into it no fewer than thirty-six saints, was commissioned by the procurator, Jacopo Carnavelli. Something of a curiosity is the altarpiece of St Anthony of Padua by that lively and rare painter in Croatia, Pietro della Vecchia (c. 1602/3–78).[69] The saint is shown in his Franciscan habit carrying the Christ Child, who stands on the Gospels holding a lily. Around the saint are fifteen predella images portraying episodes from his life. St Anthony, born in Lisbon, worked among the Muslims in Morocco, retreated for a period to a hermitage outside Forlì, and spent the remainder of his life preaching and teaching in Italy. In Dalmatia he was particularly venerated as a biblical scholar and 'hammer of heretics'.

THE PELJEŠAC PENINSULA

Immediately to the east of the island of Korčula is the Pelješac peninsula. It is forty miles long and only seven miles wide at its broadest point. With a backbone of mountains, the lower slopes and plain are rich and fertile with vineyards and citrus fruits, while in the shallow waters were and are salt pans. Inhabited by the Illyrians, colonised by the Greeks, Romans and Byzantines in turn, it was sold to the Republic of Dubrovnik in 1333, whose property it remained until 1808, when the republic was dissolved.

STON AND OREBIĆ

Ston is the town closest to the mainland and to Dubrovnik. It is still surrounded by a magnificent chain of defensive walls that were built on the orders of Dubrovnik by its own military engineers, and completed in the fifteenth century. They consist of three miles of walls, forty-one towers, seven bastions, and two forts linking Veliki Ston with St Michael's Mount and Mali Ston. These defences were erected by a succession of artists, including Michelozzo di Bartolomeo Michelozzzi of Florence (1396–1472), Bernardino of Parma and Giorgio da Sebenico, the latter justly celebrated for his great works at the cathedral of Šibenik.

Near the tip of the peninsula where one boards the Korčula ferry is the town of Orebić, and just outside the town towards Lovište is the Franciscan monastery with its church of the Assumption (or Santa Maria degli Angeli).[70] It stands on the side of Mount St Elijah (Elie/Ilija), some 150 metres above sea level, and from this vantage point there are splendid views of the Pelješac channel and the city of Korčula. The church's austere exterior has the central portal surmounted by a triangular-headed

pediment, which contains a half-length relief of the *Virgin and Child* flanked by lions, a richly carved *acquasantiera* with scallop-shell niche to the right and, above, a rose window within a triangular gable. The interior, a simple barn-like structure, is lit by semicircular-headed windows, and leads to a smaller chancel. This chancel, the original shrine of *Our Lady of All Angels*, has been much venerated for centuries by pilgrims and seamen. The church itself contains a fascinating and moving collection of votive paintings and objects associated with the miraculous interventions of the Virgin for saving the lives of sailors and travellers. The most venerable object for devotion is the diminutive early icon of the *Virgin and Child* placed within a much later Corinthian tabernacle

9.30 Gothic censer in the form of a tower, Florence?, *c.* 1460–70, unmarked silver, Monastery Museum of the church of the Assumption, Orebić. Photo: Živko Bačić.

9.31 Antonio del Pollaiuolo, study for a Gothic censer in the form of a tower, pen and wash with red-brown ink, Gabinetto Disegni e Stampe, Uffizi, Florence. Photo: courtesy of the Soprintendenza Speciale per il Patrimonio Storico, Artistico ed Etnoantropologico e per il Polo Museale della città di Firenze, Gabinetto Fotografico

and surrounded by carved figures of angels and seraphim. This must have been relocated to make way for the impressive high altar, a polyptych set within a grand frame of triumphal arch format. The main image is of the *Immaculate Conception Adored by Saints and Angels*, dated 1599, which seems to be by the Venetian Pietro Malombra (1556–1618). Above, in the attic, is an *Annunciation* and beneath, flanking the *Immacolata*, are four Franciscan saints in round-headed lateral panels, the pairs placed one above the other. There is a small museum housed within the monastic buildings that surround the fifteenth-century cloister. It contains the original of the *Madonna and Child* on the facade, which has been replaced by a copy. This sculpture may be by the so-called Master of the Marble Madonnas, who has been variously identified as Tomaso Fiamberti (fl. 1498–1524/5) or Giovanni Ricci (1470–1523), two artists who regularly collaborated. It is, however, now thought that this so-called 'Master' was not either of these sculptors, but a Tuscan working in the Marche *c.* 1470–1500. There is also a *Virgin and Child* of *c.* 1465 carved in stone by Niccolò Fiorentino or his workshop. Of particular interest is the fantastic silver censer with the upper section formed like an elaborate Gothic turret, bristling with a forest of pinnacles, crockets and pierced windows (fig. 9.30). It was made *c.* 1460–70, possibly in Florence, and is related to a variant design signed by Antonio del Pollaiuolo (1431/2–98) now in the Print Room of the Uffizi, Florence (fig. 9.31). The censer may have been made and purchased for the church at the same time as the two Madonna reliefs. Were the censer to be of Dalmatian rather than Florentine workmanship, it might well still follow a Pollaiuolo drawing, for we do know that when Giorgio da Sebenico left Squarcione's studio in Padua in 1461 to return to Zadar, he brought with him drawings by Pollaiuolo.[71]

Another treasure in this museum is a rare painting by Andrea Lilio of Ancona

9.32 Andrea Lilio, *St Francis of Paola*, signed and dated 160(?9), oil on canvas, Monastery Museum of the church of the Assumption, Orebić. Photo: Živko Bačić.

(1555–1616); this distinctive and talented follower of Barocci also worked in the Roman church of San Girolamo dei Schiavoni just beside Palazzo Borghese.[72] It is signed and dated 160(?9). This tall, narrow panel represents *St Francis of Paola*, the celebrated founder of the Minims. The venerable old friar is portrayed with bald head bowed and flowing beard. He stands within a sculpted niche and leans on his staff while holding a rosary (fig. 9.32). The saint, who is identified by the artist on an ornamental *trompe l'oeil* tablet beneath, once formed part of a triptych, but the companion panels were lost in a fire.

To sum up, this account of the Italian treasures in Dalmatia is by no means comprehensive. You will have to consult the next chapter to learn about Dubrovnik. I am very aware that some key towns and islands like Lošinj, Poreč, Cres and Lastovo have been omitted, and this was because I have written only about works that I had examined in the original. This has meant that what appears to be a superb Bartolomeo Vivarini *sacra conversazione* in the church of St Anthony in Veli Lošinj has been omitted. I have not visited Poreč to see the basilica of Euphrasius with its fine mosaics and, even more important in my context, the Antonio Vivarini polyptych in the little museum situated next door in the former Bishop's Palace. So this account should be taken only as an introduction to a complex and intriguing subject. I have discussed the work of architects, painters, sculptors, engravers, goldsmiths and potters, and I do believe this discussion proves that Italian art and artefacts were dispersed liberally all around the Adriatic and that it is short sighted, if not foolish, to believe that great Italian art is confined only to the western shores of the Adriatic. The pattern of patronage in Dalmatia *c.* 1400 to 1800 is becoming clearer, for the close connections between artists in Croatia and in Italy itself are now widely recognised.

DUBROVNIK: ITALIAN ART, *c.* 1400–1800

Timothy Clifford

The reason for treating Dubrovnik (Ragusa) separately from the rest of the Dalmatian littoral is that during the period under discussion this state was a sovereign republic and not, like the rest of Dalmatia, subjected to the colonial control of the Serenissima. This is to not to say that, as Dubrovnik was no Venetian vassal, the influence of Italian art was minimal; far from it, for the republic in matters artistic was entirely Italianate, even if a little less dependent on the paramount influence of Venice. This is in contrast to the rest of the Dalmatian coast. Dubrovnik is the most southerly city of Croatia. As an entity, the republic consisted of the ancient and strategically positioned fortified port of Dubrovnik (Grad, literally 'The City'), the tiny island of Lokrum (on which was sited a Benedictine monastery), the deep and well-protected bay of Gruž (which was where Dubrovnik built its ships after 1525), and Lapad (a forested peninsula to the west of the old city where merchants with humanist ambitions built extraordinary Renaissance villas between 1520 and 1580). The republic also comprised Ston and the Pelješac peninsula (or 'Ston Point') and inshore islands like Šipan, Lopud, Mljet (instituted as a *lazzaretto* or quarantine station in 1397) and Daksa. There were other suburban areas clustered closer around Dubrovnik like Trsteno, Lokrum, and Cavtat.[1]

Dubrovnik, as the rival trading nation of Venice in the Adriatic, suffered from a long history of war with that state and from periods of martial suppression by it. As part of the Byzantine Empire *c.* 998–1000, it was first defeated by Doge Pietro II Orseolo and had to submit to Venetian rule. After a brief respite of Norman dominance, it was again ruled by Venice between 1125 and 1145. Then, having shaken off Venetian shackles, Dubrovnik was attacked and conquered yet again by Venice in 1171, but between 1186 and 1192 it was obliged to accept Norman overlordship as a means of resisting its two major enemies of Venice and Serbia, before returning to its ancient allegiance to the Byzantine Empire. In 1202 a Venetian fleet seized Dubrovnik and for the next 150 years it was ruled by Venice with a count (or rector) and a bishop sent from there. Then, in 1358, with the Treaty of Zadar, Dubrovnik became effectively independent under the suzerainty of the Hungaro-Croatian kings, who exercised very light authority over the city. The people of Dubrovnik started to style themselves 'Republica Ragusina' and began to build for

themselves, independent of Venice, a major fleet of armed ocean-going merchantmen.

In 1374 Dubrovnik received permission from Pope Gregory IX to trade 'ad partes Saracenorum'. This papal permission to trade with the Muslim world was confirmed by the Treaty of Basel in 1433. In 1442 Dubrovnik entered upon a concerted course of non-alignment and began to pay annually to the sultan of Turkey a massive tribute (*harač*) in return for favourable trading concessions, as noted in the previous chapter. The state henceforth studiously avoided joining in Christian wars against its Muslim neighbours and remained steadfastly Catholic. This arrangement suited the Turks, allowing Dubrovnik to be the key entrepôt in the Adriatic between East and West. Like Switzerland, or perhaps even more like Hong Kong, it waxed rich and powerful. Dubrovnik, however, remained ever wary of the Turks and of its Orthodox Slav neighbours. It never felt it could depend on non-aggression pacts and treaties. Accordingly, Dubrovnik continued to build up a most powerful fleet, providing special privileges to its sailors, and above all spent a considerable proportion of its wealth in making its fortifications among the most impregnable in the Adriatic.[2]

Many artists from the fourteenth century to the mid-seventeenth century subscribed to the concept of the *uomo universale*, as envisaged by the likes of Leon Battista Alberti (1404–72). They were used to the idea of 'multiple tasking' and could be employed as architects, sculptors, painters, hydraulic and military engineers, medallists, designers (in general) and spies (in particular). Dubrovnik, for good reason, remained fearful of Venice and so employed artists who were not Venetian natives

10.1 Design by Onofrio di Giordano della Cava with sculptures carved by Pietro di Martino, *Small Fountain*, *c.* 1436, Dubrovnik. Photo: Živko Bačić.

10.2 Michelozzo di Bartolomeo, *Minčeta Tower*, 1462–4, Dubrovnik. Photo: Živko Bačić.

for key tasks. The City, apart from high and stout walls, depended upon a plentiful supply of clean drinking water and also water for industrial purposes. Onofrio di Giordano della Cava (fl. 1438–55), a Neapolitan architect and engineer, was called in by the Dubrovnik Senate in 1435–6 to build an aqueduct. He was assisted by Andreucci di Bulbito from Apulia.[3] The aqueduct carried water from a mainspring at Šumet in Rijeka Dubrovačka along a channel of 11,700 metres to the city reservoir, depending on gravity with an incline from beginning to end of only twenty metres. When completed, seventy litres of water per second could flow along it. The water was distributed within the city to reservoirs and fountains, namely Onofrio's Great Fountain which one sees soon after entering Dubrovnik from the Western (or Pile) Gate in front of the convent of the Poor Clares. This was a much more handsome fountain when first constructed, but it was severely damaged by the great earthquake of 1667. Water also flowed to Onofrio's Small Fountain by the gate of the Arsenal, placed on the eastern side of the city to supply the marketplace in the main Luža Square (fig. 10.1). Set in a round-headed niche, the octagonal basin is carved with reliefs of putti carrying emblems of the zodiac; above them is a smaller basin carved with masks through which the water gushes,

surrounded by dense foliage with a finial of dolphins suspended, rather awkwardly, by their tails. The sculptures, now coarsened from wear and weathering, were carved by Pietro di Martino of Milan. The hydraulic specialist was the same Onofrio della Cava who was later to rebuild the Rector's Palace.

In 1439 at the Council of Florence, the Orthodox and Catholic churches, faced with the imminent danger of the Turkish menace, made a pact. Emperor John VIII Paleologus of Byzantium requested help from Pope Eugenius IV, which was provided, but the resultant great Christian force that was sent out to attack the Muslims was defeated at the battle of Varna in November 1444, when its paramount commander, the king of Hungary, was killed. Then, in May 1453, Constantinople fell to the Turks. This defeat had dire consequences for the Christian world, particularly for the states bordering the Adriatic. In 1459 Serbia ceased to exist; meanwhile in 1461 the Ragusan Senate, feeling particularly threatened by the Turks, who had now begun a dramatic advance through Bosnia, turned to the urgent task of strengthening Dubrovnik's fortifications. Earlier in 1430 the Dubrovnik Senate had insisted that the construction work of the city fortifications be carried out 'non tanto per la belleza, quanto la fortezza' (not so much for beauty as for strength).[4] The new task of fortification was entrusted to Michelozzo di Bartolomeo, the great Tuscan architect and sculptor famed for building the Medici Palace in Florence, who was summoned to Ragusa on 4 May 1462. Between 1462 and 1464 he reconstructed the Minčeta Tower (fig. 10.2) on the land side of the city, which now became the highest point of the wall. This was according to a wooden model supplied by the architect in June 1461. Upon the quadrilateral base of the old tower he placed a great round tower linked to the scarp walls. On its upper storey was a series of massive gun ports to provide all-round defensive fire, while, above, a high but much narrower round tower was constructed by Juraj Matejev (Giorgio da Sebenico) of Zadar. Between 1462 and 1464 Michelozzo was also employed constructing the Puncijela Tower, the Revelin Fortress at the Ploče Gate to the east, and the Bokar Fortress on the west of the city.[5]

One might well ask why so many Italians rather than fellow Slavs were employed by the Ragusan Republic. After the fall of what are now called Bosnia and Hercegovina, Serbia and much of Croatia to Turkey, the pool of Christian Slavs available was severely reduced. The Ragusan Republic demanded the highest standards; their patricians were rich, spoke Italian and could afford to recruit people of exceptional talent. The other major Ragusan patron of the arts was the Church. The two great mendicant orders, the Dominicans and the Franciscans, arrived in Dubrovnik by 1225 and 1235 respectively, and these religious houses not only recruited their monks largely in Italy but were used to employing Italian architects, painters, sculptors and craftsmen.

Notably, Michelozzo was given the post of strengthening Dubrovnik's fortifications against the competition of two other Italians, Bernardino of Parma (who had already remodelled the harbour) and 'Pavao the Goldsmith' or Paolo of Ragusa (1420–79), the medallist who designed and cast several medals of King Alfonso V of Naples and a medal of Federigo da Montefeltro. Paolo, a sometime collaborator of Donatello, went on, like Gentile Bellini, to work for Sultan Mehmed II. In 1464 Michelozzo put forward plans for rebuilding the Rector's Palace that were rejected by the Ragusan Senate; he then flounced back to Italy. The Senate was legendary for its conservatism and prudence where monetary matters were concerned. In 1465 it appears that the Italophile Juraj Matejev also left Dubrovnik's service, and so the continuing task of refortifying the city fell to a local, Paskoje Miličević, who then went on to serve the republic faithfully for fifty-one years. The Dubrovnik senators kept up to date with the latest fortification innovations, especially to counteract the serious threats during the War of the First Holy League (1537–40). In 1538–9 they employed, through the agency of Andrea Doria of Genoa (Spain's great admiral), the services of the celebrated civil engineer Antonio Ferramolino of Bergamo. He was consulted on the Revelin Fortress, which is on the north-eastern approach to

the harbour, a building started by Michelozzo and then completed to his renewed specifications. These fortifications were erected to withstand not so much Turkish as Venetian attack.

For the period under discussion the Ragusan Republic was a complex aristocratic oligarchy under its rector (or Ragusan count), a ceremonial figurehead who served in office for one month only – he could be re-elected but not consecutively – and ruled *primus inter pares*. He controlled three councils: the first, the Major Council, was composed of all adult male patricians. They then elected the Senate and the Minor Council. Until 1401 the Senate had fifty-one members, but was later increased by ten, and it was this body that held significant power. The Minor Council was the executive body, an organ used by both the Senate and the Major Council. The term of office for all three councils was one year. All major posts in government and administration were held by patricians. By this quasi-democratic series of checks and balances no tyrant could exercise supreme power, and power remained firmly in the hands of the patrician class. It was a system of government, indeed, not unlike that of Venice.[6]

Many of the magistracies were also based on Venetian equivalents. The three Proctors of St Mary ('Procuratori di Santa Maria') were appointed for life to supervise the income and expenditure of the cathedral and to provide for the poor, much like the Venetian Procuratori di San Marco. Six Dubrovnik nobles called Lords of the Night ('Signori della Notte') were designated to keep the town secure and orderly after dark, and they also had counterparts of the same name in Venice. The city doctors were never Ragusans and always either Jews or Italians, while the most important non-noble and non-Ragusan officers were the six chancellors or secretaries of the Ragusan government. Five out of these six were customarily Italian. Dubrovnik's schoolmasters were also usually Italian. Even in times of the greatest danger to the republic, Italians were employed in key strategic posts: for example, in 1463 an Apulian *condottiere* was employed as commander of the republic's pikemen, while in 1655 the chief bombadier of the city was Antonio Vanini, who was probably from Tuscany.[7]

We approach the city by its main entrance, the Pile Gate, on the west over the dry moat across a stone bridge. The first form of this bridge was built in 1397 by Giovanni da Siena, but its replacement was constructed by the local fortifications expert, Paskoje Miličević. We pass under an arch with a statue of St Blaise (Sv. Vlaho) set in a richly decorated niche. The hieratic figure of the bishop is flanked by Corinthian pilasters which support a frieze ornamented by two putti supporting a column. The frieze with flying putti is taken from *ephoebe* (spirits) carved on Roman sarcophagi, a form frequently borrowed by Donatello and his circle. Although the gate in its present shape dates from 1537, the earlier 'Gothic' gate was built in 1460, and I suspect that the tabernacle of St Blaise was simply reused on the present facade. We pass to the right of the Great Fountain by Onofrio della Cava

houses of uniform proportions, three storeys high, four bays wide with two shops below *na koljeno* (literally, 'on the knee' or *inginocchio*). They were all built after the great earthquake which struck on the morning of 6 April in Holy Week, 1667. The combination of earthquake, tidal wave and fire wrought terrible damage to the fabric of the city and resulted in massive loss of life. The late medieval and Renaissance *palazzi* which flanked the Placa were nearly all destroyed, as were several churches including the cathedral. The Placa as we see it today was built to the plan and elevation of the Roman civil and military engineer Giulio Cerutti (fl. 1660–98), who arrived in the summer of 1667 and was recruited by Stjepan Gradić in Rome. Gradić, the key figure in the rebuilding of Dubrovnik, will be discussed later.[8]

The first church we pass on the left-hand side is the church of the Holy Saviour (San Salvatore, Sv. Spas), a tiny votive structure erected by order of the Senate in 1520 in gratitude for the city being spared from destruction by an earlier earthquake on Ascension day, 17 May 1520. It was built by Petar Andrijić of Korčula (fl. 1492–1553) in the Venetian manner, following the Mauro Codussi formula much favoured in Dalmatia, of three bays with a rose window in the attic flanked by pilasters, and crowned by

10.3 Pierantonio Palmerini, *The Ascension, c.* 1527, oil on canvas, church of the Holy Saviour, Dubrovnik. Photo: Božo Gjukić.

(1438) and look straight ahead down the Placa or Stradun (Latin *platea* = street), the great wide street that divides the city into northern and southern halves from the Pile Gate down to the bell tower and Luža Square. The street was created at the end of the eleventh century. By the close of the following century, the city was surrounded by a high single wall. The Placa, as we now see it, is flanked to the north and south by a row of elegant

a clover-leaf gable. The interior boasts a handsome, although rather archaic, altarpiece appropriately of the *Ascension* (fig. 10.3) painted *c.* 1527 by that rare Marchigian artist Pierantonio Palmerini (fl. 1518–38), who was taught by Timoteo Viti (1469–1523), although he was also much influenced by the Urbino court painter Girolamo Genga (*c.* 1476–1551). He rented a house in Dubrovnik in 1526. In the agreements Palmerini was

10.4 Giovanni Toschini, *Risen Christ*, marble, Franciscan church, Dubrovnik. Photo: Božo Gjukić.

10.5 Pharmacy with apothecary jars, Franciscan church, Dubrovnik. Photo: Živko Bačić.

assisted by the unknown Jacopo di Marco. Here the Virgin kneels surrounded by the twelve apostles, her head raised pleading in intercession for the city of Dubrovnik (situated in the background left) towards the ascending Christ in a golden mandorla, who is surrounded by angels and putti throwing down bunches of roses. Painted in 1527, it cost 150 scudi and follows closely the *bozzetto* by Palmerini now in the Pinacoteca Comunale, Fossombrone, which it is thought may have come originally from the local church of San Filippo. The main differences between the *bozzetto* and the altarpiece are that there is a pool of water and a dog in the foreground of the altarpiece that are omitted in the *bozzetto*, the background buildings are omitted in the *bozzetto*, and there are marked differences in the shape of the clouds.[9] The form and disposition of Christ and the cherubim are so like a red chalk drawing by Genga in the National Gallery of Scotland that one might be excused for presuming that Palmerini was here using an idea, or maybe even a cartoon, by Genga.[10]

Next to the church of the Holy Saviour is the Franciscan monastery. This complex was erected from 1317 on its present site, but the monastic church was destroyed in the great earthquake of 1667, leaving the cloister and some of the conventual buildings untouched. The handsome main portal facing onto the Placa of *c.* 1498 is by the local masons Leonard and Petar Petrović. It consists of pilaster strips ornamented with three tiers of tabernacles, empty but for blind traceries, the upper tier containing statues of St Jerome and St John the Baptist, flanking a flamboyant lunette enclosing a carved Pietà (following a German prototype), and culminating in a corbel supporting an image of God the Father. This portico was saved from the ruined church, and re-erected when the church was rebuilt. In design it follows the much grander Porta della Carta of the Ducal Palace, Venice.

The Franciscan church (Chiesa dei Frati Minori) has an undecorated facade fronting the Placa with five triangular-headed windows springing from a string course that light a sequence of symmetrical baroque side altars from above. At the west end is a handsome organ and choir loft, while at the high altar, at the east end, is a fine full-sized statue of the *Risen Christ* standing within a tabernacle supported by salamonic, or barley sugar, columns (fig. 10.4). The *Risen Christ* was carved by Giovanni Toschini (fl. 1690–1735), a sculptor from Carrara who had once worked alongside Domenico Parodi of Genoa, sometime assistant of Bernini. Certainly, the pose and disposition of the drapery is reminiscent of Bernini. There are four tabernacle side altars carved in 1685 by one 'Iseppo Sardi', who was Giuseppe Sardi, a minor sculptor of Venice (1631–99). One of these tabernacles encloses a magnificent image of the *Immaculate Conception and God the Father*, the finest painting in the church, which is ascribed to Carlo Maratti (1625–1713) but which may be Neapolitan and seems closer to Massimo Stanzione (*c.* 1585–*c.* 1658). It is reminiscent of Stanzione's *Coronation of the Virgin* at San Giovanni Battista delle

Monache, Naples. We should not overlook the carpentry of the confessionals, which is elegantly Borromini-like with handsome, shapely, broken cornices.

The Franciscan apothecary next door to the church is historically of considerable antiquity. Started in 1317, it is claimed to be the third oldest continually functioning apothecary in the world. The wooden shelves and cupboards, redecorated in the mid-nineteenth century, contain wet and dry drug jars including many from the Marche and Abruzzi, including handsome tall-necked globular bottles with inscribed banderoles that appear to have been made in Urbino or Pesaro in the early sixteenth century (fig. 10.5). Another eight drug jars decorated with identical banderoles are in the Museo Communale, Città di Castello.

The sacristy to the north-west contains an unusual reliquary cupboard in the form of a polyptych, also by Pierantonio Palmerini, for which there are payments of 18 August 1528 in the Ragusan archives.[11] This cupboard, currently in the course of conservation, is both an unusual structure and also of special interest as being by this rare named artist. The interior consists of thirty-three pigeonholes that contained reliquaries; the covering polyptych is made up of three doors, the inside faces of which have full-length figures of *St Blaise Holding a Model of Dubrovnik*, *St Jerome Holding a Model of the Franciscan Church* and *St Francis in Ecstasy*. The outside face is painted with the *Resurrection* flanked by standing figures of *St Michael* and *St Luke* and, above, the *Annunciation to the Virgin*. The elaborately carved frame incorporates in the bottom corners an armorial (a ladder *or*, on a field *gules*, in the canton an eagle displayed *sable*, on a field *or*). These arms, which are of the patron Luka Bunić, also recur in some of the capitals of the stone pilasters in the sacristy. The sacristy also contains an elaborate stone *lavabo* with a central stone beam carved with three putto heads.[12] It is almost certainly Italian work of around 1520, as is the elaborate intarsia panelling decorated with *grottesche*, candelabra motifs and confronted griffons.

The conventual buildings to the north-east contain a gallery filled with works of art. There is a fine *Ecce Homo* by Francesco Raiboldini, called 'Francia' of Bologna (1450–1517), painted *c.* 1498, showing the head and shoulders of the weeping Christ as the Man of Sorrows.[13] He is tied to a column with a glimpse through a window to the left showing a mountainous Italianate landscape. The panel is finely preserved, demonstrating Francia's goldsmith-like attention to minutiae (he was trained as a goldsmith) with the fine delineation of Christ's curling hair and biforcate beard, the reflections in his watery tears and his forehead with thorns driven into the living flesh. It is a moving image of the Saviour suffering not so much from his own wounds as from the sins of the whole world.

10.6 Here attributed to Giovanni Battista Gaulli, called 'il Baciccio', and studio, *St Francis and St Helen Adoring the True Cross*, oil on canvas, ?*c.* 1685–6, Franciscan monastery museum, Dubrovnik. Photo: Vlaho Pustić.

10.7 Beltrand Gallicus, relief of two flying angels supporting the Holy Name of Jesus, 1520–1, Sponza Palace courtyard, Dubrovnik. Photo: Živko Bačić.

10.8 Anonymous Italian sculptor, relief of two kneeling angels supporting the Holy Name of Jesus, 1481, Ruđer Bošković Square, Dubrovnik. Photo: Vlaho Pustić.

Upstairs in the Friars Minor library, which contains 20,000 books including 137 incunables, there is a good copy of *Christ and the Samaritan Woman* after the original at Capodimonte, Naples, by Lavinia Fontana (1552–1614). Downstairs there is a good old copy of the *Virgin and Child with St John and St Anne* painted by the Bolognese Annibale Carracci (1560–1609) of *c.* 1597–8, of which the original, formerly in the Peretti-Montalto collection, is in the National Gallery, London. An old copy is in the Strossmayer Gallery, Zagreb (cat. no. 170), but excludes the figure of St Anne. Of much greater interest is the major altarpiece removed from the monastic church next door, which shows *St Francis and St Helen Adoring the True Cross* (fig. 10.6). It is superscribed with the initials IHS and, beneath, the sacred heart pierced by three nails. Below and between the two kneeling saints sits a putto holding a crown, which is very similar in form to the Hungarian crown that surmounts the coat of arms of the Ragusan Republic. It does not seem to have been noted before that this is a major altarpiece by Giovanni Battista Gaulli, 'il Baciccio'

(1639–1709). This celebrated Genoese artist was much favoured by Bernini in Rome, and the *bozzetto* for it is in the Pinacoteca Comunale at Deruta. The *bozzetto* originally belonged to the artist's biographer, Lione Pascoli of Perugia, and is inscribed on the back in what appears to be Pascoli's own hand: 'de Batista Gaulli do. Baciccio [u]omo eccelentissimo'. The same museum also contains a *bozzetto* of the *Lawgivers and Leaders of Israel* by Baciccio for his fresco in the Gesù, Rome, and the *Four Evangelists* also for the Gesù, both from Pascoli's collection. They date from *c.* 1676, which led Professor Engass to date the *bozzetto* to this same period.[14] Certainly, the Dubrovnik picture would appear to have been painted after the earthquake of 6 April 1667, and perhaps as late as the *Putto with the Emblems of Ludovico Gaulli* in the Collegio Nazareno, Rome, which was commissioned as late as 1686.[15] We also know that what was probably its original marble altar frame (now containing a nineteenth-century replacement) was supplied to the Franciscan church by Giuseppe Sardi in 1685–6. The patron is as yet unclear, but it may have been commissioned by the Ragusan Confraternity of the Holy Name of Jesus. We must pause to consider how such a picture would have been commissioned in Rome after the great earthquake. Certainly, the key figure from Dubrovnik would have been Stjepan Gradić (1613–83) in Rome. Gradić was a Ragusan aristocrat, cleric, diplomat, scholar and patriot. He had received a scholarship from the Ragusan Republic to study in Rome and, by the time of the earthquake, was already deputy keeper of the Vatican Library and the most important Croatian within the Vatican. He befriended several cardinals, including the future Pope Alexander VII Chigi (1655–67) and Pope Innocent XII Pamphilij (1691–1700). On four occasions he served as the president of the Croatian Confraternity of St Jerome and worked tirelessly on overcoming the problems of setting up the Jesuit College in Dubrovnik. At this time he was working as the subordinate of the cardinal protector

10.9 Maso di Bartolomeo and others, *Great Cloister*, 1456–83, Dominican monastery, Dubrovnik. Photo: Milan Pelc.

10.10 Paolo Veneziano, *Crucifixion with Symbols of the Four Evangelists Flanked by the Virgin and St John the Evangelist*, c. 1348–52, tempera and gold leaf on panel, church of St Dominic, Dubrovnik. Photo: Živko Bačić.

situated, hence the name Sponza (Spongia-Alluvium). It later housed the customs house, bonded warehouses, the mint, the bank, treasury and armoury. Its design (built 1517–23), which is very Italianate, part Gothic and part Renaissance, was by Paskoje Miličević of Ragusa, deriving partly from Venetian models. The main facade onto the Placa consists of an open, round-headed loggia supported on Corinthian columns of five bays on the ground floor with, on the *piano nobile*, a large rectangular window, its Gothic tracery supporting three quatrefoils. This window is, incidentally, copied directly from that on the Palazzo Loredan dell'Ambasciatore on the Grand Canal, Venice. The Sponza Palace window is flanked by two flamboyant Gothic windows, while a third storey, lit by simple bolection moulded rectangular windows, is interrupted in the central bay by a tabernacle housing a statue of St Blaise. The building has a hip roof, the cornice decorated by free-standing palmette antifixes.

of Dubrovnik, Giulio Barberini. By Gradić's diplomatic devices he skilfully ensured that the republic was not involved in Pope Alexander VII's anti-Ottoman schemes. From the correspondence it is clear that Gradić was deeply concerned in all aspects of the restoration and beautification of Dubrovnik after the earthquake.[16]

The Franciscan monastery contains a fine cope and hood in crimson and yellow cut-silk velvet decorated with coronets surmounted by rosettes, palm fronds and laurel. This is reminiscent of velvets designed by Gianlorenzo Bernini and his assistant Giovanni Paolo Schorr (1605–67) for Pope Alexander VII. It is like a *Study for Embroidery with the Chigi 'Stemma'* in the Gabinetto Nazionale delle Stampe, Rome.[17]

Leaving the Franciscan monastery and continuing on down the Placa to the end, one sees the Sponza Palace (or Divona), which contains the State Archives. The building was originally where a massive communal cistern for collecting rainwater was

The carved decoration (post-1516), is all by the brothers Nikola and Josip Andrijić of Korčula. The interior courtyard, consisting of two storeys of round-headed arches, culminates high up on the northern wall with a handsome low-relief carving of two flying angels supporting the Holy Name of Jesus within a wreath of fruit, an entirely Florentine device deriving ultimately from Verrocchio but carved by a certain (otherwise unknown) Frenchman, Beltrand Gallicus or 'Boltranius Francigena', in 1520–1 (fig. 10.7). This composition has, however, a direct Dubrovnik precedent, a yet finer relief of the same subject in Ruđer Bošković Square beside the Jesuit church. Dated 1481, it has clearly been resited, having been salvaged after the great earthquake, and formed a lunette over a doorway. It does seem to be by a Tuscan hand (fig. 10.8).

Passing behind the Sponza Palace to the north-east, one finds the Dominican monastery with its outer northern wall being one and same as the city wall.[18] The monastery was started in 1225

10.11 Antonio de Bellis, *Virgin with St Blaise and St Francis with a View of Dubrovnik*, *c*. 1657–8, oil on canvas, Dominican Monastery Museum, Dubrovnik. Photo: Živko Bačić.

and not completed until 1314. The church, begun in 1301, like a massive barn, follows the 'hallenkirche' formula used by the mendicant orders, and culminates in a polygonal apse at the east end (like the basilica of St Francis at Assisi). It is separated from the nave by three tall Gothic arches, the high altar lit by two lancet windows. The interior is now once again austere and simple, for all subsequent baroque decorations have been removed. As it is now, it resembles closely the interior of the Franciscan church of the late thirteenth century at Pula. The bell tower (*c*. 1390) was designed by a certain Checo di Monopoli. It contains, among other bells, one cast by Bartolomeo di Cremona (1458). The Great Cloister (fig. 10.9), loosely based on Michelozzo's designs for a cloister wall in Santa Croce, Florence, was built by a squad of local masons to the design of the Florentine sculptor and bronze castor Maso di Bartolomeo (1406–56), an associate of Donatello, Michelozzo, and Luca della Robbia. He was principally employed

as the official founder/smelter of weaponry for the republic. The greatest treasure of the church is the Rood, a crucifix within a lacy, florid frame with trefoil terminals decorated with the symbols of the Evangelists flanked by attenuated figures of the Virgin and St John the Divine, both within crocketed, shaped panels, terminating in poppy heads (fig. 10.10).[19] Donated according to the will of Šimun Restić of 1348, it is a masterpiece by Paolo Veneziano (*c*. 1300–62) dating from *c*. 1348–52, and must number among the most refined and magical treasures in Croatia.

The church would once have been rich in altarpieces; most of these have been removed and are now displayed in the Dominican monastic museum. The church was heavily damaged by the 1667 earthquake, and the interior was largely restored in the classical baroque taste with a series of stone Corinthian tabernacles enclosing altarpieces, including two large oils (*c*. 1680) by a Neapolitan pupil of Domenichino, Francesco di Maria (1623–90). One shows *St Anne Surrounded by St Andrew, the Blessed Margaret of Savoy, St Catherine of Siena, St Anthony Pierozzi, St Raymond of Penaforte and St Hyacinth*. The second, a poorer picture, shows the *Virgin and Child with Saints* and includes a crude image of St Thomas Aquinas added by a certain Carmelo Reggio (d. 1819) at the request of the monastery. Also in the monastery museum is a masterpiece by Antonio de Bellis of Naples (fl. 1640–60) of the *Virgin with St Blaise and St Francis with a View of Dubrovnik* (fig. 10.11), painted before the 1667 earthquake and so providing an invaluable document of what the city must have looked like *c*. 1657–8. It would be interesting to know why the Dominicans were commissioning so many pictures at that time from Neapolitans. One of the most significant masterpieces is the recently conserved *Mary Magdalen with St Blaise, the Archangel Raphael, Tobias and a Donor* by Titian (Pieve di Cadore, 1488/90–1576) (fig 10.12), a work – sadly maltreated in the past – that was sensitively conserved in 2001–6 by the Croatian Conservation Institute, Zagreb.[20] The composition shows, upon a low step, St Mary Magdalen, centre, standing wearing a white shift, her hands clasped in prayer, looking up to heaven. To the left is the vigorous figure of the mitred St Blaise, with venerable white beard, in full canonicals holding a model of Dubrovnik. He turns in profile to the right looking towards the Magdalen, his short crimson velvet cope swirling to reveal his white cassock. The Archangel Raphael and Tobias with his fish protect the sombre kneeling figure of the donor wearing black. Thunderous steel-grey clouds silhouette a golden sunset. The painting was first recorded as 'a work of the celebrated Titian' by the Dominican Serafino Razzi in *La Storia di Ragusa* (Lucca 1595) when it was in the Dominican church on the altar of St Mary Magdalen. The picture's patron is undocumented, although he is

10.12 Titian, *Mary Magdalen with St Blaise, the Archangel Raphael, Tobias and a Donor*, ?*c*. 1549, oil on canvas, Dominican Monastery Museum, Dubrovnik. Photo: Vidoslav Barac, Croatian Conservation Institute.

10.13 Follower of Lorenzo di Credi (perhaps the so-called Tommaso), tondo of the *Holy Family*, mixed technique on panel, Dominican Monastery Museum, Dubrovnik. Photo: Živko Bačić.

the powerful influence of Leonardo at this moment on Florentine painting. Much later, and quite unexpected in a Croatian context, is the superb altarpiece of the *Descent of the Holy Ghost* (fig. 10.14) by Santi di Tito (1536–1603), also a native of Florence. This major altarpiece shows the apostles and disciples kneeling in an upper room (of elegant Vasarian architecture), with the Virgin Mary in the centre, all looking up as the Holy Ghost appears in a burst of flame. In the right-hand corner the venerable bearded donor, Vice Stjeporić Skočibuha (1534–88), humbly kneels. A drawing of the same subject by Santi di Tito is in the Uffizi, Florence, while the subject was painted again in 1593–8 for the Company of Santo Spirito, a confraternity associated with the church of San Vincenzo Martire at Prato.[22]

Before the earthquake of 1667, the interior of the church must have looked spectacular. The main altar of the fifteenth century was paid for by Anne, widow of Jakov Menčetić. It was of porphyry articulated by pillars with elegantly shaped capitals and arches. In 1422 a *paliotto* ornamented with silver-gilt sculptures of saints was ordered for it from Nicola di Lorenzo of Florence, then living in Dubrovnik. The Dominicans, not entirely satisfied with this, erected an even grander one ornamented with figures of Saints Peter, Paul, John, Dominic, Peter Martyr, Thomas Aquinas, Blaise, Mary Magdalen and other saints (up to eighteen large figures and some smaller figures of angels and prophets). It was partly paid for by the goldsmith Pietro Panifani of Sermoneta in Lazio. Serafino Razzi wrote of it in 1595: 'The altar is so beautiful that – they say – together with the other silver, it is worth 100,000 ducats … It is exhibited only during important religious holidays; otherwise it is locked away in a wooden cabinet that is decorated with fine paintings of the same number of figures.' After 1667 the silver was sadly sold to raise funds for renovating the partly ruined monastery.[23]

Leaving the church you pass by the little church of Our Lady of the Rosary, which is affiliated to the Dominican monastery. It contains the tomb of the celebrated Sienese writer Camillo de Camillis (d. 1615), who was tutor to the great Croatian poet Ivan (Djivo) Gundulić. It also contains a handsome altarpiece, the *Virgin of the Rosary between St Dominic and St Catherine of Siena*, the hovering angels reminiscent of Guido Reni, and perhaps painted by Domenico Peruzzini (fl. 1640–61), working in Pesaro and Ancona, or his brother Giovanni Peruzzini (1629–94), who were both associates of Guido's main follower, Simone Cantarini. Certainly, a 'Peruzzini' appears in the monastic archives.

generally believed to have been a member of the patrician Pucić-Pozze family (possibly Damiano Pucić), but others have argued that it was commissioned by a member of the family of Count Gozzi. The presence of Tobias and the Archangel Raphael in association with the donor suggests, as is found with similar Florentine quattrocento images, that the donor is about to leave his native city journeying to foreign parts, and that the Archangel Raphael with Tobias will act as his interlocutors and guardians. At Dubrovnik it is argued that this Titian dates from the end of the fifth or beginning of the sixth decade of the sixteenth century, but I would argue rather earlier, perhaps a little before 1550, and it is, in my opinion, to a large extent autograph.

The museum also contains a precious small tondo of the *Holy Family* by a follower of Lorenzo di Credi (1456–1537) (fig. 10.13).[21] The composition shows the Virgin in a landscape within classical ruins, kneeling in prayer. She gazes at the Christ Child, bottom centre, who lies on his back playing with St John the Baptist to the right, while St Joseph, seated behind to the left, appears to shy away in consternation. The picture demonstrates

10.14 Santi di Tito,
*Descent of the Holy
Ghost*, oil on canvas,
Dominican Monastery
Museum, Dubrovnik.
Photo: Živko Bačić.

10.15 Marino Gropelli, portal of the House of the Main Guard, *c.* 1706–8, Dubrovnik. Photo: Vlaho Pustić.

RIGHT 10.16 Marino Gropelli, façade onto the Placa of the collegiate church of St Blaise with statues of Religion and Hope on balustrade, *c.* 1706–15, Dubrovnik. Photo: Jurica Skudar, Croatian Conservation Institute.

Retracing our steps from the complex of the Dominican monastery to the Placa, we see, to our left, the remarkable portal of the House of the Main Guard (fig. 10.15), a martial conceit, which is now the grandiloquent entrance to the Arsenal Wine Bar. The banded Tuscan Doric columns flank a rusticated arch with a head of the helmeted Mars as the keystone. The entablature sports four grenades and a most realistic looking mortar. It was originally intended for the gateway to the admiral's residence and is by the Venetian architect and sculptor Marino Gropelli (1662–1721) from 1706–8. Next to it is Onofrio's Small Fountain that has already been discussed. If one turns one's back on the fountain and looks to the right across Luža Square, one can see the collegiate church of St Blaise. The earlier church dating from the Romanesque period was badly damaged by the 1667 earthquake and then destroyed by fire on the night of 24–5 May 1706. It was rebuilt in 1706–15 in the baroque style also by Marino Gropelli (fig. 10.16). This centrally planned domed building is three bays wide and of two storeys. It is raised on a balustraded podium and approached by a wide flight of steps, providing an open-air stage for the pageantry of grand civic and religious functions. The facade onto the Placa, best described as neo-Palladian, follows the

format of a triumphal arch. It has a broad central bay pierced by a richly carved pedimented Corinthian doorway, flanked by two slightly narrower bays enclosing high, plain, rectangular windows with carved ornamental tablets beneath and, in the frieze above, crossed palm fronds. The richly carved cornice and entablature is supported by gigantic Corinthian cluster columns. The central bay of the upper storey consists of a Diocletian window, crowned by a statue of St Blaise supported on a rich console, with a balustraded parapet. The flanking bays terminate with statues of Religion and Hope (see fig. 10.16).

Both the building and its sculptural enrichments are by Marino Gropelli. He was the eldest son of the sculptor/mason Giovanni Battista Gropelli (1640–1714); Marino's sons Giuseppe and Paolo were also in the family sculpture business. Gropelli was called to Dubrovnik to reconstruct the church of St Blaise and was in the city by November 1706, remaining there until the end of 1715. When he arrived at Dubrovnik, Gropelli was already a well-attested sculptor in Venice, having carved six angels (1691–2) for the high altar of Santa Croce della Giudecca, now in San Antonio Abate at Lussingrande (Veli Lošinj). He also worked in 1693 on the facade of San Stae, Venice. In 1704 he was paid for the *paliotto* of the high altar of the marine sanctuary of Isola di Barbana in the Grado Lagoon, and in 1704–5 sculpted an angel for the high

10.17 Bishop's throne, Venice, *c.* 1715–20, carved and gilded wood, collegiate church of St Blaise, Dubrovnik. Photo: Božo Gjukić.

10.18 Salvi di Michele, façade of the Rector's Palace, 1467 onwards, Dubrovnik. Photo: Živko Bačić.

altar of the parish church of Fratta Polesine. Between 1702 and 1708 he carved the very fine relief of the *Victory of the Dardanelles* for the Valier monument in San Giovanni e Paolo, Venice. After completing St Blaise, Marino Gropelli returned to Venice, and worked at Udine and for the Russian court at St Petersburg. The quality of Marino's sculptural work in Dubrovnik is variable, which must suggest considerable workshop assistance.[24] St Blaise also contains early replicas of the *Four Evangelists* by, or after, the Neapolitan Mattia Preti (1613–99), which are identical to those in Our Lady of Carmel. Also notable is the splendid Venetian bishop's throne of the early eighteenth century richly carved with elaborate scrolled arms and feet incorporating demi-putti (fig. 10.17).

Passing down the east side of the church into Prid Dvorom we see, to the left, the Rector's Palace (Knežev dvor), perhaps the most venerable and splendid building in Dubrovnik (fig. 10.18), and like the Sponza Palace nearby, it combines elements of the Gothic and the Renaissance. The western facade is eight bays wide in two storeys, with the upper storey lit by Gothic two-light windows. On the lower storey the end bays are split into two with paired rectangular windows on the ground floor and paired Gothic arched windows above on the mezzanine. The centre of the lower storey consists of an open arched loggia articulated by five massive columns and two pilasters at either end, with plain shafts and elaborately carved capitals, from which spring round-headed arches. Its history is complex: the original building was part fortress, part palace, and where the count (and subsequently the rector) lived with the administration. It was also where weapons and large quantities of gunpowder were kept. On the

10.19 Pietro di Martino, Aesculapius capital (detail), Istrian stone, Rector's Palace, Dubrovnik. Photo: Goran Vranić.

10.20 Salvi di Michele, capital carved with fruit, foliage and putti, c. 1467, Istrian stone, Rector's Palace, Dubrovnik. Photo: Vlaho Pustić.

10.21 After Lelio Orsi da Novellara, *Lamentation*, c. 1563–9, oil on canvas, Rector's Palace museum and gallery, Dubrovnik. Photo: Miro Dvoršćak.

night of 10 August 1435 the ammunition supply ignited, destroying most of the structure. Onofrio della Cava of Naples was asked to design and build the new palace. The columns, from a quarry in Korčula, had capitals richly carved by Pietro di Martino from Milan. Many of these capitals depicted scenes of special allegorical significance. One surviving shows, for example, Aesculapius (fig. 10.19), the physician who was thought to have lived in Epidaurus (which was confused with Epidaurum/Cavtat), and a relief of the Judgement of Solomon, symbolic of the justice administered by the Ragusan patriciate. A figure of Justice at the top of the staircase which leads to the courtroom has the inscription: 'Iussi suma mei sua vos cuicumque tueri' (My highest duty is to protect your right). The administration had clearly not learnt from its earlier mistake of storing gunpowder, and the palace again blew up on the evening of 8 August 1463, damaging much of the southern part of the building. It was restored but then damaged again by the earthquakes of both 1520 and 1667. After the 1463 explosion, the Florentine Michelozzo submitted plans for the rebuilding of the palace, but these were rejected by the Major Council on 5 May 1464. The work was entrusted to local builders, with many of the capitals carved with fruit, foliage and putti (fig. 10.20) by Salvi di Michele of Florence, who also directed the reconstruction works from 1467.[25]

The interior now contains the museum and picture gallery. On display is an oil of the *Lamentation* of c. 1563–9 (fig. 10.21), an excellent early copy after Lelio Orsi da Novellara (1511–87), of which the original is now in the Museo di Palazzo Venezia, Rome.[26] The museum also contains a superb Neapolitan cabinet with painted drawer fronts on glass, framed by mouldings of ebony and tortoiseshell, supported on an elaborately carved and gilded stand (fig. 10.22).[27] Such cabinets, usually made in pairs, date from c. 1670–80, and the paintings are frequently copied from compositions by the Neapolitan Luca Giordano (1634–1705). Elsewhere a document of 1679 refers to a payment made to a certain Giovanni Battista Tara in Naples for a pair of such cabinets.[28] Similar ones were bought on the Grand Tour by Sir Thomas Isham and remain at

10.22 Cabinet, Naples, *c.* 1670–80, ebony, painted glass panels on carved and gilded wooden stand, Rector's Palace museum and gallery, Dubrovnik. Photo: Božo Gjukić.

10.23 Night clock, Roman, *c.* 1675–80, ebony with copper dial painted with *Cephalus and Aurora*, Rector's Palace museum and gallery, Dubrovnik. Photo: Božo Gjukić.

Lamport Hall, Northamptonshire, while another pair belongs to the Sitwells at Renishaw Hall, Derbyshire. The museum also owns one of those curious night clocks ('orologio della notte'), which has its copper dial painted with *Cephalus and Aurora*, perhaps by Gaulli's follower, the Roman Giovanni Odazzi (1663–1731) (fig. 10.23). The escapement is pendulum driven but, importantly, the hours are not struck. The dial is enclosed within an ebony altar-shaped frame, and the special feature is that a candle was placed behind the lug-shaped chapter ring, with the candlelight shining from the back through pierced Roman numerals. These silent clocks often had their dials painted by the most distinguished Roman artists of their day. They were invented by the Campani family of Genoa and Rome, and made originally to the order of Pope Alexander VII Chigi, who suffered from acute insomnia.[29] Stjepan Gradić of Dubrovnik, who was living in Rome in and after the great earthquake of 1667, had been a good friend of this pope, so one might have thought it was through Gradić's good offices that this clock came to the Rector's Palace. However, I now find it was acquired relatively recently with no such distinguished provenance recorded.

If we leave the Rector's Palace and turn to the left, we see

the great baroque cathedral. It originally dated from the eighth century but was destroyed in the 1667 earthquake. As we see it now, it was rebuilt (1671–1713, fig. 10.24) by Andrea Buffalini of Urbino (fl. 1656–73), an architect provided on Gradić's advice.[30] Much of the money for the rebuilding was raised by Gradić himself. It was completed long after Gradić's death, but his key role is recalled by the plaque that was placed by the grateful Senate on the cathedral's facade. The building is a Greek cross structure with a dome over the crossing. The pretty Corinthian facade of five bays and two storeys is in the Roman taste and very conservative. Its inspiration reflects many of the same forms and ideas of Carlo Maderno's delightful facade of Santa Susanna, Rome (1597–1603). The Ragusan Senate, if not knowing Santa Susanna, would at least have been familiar with Maderno's monumental facade of St Peter's of *c.* 1606.[31] Buffalini's plans were accepted in 1671, and work started in 1672 using, first, Paolo Andreotti of Genoa as master of works, followed by Antonio Bazzi of Genoa and then Friar Tommaso Napoli of Palermo. The cathedral was completed by a local architect and mason, Ilija Katičić, in 1713. Antonio Bazzi complained in 1680 when he left Dubrovnik that he had not been fully paid, and this we know greatly irritated Dubrovnik's cardinal-protector in Rome, Giulio Barberini. Stjepan Gradić continued to work tirelessly on the restoration of the city. Recently, Robin Harris observed of Gradić:

'It is, though, easy to imagine that those who received his exhortations and criticisms must have been heartily irritated by them. Gradić's starting point always seemed to be that everything in Italy was done better and that the provincials back home must copy it. The Ragusans were thus advised to use Italian-style carts to carry stones and rubble, to build Italian-style houses for the poor and to institute an Italian-style state bank. They should modernise their attitudes and institutions, widening the ranks of the patriciate, encouraging immigrants to settle and abandoning Erastian tendencies towards the Church …'[32]

The interior of the cathedral contains many rather lugubrious marble altar tabernacles, mostly by Italians. Among the finest is that erected to St Bernard (1686–8) and paid for by Archdeacon Bernard Dordić, which was supplied by Carlo degli Frangi of Naples. It encloses a fine painted altarpiece, much in the manner of Carlo Maratti but by the Dubrovnik artist Pietro Mattei (Petar Matejević, fl. 1670–1726), of *St Bernard Kneeling before Christ and the Virgin*, signed 'Petrus Mattei Ragus pingebat 1721' (fig. 10.25).

The high altar is graced by a polyptych from Titian's workshop of the *Assumption* with flanking panels to the left of *St Blaise and St Lazarus* and to the right of *St Nicholas and St Benedict*. Above these pairs of saints are panels of the *Angel Gabriel* (left) and the *Virgin Annunciate* (right). Despite Titian's signature on

10.24 Andrea Buffalini, cathedral facade, 1671–1713, Dubrovnik. Photo: Vlaho Pustić.

10.25 Pietro Mattei, *St Bernard Kneeling before Christ and the Virgin*, signed and dated 1721, oil on canvas, Dubrovnik Cathedral. Photo: Božo Gjukić.

the sarcophagus of Mary ('TIZIANUS. F.R.R.'), it is difficult to recognise much of Titian's own hand.[33] The altarpiece was painted *c.* 1550 for the Brotherhood of St Lazarus for their church of St Lazarus at Ploče. As the cathedral after the 1667 earthquake had lost its high altar, and as it was dedicated to Maria Assunta, the Ragusan Senate decided to move the polyptych to its new location in 1711–12. The Senate's decision was confirmed by Vicar General Sebastian Bunić on 25 November 1712.

The cathedral contains several intriguing altarpieces which can easily be overlooked. One by Pellegrino Broccardo of Genoa (fl. 1555–90) shows *St Matthew before Christ and the Virgin Mary* (1588) (fig. 10.26). The Evangelist is seated in the foreground looking upwards and gesturing with his left hand towards his Gospel, held by a putto. He is seated on a stool which stands on an inlaid marble pavement. In the middle distance is a cityscape, presumably a view of the Dubrovnik Placa, flanked to the left by a statue in grisaille of the *Sacrifice of Isaac all'antica* while

above, seated in clouds, are the Virgin and Child surrounded by putti. The group of the Virgin and Child is taken directly from an oil by Perino del Vaga (1501–47) of the *Holy Family*, now in the collection of the Prince of Lichtenstein, Vaduz, which is thought to date from *c.* 1540. The figure of St Matthew is adapted from the figure of St Luke also designed by Perino del Vaga but executed in fresco by Daniele da Volterra 1540–3 for the vault of the Cappella del Crocifisso, San Marcello al Corso, Rome.[34] Presumably Broccardo had been one of Perino's pupils in Genoa. Perino was, we know, one of Raphael's most distinguished pupils, and it occurs to me that Perino may also have been responsible for the excellent copy of Raphael's *Madonna della Sedia* (original in Pitti Palace, Florence) which is in the cathedral treasury. The additional painted figures of the Evangelists in the spandrels are certainly reminiscent of Perino. We know that Broccardo was employed briefly by Archbishop Beccadelli, a poet and friend of Michelangelo, Cardinal Reginald Pole and Pietro Bembo. He stayed with the archbishop at his summer villa on Šipan, where Beccadelli had founded a sort of academy.

Broccardo is an intriguing figure – a painter, draughtsman, musician and churchman. He was born in Imperia (Liguria), and worked in Dubrovnik 1555–60, save for a trip to Egypt in 1556. A topographical drawing by him of Cairo is in the State Archives of Turin. In 1560–1 he returned to Rome and painted a portrait of the English Cardinal Reginald Pole, copied from the original then belonging to Cardinal Morone. In 1576 he became a canon of the cathedral of Genoa and died on 8 February 1590 at Ventimiglia. Broccardo's patron, Bishop Ludovico Beccadelli, born in Bologna, was apostolic legate to Venice 1550–4 and nominated by Pope Paul IV Carafa as archbishop of Ragusa in 1555, where he remained until 1563. He then returned to Italy, employed by Grand Duke Cosimo I de' Medici to train his son Ferdinando for the religious life. Beccadelli lived in Prato and died in 1572. His portrait was painted by Titian and is now in the Uffizi Gallery, Florence, signed and dated 1552 (inv. no. 1457).

There exist two other fascinating altarpieces painted in oil on canvas, one representing the *Adoration of the Shepherds* (Fig. 10.27). It shows the Christ Child, bottom centre, adored by St Joseph and the Virgin Mary kneeling to the left, lit by Christ's divine light as described by St Brigid of Hungary in a vision. The shepherds appear from the right, the foremost shepherd doffing his hat respectfully towards the Infant Christ and carrying behind him, as a gift, a lamb in his left hand. Above, in the heavens, circle fluttering cherubim and seraphim holding a banderole inscribed: 'GLORIA/ IN EXCELSIS/ DEO/ ET/ IN TERRA'. Traditionally the picture had been attributed to Correggio, but in 1964 Grgo Gamulin published the altarpiece, wrongly in my view, as a work by Luca Cambiaso of Genoa painted *c.* 1565–70.[35] The plump

10.26 Pellegrino Broccardo, *St Matthew before Christ and the Virgin Mary*, 1588, oil on canvas, Dubrovnik Cathedral. Photo: Božo Gjukić.

10.27 Here attributed to Orazio Sammacchini, *Adoration of the Shepherds*, oil on canvas, Dubrovnik Cathedral. Photo: Božo Gjukić.

10.28 Sebastiano Ricci, *Madonna and Child with St Simon Stock and St Theresa of Avila*, *c*. 1700–10, oil on canvas, Dubrovnik Cathedral. Photo: Miro Dvorščak.

10.29 Andrea Vaccaro, *St John on Patmos Witnessing the Coronation of the Virgin*, oil on canvas, Our Lady of Carmel, Dubrovnik. Photo: Vidoslav Barac.

putti with their artfully foreshortened format, however, suggest an artist trained in Emilia at much the same time, probably Orazio Sammacchini (1533–77).

The other altarpiece, now hanging on a side wall, is of the *Madonna and Child with St Simon Stock and St Theresa of Avila* (fig 10.28). Here the Virgin, reclining in clouds with the Christ Child in her lap, suspends the scapular which is kissed by St Simon Stock, bottom left, while St Theresa of Avila swoons to the right, a red hot arrow about to pierce her breast held by an attendant angel. Sebastiano Ricci (1659–1734) probably painted it *c*. 1700–10 before his departure for England. It numbers among his greatest early altarpieces.[36] Ricci's painting came from the church of Our Lady of Carmel (Karmen), and was the altarpiece

to the left of the high altar. The church itself is being restored, and this, along with all its other altarpieces and decorations, will be returned to their original destinations.[37] The ceiling of Our Lady of Carmel was painted with the *Assumption of the Virgin*, a large rococo canvas by Bartolomeo Litterini of Venice (1669–1748), an artist also represented in Cavtat, Brsečine, and Ston.[38] The high altar was graced with a so-called *pala portante* incorporating a Romanesque image of the Madonna of Carmel, set into a later canvas, with the venerable image adored by St John the Divine and St Simon Stock, St Nicholas of Myra and St John the Baptist. Signed and dated '10. ANGELUS CANINI/ ROM. FACIT 1641', it numbers among the earliest major works of the Roman artist Giovanni Angelo Canini (1617–66).[39] To the right

10.30 Mattia Preti, *St Mark* (during restoration), oil on canvas, Our Lady of Carmel, Dubrovnik. Photo: Vlaho Pustić.

Philistines, the *Flight into Egypt*, the *Massacre of the Innocents* and the *Descent of Christ into Limbo*.[41] The set, which appears to date from the second decade of the seventeenth century, should be compared with Padovanino's fine signed altarpiece of the *Madonna with St Nicholas and St Blaise* at Santo Spirito, Hvar (Lesina) and paintings of the *Magdalen* and the *Deposition* in the cathedral of Trogir (Traù), which Berenson, on a visit to Dalmatia, first attributed to the master.

The highlights of the cathedral's applied art possessions are housed in the magnificent reliquary treasury, built by Marino Gropelli 1717–21, which is situated opposite the vestry in the crossing to the south. All the relics were removed to this location from the security of the Revelin Fortress in 1721. They consist of some 182 specimens collected by Ragusa over the last thousand years. Many of them are also considerable works of art of Italian craftsmanship, and are very ancient. The most notable from our period is the silver-gilt and ebony crucifix (Fig. 10.31), which incorporates in its plinth a reliquary of St Philip Benizzi (1233–85). The relic was remounted in Rome in 1671 to commemorate the canonisation of the saint, during the period of Bishop Vicenza III from Lucca (1669–93). The corpus of the *Cristo vivo* is a variant from a known model of Alessandro Algardi (1598–1654), the great Bolognese sculptor, who became Bernini's chief rival in Rome. Algardi was much patronised by Pope Innocent X Pamphilij, the friend of Gradić. The corpus closely resembles those in Rome at Santa Maria del Popolo (bronze), San Carlo ai Catinari (gilt bronze) and in the Gèsu (wood). We know that Algardi first supplied such a crucifix in silver, three palmi high, to Pope Innocent X in 1646. This crucifix is now lost, but the Dubrovnik corpus may have been similar but

of the high altar was an altarpiece of *St John on Patmos Witnessing the Coronation of the Virgin* by the Neapolitan painter Andrea Vaccaro (1604–70), signed in monogram and commissioned by the Dubrovnik patrician family of Restić (fig. 10.29).[40] The church also contains a good set of paintings on canvas of the *Four Evangelists* (including *St Mark*, fig. 10.30) by the Neapolitan Mattia Preti (1613–99). When restored and reconstituted, Our Lady of Carmel will be one of the finest small church interiors furnished with Italian art in Croatia.

Hanging high up in the cathedral choir are a set of four landscape-shaped oils on canvas by Alessandro Varotari, called 'il Padovanino' (1588–1648), which represent *Samson and the*

smaller and a later casting.[42] Vinicije Lupis of Dubrovnik, the archivist and connoisseur of silver, has researched, identified and published a major group of baroque and rococo silver preserved in Dubrovnik and the environs supplied by Roman makers.[43] In the cathedral there are, for example, a monstrance and six large silver candelabra by the Roman goldsmith Bartolomeo Boroni (1730–87). There is a reliquary of the hand of St John the Baptist from the Roman workshop that used a halberd as its hallmark. In the Franciscan church are a chalice made by Benedetto Andronico (fl. 1762–87) and a monstrance, the work of Domenico Ridolfi (1672–1712). The Dominican church boasts a reliquary made by Antonio Capeletti (1804–38) and a chalice by Baldassare Pieri

(1749–89), while the church of St Blaise has a fine monstrance also by Pieri as well as an embossed silver bound missal from the former church of St Anthony Abbot, which is hallmarked by Benedetto Andronico.

It would be misleading to believe that all the baroque and rococo silver in Dubrovnik was made in Rome, for Naples was clearly the rival supplier. In the cathedral there are several reliquaries by the Neapolitan Cristoforo Angeli (fl. 1729). The Franciscans have a chalice by the Neapolitan goldsmiths' consul Sebastiano Avitablo (fl. 1715–26); the Dominicans have several liturgical items including a handsome bell, while the collegiate church of St Blaise has the most extensive collection, with works by the anonymous 'A.P.' and a series of silver *palmi* (repoussé bunches of flowers as altar ornaments) by Biagio Giordano (fl. 1774–1807). The most magnificent Neapolitan piece is undoubtedly the reliquary of the *Christ Child's Swaddling Bands*, attributed to Antonio Avitablo, in the form of a rectangular casket supported on demi-putti, with scrolling feet surmounted by seated angels at the four corners, the sides pierced with windows of rock crystal (fig. 10.32). The hinged cover is ornamented with the heads of cherubim and kneeling putti, and surmounted by a statuette of the *Blessed Virgin Mary*.[44]

The appearance of quantities of Roman and Neapolitan silver, in the same sort of proportions as the surviving painted altarpieces, confirms how close Dubrovnik's artistic and commercial ties were to these two Italian cities during the late seventeenth and eighteenth centuries, Venetian artefacts being notably scarce. We must remember that the Ragusans had

10.32 Attributed to Antonio Avitablo, reliquary of the *Christ Child's Swaddling Bands*, Naples, ?*c.* 1675, silver and rock crystal, Treasury Museum of Dubrovnik Cathedral. Photo: Božo Gjukić.

LEFT 10.31 *Crucified Christ* after a model by Alessandro Algardi, 1671, silver-gilt and ebony crucifix, Treasury Museum of Dubrovnik Cathedral. Photo: Božo Gjukić.

always been particularly fearful not only of the Sublime Porte but above all of the Serenissima. After the defeat of the Turks outside Vienna on 12 September 1683, Dubrovnik was aware of the Turks' comparative weakness, and so decided to enter into secret negotiations with the king of Hungary. The Spanish ambassador to the Habsburgs, Carlo Emmanuele d'Este, marquis of Borgomanero, urged on these negotiations. On 2 September 1686 Buda fell to the Austrians, and Dubrovnik switched alliance and began paying its annual tribute to Vienna. Then, during the so-called Long War (1683–99), Herceg-Novi in October 1687 and Belgrade in September 1688 also fell to the forces of the Christian League. Dubrovnik feared that Hercegovina would

10.33 Pietro Passalacqua, flight of steps to the Jesuit College, 1738, Dubrovnik. Photo: Damir Fabijanić.

be taken over by Venice rather than Hungary, so they resolved openly to support Hungary, only to find themselves blockaded by a powerful Venetian fleet.[45] Eventually, in 1701, the Venetians and Turks made peace. Venetian pressure on Dubrovnik was now temporarily lifted. In these circumstances, it is hardly surprising that Dubrovnik was not inclined to commission Venetian architects or, for that matter, buy Venetian paintings or silver.

The bishop's picture gallery, currently in store, contains a good *Virgin and Child with an Angel* by the Florentine Domenico Puligo (1492–1527), which is closely comparable to a version in the Pitti Palace, Florence.[46] There is also a rather disappointing half-length of *St Catherine of Alexandria* attributed to Palma Vecchio (fl. 1510–28)[47] and an interesting *Christ at the Column* by Francesco Ubertini, called 'il Bacchiacca' (1495–1557), but the latter may be by that obscure artist Visino, who worked in Florence and Hungary *c.* 1510.[48] The so-called Bacchiacca, when I saw it, was very dirty, but seemed closer to the *Leda and the Swan* attributed to Visino in the Uffizi, Florence.[49]

Leaving the cathedral and walking around behind the apse to the west, a very short walk will bring one to a handsome baroque flight of steps which lead from the south side of Gundulić Square (Gundulićeva poljana) to Ruđer Bošković Square, the church of St Ignatius, and the Collegium Ragusinum or Jesuit College. The author of these steps (Skalinada, fig. 10.33) was the Roman architect Pietro Passalacqua (d. 1748), and they were designed in 1738, shortly after the more ambitious and justly famous Spanish Steps in Rome linking the Piazza di Spagna with the church of Santa Trinità dei Monti, constructed between 1723 and 1726 to the design of Francesco de Sanctis (d. 1731). Passalacqua was a really interesting rococo architect whose works can be a delight, like the oratory of SS. Annunziata in Rome built 1744–6, or his work with Domenico Gregorini on the more austere facade of Santa Croce in Gerusalemme, Rome (1741–4).[50]

The Jesuit church of St Ignatius was built to the designs of the celebrated Jesuit painter and architect Fratel Andrea Pozzo (1642–1709). He started on the project in 1699, finishing it in 1703, but the actual building work was not completed until 1725. The sombre dignity of this classical facade reflects the grandeur and authority of the mother church in Rome as designed in the sixteenth century by Giacomo Barozzi da Vignola (1507–73), rather than the revised facade as built to the design of Giacomo della Porta (*c.* 1537–1602). The austerity is broken by the introduction of a lively carved angel added by Gropelli to point to the escutcheon with the Holy Name of Jesus placed above the main door. The sanctuary is decorated with coarse illusionistic frescoes of the life of St Ignatius, the founder of the Jesuit order, by Gaetano Garcia of Sicily.

Beside the church, the Jesuit College is a severe looking seminary. The interior on the ground floor has a grand corridor with a series of doorways opening onto it surrounded by intricate and complex geometric mouldings worthy of Francesco Borromini, which I suspect might also be by the talented Pietro Passalacqua.

Finally, there is the church of the Domino, 'Our Lord'. (The church is commonly known as the 'Domino', but it is formally dedicated to All Saints, and stands on the Široka ulica (meaning Broad Street) crossing with the Iza Roka street (meaning behind Rocco, because of the St Roche church). In itself it is not a remarkable building, but it contains a good altarpiece by Andrea Vaccaro of Naples (1605–70), showing *All Saints Adoring the Virgin Seated between Christ and God the Father*, which is not unlike the finer *St John on Patmos Witnessing the Coronation of the Virgin* by the same artist that was painted for the Carmelite church and has previously been discussed (see fig. 10.30).

In conclusion, Ragusa, this tiny Croatian state whose capital was the fortified city of Dubrovnik, wielded astonishing power and influence. Politically, as a free merchant republic it operated as an enlightened oligarchy based upon a constitution established in 1272 but ruled by Venice until 1358. The state survived on its diplomatic skills, agilely playing off the Normans, the Byzantines, the Hungarians, then the Venetians and the Turks. The substantial profits made from trade were invested in beautifying the state and establishing a proto-welfare system that provided medical care (1301) and a home for the elderly (1347) and abolished the slave trade (1416). Under such enlightened rule, humanism flourished and sophisticated suburban villas sprang up after the classical model that must have been the envy of their Italian neighbours. The state survived until 1808, when it surrendered to French forces and then, in 1815, was ceded by treaty to the Austro-Hungarian Empire.

Art in Dubrovnik flourished, and unlike most of Croatia, a distinctive native school of painting developed in the late fifteenth century with lyrical artists like Lovro Dobričević (*c.* 1420–78) and Nikola Božidarević (fl. 1476–1517), who betray not only strong Italian influence, but also that of Spain, Hungary and Germany. One of the finest of these Ragusan artists was Mihajlo Hamzić (fl. 1504–18), who for a time even collaborated with the Venetian Pietro di Giovanni. However, the strongest influence on Ragusan artists like Dobričević or Božidarević seems not to have been from Venice but from their rivals Genoa, with the likes of little-known masters like Giovanni di Barbagelata and Nicolò Corso.[51]

Above all, the art commissioned in Dubrovnik was Italian, and although the state, with justification, greatly feared Venice, paradoxically Venetian ideas of government and of architecture could not fail to attract them. However, the discerning Ragusans fiercely valued their independence and delighted to commission major buildings, sculptures, paintings and works of art from a wide variety of talented Italian artists. It is this combination which makes Dubrovnik today so memorable and so extraordinary.

CASTLES & MANOR HOUSES OF CROATIA: WINNING OR LOSING

Marcus Binney

There is not a country in Europe, at least none I have yet found, which does not boast its own distinctive collection of castles, manor houses and ancestral seats. Yet little more than half a century ago Armageddon arrived in much of Europe, and the traditional landowning families which had built and owned these houses over centuries were forced to flee or were evicted. It happened in Britain with the Second World War requisitioning of practically every major country house. It happened over much of Central and Eastern Europe as the tide of battle swept into Russia and then back again. Great historic houses were plundered and stripped of their contents. The owners fled.

At best the houses were taken over as cheap floor space by institutions – schools, hospitals, orphanages, old people's homes or agricultural collectives. In most of Eastern Europe very few (except in the Czech Republic) were taken over as museums and opened to the public. Croatia, rich in ancestral homes from the Middle Ages onwards, suffered more severely than most, enduring the triple blows of damage during the Second World War, confiscation under Communism and then severe damage to a significant number of houses during the War of Independence of 1991–5.

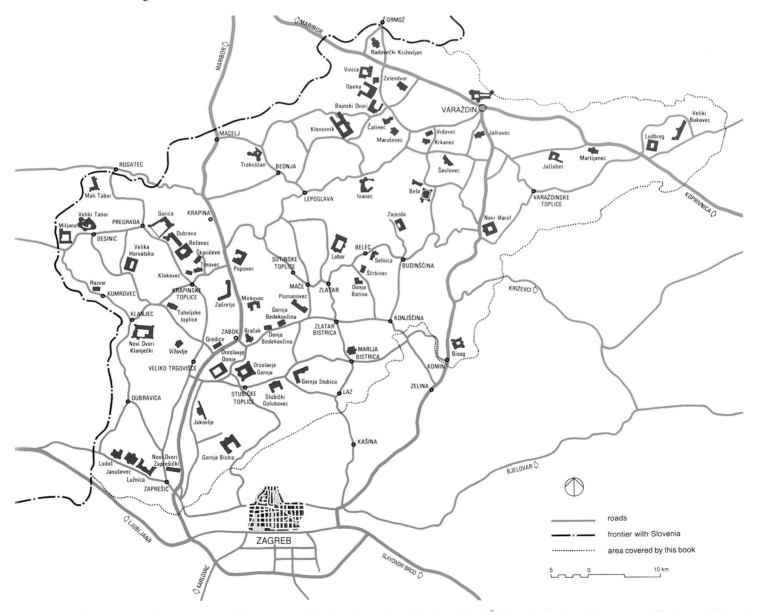

11.1 Map of the Zagreb region showing all the places visited by the author (Mladen Obad Šćitaroci, *Castles, Manors and Gardens of Croatian Zagorje*, Zagreb 1996, between pp. 32 and 33, map by Bojana Bojanić Obad Šćitaroci, assisted by Nada Ivanković)

11.2 View of Trakošćan Castle and lake. Photo: courtesy of the Trakošćan Museum.

11.3 Trakošćan Castle, interior showing the library. Photo: courtesy of the Trakošćan Museum.

For a relatively small country – small at least in terms of population – Croatia has a remarkably varied collection of historic castles and manor houses ranging from impressive medieval fortifications to grand Renaissance and baroque residences. There are numerous late eighteenth-century and early nineteenth-century classical houses and a series of mansions in castle style reflecting the strength of the Romantic movement all over Europe. In Osijek I encountered a splendid run of opulent art nouveau town houses. Not far from the town stands a most intriguing 1920s hunting lodge, Tikveš, built between the two world wars.

We set out on a Sunday morning in late October on a grand loop around the mountain north of Zagreb (fig. 11.1). Trakošćan Castle is the pride of continental Croatia and a major destination for visitors (figs 11.2 and 11.3). You catch a romantic view of it perched on a crag with a large lake below. All around the trees were turning gold in the late autumn.

Though medieval in origin, the castle took on its present appearance in the mid-nineteenth century when it was remodelled in Gothic style with a quantity of rich woodwork and panelling, much of it in a spirited flamboyant Gothic style. The interior is arranged so that you make a satisfying circuit of both the main stories through state and family rooms, most retaining furniture. There are richly carved ogee arched doorcases inset with coats of arms. The dining room has a magnificent built-in baroque sideboard with corkscrew columns. My interest was seized by a set of paintings of the *Four Continents* by Michael Story, evidently seen as an opportunity to hang some extremely voluptuous nudes. Lively texts added constant interest. Beneath the entrance I learnt that the Drašković family 'had so-called Regal rights … the right of the sword, of selling wine, the right to transport, to collect tolls, to hold fairs and the patronage of prisoners held for ransom in relatively good conditions' (they lost their value if they died). In the Victorian kitchen was a large island stove from which fumes were extracted under the floor and up a chimney in the wall. A quotation humorously reminded us of good living in past times: 'We aristocrats eat partridges and other fine meat and hence we are more intelligent and sensitive than people who eat beef and pork.'

Even so, thanks to sustained efforts by the national monuments services, the majority of ancestral seats survived these harsh years, enough to fill the two handsome volumes by Mladen and Bojana Šćitaroci: *Castles, Manors and Gardens of Croatian Zagorje* and *Manors and Gardens in Croatia*, referred to here as the Gold and the Red Books, the first on the province around the capital of Zagreb, the second on Slavonia.[1] From these I made a selection of houses covering all periods which were of striking architectural quality, set in fine grounds, or apparently retaining interesting interiors. Some were self-evidently in a sad state; others had potential to earn their keep if sold or put to enterprising new uses.

11.4 Oroslavje Donje, exterior. Photo: Goran Bekina, Ministry of Culture.

11.5 Gornja Stubica, exterior showing corner portico. Photo: Goran Bekina, Ministry of Culture,

11.6 Stubički Golubovec, garden front. Photo: Goran Bekina, Ministry of Culture.

Driving on to Sveti Križ Začretje, I came face to face with the blunt reality of a situation I was to encounter again and again. The eighteenth-century house stood in a pleasant grove of trees in the centre of the village. But the setting had been cruelly eroded by a large villa built less than a hundred metres from the house. Nonetheless, it had been bought recently by a family from Zagreb who were holding concerts in the house. Repairs had begun but the house was unoccupied. The boomerang plan, with wings extending at an angle from a central pavilion, suggested it was practical to phase the work and introduce a range of uses.

A few miles on, Oroslavje Donje proved to be a charming late eighteenth-century Austrian-looking hunting lodge with steep tiled roof (fig. 11.4). The grey architectural trim stands out like a livery from the strong butter-yellow walls with horizontal banding on the low ground floor and pilasters and tweaked pediments on the *piano nobile*. The entrance range had a new roof, but the first floor windows were broken. A carriage archway leads through to an inner courtyard with an exit in the back range. Though most of the house was empty, a plume of smoke rose from a cottage at the back. This could be a private house again. The house is very much in the centre of the town, but given seclusion by a grove of trees.

Next came Gornja Stubica, an unusual L-shaped manor (now a museum) with a stone paved ramp leading down to grand archway carrying a date of 1756. The courtyard with two-storey Renaissance arcades is of a kind often seen in Central Europe, plainly detailed but nobly proportioned. The chapel was gloriously frescoed in the manner (and light palette) of Tiepolo with a convincing illusionist dome. Inside, an enfilade of rooms on the *piano nobile* showed changing styles in decoration and furniture with a splendid model of the castle of Veliki Tabor. An unusual feature is the elegant Greek Doric portico set oddly at the corner, not the centre, of the garden facade (fig. 11.5). This appeared to be a summer loggia rather than an entrance portico, a place where you stepped out of the saloon rather than into it.

11.7 Marija Bistrica, Hellenbach Manor, exterior. Photo: Goran Bekina.

Stubički Golubovec, dating from the 1790s, is built on a U-plan with neoclassical garlands over the windows. In other ways it is distinctly old-fashioned for this date with a steep roof and shallow baroque entrance arch and an onion cupola on the left wing. We met Davor Vlajčević, who explained his ambitious plans for the manor. Determined to revive the estate, he had toured Europe to look for innovative ideas and found inspiration in a horse dairy farm in Belgium. His plan was for a farm with a hundred mares providing milk. The milk of mares, he explained, was especially healthy and sought after. He had obtained an interest in the property but not yet full title. The question evidently was whether all this could be sorted out on a reasonable timescale. Inside, though empty the house was in a reasonable state, and evidently in use for occasional exhibitions. The prettiest aspect of Stubički Golubovec is the garden front with bold pedimented centre and a single-storey portico with paired Doric columns (fig. 11.6). The garden had run wild, and one had to inch along the stone plinth which surrounded the house to reach it.

Marija Bistrica (figs 11.7 and 11.8) is unique in Croatia, and indeed in most of Eastern Europe, in remaining in the hands of the family throughout the hard years of Communist rule. Today it still retains its nineteenth-century furnishings, though funds are desperately needed for repairs. The house stands at the top of a small park, shielded from the main road below by a line of mature trees.

The house is a wonderfully preserved and remote example of the idealised villa plan as built by Palladio and his disciples

11.8 Marija Bistrica, interior showing central hall. Photo: Miljenko Marohnić.

all over Europe. It has all the quintessential features of a perfect Renaissance or neoclassical villa – a pedimented portico and *piano nobile* above a basement. It is a perfect square, standing free so it can be admired in temple-like isolation. Curiously little seems to be known of its design or even date, let alone the name of the architect, but it appears to date from the 1780s when the estate was owned by Count Petar Sermage, who inherited it from his first wife Josipa, née Keglević.

11.9 Novi Dvori Zaprešićki, manor house. Photo: Vidoslav Barac.

partitions set well below the ceiling, carefully balanced on the other side.

The central hall is faced with shallow giant pilasters carrying a full entablature. Above, the clerestory has windows on all four sides. The dado is marbled, as are the door surrounds, which are adorned with red valences suspended from brass rods. Over the doors there are panels of arms and armour, musical instruments and symbols of the arts, all superbly crisp and in quite high relief. Inset on the walls between are two oval frames containing painted scenes in the manner of Claude Lorrain. The compass pattern floor is a handsome legacy from a film production. The salon beyond has three arched doors opening onto the portico, each arch inset with palm fronds. With so many doors and windows, the fireplace had to be set in a corner surmounted by a large red marbled niche and distinctive Louis Seize urn above. This is complemented by relief panels of wreaths and garlands over the doors. The library to the right, like the salon, has a herringbone parquet floor as well as elegant tall glass-fronted bookcases set flush with the walls. An intriguing detail is the pop-up metal clips or fasteners in the sills which hold the windows open when required.

The urgent need for funds became fully apparent outside, where the stucco window surrounds have disintegrated in many places. A sum of 500,000 euros, I was told, was required to stabilise the villa and do the essential and long overdue repairs to its structure. Since the mid-nineteenth century, the property has belonged to the Barons Hellenbach, descending from Zdenko Hellenbach to his daughter Gizela and then to her daughter Ruth, who lives there with her husband and two children today. Though land was confiscated in the Communist years, the family lived on alone in extreme cold and considerable discomfort. Today it is self-evident that whatever funds are available are spent on the building rather than modern conveniences. It is absolutely vital that the house remains complete with its furnishings and family connections.

West out of Zagreb a string of four houses were marked in close succession on the map in the Gold Book. First came Novi Dvori Zaprešićki (fig. 11.9), still in the outer suburbs. The approach reminded me of the distinctive Herrenhauser in

Marija Bistrica is on a typical Palladian plan with a central toplit hall and three rooms along each main front. The plan is sophisticated and accomplished with the internal doors set in line to form an enfilade along all four fronts. Internally, the style is Louis Seize with many plasterwork features clearly taken from engravings. There is a certain chunkiness or exaggeration to some of the details, but they are otherwise correct and indeed sophisticated in their use of classical motifs. The front door with pretty fanlight opens into an octagonal hall surmounted by an exquisite shallow octagonal dome painted with classical coffering which diminishes in size towards the centre. The treatment of the walls is very architectural with double doors and large niches, but beside the entrance a bathroom has been contrived within

11.10 Novi Dvori Zaprešićki, Granary, today Gallery of Naive Art. Photo: Jadranka Beresford-Peirse.

11.11 Lužnica, exterior. Photo: Miljenko Marohnić.

11.12 Lužnica, Neo-gothic stove. Photo: Miljenko Marohnić.

Schleswig-Holstein, where farm buildings are lined up on either side of an arrow-straight drive to lend grandeur to the approach. Here the manor is reached along a stately avenue of chestnuts with the farm buildings set back behind broad grass verges. I was told the house was owned by the municipality, and though there were some serious signs of neglect and decay, the grounds were well kept. There were obvious development opportunities so close to the town. The big question as always in such situations was whether the two could be combined to advantage.

On the right of the avenue stood a granary with distinctive squared timber-framing (fig. 11.10). This had been smartly restored as a gallery. On the left was a barn with diamond ventilation holes, and beyond it another long barn where the roof had collapsed in two places leaving gaping holes. It appeared to have been constructed as stables or mangers below with haylofts above. Opposite were pergola-like frames on which to hang maize out to dry. The manor house, newly reroofed, was set to the right of the avenue and at an angle, standing amidst extensive grass and backed protectively by trees. It consisted of

a long range of twelve windows with central rather rudimentary porte cochère and stepped gable behind. Windows on the upper floor had Tudor hoodmoulds. The manor had taken on its present proportions by the first half of the nineteenth century – it is shown as it is today in a drawing in the sale contract of 1852 when Count Erdödy bought the house from Ban Jelačić.

Lužnica (fig. 11.11) came into view across a large expanse of broad flat meadow standing on rising ground and framed by a cut in the trees. The gabled centre surges through the main cornice in best baroque fashion. At the corners are the pepper pot towers or *poivrières* often found on chateaux in France. Today the house belongs to the nuns who bought the estate in 1925. It is approached from the other side past a self-confidently new residential block recently built for older nuns to retire to. The entrance front forms a three-sided courtyard with distinctive pinched pediments over the windows.

Inside craftsmen were at work in the ground-floor rooms, nearing the completion of a very extensive renovation. A sister descended the stairs to take us on a tour. It is quickly apparent that all the work has been done to a very high specification. The stair had wooden steps with delicately carved risers and a bold baroque balustrade on the landing. The centre saloon was arranged with curving rows of chairs for a lecture. At the back is a very handsome Gothic stove with pretty gilded ornament (fig. 11.12). Beside the windows are neat built-in cupboards with Louis Seize detail retaining hinges and locks. The rooms on either side of the saloon are sympathetically furnished, and a large corner room has a refectory with modern servery. One of the corridors terminates in a small pretty chapel. An enfilade with double doors leads from one room to another.

Evicted in 1945, the nuns returned in the 1980s. To finance the work they sold some outlying land, received help from the Ministry of Culture, and raised donations from local businesses, but the major part came from a German foundation which supports monasteries.

Januševec (fig. 11.13) is described as the most beautiful manor in the whole of Croatia by Gjuro Szabo in his 1939 study, *Through the Croatian Zagorje*. You catch a sudden glimpse of it above the road, all shining white stucco like the White House in Washington, DC. It was built about 1830 by Baron Josip Vrkljan, a retired general who was in charge of the finances of Marie Louise, grand duchess of Parma and second wife of Napoleon. He was well acquainted with the handsome porticoed villas of the Veneto, and his architect was probably the talented Bartolomej Felbinger. There are porticoes on three sides, each different. The entrance front has a portico of giant Corinthian columns, mirrored at the back, while the flank has a portico *in antis* recessed behind more columns.

The house was severely damaged in the Second World War when the splendid domed rotunda was destroyed. Today the house has an unusual and rather special guardian, none other than the gardener who had arranged a splendid display of window boxes overflowing with cascades of geraniums. Even the children's swing on the lawn is decorated with hanging baskets. These are all evidently a brilliant deterrent against casual vandalism and spray-painted graffiti.

11.13 Januševec, exterior. Photo: Jadranka Beresford-Peirse.

11.14 Laduč, exterior. Photo: Marko Ćolić.

11.15 Miljana, exterior with courtyard. Photo: Jadranka Beresford-Peirse.

11.16 Miljana, dining room. Photo: Marko Ćolić.

Beyond was Laduč, a chaste and rather pretty stucco house dating from the first half of the nineteenth century, which belonged to the Vranyczany family (fig. 11.14). The entrance doors are set within a two-storey porch with masonry arches below and slender iron ones above. Today it is an orphanage, but by contrast to the rather grim image of such institutions in Central and Eastern Europe, this appears very well kept. Twin drives lead up to the main front framing islands of turf inset with formal bedding. We rang the bell and called out, but failed to summon anyone though we heard distant voices in the kitchen. Peering through the windows of the entrance hall, we saw a grand staircase ascent framed by a double row of arches. This house for once appeared fully used and in safe hands, even if rather less well tended at the back.

On the way towards the Slovenian border we made a brief stop at the preserved village of Kumrovec. This has the feel of an open-air museum in the Scandinavian mould, but the collection

11.17 Veliki Tabor, exterior. Photo: Vidoslav Barac.

of farmhouses, cottages and barns have not been scooped up from elsewhere. They are the originals. A number of interiors are open and furnished in traditional peasant style, all very sympathetically done. One of the larger houses is Marshal Tito's birthplace and childhood home.

Driving on we passed Razvor Manor, a delightful small baroque building set back from a bend in the road with distinctive stucco banding on the ground floor and tweaked pediments over the upper windows. It has been recently painted in a smart yellow and white livery, and may be used as a restaurant.

Our goal is Miljana, the former manor house of the Ratkaj family. The road winds through a village of scattered houses set in pasture. The house is at the end, standing on rising ground which shows off its distinctive layout to good advantage. The entrance is beneath a clock tower. The house behind is painted a distinctive charcoal colour with white trim. The garden in front is filled with pretty roses which are in bloom even now in October.

Miljana is in an impressive state due to Dr Franjo Kajfež, a successful and renowned biochemist who worked in the cosmetics industry. Having made a large fortune abroad, he bought the house in 1980, lavished money on it, opened it to the public

and held exhibitions. Here he established his own large research library largely arranged in the attics around the courtyard.

The courtyard is paved in squares of pebbles with two large sundials painted on the walls (fig. 11.15). On the far side is a double arcade with broad arches and piers below and squat columns above in the Central European Renaissance manner. The arcades are now glazed in and furnished with an impressive group of early gramophones on the ground floor. Broad stone steps rise leading to the *piano nobile*. The front door has bold chevron pattern boarding.

Inside it is warm and well furnished. The rooms open one into another, adorned with a splendid series of porcelain stoves looking like overgrown chessmen. The furniture is heavy but appropriate, comfortable or *gemütlich* in the German sense. Carved sofas, massive wardrobes and writing desks crowd the walls. Some of the rooms have pretty painted window reveals bursting with rich rococo shellwork. One of these rooms is vaulted. The best is the dining room with windows on two sides and *galante* scenes of courting couples (11.16). The main roofspace is formed into an exhibition gallery open from end to end.

The medieval castle of Veliki Tabor is preserved and proudly displayed as an ancient monument (fig. 11.17). The central tower was reopened a week earlier, but this time we are too late, meeting a convoy of curators driving home with gusto.

The final stop of the day is Bežanec, a stuccoed eighteenth-century house laid out on four sides of a central courtyard (fig. 11.18). It stands on a knoll above the road. We park close to a hollow lime tree of staggering girth which must be centuries old. Bežanec is now a hotel. The carriage arch has become the entrance hall, and we are ushered down the corridor to meet the proprietor, Siniša Križanec. He tells us he started work in 1990 and finished in a year. The hotel now has twenty-five double rooms, three suites and 3,500 square metres. He had previously been in government protocol and had run a small restaurant nearby. At Bežanec he has worked closely with the diplomatic corps providing conference facilities and catering at a 'high level'. Young people come to be married. He continues: 'I am not the owner, but then nobody is. But now I can't cope any longer. I'm fed up with all the bureaucracy. I've lost the will to fight the system.'

Sitting in his office it is hard to assess all this, but we now set off on a tour. To furnish the bedrooms he went to sales and warehouses. Each room is different, and furnished with lavish suites of furniture in a host of styles, with matching bed, cupboard, dressing table, sofa and chairs. It is a world away from IKEA, a window on a vanished world giving the rooms a personality. The bedrooms are lofty and freshly painted, and the bathrooms have the smartest fittings available, including hexagonal baths. There is a handsome dining room at one corner of the quadrangle looking out over the garden. In the basement we find the vaulted cellar is a large nightclub with strobe lighting and smart low banquet seating.

11.18 Bežanec, exterior. Photo: Marko Ćolić.

The next day we drive north-east. We make an unscheduled stop driving through a large village when a fine eighteenth-century house opens up to view on the right framed by brick gatepiers. The house is Donji Martijanec (fig. 11.19), which stands on axis with a double-height portico and farm buildings on either side. But what a state it is all in. The house has no doors or windows. We can walk straight in. The farm buildings on the right are equally battered, with an ugly recent addition at the near end. The large barns on the left are a different matter. Huge structural work has taken place. The ground has been excavated to basement level. There is a new roof but work seems to have halted. We are baffled. Only later do we learn that the new owner is installing a major gallery here. A substantial amount has been invested, an impressive commitment to the village. The big question is, will it happen in time to rescue the house? The upper portico with slender Ionic columns is finely detailed. The walls are faced in stucco with channelled rustication below and quoins above.

Our destination is the conservation centre of the Croatian Conservation Institute established in Ludbreg, the large seat of the Batthyany family. It is a Renaisssance schloss laid out around a courtyard, recased in a severe classical style in the second half of the eighteenth century. Ludbreg dominates the town, being four storeys high. It has been restored to a high specification with crisp and

11.19 Donji Martijanec, exterior. Photo: Ivana Peškan, Conservation Department, Ministry of Culture, Varaždin.

11.20 Veliki Bukovec, exterior. Photo: Ivana Peškan, Conservation Department, Ministry of Culture, Varaždin.

newly painted stucco. The age of the building is more apparent inside, where we are taken into a large chapel with ravishing rococo decoration. The arches spanning the ceiling are painted with rich rocaille shellwork. The illusionist architecture is open to the skies, framing scenes of heavenly hosts floating in the sky.

Throughout the twentieth century the mansion had a troubled history, used as a factory and then by the military. Now it is home to a series of well-equipped and staffed conservation workshops. We see exquisite seventeenth-century carved and gilded wooden ceiling work brought for treatment from the Rector's Palace in Dubrovnik. Other studios are devoted to altarpieces and textiles. It is slightly alarming to be led to a gas chamber, but this is for treating works of art suffering from fungal attack.

Veliki Bukovec (fig. 11.20) is a large manor house standing by the road at the edge of a village of the same name, built for Josip Kasimir Drašković in 1745–55, who had risen to the rank of Imperial Chamberlain and Confidential Imperial Councillor. The end of the building is occupied by an inn, but when we walk into the park the long flank looks derelict. Continuing round the end of the house, it is a surprise to find the entrance pavilion smartly painted with cars in front. Here we find the factor, who explains the situation. The house had become a school in 1950, which saved it from collapse. When the school moved out in 1980, the house was turned over to storage for locally made baskets. Left empty during the political upheavals of the 1990s, the local community had decided to offer it back to the last count, Dr Karl Graf Drašković, who was now 84. He had given it in turn to his son Nikola. For a long time it had proven impossible to do any

11.21 Klenovnik Castle, aerial view. Photo: Milan Babić, from the book: Mladen Obad Šćitaroci, Manors and Gardens of Croatian Zagorje

11.22 Bajnski Dvori, exterior. Photo: Ivana Peškan, Conservation Department, Ministry of Culture, Varaždin.

ourselves in a large top-lit staircase hall with colonnaded landings and handsome sturdy oak balustrades. But this was to be the low point of my tour. There had been a spate of burglaries, and two ancient retainers were struggling with a stepladder to take the tapestries off the walls. Only they were not tapestries but painted cloths portraying hunting scenes. It was hard to see they had any sale value, and sadder still was to see the wooden frames being unscrewed and levered off and dropped to the floor. How tragic it had come to this after all the house had survived.

Our next castle, Klenovnik, is illustrated in a striking aerial photograph in the Gold Book (fig. 11.21). This shows a grand courtyard house, extended by wings set proudly on a hilltop encircled by trees. It was built in the seventeenth century in two stages by the Drašković family, and completed in 1667. A charming inscription in the garden, coinciding with the start of work, runs: 'May this building stand until an ant drinks up the sea and a tortoise circles the earth.' By the twentieth century the house was too large to live in, and in 1925 it was sold to the Zagreb Workers' Insurance Centre. Since 1925 it has been a hospital for tuberculosis and lung diseases.

Numerous large houses such as this have been taken over as hospitals in Western Europe, notably in Britain, where the inexorable pattern is that after the buildings have been hugely extended and usually disfigured by additions, the authorities suddenly decide the institution is no longer fit for purpose and close it down. Thereafter, their sole interest in the property is to sell it for as much money as possible, if necessary by dividing much of the surrounding land into building plots.

The saving grace of such large buildings often lies in their settings, and so it is here. The drive circled up through grounds planted with numerous handsome trees, an approach with more than a touch of Rothschild grandeur. From the top there are naturally splendid views, though some have been obscured by trees, as well as garden court and terraces. With its ancillary accommodation, the castle will convert readily into a conference hotel or training college should the hospital leave.

We next stopped briefly at Bajnski Dvori (fig. 11.22), a charming fragment of a house burnt down by miners in the uprising which followed the fall of Austro-Hungarian Empire in 1918. Dating from the mid-nineteenth century, it has hood moulds to the windows, diamond pattern glazing, and buttresses – shades of the English Tudor style. Standing in pleasant grounds, it could either become, in due course, a private house or be adapted as for holiday lets. It served as a hospital until about ten years ago and now belongs to the state. We heard that the heirs of the former owners have put in a request for the return of the property.

work because of bureaucratic delays. The village had simply made a present of a big problem. Not the least problem was that the house now has nine hectares rather than the original 1,000, much of which had been sold after the First World War. The family had continued to come here for summer holidays and for hunting in winter, but all this had come to an end in 1945.

We entered a smart vaulted hall with antlers on the walls. The factor had a small comfortable office and the count a ground-floor flat. The appeal of this seemed to be that it was relatively easy to keep warm. Ascending the main staircase, we found a parade of fine rooms with parquet floors and decorative plaster ceilings, all awaiting restoration. It was heroic for the family to have returned at all, and excellent that the factor was installed.

We drove on to Maruševec, which had been bought in 1873 by the Prussian Count Schlippenbach, who had remodelled the house in romantic castle style. His coat of arms with an eight-point coronet carries the date 1877 and marks completion. The composition is dominated by a massive donjon tower with bartisan turrets corbelled out from the corners. Beneath it is a carriage arch set low and seemingly groaning under the weight of the masonry above. Stepped gables and pepper pot towers add further romance to the skyline.

After 1945 the house had been used for a while by the commune and in 1969 leased to Christian Adventists. They remained there until 1999, when the house reverted to the commune. A year or two ago, the house was returned to the legal owner, Dr Oscar Pongratz. We entered expectantly, finding

11.23 Opeka, the ruined house. Photo: Jadranka Beresford-Peirse.

11.24 Opeka arboretum. Photo: Ivana Peškan, Conservation Department, Ministry of Culture, Varaždin.

Opeka is a famous arboretum planted principally by Count Marko Bombelles with seeds and specimens he had culled from travels all over the world. The gardens begin on the flat but then climb the hillside, first gently, then above the manor increasingly steeply and dramatically. Opeka without question is

an international marvel, a place of astonishing beauty, richness and variety in terms of its planting. At the end of October the autumn colour was mesmerising, not the reds of New England but every shade of yellow, gold and russet brown. Yet what a tragic site too. The house was boarded up and half-way to ruin (fig. 11.23). Worse, the spiral of decay was taking over the gardens. On the lower levels the grass was still regularly cut and paths maintained, but above the house the grounds were becoming a jungle. Trees lay where they had fallen, blocking paths. An increasing part of the grounds were fast become inaccessible. Yet just opposite the gates we found a flourishing well-maintained school of horticulture. Could they not spare some students for a few hours a week for some practical work?

The park at Opeka contains trees and shrubs from Japan, China, Tibet, the Caucasus, North America and many parts of Europe (fig. 11.24). The 1963 plant census recorded 4,927 deciduous trees and 8,651 conifers – in all 14,016 varieties of trees and shrubs. Exotics included tulip trees, black walnut, royal paulownia, *Pterocarya* and the pagoda tree. In the prosperous, well-supported and fashionable world of international gardens, Opeka could surely find some friends willing to put project money into its revival. This is a case where rescue of the garden should take precedence over the house, for once Opeka is on the mend it will attract increasing numbers of visitors and the house will need to be repaired to accommodate them.

On the long drive to Osijek (fig. 11.25), our first stop was the castle of Stari Grad at Đurđevac, standing in flat fenland at the edge of the village (fig. 11.26). The remarkable story of the castle's stand against the Turks is told with relish. When the garrison faced starvation, they decided in a magnificent show of bravura to fire their last chicken at the besiegers. The Turks, taking this as a sign that supplies were plentiful, promptly lifted the siege. Looking at Đurđevac today, it is hard to see how so small a castle could have successfully held out against the Turks at all. The explanation must be that in the seventeenth century this was highly treacherous marshland, only later drained by a system of dykes. Inside the castle is not what you might expect – a fortress where you visit dungeons, ascend narrow spiral staircases and look out through arrowslits and gunloops. The interior is a modern picture gallery forming a continuous circuit around the central courtyard with no cross walls.

Driving on to Virovitica, I am dropped in front of Pejačević Castle (fig. 11.27). It is splendidly sited in the centre of the town on rising ground amidst the now familiar grove of trees. There is a baroque geometry in the layout with an approaching main road aligned on the entrance tower for at least a mile, while the road from Zagreb to Osijek intersects at a right angle. The castle is shabby, and the characteristic Austrian livery of butter yellow with white trim is pockmarked and flaking. The main front with grand pavilion centre and ends has a depressing institutional feel. Across the road is an impressive baroque church lined with

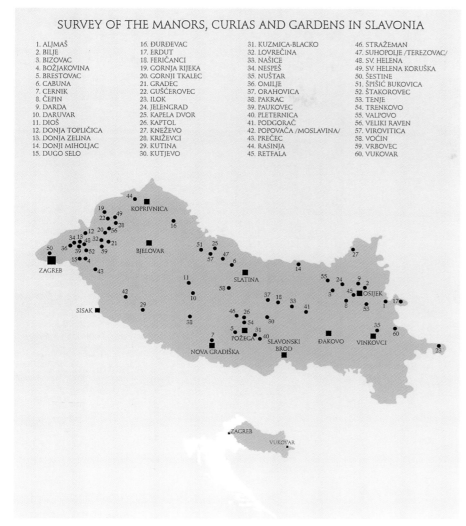

SURVEY OF THE MANORS, CURIAS AND GARDENS IN SLAVONIA

11.25 Map of Slavonia from Zagreb to Vukovar, Mladen Obad Šćitaroci and Bojana Bojanić Obad Šćitaroci, *Manors and Gardens in Croatia*, Zagreb 2001, p. 70.

11.26 Đurđevac Castle, exterior. Photo: Milan Pelc.

a stunning series of baroque altars carved in wood and adorned with statues painted to look like the smoothest Carrara marble. One altar contains a cage of lost souls being burnt in hell. The magnificently ornate pulpit is dated 1759.

Returning to the castle I walk through the many columned carriage entrance to make some most unusual discoveries. First, the cellar to the left is now a bierstube with two-lane bowling alley neatly fitted into the long brick vault. In the sunken garden beyond the main terrace is the town lido, a large and rather splendid outdoor pool, cleverly just below the line of sight. Ascending to the great hall, I rub my eyes in disbelief at an exhibit of modern traffic signs with sample road surface and markings running diagonally across the floor. The room is absolutely bare, no panelling, pilasters, not even a cornice or a skirting. Then I spot little windows opened up by scrapes in the white paint showing colourful decorative painting. The main rooms are mostly devoted to archaeological display. Asked what she would do if funds were available, the curator said: 'Put the castle back as it was.' The present plans are slightly different – for the mayor to move here from the town hall. But it might be no bad thing for the castle to be the focus of civic life and host to major civic receptions. The mayor should begin by restoring the decorative scheme in one room to give us an idea of vanished splendour, perhaps creating an appetite for more. Certainly, the castle has a fascinating history. Old engravings show a formidable walled and moated fortress on the site.

Janković Manor stands on rising ground in the centre of the town of Suhopolje in a large and splendid grove of trees. It is a fine house just seven or so windows wide which could be adapted to any number of uses – as a museum or gallery, restaurant cum hotel or as a series of apartments. Yet the plaster is peeling from the walls, and there is not a pane of glass in the windows. You can walk in through any number of doors or simply step through the windows. Ironically, a start was made on the Gothic gate screen which leads through to the front courtyard. It has a blue tin roof and Disney-looking turrets. Though trees shelter the house, there is a large sports arena barely 100 metres away and to the side below the outbuildings a bierstube with numerous outdoor tables.

It is hard to see how the house can ever be given sufficient land to make it suitable for residential use, nor how the town can find sufficient funds to restore it and run it as a museum. Yet it remains a landmark with an interesting history – the solution perhaps is to make

11.27 Pejačević Castle, Virovitica, exterior. Photo: Marko Ćolić.

11.28 Donji Miholjac, exterior. Photo: Marko Ćolić.

windowless. On one side were pleasant wooded hills, on the other the drone of traffic as it crossed a bridge. Yet someone should make something of this ruin, perhaps as a small emporium of shops and restaurant for travellers. The walls are robust, and internal reconstruction could be straightforward.

In the town of Slatina, opposite a large factory, a tall chalet-like house stood beside the road, a sign announcing it as Dvorac Drašković (Drašković Manor). This was a splendid essay in Greek Revival style painted in Pompeian red and cream. A pair of stately caryatids held up the main gable. The house is clearly the work of an architect of talent and imagination. Yet windows were broken and the house unsecured. Help is urgently needed.

Donji Miholjac (fig. 11.28) is a splendid baronial nineteenth-century house such as you find in the Sologne south of Orleans or in Scotland. Designed by the Hungarian architect Istvan Möller and built in 1905–14, it is in full romantic mode, bristling with gables and turrets and a very grand line of single-storey outbuildings. Once again it is in the centre of the town, in a large well-tended park which takes the form of a shady grove of trees. Close to the house the formal planting of the garden remains.

I am met by Melia Vidaković, full of bonhomie and enthusiasm with all the energy needed for a European minister of tourism. The house is used by two branches of government, so I enter with some trepidation. The office workers have gone home, but a posse of good natured cleaning ladies are at work, and kindly admit us to all the main rooms. The heating is full on, and I voice my fears that the atmosphere is so dry that the panelling may soon start to

it a kind of hostelry. I began to think of the Spanish paradors or rather the Portuguese pousadas, which are more modest in size but also state-funded hostelries. Croatia has many calls on funds, but might not an organisation on these lines perhaps bring in some investment into a few of these houses? On the edge of the town is a very splendid neoclassical church with huge dome and inside an extraordinary rockwork pulpit and stately temple-fronted organ.

Driving on I saw the shell of a handsome brown brick house across the fields, distinctly English in its restrained Georgian proportions and detail. This is Cabuna. We drove up to find the roof collapsed but the facade at the back largely intact though

shrink and crack. The main interiors are wonderfully complete with a wealth of handsome panelling and woodwork, as well as stone vaulting and balustrades and a splendid Puginesque brass chandelier in the main hall. As tourism grows, there is a case for Donji Miholjac to be opened to the public as a grand stately home or hotel. A big surprise emerges on the second floor in the cavernous space beneath the roof. The huge timbers rise nearly three stories; there is no floor but instead a wooden deck which allows you to walk the length of the space. From here we ascended an elaborate wooden stair to an observation chamber in the tower with panoramic views of the town through windows on all four sides.

11.29 Bilje, exterior. Photo: Goran Bekina.

11.30 Darda Manor, exterior. Photo: Goran Bekina.

offices, and the numerous doors around the courtyard (pleasantly shaded by plane trees) make conversion to other uses such as a hotel or series of cottages very straightforward. A splendid coat of arms with banners, cannons and muskets survives on the inside of the archway. Steps lead down to extensive cellars which are said to be connected by tunnel to a nearby barracks.

The manor at Darda (fig. 11.30) in Turkish times had been linked to Osijek by a famous pontoon bridge, the Suleiman Bridge, eight kilometres long across the marshes, burnt down in 1664 when the Turks retreated. Darda is approached by a long straight estate road and stands fronted by gates opposite a range of farm buildings. It is an impressive three-sided composition fronted by a double-height portico with the upper stage glazed in like a conservatory. Its appearance is early nineteenth century.

Today it is a sorry sight as every single pane of glass is broken, though the roof has been patched with the correct fish-scale tiles at the back. This is all the more poignant as here I find fishermen perched contentedly by the water of the canal. Immediately beyond, a tractor is mowing a large sports ground. For how long must the house stand decaying? There is clearly some land which could be assigned to the house, including an attractive grove of trees to one side. In due course, if the roof remains sound, it could surely be let or better sold for a range of uses ranging from residential to hotel or offices.

We drove on to Vukovar to look at Dvorac Eltz (Eltz Manor), a grand eighteenth-century residence begun by Count Kueffstein in 1728 and completed

Bilje (fig. 11.29) is a hunting lodge built for Prince Eugene of Savoy, the scourge of the Turks at the turn of the eighteenth century. His grateful hosts had bestowed large estates upon him, but the restless warrior never returned to enjoy them. The lodge is laid out on a courtyard plan with a tower over the entrance arch. Bilje is entirely surrounded by a deep, wide, dry moat and approached across a brick arch bridge. The moat is walled around the inner side, preventing stock from approaching, and there are pointed bastions at the corners. On one of these stands a delightful domed sentry box or look-out point. At the back, vaulted chambers open onto the moat like the basement coal cellars of a London town house. The lodge is now used as

by Count Eltz after he acquired the estate in 1736 (fig. 11.31). It stands in a splendid position on the west bank of the river Danube. The main approach was originally by water so the principal front faces the river. Tragically the house was fiercely shelled by the Yugoslav army and Serbian paramilitaries during the War of Independence (fig. 11.32). The bright butter-yellow stucco shown in photographs has vanished, leaving pockmarked brickwork. Funds for a new roof were raised at a concert held in London's Royal Festival Hall. Across the road on the land side, the extensive series of outbuildings are also badly shot up and mostly roofless. Nonetheless, a determined start has been made. The orangery is restored and repainted with a modern art gallery

11.31 Eltz Palace, Vukovar, the Town Museum, before destruction. Photo: V. Červenka, courtesy of the Town Museum, Vukovar.

11.32 Eltz Palace, the Town Museum, Vukovar, after destruction. Photo: V. Červenka, courtesy of the Town Museum, Vukovar.

renovated the castle in Italian style, and later generations recast the park in French and English style with both terraces and informal planting. The Odescalchis extended the wine cellars under their residence and introduced new grape varieties such as Sylvaner and Traminer. They also initiated the sale of wine in bottles. Special pride is taken in the serving of Ilok wine at the wedding of Princess Elizabeth of England in 1947, who was crowned queen six years later. The cellars are lined with large barrels (fig. 11.34), including a glass one supplied from Vienna in 1909 and containing 36,140 litres. The residence will reopen as a hotel aimed at attracting visitors interested in wine. The noble nineteenth-century church nearby has been superbly restored and has a very fine painted interior with trails of flowers and vines painted on a pale beige ground.

On the edge of the town of Osijek is Retfala, a grand eighteenth-century residence of the Counts Pejačević, whose name occurs so frequently in these parts. It is set back behind a screen of railings with a large forecourt where building work is going on in earnest. The house has a raised pedimented centre with an inset arcade. On either side are lower L-shaped wings with mansard roofs and temple-front ends echoing the main pavilion. It had just been bought by a leading

within. Inside the house the shelling has done appalling damage. Yet tantalisng fragments remain of stucco ceilings and fireproof vaults above, as well as a marble chimneypiece.

Along the river to Ilok (fig. 11.33) there is a large four-square baroque palace carrying the name of one of the great papal families, the Odescalchi. It stands within the medieval walls of what was once the second largest walled town in Croatia. The position is impressive, though not the smoking factories built on the far bank in Serbia. Yet the setting of the castle remains green with extensive gardens and trees within the walls. Within the walled enceinte there are monastery buildings as well as the remains of a Turkish bath. Summer excavations are revealing the remains of a major twelfth-century basilica sixty metres in length. When Ilok was liberated from the Turks in 1688, it was given to Pope Innocent XI, who gave it to his nephews. They

local businessman, who is to make it his home. The position is conspicuous on the main road out of town, so this sounds a good solution. After confiscation in 1945, Retfala became a hospital, which had continued here until 1990.

Valpovo is a rare medieval castle which escaped destruction by the Turks (fig. 11.35). It stands in the centre of the town, an enceinte of high walls with a tall medieval tower at one end and baroque clock tower at the other. The clock tower fronts an impressive baroque entrance range with giant pilasters which raises hopes of eighteenth-century state rooms within. Entering through a carriage arch, a concert platform inside shows the courtyard is in regular use for events. The chapel is deconsecrated and used for exhibitions. It is bright and white within, retaining an unusual drum-shaped pulpit set impressively at the top of a long straight flight of steps, all in black ironwork.

11.33 Ilok. Photo: Mario Romulić.

We then ascended the medieval tower, where each level contains a saucer domed chamber with brick floors neatly laid in concentric circles. The second-floor chamber has handsome stone window seats in best medieval manner with a chamfered stone archway to the door. Emerging on the top of the tower, we admire castle grounds extending beyond the immediate public park into woodland – a remarkable green lung for the town. On one side is a large stable block which I am told is owned by a bank. There is a possibility that the central pavilion could become a theatre.

11.34 Wine cellars at Ilok. Photo: Marko Ćolić.

Descending to the courtyard, I am now looking forward to seeing the rooms in the entrance range. But no, we cannot enter. It was occupied by troops during the War of Independence, and all the furniture vanished as well as the staircase. Instead, we ascend an outdoor flight of steps to a first-floor balcony with iron railings and arches carrying lights. This opens into the former family apartments, a series of arch-vaulted rooms with bold baroque plaster panels in the ceilings and pretty neo-rococo porcelain stoves. There is some charming grisaille panelling, part classical, part Gothic. As we leave, strains of piano music fill the courtyard. The opposite range was used as a music school.

Like other castles, Valpovo was nationalised after the Second World War. Though money has evidently been spent at various periods on repairs, the castle looks in decline with no clear plans for its future use. The best hope appears to lie with the Prandau family, now based in Germany or Austria, who had contacted the town authorities to enquire if they could take back the castle. This strikes me as a prime case for re-establishing the family connection, hopefully bringing in both investment and a family presence, and no less important some heirlooms in the form of portraits or furniture. These negotiations I had learnt elsewhere are very complex and not always fruitful. There is no clear policy on restitution as in the Czech Republic, and families shy away

11.35 Valpovo Castle, exterior. Photo: Marko Ćolić.

11.36 Large manor of Pejačević family, Našice. Photo: Marko Ćolić.

of the high street. The ground descends steeply, providing impressive vistas across the valley below to the Hungarian hills. The large manor was built in 1811–12 for Count Vincencije Pejačević and extensively enlarged and remodelled in the 1860s (fig. 11.36). The house is in the familiar butter-yellow stucco with white architectural trim. The centre breaks forward boldly, containing an arched porte cochère and flanked by delightful domed corner towers added in 1865. A grand sweeping roof adds a further impressive flourish.

The entrance hall is ablaze with *belle époque* opulence, filled by a brilliant white sweeping horseshoe staircase. The balustrade is baroque, the wall panels Louis Seize with occasional details that are almost Vienna Secession. The salon at the top, overlooking the park, has a wooden inlay floor and a star-pattern ceiling. There is a magnificently ornate late nineteenth-century sideboard, presumably Viennese, encrusted with trophies of game. Three rooms are memorials to local celebrities, one of whom is Dora Pejačević, the Croatian composer. The interiors are as well looked after as money allows and a proud municipal possession. Here, too, there have been discussions with the Pejačević family as to whether they might return. Back in England I learn the conditions are considered very onerous and nothing is likely to happen.

The little manor was built in 1905–7 because the then Count Pejačević disapproved of his son's bride. The house is a pavilion, set 200 metres to the side of the large manor, screened by trees and with its own axial vista over the valley. There is no doubt that this would make an enchanting family house or indeed small hotel or elegant restaurant. If a private house, it would need to be given the privacy of its own gardens. Currently it is used by a broadcasting company which has ensured it is well maintained and allows the public to appreciate its architecture as they walk round the park. The entrance front has a pretty colonnade of paired wooden columns. On the garden side a series of stepped terraces are visible beneath the grass – the ornamental planting is shown in old photographs.

because negotiations are slow in the extreme and the liability enormous with little incentive to invest. Valpovo, being largely empty, appears a good place to explore a gradual transition.

At the bustling town of Našice two important mansions of the Pejačević family stand in extensive grounds on one side

The Franciscan monastery on the other side of the high street contains a pretty trellised gallery overlooking the choir from which the Pejačević ladies could watch the Mass in seclusion. There are also two splendid marbled baroque altars, one red, the other black. Standing proudly above a road on the edge of town is a Gothic funerary chapel designed by Herman Bollé, the architect who remodelled the cathedral in Zagreb.

Over the hills in Kutjevo, Turković Manor stands in a commanding position at the top of one of the main approaches to the town (fig. 11.37). It is set in a large circle of grass shaded by some fine trees with railings along the road but very much on show. Wide expanses of grass on surrounding roads add to the pastoral feel. With its commanding onion-domed tower Turković Manor is ideally placed to become a hotel, and indeed this is precisely what is planned. But all is far from well. The company carrying out the conversion has run into financial trouble, and work has ground to a halt. The property now belongs to an insurance company, and a further sum of one million euros is needed to complete the work.

It rapidly becomes apparent that the conversion work has been completely out of sympathy with the old building. Dormers have been added to light bedrooms in the attics, but though they are large and clumsy, the actual windows are tiny and mean, hardly an attractive prospect for future guests. Inside it is more dismal still. Not a trace of old fabric remains, not a stone step, a doorcase, a floorboard or a ceiling beam. Every surface is bare concrete. The rooms have lost their traditional pleasant proportions, as in each one an ugly bite has been taken out to install a windowless bathroom. 'It is quite impossible to undo this condition,' says my guide.

We walk round the back to find a very large factory has been built against the manor – one small consolation is that none of the bedrooms look out this way. We are taken round to the factory gate, where we have been told we can sample the local wine. There is a grim office block ahead, but instead we descend to a magnificent cellar running beneath the manor. The arch vault is so darkened it is hard to see if it is in brick or stone. It contains a splendid series of barrels, one dated 1918. On the lower level is a still wider double-aisled cellar apparently dating from the seventeenth century. At the end are a series of large barrels with ends carved with scenes in folk style telling the story of wine making in the area, beginning with the arrival of the Cistercians, continuing with the Turkish wars and the coming of the Jesuits. The Turković family, who arrived in the nineteenth century, sold their oaks to shipyards.

After a week I was left with some very sharp impressions. First, despite over sixty harrowing years of neglect and rough treatment, numerous castles and manor houses remain, stripped of their contents and often interiors too, but many still in pleasant grounds. The Communists deliberately allowed development close to some houses to score a political point. This restricts the range of potential uses in some cases.

In Britain conversion of grand houses and their outbuildings into a number of self-contained houses, apartments and cottages has been the saving of many overlarge houses. In Croatia house prices at the moment are too low to generate this level of investment, though the market may rise rapidly as the economy catches up with Western Europe.

Clearly, there is some potential for encouraging the pre-1945 owners to return, though this is unlikely to happen unless the terms allow them to see some increased value in their investment. Some of the properties in question are so decayed that they have a zero or negative value. Re-establishing the family connection is not going to be easy or to happen in more than a few cases, but it deserves exploring and encouraging.

A larger number of houses are likely to be acquired by investors and developers, and it is vital to exert firm planning controls to ensure there is no further erosion of the character of these places, whether through random subdivision or unsuitable new building nearby. Croatian castles and manor houses have potential to contribute to tourism, whether as places to visit or to stay. In encouraging tourism, Croatia has the attraction of scenery, sun and excellent and moderately priced food and wine. Its castles and manor houses deserve government support and promotion.

One special challenge is that many of the documents which tell the story of these houses and estates are not in Croatia but in Vienna or Budapest. In addition to the excellent Croatian scholarship which has illuminated the history of these houses, there are new seams of history to be explored which should yield information about owners and architects and what appears so rare – architects' drawings. Every castle and manor house that I have seen in Croatia is worthy of an effort to save it or ensure that it continues to flourish. Despite depradations, this is still a rich heritage, rewarding to explore.

11.37 Turković Manor, Kutjevo. Photo: Marko Ćolić.

MUSEUMS OF ZAGREB

Brian Sewell

Zagreb, capital of Croatia, small though it is, might well be described as a city of museums, so many are there within its walls devoted to so many subjects, their range reaching from the fine and applied arts to science, engineering and technology, from archaeology to the natural sciences, from musical instruments to the botanical gardens (fig. 12.1). In this they reflect the nineteenth-century extension and consolidation of intellectual interests first logically and scrupulously explored, classified and catalogued in the Age of Enlightenment that was the previous century; they reflect, too, the growth of intellectual equality with Vienna that was so much a sign of increasing independence, first from Austria and later from the Austro-Hungarian Empire. Croatia – one of the strongest voices in the argument for political independence among the full half of the empire's population that was neither Austrian nor Hungarian – did not, of course, achieve it even after Austria's defeat in the First World War, but was instead frustratingly subsumed in the newly formed Yugoslavia. Not until a decade after the death of Marshal Tito in 1980 did Croatian nationalists succeed in breaking away from the by then disintegrating union, and the country's independence was at last recognised by the European Union in 1992. The subsequent hostilities with Serbia and Bosnia, so damaging to the country's cultural monuments, would never have occurred had an independent Croatia been one of the consequences of the Treaty of Versailles in 1919 – as it could easily have been had British politicians maintained the interest in Croatia continuously demonstrated by William Gladstone when prime minister in the nineteenth century.

THE MIMARA MUSEUM

The most imposing of Zagreb's museums has, however, nothing to do with Croatian history, nor the Enlightenment, nor the broad historical sweep of Austrian intellectual, cultural and religious influences. Rather it is a recent donation to the city by the multimillionaire Ante Topić Mimara, a private collector and dealer who was for many years a close confidant of Marshal Josip Broz Tito.

I write of it first because, housed in what might easily be mistaken for a vast neoclassical palace (it was a school) with three pavilions connected by wings twelve bays in length, it is not only the most imposing museum in the city, but the newest and the most extravagantly conceived and subsidised by the state, 'MIMARA' written grandiloquently across the central pavilion. At a time when guidebooks are too often based on received rather than researched information, it is the museum given the most prominence in the most accessible literature: one guide, listing the city's 'Top Ten' museum exhibits, offers nine that are of great distinction, but as the tenth it proposes a portrait in the Mimara collection attributed to Velázquez that has been accepted as genuine by no art historian with expertise in Spanish art.

I write of the Mimara Museum first because Mimara also had some influence over what, for a century, had been Croatia's equivalent of a national gallery, and his interventions there cannot be understood without some awareness of the nature of the man; in doing what he did, he lent his collection, and himself, undeserved credibility. I write, too, because I have had personal knowledge of Mimara since the mid-1960s and have much unpublished information that casts a shadow on his collection; he and his museum are, to use a vulgar idiom, the elephants in the room, and I wish to drive them out of it.

12.1 A view of Zagreb: the Arts Pavilion in the foreground, built in 1896 to represent Croatia at the International Exhibition in Budapest, was set in this site in 1989 by Ferdinand Fellner and Hermann Helmer. Photo: Ivo Pervan, courtesy of the Croatian Tourist Board.

Few art specialists anywhere knew anything of Mimara, though he claimed to have begun collecting when a child and to have bought his first important antiquity in his very early twenties. In 1963, Thomas Hoving, then curator of the Cloisters in New York, the medieval department of the Metropolitan Museum, and later director of the museum itself, brought Mimara out of the shadows when he purchased from him the *Bury St Edmunds Cross*, a twelfth-century ivory carving that has no recent provenance and almost certainly nothing to do with what was once one of England's earliest and richest abbeys. As the price – 600,000 US dollars – was then among the highest ever paid for a work of art, rumour and insinuation multiplied, boosted by Mimara's boast that he had been the art adviser and friend of Hermann Goering, the rapacious Nazi leader whose collections of paintings and objects he had helped to form both before and during the Second World War. Of this there is no proof, but there are many indications that Mimara was in Germany throughout the war, himself in possession of a constantly increasing collection – the broker's cut – and that in the pan-European confusions of the post-war years it grew at an even faster pace. Appointed to the Yugoslav Military Mission in Berlin in 1946, his task was to supervise matters of cultural restitution, and he was given a diplomatic passport that enabled him to travel anywhere he wished in the vast range of ravished Europe. He was subsequently accused of transferring to Yugoslavia, primarily Serbia, works that had been erroneously identified in Italy, France, Czechoslovakia and other Central European countries. By the mid-1950s his own collection was enormous, and of this he presented a substantial part to the then Socialist Republic of Croatia in October 1973.

When, early in 1983, I learned that in September his gift was at last to be accessible to the public and that a catalogue had been published boasting paintings by Raphael, Michelangelo, Parmigianino, Castagno, Caravaggio, Giorgione, Titian, El Greco, Velázquez, Rembrandt, Rubens, Van Gogh and most of the Impressionists, I went to see the collection, very puzzled by the valuation then put on it of only three million pounds. Housed in the Villa Zagorje some distance from the centre of the Croatian capital, it proved to be not the boasted Louvre of Zagreb, but an embarrassing assembly of pictures wrongly attributed and heavily and recently reworked.

There was, however, still room for hope that the collection might be, in some sense, significant, for in the Villa Zagorje there had been room to display only a hundred or so paintings and a selection of Mimara's Chinese, Japanese and European works of art, porcelain, ivories, antiquities, sculptures, glass and carpets – perhaps a tenth of the collection. His impassioned plea that the public and the experts in these fields should support him in his ambition to exhibit the remainder was realised in July 1987, shortly after his death, with the opening of 'The Art Collection of Ante and Wiltrud Topić Mimara' in the late nineteenth-century neo-Renaissance palace on Roosevelt Square in central Zagreb. Its

3,754 exhibits, it was then claimed, were 'an art collection of worldwide renown … an artistic treasure … for the entire world', and Mimara's unprincipled activities as an acquirer were presented in terms of aesthetic conviction, indefatigable labour, scholarship, and the fulfilled certainty that in forgotten collections in remote corners of Europe great masterpieces had lurked undiscovered until he, Mimara, had found them – a noble ideal of which he never wearied, as related in the 1989 Mimara catalogue: 'From his sojourn in foreign lands he returned bearing gifts on an unprecedented scale.'

In the 1989 revision and enlargement of the collection's catalogue, among half-a-dozen essays of post-mortem praise and adulation, a brief curriculum vitae is included, from which we learn that Mimara, born in 1898, was apprenticed in Rome at the age of twenty or so to Antonio Mancini, a fashionable portrait painter whom John Singer Sargent thought the best of his Italian contemporaries; he also 'took instruction in the craft of picture restoring'. These two facts perhaps explain the consistency of the many later interventions, alterations and subversions that corrupt the ambitiously attributed paintings in the Mimara Museum. It is excessive to assume that every painting in Mimara's collection has in some sense been falsified, but the informed visitor's response is too often disrupted, even overwhelmed, by his attributions, often to the greatest painters in the history of art. In every gallery and museum the connoisseur is confronted by a handful of questionable attributions and with problems of wear, abuse and restoration that not only obscure the original state and intention of paintings but distort our perception and interpretation of them, but in the Mimara Museum we are dumbfounded by their number. The only reasonable approach is to ignore the labels, the signatures and the catalogue, to set aside not only the many paintings that are obviously intended to deceive but the hostility and prejudice that they engender, and to treat the remaining pictures as unattributed, though not unattributable, and make our own suggestions. Only by adopting this stratagem can the visitor be dispassionate enough to derive benefit from the collection.

The benefit is very small. In the museum's first room a handful of trecento panels, though jostled by worthless icons, raise the visitor's expectations. A painting of *Christ's Circumcision* attributed to Pietro Lorenzetti has some serious quality; probably a panel from a polyptych, this surprisingly dramatic and expressive narrative is by neither of the Lorenzetti brothers, but by a more than competent follower later in the century. The *St Lawrence*, too, attributed to Simone Martini, has quality, but it is so distant from Simone that the attribution disrupts our perception. A *Virgin and Child with Saints* given to Niccolo di Pietro Gerini (though not by him) sustains our hope that perhaps the Mimara collection is not quite so bad, but then a *Virgin and Child* listed as English fourteenth century dashes the hope, and no picture deeper into this vast and functionally splendid palace revives it. The art historian may find momentary relief from

12.2 *St Luke*, mid-sixteenth century, oil on wood, 156 x 96 cm, Mimara Museum, Zagreb. Photo: Nedeljko Čaće.

scepticism in a *Ruth and Boaz* signed and dated Gerbrand van den Eeckhout AD 1661, though it is not of international museum standard, only then to be outraged by pictures attributed to his master, Rembrandt; and though the attribution of a large *St Luke* to Raphael (fig. 12.2) could hardly be more mistaken, it is at least a mid-seicento picture of some quality, though neither Florentine nor Roman. In all the hundreds of pictures on view (not by any means the complete collection), not more than twenty are worth a second glance; with so much dross the intelligence of the experienced visitor is insulted, and the inexperienced visitor and the student of art history are deceived.

On the Mimara Museum's lower floors, however, the ratio of masterpiece to rubbish is more even. Mimara's small holding of early antiquities is not to be trusted – indeed, many of his Egyptian and classical objects are risible – but among his Christian ornaments, and particularly his glass, some fine things

are to be found, and a few of his ivories are intriguing enough to remind us of the *Bury St Edmunds Cross* that first brought him to international notice. But what virtues his holding of art objects and the applied arts may have are not significant enough to compensate for the scandal embodied in his pictures. Croatian scholars are well aware of the international embarrassment they suffer while the museum continues to exist, promoted as a jewel among the intellectual attractions of their capital, and it is to be hoped that in the not too distant future the political authorities of Croatia will close the building, transfer the few fine paintings and works of applied art to the academy of which the Strossmayer Gallery of Old Masters is a part, and dispose of the remainder. Mimara himself provided a precedent for such a transfer.

THE STROSSMAYER GALLERY OF OLD MASTERS

In the debate over Mimara's connoisseurship as demonstrated in his eponymous museum, perhaps the most disconcerting argument is engendered by the eighty-two paintings that much earlier (in 1948 though not confirmed until 1967 and integrated only in 1971) he donated to the Strossmayer Gallery in Zagreb, for though among these a handful are of serious merit or museum quality, the remainder are typical of Mimara in their doubtful authenticity and the ambition of their attributions. The authorities of the gallery were unwise to accept the gift (and indeed did not accept all the pictures that were offered), for it dramatically weakened what had been an intriguing and important example of a gallery formed by one man, Bishop Josip Juraj Strossmayer, for political, nationalist and educational purposes at much the same time as not dissimilar collections were formed, initially for more personal reasons, in Western Europe – witness the Wallace Collection and the Jacquemart-André, Poldi Pezzoli, Lazaro Galdiano and Bowes museums.

Josip Juraj Strossmayer, born in 1815 into a merchant family of Austrian origin (his parents came from Linz), was a man of brilliant and precocious mind – at eighteen, in 1833, a doctor of philosophy, at twenty-three a priest, at twenty-seven a doctor of theology and a university professor in that discipline, at thirty-two court chaplain in Vienna and at thirty-five bishop of Đakovo in eastern Croatia, near his birthplace of Osijek and the frontier with Hungary. His official title was bishop of Bosnia, Slavonia and Sirmium (north-western Serbia), and it was in this diocese that he remained until his death in 1905, deeply involved in the politics of Slavonic nationalism within the Austro-Hungarian Empire. This he fostered throughout Croatia-Slavonia, among the Slavs of southern Austria, and in Dalmatia, recognised as the leader of the opposition to Hungarian predominance, gaining international support from many European leaders, among them Gladstone, with whom he maintained an extensive correspondence. To enhance the integrity of Croatian culture he published collections of national songs and stories, insisted on the reorganisation of the whole educational system to equal that of Austria itself, established schools, libraries and learned societies together with scholarships and other educational funds for the impoverished, achieved recognition in Vienna for the University of Zagreb (then known as Agram), and both founded and funded in that city the Yugoslav Academy of Arts and Sciences, and the gallery that has always born his name.

Further afield he was admired not only for these achievements, but for the constancy of his hostility to Hungarian dominance and his sympathy with Russia, his denunciation of the Jesuits (who became his bitter enemies), his long and energetic opposition to the doctrine of papal infallibility, and for his winning papal recognition of the right of his congregation to have a Slavonic rather than a Latin liturgy. In spite of these last, he enjoyed the confidence of Pope Leo XIII (himself something of a social and political reformer), who elevated him to the rank of archbishop and saw that he was appointed count of the Holy Roman Empire.

The Strossmayer Gallery of Old Masters opened in the autumn of 1884, occupying a whole floor of the academy and reinforcing its devotion to the arts. The academy itself, approved by Emperor Franz Josef in 1866, with Strossmayer as patron, had begun to function without dedicated premises in 1867, the year in which the bishop also began the construction of a cathedral and palace in Đakovo, the small town from which his diocese derived its name. Despite vigorously efficient management of the diocesan property from which came the funds for all his social, educational, political and ecclesiastical endeavours – and how much more might he have done had Croatia's Hungarian masters not taken in taxation half the income of its subject province – Strossmayer was unable to make funds available for a suitable building for the academy until 1875; the building was begun in 1877 and completed in 1880, with an empty floor to accommodate his pictures when he died. The completion of this typically Viennese neo-Renaissance palace by Friedrich von Schmidt, an architect of great eminence in Vienna (though best known for Gothic Revival designs), seems, however, to have triggered in Strossmayer the wish to see for himself the installation of his pictures there, and the donation was brought forward.

12.3 *St Peter Enthroned*, tempera on wood, 176 x 87.6 cm, Strossmayer Gallery, Zagreb. Photo: courtesy of the Strossmayer Gallery of Old Masters.

The bishop had been buying pictures for fully thirty years. On his appointment as bishop of Đakovo in 1850 he had found a number of old paintings in his official residence there, and in 1854 decided to buy more, at first systematically, pursuing what he thought to be the main streams of Italian art history, principally those of Renaissance Florence and Venice. In the 1870s, however, he diversified into the schools of northern Europe and the seventeenth-century while continuing to nourish his enthusiasm for earlier Italian painting. He relied, as did most rich amateurs, on the advice of the experts of the day, few of whom were in any way qualified to suggest or confirm an attribution. His 253 paintings were, nevertheless, diverse and interesting enough to be of great value to the new university's infant department of art history, members of which ensured that few of the early attributions survived long into the twentieth century. Such a significant nucleus attracted further benefactions, some of which, of work by then contemporary artists, led in 1934 to the foundation of a Gallery of Modern Art in Zagreb, thus maintaining the integrity of Strossmayer's benefaction as one of 'Old Masters' of art historical interest and importance.

The most serious upheaval of the founder's intentions occurred with the integration of Mimara's gift in 1971, when space for many of Strossmayer's paintings was usurped for his; the single floor of the academy's palace was suddenly too small to accommodate both. To the author of the gallery's 1982 catalogue, the Mimara donation, which he imagined to have been subject to the most recent findings of art history, 'their attributions established without vain pretension', refreshed and enriched that of Strossmayer and had to be given primacy; but at a stroke the period quality of the collection and its kinship with its fellows in Western Europe was mangled, though not beyond recovery. It should be possible to remove from view Mimara's El Greco, an arrant fake, the Fragonard self-portrait, the Ruisdael landscape and every other picture that in terms of authenticity, condition, integrity and quality defeats the declared educational purposes of Strossmayer; this would leave a handful that support and even enhance the quality of the founder's gift, for one painting, though an obstinate mystery, is truly outstanding.

This we must presume is a panel from an ornate, pierced and double-sided ecclesiastical screen; on both sides a sculptural image of *St Peter Enthroned* (fig. 12.3) as the first pope is almost illusionist in the skill with which it is set against the complex ogee arch of the screen elements that frame it. It is an irony that one of the most important and impressive pictures in the Strossmeter Gallery should have been presented by Mimara. His attribution was to a fifteenth-century member of the School of Avignon (for which there is not the slightest evidence), but in the 1985 catalogue an equally unacceptable attribution to the south Netherlandish painter Jean Bellegambe is proposed, with a date in the early decades of the sixteenth century, though the figure of St Peter is far too observed and monumental for so archaising a sensibility as his. We should, perhaps, think of the panel in the context of Hispano-Netherlandish painting towards the end of the fifteenth century. Mimara also gave the gallery a decent early sixteenth-century painting of the *Woman Taken in Adultery* very close to the Ferrarese painter Lodovico Mazzolino (his attribution) but more probably by Ortolano, a characteristic Pittoni of the *Adoration of the Shepherds*, an intriguing later seventeenth-century picture of beggars quite certainly not by Ribera (to whom he attributed it), and a landscape attributed to Wynants. This last is of peculiar interest in the context of Gainsborough: Mimara, of course, had the seventeenth-century Dutch painter Jan Wynants in mind (as do most art historians

writing of Gainsborough's early years). It is in fact by Francis Wynants, a landscape painter working in Suffolk when Gainsborough was a boy, and makes the point, yet again, that provenance might be useful – but nothing that belonged to Mimara has any earlier history.

I doubt if any of the paintings collected by Strossmayer is a fake, though he was collecting at a time when forgeries were being made on an almost industrial scale; I am, however, puzzled by three small panels of *Christ and the Twelve Apostles* attributed to Lorenzo di Alessandro, a painter from the Marches in the later quattrocento, for they are uncommonly, even astonishingly, free in their facture and modern in their physical types. They were bought in Rome before 1885, then thought to be by Carpaccio, but subsequently demoted to Venetian and then Central Italian schools until given to Lorenzo in 1926. They bear not the slightest resemblance to the signed and indisputably authentic *Mystic Marriage of St Catherine* by Lorenzo in the National Gallery in London. The current catalogue of the Strossmayer donation, published in 2006, lists them with a question mark and is, in general, much less assertive in tone than its 1985 predecessor, which included the Mimara donation; the words *način* (manner), *radionica* (workshop), *krug* (circle), *sljedbenik* (follower) and *neznani slikar* (unknown painter) appear with comforting frequency – they do not appear at all in any Mimara catalogue.

Among a small group of trecento and early quattrocento panel

12.4 *Stigmatisation of St Francis and the Death of St Peter Martyr*, tempera on wood, 24.3 x 43.8 cm, Strossmayer Gallery, Zagreb. Photo: courtesy of the Strossmayer Gallery of Old Masters.

12.5 Filippo Mazzola, *Christ at the Column*, tempera with oil on wood, 60.5 x 42.4 cm, Strossmayer Gallery, Zagreb. Photo: courtesy of the Strossmayer Gallery of Old Masters.

Cleopas, the mother of St James, and Mary of Bethany?), and perhaps the representative of a female order responsible for commissioning it. The *Holy Trinity* is attributed to the Master of the Virgo inter Virgines – an attribution adhered to by Friedländer – and is in remarkably fine condition for a late fifteenth-century painting on panel. The *sacra conversazione* (fig. 12.7) is by Girolamo da Carpi and combines Ferrarese idiosyncrasies with the formalities of Rome and Bologna. Through the bold devices of eye contact and a turning pose, the Baptist engages directly with the spectator, drawing him into the event while a putto diverts attention to the lamb; the Christ Child is cast in the character of the putti at the base of Raphael's *Sistine Madonna*. These two paintings encapsulate the best of Strossmayer's connoisseurship; as with many collectors of his period – Ludwig Mond in London is a parallel – he knew too little, depended too much on advisers who knew no more, and was seduced by names, but often enough was blessed with strokes of luck. The collection as a whole offers a fascinating insight into taste and judgement Europe-wide in the later nineteenth century.

Strossmayer was not without interest in the painters of his day. His museum still contains the portrait painted of him in 1892 by Vlaho Bukovac (fig. 12.8), the most significant and internationally known Croatian painter of the time. This pupil of Cabanel was resident in Paris from 1877 until 1893, when he returned to Zagreb, but was essentially a Salon painter with no interest in the

paintings of which the significant quality and interest should not be obscured by largely wayward attributions, a single predella panel illustrating the *Stigmatisation of St Francis and the Death of St Peter Martyr* (fig. 12.4) is hauntingly beautiful. It is attributed without qualification to Fra Angelico, but was rejected by Laurence Kantner when the Metropolitan Museum, New York, held its Fra Angelico exhibition in 2005, as 'a mysterious panel … difficult to characterise stylistically'.[1] It is certainly of the period and is in a fine state of conservation and of high museum quality. A half-length figure of *Christ at the Column* (fig. 12.5) is beyond speculation so prominent is the signature of Filippo Mazzola, a Parmesan painter, possibly a pupil of Alvise Vivarini, achieving in this panel something of the gravity of Antonello.

Strossmayer's most imposing Renaissance paintings are altarpieces – a *sacra conversazione* of the *Virgin and Child with Saints John the Baptist and Jerome* and an iconographically intriguing *Holy Trinity* (fig. 12.6) with Christ lying dead in the lap of God the Father, St John the Evangelist comforting the Virgin Mary, three other Marys of the New Testament (the wife of

12.6 *Holy Trinity*, oil on wood, 146 x 128 cm, Strossmayer Gallery, Zagreb. Photo: courtesy of the Strossmayer Gallery of Old Masters.

12.7 Girolamo da Carpi, *Virgin and Child with Saints John the Baptist and Jerome*, oil on wood, 137.6 x 140.4 cm, Strossmayer Gallery, Zagreb. Photo: courtesy of the Strossmayer Gallery of Old Masters.

12.8 Vlaho Bukovac, *Bishop Strossmayer*, 1892, oil on canvas, 144 x 112 cm, Strossmayer Gallery, Zagreb. Photo: courtesy of the Strossmayer Gallery of Old Masters.

Impressionists, though towards the end of his life he became something of a post-pointillist (he died in 1922). He was a popular portrait painter in England, particularly in the north, and had two campaigns of painting here in 1886 and 1888; I have no doubt that had his masterpiece of history painting, the *Dream of Gundulić* of 1894 (fig. 12.9), been exhibited here, wild enthusiasm from an audience accustomed to Alma-Tadema, Millais and Leighton would have been the consequence. Still catalogued as part of Strossmayer's collection, this is one of the two vast narrative paintings that in the first room of Zagreb's Gallery of Modern Art introduce the visitor to Croatian art of the twentieth century.

THE GALLERY OF MODERN ART

Founded in 1919 as a national museum for modern Croatian xart and in its palatial building since 1934, the museum was refurbished in its current cleverly chronological order in 1990, the means and methods of display changing sympathetically as it moves through the century. The donation of Bishop Strossmayer's later nineteenth-century paintings helped to give it a sound start and the *Dream of Gundulić* by Vlaho Bukovac confronts a particularly powerful and unremittingly bloody *Bacchanal* (fig. 12.10) by Celestin Medović, three of whose pictures Strossmayer also bought. Between them, these two paintings are a match in idea, narrative power and execution for all the pictures by their British contemporaries with which Henry Tate founded his gallery on Millbank. Tate could well, indeed, have been one of Bukovac's patrons; from the later 1880s almost until the outbreak of the First World War, the painter had a close and affectionate circle of friends and patrons in Britain, for two of whom at least collecting paintings was a consuming interest. These were Samson Fox of Harrogate and Richard LeDoux of West Derby near Liverpool, both of whom saw Bukovac as one of the leading painters of the day and were thus avid collectors of his work. Tate also hailed from Liverpool, and it can hardly have been by chance that in 1886 LeDoux bought Tate's house there. A London art dealership, Vicars Brothers, bought and sold pictures by Bukovac, and may have been the agents for the twenty portraits that he claimed to have painted of London sitters. A checklist of his paintings in British collections within his lifetime – fifty-five in number, most of them now untraced and probably languishing under false attributions – was published as an addendum to a formidable 'resurrection' article by Alex Kidson of the Walker Art Gallery, Liverpool.[2]

Further into the gallery are more of the bishop's paintings by Bukovac and his contemporary, Nikola Mašić. While Bukovac brought something of the Salon and the Royal Academy to Croatian painting, Medović brought the Munich School to Zagreb, a school even more celebrated than Paris at the time. Its influence is evident in the romantic light that he chose, as well as in handling of paint and colour; he was, however, a troubled soul who, having been ordained a priest, spent his later years in

12.9 Vlaho Bukovac, *Dream of Gundulić*, 1894, oil on canvas, 185 x 308 cm, Gallery of Modern Art, Zagreb. Photo: Luka Mjeda.

isolation. Mašić studied in both Munich and Paris, painted Croatian landscapes *en plein air*, and was damned by critics when he took to anecdotal realism.

These three painters were the founders of modern painting in Croatia, yet in their respect for the ancestral traditions of European painting, their work might look happier in the context of Strossmayer's collection of Old Masters – a strong and vigorous conclusion to it – for after their deaths younger Croatian painters tended to reflect rather than rival the movements that developed elsewhere in Europe. Symbolism and German Expressionism were particularly powerful influences, with frequent hints of Van Gogh, Cézanne, Derain and even Mondrian. Ideological Social Realism was paramount for some years after the Second World War, but with growing independence from Russian political influence, forms of abstract art began to dominate, and by the end of the twentieth century conceptual art, installation, video and all other international idioms of contemporary art were in the ascendant.

With the construction of an entirely independent new gallery designed specifically for the purpose and already nearing structural completion, Zagreb will very soon join the major European capitals in the ability to mount internationally important retrospective, monographic and encyclopedic exhibitions, thus complementing the intellectual and aesthetic foundations laid ninety years ago in the Gallery of Modern Art.

THE HOUSE AND STUDIO OF IVAN MEŠTROVIĆ

Of twentieth-century Croatian artists none is more celebrated outside his country than Ivan Meštrović, an instinctive and prolific sculptor born of peasant stock in 1883. There is some truth in the tale of the brilliant boy discovered by chance in a Dalmatian village and the clubbing together of friends and supporters to pay for his formal training in Vienna, but it is a not uncommon myth in the history of art – witness Vasari's report of Cimabue's discovery of Giotto as the shepherd boy drawing his master's sheep. In Vienna Meštrović gathered the lively Central European influences of the day, and while still a student exhibited with the Secession in 1902, continuing to do so until 1909. His first major work was the *Well of Life* (fig. 12.11) in the Theatre Square (now Marshal Tito Square) in Zagreb, erected in 1905, a year after he left the Vienna Academy. In this, many critics perceive the influence of Rodin, but Meštrović first made contact with the great French sculptor only in 1907 when in Paris for some months into 1908. He could only have seen those sculptures that, to great acclaim, Rodin sent to the Vienna Secession in 1901, Meštrović's first year as a student in the city, and sculptures illustrated in the many art publications of the time, but these were enough to shape the *Well*. It is set low in a hollow in the ground, visible only to visitors crossing the footpaths of the square and easily missed, yet, human and humanitarian in subject, this imposing bronze of large figures gathered in emotional attitudes in high relief about the well-head is the most important free-standing sculpture in the city, for it is a work of art, not a thing of propaganda and historical bombast.

In Paris Meštrović also met Bourdelle and Maillol, and in the Louvre he studied Assyrian, archaic Greek and Egyptian sculpture, adding these influences to his growing compendium of inherited styles, Balkan Byzantine not least among them. In this he has some parallel with Henry Moore half a generation later, but unlike Moore he remained loyal to the subject, often highly emotional, often Christian or historical, and at no point in his career did he pursue any aspect of abstraction. After an exhibition at the Victoria and Albert Museum in London in 1915, an English critic felt inspired to write of him as 'a prodigy and wonder … a wholly new force in sculpture … whose facility knows no limits'. Between the wars, however, he contributed nothing to any avant-garde movement in sculpture, but was nevertheless important in maintaining, in the sense of contemporary high style, the acceptable face of monumental sculpture, always making it intelligible to the passer-by to whom it was addressed; in this field he was both praised for his expression of energy and power and damned for his excess of 'storm and fury'. His reputation, once so high, flagged after the Second World War, and his last years were spent in the USA as professor of sculpture at the University of Notre-Dame, Indiana. There he died in 1962. 'He had so many styles', wrote one critic, 'that it was hard to detect which was his own' – a sad end to a once so promising career.

His surprisingly subtle monument in Zagreb is the house in the upper town in which he lived from 1922 to 1942, when – a year after Croatia was overrun by Nazi forces – he fled to Switzerland (fig. 12.12). That the house has been on the site since the seventeenth century is evident in some aspects of its architecture and construction, particularly its stout tree-trunk beams, but it was re-jigged for Meštrović (to his own design) as a spacious family residence with a studio attached. With some 300 sculptures in bronze, wood, stone and plaster, together with an archive of photographs and documents, the remaining furniture all to his design, it was his gift to the city. It has an extraordinary atmosphere of peace and repose quite unlike his monumental sculpture, examples of which are in the studio and garden; smaller pieces, drawings and prints – all made before his departure in 1942 – decorate the house, which throws a gentle light on an often seemingly aggressive sensibility.

THE ARCHAEOLOGICAL MUSEUM

By far the greatest and aesthetically most important work of art in Zagreb is the *Apoxyomenos* (fig. 12.13), a more than life-size figure of an athlete in bronze recovered from the sea in 1999. The intended place for its permanent display is a dedicated museum yet to be built on the island of Mali Lošinj, where it was discovered, but for the time being it is to be found in the capital's

Archaeological Museum, where it adds Greek glory to a significant collection of classical antiquities that are primarily provincial Roman. After stripping the heavy marine inscrustations and repairing bronze made fragile by the hazards of two millennia spent between rocks on the bed of the Adriatic Sea, it is now presented as an almost unblemished sculpture of a nude male figure of nobility and grace, an ideal profoundly informed by realism. Other versions exist – in marble and basalt as well as bronze – and no claim is made that this is the prime original. The

12.10 Celestin Medović, *Bacchanal*, oil on canvas, 202 x 357 cm, Gallery of Modern Art, Zagreb. Photo: Luka Mjeda.

earliest of the type is thought to date from *c.* 350 BC or slightly earlier and thus late classical or Hellenistic; this version is interpreted as an early replica of *c.* 100 BC.

The sculpture offers no clue to the athlete's particular skill; he has held no javelin or discus, and as his ears and nose are perfect, he cannot have been a boxer; heavily built for a runner, he was more probably a wrestler. We see him after his exercise or competition, relaxed, scraping oil and dust from his left thigh with a strigil held in his right hand, the action introducing a faint and

informal hint of *contrapposto*; with downcast gaze and sweat-curled hair pushed back from his brow, he is caught in a moment of absolute concentration on the simple but necessary and quotidian business.

In broader cultural terms, however, the importance of the *Apoxyomenos Zagrabiensis* is outweighed by the far less spectacular *Liber Linteus Zagrabiensis* (fig. 12.14). In 1862 the then national museum in Zagreb inherited a mummy and her wrappings from a Croatian collector who had been to Egypt in

12.11   Ivan Meštrović, *Well of Life*, 1905, bronze, Marshal Tito Square, Zagreb. Photo: Boris Cvjetanović.

1848. The mummy, poor woman, was of scant importance, but her wrappings were, for a German professional Egyptologist soon recognised that they bore some kind of script that was not based on the Egyptian hieroglyph. Over the fourteen metres of this unwound strip of linen, some of it in fragments, there was evidence of an order, perhaps alphabetical, that could not be identified with anything Egyptian. By 1892 it had been identified as the longest known script in the Etruscan language, with some 1,200 words in columns along the length of the linen, which had originally been rolled like a scroll. It is now displayed like the lines of text in an old telegram; the only book of its kind, though stained with what are mischievously described as 'mummy juices',

12.12 War damage to the Meštrović House Museum, Zagreb. Photo: Boris Cvjetanović.

much of it is clean and clear. Unlike the Rosetta Stone in the British Museum, which led to our ability to understand Egyptian hieroglyphics because it had a parallel text in Greek, Zagreb's *Liber Linteus* offers no such key to assist our comprehension. As far as we understand it, it is a liturgical calendar of religious laws and the dates on which sacrifices must be made to particular gods.

To the question 'Why should an Egyptian mummy be wrapped in an Etruscan manuscript?' there is no answer, nor to further questions provoked by this mystery; research continues and we know only that scientific examination suggests an origin *c.* 400 BC for both mummy and book. Both are displayed in the context of a wide-ranging collection of Egyptian antiquities and artefacts connected with burial rituals, votive cults and Books of the Dead.

The extensive Greco-Roman collection of some 40,000 objects primarily reflects excavations in the neighbourhood of Zagreb and the Panonian-Illyrian region, and consists of provincial sculpture, small bronzes, armour, pottery, jewellery and coins. The most outstanding sub-collection is of some 1,500 Greek vases, of which the largest group is fourth-century BC red-figure examples of Apulian and Lucanian origin. Many of these have a British connection in that they, together with Greek statuettes and Roman sculptures of the quality commonly found in the further flung corners of the Roman Empire, came from the collection of Lavall Nugent, an Irishman born in 1777 in Ballynacor, who became a field marshal of the Austrian imperial army, a knight of the Golden Fleece and, in 1849, commander of the Military Frontier of Croatia formed to provide a Balkan bulwark against the Ottoman Empire. When, in 1862, calling himself Count Lavall Nugent, he died in Croatia, he owned four castles there and lived in one with this collection.

The museum also exhibits smaller collections of prehistoric, Celtic, medieval, pre-Columbian and numismatic material.

ZAGREB CITY MUSEUM

From its ancient origins on an easily defended hill (the views both panoramic and enchanting) almost to the present day, the history of the city of Zagreb is elegantly enshrined in this converted eighteenth-century convent of St Clare and adjacent older buildings. The collections date far back and suggest origins seven millennia past, but the museum's individual strength lies in its relics of the turbulent Middle Ages and, particularly, in the exhibits that connect Croatia with its Austrian and Austro-Hungarian heritage, rooted in flamboyant mid-European baroque and the coy classicism of the Biedermeier decades of the earlier nineteenth century. In both, the museum offers extraordinary insights on the civilised provincial fringe of one of the great powers of the day.

MUSEUM OF ARTS AND CRAFTS

This first cousin to the Victoria and Albert Museum (and infinitely more intimate) is a place of pure pleasure for anyone interested in the history of furniture and glass (fig. 12.15). It opens with a handful of paintings ambitiously attributed to Old Masters; two given to the seventeenth-century painter Guercino, *David with the Head of Goliath* and *David Playing the Harp*, are by entirely different hands, both of them painted two centuries later, but *Pharaoh's Daughter Handing the Infant Moses to his Sister Miriam*, if not by Ferdinand Bol (to whom it is attributed), is at least a work of museum quality by a painter distantly influenced by Rembrandt. The Gothic and baroque sculpture is overwhelmingly impressive, ablaze with gold leaf and polychrome, and visible in a way that is never possible in the original ecclesiastical positions for which these minor masterpieces were intended. In furniture galleries devoted to examples of impressive quality, we encounter the Central European traditions at their most robust and independent of French *ébénistes* in their Parisian heyday. An even more independent spirit is evident in the furniture of the Biedermeier period and the subsequent Secession. Other galleries are dedicated to clocks and watches, musical instruments and, on the upper floors, an astonishing collection of glass, both decorative and functional.

CROATIAN MUSEUM OF NAIVE ART

Founded in 1952, this claims to be the world's first museum of its kind; its contents are predictably – since leaders of this Croatian school exhibited their work in Paris when enthusiasm for the genre was at its highest – close to the naive art of Le Douanier Rousseau, Louis Vivin and that now all but forgotten group, Les Instinctifs. The self-consciousness of their deliberate primitivism brings them closer to the British painters Helen Bradley and Beryl Cook than to the simple honesty of Alfred Wallis, but there are, nevertheless, a few painters whose naivety is genuine and, occasionally, spiritual. There are some 1,500 works in the collection.

12.13 *Apoxyomenos*, copy of Greek original from *c.* 350 BC, bronze, Archaeological Museum, Zagreb. Photo: Vidoslav Barac, courtesy of the Croatian Conservation Institute.

OLD ZAGREB

The ancient core of Zagreb, on the hill above the nineteenth-century grid-plan expansion to the river, is itself a museum and should be explored, particularly for churches, of which the largest is the cathedral dedicated to the Assumption of the Blessed Virgin Mary. For this the claim is made that it is the most monumental Gothic church to the south-east of the Alps, combining both French and German elements – and so indeed it does in terms of ferocious restoration as well as its thirteenth-century beginnings. Its ornate facade and twin towers are a late nineteenth-century design, completed in 1902, by Hermann Bollé, a German architect much active in Croatia after contributing to the restoration of the Stephansdom in Vienna. An earthquake in 1880 gave him his greatest opportunity in Zagreb, not only for restoring the cathedral but for clearing away (that is, deliberately destroying) many provincial baroque and other buildings in its immediate area, Kaptol, and in Gornji Grad nearby. Purist in approach, Bollé had no sympathy for the complex organic accretions over the centuries that make so many buildings interesting, and removed all that was Renaissance and baroque, including the ribbed vaulting and the original portal of 1640 by Kozmas Müller, a Slovenian sculptor and stonemason whose only documented work it was.

The stripped interior still has its grandeurs, but everywhere there is the sense that a Viollet-le-Duc has been at work on everything architectural. The Renaissance pews survive, so too a late baroque marble pulpit by Mihael Kusse (probably from Ljubljana), his most beautiful work, a decent painting of the Virgin by Carlo Bononi and three mid-eighteenth-century altars by Francesco Robba, a Venetian sculptor who spent most of his working life in Ljubljana and Zagreb.

Another example of Bollé's neutering approach to the past is his treatment of the small church dedicated to St Catherine in the Upper Town, built between 1620 and 1632. The classical facade, based on Vignola's Il Gesù in Rome, as befits a provincial Jesuit church, is very restrained and the interior simple; the baroque character of the interior was applied a century later with embellishments in stucco on walls and ceiling by Kristofor Andrija Jelovšek, another native of Ljubljana, who was also responsible for the astonishing illusionist painting of the apse, *St Catherine among the Philosophers of Alexandria*. The complex baroque altar dedicated to St Ignatius is again by Francesco Robba.

The church of St Mark should also be explored (fig. 12.16). It dates from the fourteenth and fifteenth centuries, has a fine Gothic portal, contains sculptures by Meštrović, wall paintings by his near contemporary Jozo Kljaković, and ecclesiastical treasures in precious metals. The colourful roof in faience tiles bears the arms of Zagreb, Croatia, Dalmatia and Slovenia.

That he should poke his nose into every church and public building upon which he stumbles unexpectedly (and some that are private) is the rule for every experienced traveller – the worst is that he is ejected, the best that with an exchange of smiles he discovers something of which he was unaware. In the late 1970s, pursuing this rule with a Croatian friend – we were on foot, knapsacked and unwashed – in search of monasteries, churches, palaces and houses, we were everywhere received with kindness and amusement. We found no great works of art, no forgotten Raphaels, but in the provincial architecture, paintings and sculpture we identified evidence of Byzantine and Venetian influence, of early Dominican, Franciscan and Jesuit theology and practice, of the spread of Austrian metropolitan culture, all telling of Croatia's cultural role on the edge of Catholic Christendom for five full centuries. This is as possible in Zagreb as in the wider countryside: never hesitate to knock on doors, or even open them.

CODA

During the recent war with Serbia six museums in Zagreb were damaged in air raids, among them the house of Ivan Meštrović in October 1991, its great timbers cracked, the studio all but destroyed (see fig. 12.12). Both it and the other museums hit by rockets have been repaired and reopened. But there is more to Croatia than its capital, and many outlying institutions were more severely damaged; the publication *War Damage to Museums and Galleries in Croatia* (Zagreb 1997), though issued over a decade ago, is a melancholy and, in many cases, still accurate record. The country's cultural heritage – very different from the Balkan states to the south, Catholic rather than Orthodox – was in part wantonly and deliberately destroyed, in part damaged, and in part stolen; now, with losses far greater and more significant than over the five centuries of Ottoman threat and the two world wars of the twentieth century, Croatia struggles with the costs of restoration and repair not only of its museums and galleries but of its churches, monasteries and palaces. Visitors to Croatia in future decades may find a happier situation and should, at the very least, enquire how things stand in the many museums and galleries omitted from this brief survey of the capital – those in Dubrovnik, Karlovac, Osijek, Otavice, Petrinja, Vinkovci, Vukovar and Zadar.

12.14 *Liber Linteus Zagrabiensis* (Etruscan mummy binding), *c.* 400 BC, Archaeological Museum, Zagreb. Photo: courtesy of the Archaeological Museum, Zagreb.

12.15 Hermann Bollé, Museum of Arts and Crafts, 1888, Zagreb. Photo: Srećko Budek.

12.16 St Mark's church, Zagreb. Photo: Ivo Pervan, courtesy of the Croatian Tourist Board.

NOTES

2. ANCIENT GREEKS IN CROATIA

Further reading

S. Bilić Dujmušić, 'The archaeological excavations on Cape Ploča', in *Grčki utjecaj na istočnoj obali Jadrana* (Greek Influence along the East Adriatic Coast), ed. N. Cambi, S. Čače and B. Kirigin, Split 2002, pp. 485–97.

M. Bonačić Mandinić, *Greek Coins Displayed in the Archaeological Museum Split*, Split 2004.

L. Bracessi, *Grecità adriatica*, Bologna 1979.

J. Brunšmid, *Die Inschriften und Münzen der griechischen Städte Dalmatiens*, Vienna 1898.

S. Čače, 'Promunturium Diomedis (Plin. Nat. Hist. 3, 141)', *Radovi Filozofskog fakulteta u Zadru* 35, no. 22 (1997), pp. 21–44.

N. Cambi, *Antika*, Zagreb 2002.

N. Cambi, S. Čače and B. Kirigin, eds, *Grčki utjecaj na istočnoj obali Jadrana* (Greek Influence along the East Adriatic Coast), Split 2002.

B. Čargo, *Issa: A Historical and Archaeological Guide*, Split and Vis 2004.

S. Dimitrijević, T. Težak-Gregl and N. Majnarić-Pandžić, *Prapovijest*, Zagreb 1998.

S. Forenbaher and T. Kaiser, *Spila Nakovana – Ilirsko svetište na Pelješcu*, Zagreb 2003.

P. M. Fraser, 'The family tombstones of Issa', *Vjesnik za arheologiju i historiju dalmatinsku* 84 (1991), pp. 247–74.

V. Gaffney, S. Čače, B. Kirigin, P. Leach and N. Vujnović, 'Enclosure and defences: the context of Myceneaen contact within central Dalmatia', in *Defensive Settlements of the Aegean and the Eastern Mediterranean after 1200 BC*, ed. V. Karageorgis and C. E. Morris, Nicosia 2001, pp. 137–56.

V. Gaffney, J. W. Hayes, T. Kaiser, B. Kirigin, P. Leach, Z. Stančič and N. Vujnović, *The Adriatic Island Project, Volume 1: The Archaeological Heritage of Hvar, Croatia*, British Archaeological Reports, International Series 660, Oxford 1997.

B. Kirigin, 'The Greek background', in *Dalmatia – Research in the Roman Province 1970–2001: Papers in Honour of J. J. Wilkes*, ed. D. Davison, V. Gaffney and E. Marin, British Archaeological Reports, International Series 1576, Oxford 2006, pp. 17–26.

B. Kirigin, 'The Greeks in central Dalmatia: some new evidence', in *Greek Colonisation and Native Populations*, ed. J. P. Descoeudres, Canberra and Oxford 1990, pp. 291–321.

B. Kirigin, 'The Greeks in central Dalmatia', in *La Dalmazia e l'altra sponda: Problemi di archaiologhia Adriatica*, ed. L. Bracessi and S. Graciotti, Florence 1999, pp. 147–64.

B. Kirigin, *Issa*, Zagreb 1996.

B. Kirigin, *Pharos: An Archaeological Guide*, Stari Grad 2003.

B. Kirigin, *Pharos, the Parian Settlement in Dalmatia: A Study of a Greek Colony in the Adriatic*, British Archaeological Reports, International Series 1561, Oxford 2006.

B. Kirigin, ed., *2001 Archaeological Sites on the Central Dalmatian Islands: Do They Have Any Future?*, Hvar and Split 1998.

B. Kirigin and S. Čače, 'Archaeological evidence for the cult of Diomedes in the Adriatic', *Hesperia* 9 (1998), pp. 63–110.

B. Kirigin, B. Djurič, P. Kos and B. Teržan, *Issa – otok Vis v helenizmu*, Ljubljana 1986.

B. Kirigin and V. Gaffney, eds, *Archaeological Heritage of Vis, Biševo, Svetac, Palagruža and Šolta*, British Archaeological Reports, International Series 1492, Oxford 2006.

I. Mirnik, 'Votive figural ara from Trogir', *Archaeologuica Iugoslavica* 15 (1974), pp. 38–41.

D. Radić and B. Bass, 'Current archaeological research on the island of Korčula, Croatia', *Vjesnik za arheologiju i historiju dalmatinsku* 90–1 (1999), pp. 361–403

Z. Stančič , N. Vujnović, B. Kirigin, S. Čače, T. Podobnikar and J. Burmaz, *The Adriatic Island Project, Volume 2: The Archaeological Heritage of the Island of Brač, Croatia*, British Archaeological Reports, International Series 803, Oxford 1999.

J. J. Wilkes, *Dalmatia*, London 1969.

J. J. Wilkes, *The Illyrians*, Oxford 1992.

J. J. Wilkes and T. Fischer-Hansen, 'The Adriatic', in *An Inventory of Archaic and Classical Poleis*, ed. M. Herman Hansen and T. Heine Nielsen, Oxford 2004, pp. 321–37.

3. ROMAN ART IN CROATIAN DALMATIA, FIRST TO THIRD CENTURIES AD

Appendix

Catalogue of objects

1 Nenad Cambi, *Imago Animi: Antički Potret u Hrvakskoj*, Split 2000, p. 142, cat. no. 16

2 Cambi, *Imago Animi*, pp. 142–3, cat. no. 20

3 Cambi, *Imago Animi*, p. 146, cat. no. 24

4 Cambi, *Imago Animi*, p. 147, cat. no. 25

5 Cambi, *Imago Animi*, p. 147, cat. no. 26

6 Cambi, *Imago Animi*, p. 147, cat. no. 27

7 Cambi, *Imago Animi*, p. 147, cat. no. 28

8 Cambi, *Imago Animi*, pp. 147–8, cat. nos 29–30

9 Cambi, *Imago Animi*, p. 148, cat. no. 31

10 Cambi, *Imago Animi*, p. 148, cat. no. 32

11 Cambi, *Imago Animi*, pp. 148–9, cat. no. 33

12 Cambi, *Imago Animi*, p. 149, cat. no. 34

13 Cambi, *Imago Animi*, pp. 150–1, cat. no. 45

14 Cambi, *Imago Animi*, p. 151, cat. no. 44

15 Cambi, *Imago Animi*, p. 151, cat. no. 46

16 Cambi, *Imago Animi*, pp. 151–2, cat. no. 47

17 Cambi, *Imago Animi*, p. 152, cat. no. 48

18 Cambi, *Imago Animi*, p. 154, cat. no. 56

19 Cambi, *Imago Animi*, p. 154, cat. no. 57

20 Cambi, *Imago Animi*, p. 155, cat. no. 58

21 Cambi, *Imago Animi*, p. 155, cat. no. 59

22 Cambi, *Imago Animi*, p. 156, cat. no. 60

23 Cambi, *Imago Animi*, p. 157, cat. no. 65

24 Cambi, *Imago Animi*, p. 158, cat. no. 66

25 Cambi, *Imago Animi*, p. 157, cat. no. 67

26 Cambi, *Imago Animi*, p. 158, cat. no. 68

27 Cambi, *Imago Animi*, p. 159, cat. no. 69

28 Cambi, *Imago Animi*, p. 163, cat. no. 82

29 Cambi, *Imago Animi*, p. 163, cat. no. 83

30 Cambi, *Imago Animi*, p. 164, cat. no. 84

31 Cambi, *Imago Animi*, pp. 168, cat. no. 101

32 Cambi, *Imago Animi*, pp. 170–1, cat. nos 106–7

33 Cambi, *Imago Animi*, p. 169, cat. no. 102

34 Cambi, *Imago Animi*, p. 169, cat. no. 105

35 Cambi, *Imago Animi*, p. 143, cat. nos 17–19

36 Cambi, *Imago Animi*, p. 144, cat. no. 21

37 Cambi, *Imago Animi*, p. 149, cat. no. 37

38 Cambi, *Imago Animi*, p. 149, cat. no. 38

39 Cambi, *Imago Animi*, p. 149, cat. no. 39

40 Cambi, *Imago Animi*, p. 152, cat. no. 49

41 Cambi, *Imago Animi*, p. 153, cat. no. 54

42 Cambi, *Imago Animi*, p. 153, cat. no. 55

43 Cambi, *Imago Animi*, p. 160, cat. no. 76

44 Cambi, *Imago Animi*, p. 166, cat. no. 93

45 Cambi, *Imago Animi*, p. 166, cat. no. 94

46 Cambi, *Imago Animi*, pp. 166–7, cat. no. 95

47 Cambi, *Imago Animi*, p. 167, cat. no. 96

48 Cambi, *Imago Animi*, p. 167, cat. no. 97

49 Cambi, *Imago Animi*, p. 172, cat. no 108

50 Cambi, *Imago Animi*, p. 173, cat. no. 110

51 Cambi, *Imago Animi*, p. 162, cat. no. 77

52 Cambi, *Imago Animi*, p. 162, cat. no. 79

53 Cambi, *Imago Animi*, p. 164, cat. no. 85

54 Cambi, *Imago Animi*, p. 172, cat. no. 109

55 Cambi, *Imago Animi*, p. 162, cat. nos 81–2

56 Cambi, *Imago Animi*, pp. 164–5, cat. no. 88

57 Cambi, *Imago Animi*, p. 165, cat. no. 89

58 Cambi, *Imago Animi*, p. 165, cat. no. 87

59 Cambi, *Imago Animi*, p. 157, cat. no. 64

60 Cambi, *Imago Animi*, p. 160, cat. no. 70

61 Cambi, *Imago Animi*, p. 144, cat. no. 22; Anna and Jaroslav Šašel, *Inscriptiones Latinae quae in Iugoslavia …. repertae et editae sunt* (Situla 5, 19 and 25), Ljubljana 1963, 1978 and 1986, no. 2203 (epitaph)

62 Cambi, *Imago Animi*, p. 144, cat. no. 23

63 Cambi, *Imago Animi*, pp. 149–50, cat. no. 40

64 Cambi, *Imago Animi*, p. 150, cat. no. 41

65 Cambi, *Imago Animi*, p. 150, cat. no. 42

66 Cambi, *Imago Animi*, p. 160, cat. no. 74; *Corpus Inscriptionum Latinarum*, Berlin 1863–1902, vol. III, no. 2491 (epitaph)

67 Cambi, *Imago Animi*, p. 159, cat. no. 72; CIL III, no. 8441 (epitaph)

68 Cambi, *Imago Animi*, p. 156, cat. no. 62; Šašel, *Inscriptiones Latinae*, no. 869 (epitaph)

69 Cambi, *Imago Animi*, p. 150, cat. no. 53; Šašel, *Inscriptiones Latinae*, no. 207 (epitaph)

70 Cambi, *Imago Animi*, p. 150, cat. no. 43

71 Cambi, *Imago Animi*, p. 165, cat. no. 90

72 Cambi, *Imago Animi*, p. 174, cat. no. 112; *L'Année Épigraphique* 1996, no. 1208

73 Cambi, *Imago Animi*, p. 168, cat. no. 103

74 Cambi, *Imago Animi*, p. 152, cat. no. 50; CIL III, no. 2030 (epitaph)

75 Cambi, *Imago Animi*, 152–3, cat. no. 52; *L'Année Épigraphique* 1991, no. 1291 (epitaph)

76 Sergio Rinaldi Tufi, 'Stele funerarie con ritratti di eta romana nel Museo Archeologico di Spalato', in *Atti della Accademia Nationale dei Lincei CCCLXVIII* (Mem. di scienze morali, ser. VIII, vol. XVI, fasc. 3), Rome 1971, no. 10 (For rereading of name see G. Alfoldy, *Situla* 8, Ljubljana 1965, pp. 95–6)

77 Cambi, *Imago Animi*, p. 156, cat. no. 61; CIL III, no. 14934 (epitaph)

78 Cambi, *Imago Animi*, p. 152, cat. no. 51; *L'Année Épigraphique* 1980, no. 689 (epitaph)

79 Cambi, *Imago Animi*, p. 159, cat. no. 71; CIL III, no. 2722 (9729) (epitaph)

80 Cambi, *Imago Animi*, p. 157, cat. no. 63; CIL III, no. 9782 (epitaph)

81 Nenad Cambi, 'Kiparstvo (Sculpture)', in *Longae Salonae*, ed. Emilio Marin, vols I–II, Split 2002, pp. 134 and 169, pl. 82; CIL III, no. 2010 cf. 8576 (epitaph)

82 Cambi, 'Kiparstvo (Sculpture)', pp. 121 and 164, pl. 16 (Jupiter)

83 A. Starac, *Proceedings of the 8th International Colloquium on Problems of Roman Provincial Art: Religion and Myth as an Impetus for Roman Provincial Sculpture*, Zagreb 2005, pp. 197–200

84 Sergio Rinaldi Tufi, *Dalmazia* (Museo della Civiltá Romana, Le Province dell'Impero 2), Rome 1989, p. 79, fig. 78 (Fortuna); Cambi, 'Kiparstvo (Sculpture)', pp. 133 and 169, pl. 75 (Tyche)

85 Cambi, 'Kiparstvo (Sculpture)', pp. 140 and 172, pl. 108

86 Tufi, *Dalmazia*, pp. 78–9, figs 76–7 and 79

87 Cambi, 'Kiparstvo (Sculpture)', pp. 118 and 163, pl. 3

88 Cambi, 'Kiparstvo (Sculpture)', pp. 120 and 164, pl. 10 (Apollo or Dionysus); pl. 13 (naked youth); pl. 11 (boy); pl. 12 (female head); 124 and 165, pl. 29 (divinity); pl. 30 (divinity with diadem)

89 Cambi, 'Kiparstvo (Sculpture)', pp. 127 and 166, pl. 39 (female torso); pl. 38 (Flora or Persephone)

90 Cambi, 'Kiparstvo (Sculpture)', pp. 119 and 163, pl. 9

91 Cambi, 'Kiparstvo (Sculpture)', pp. 63–4 and 167–8

92 Cambi, *Imago Animi*, pp. 133 and 169, pl. 76

93 Cambi, 'Kiparstvo (Sculpture)', pp. 125–6 and 166–7, pl. 31 (Dionysus); pl. 32 (Jupiter); pl. 42 (Polycleitan Dionysus); pl. 43 (Dionysus with grapes and panther)

94 Cambi, 'Kiparstvo (Sculpture)', pp. 129 and 167, fig. 57 (weary Heracles); fig. 58 (Heracles with Apples of Hesperides)

95 Cambi, 'Kiparstvo (Sculpture)', pp. 126 and 166, pl. 37

96 Cambi, 'Kiparstvo (Sculpture)', pp. 123 and 165, pl. 21 (Silvanus from near Klis); pl. 22 (Silvanus from Salona); 132 and 169, pl. 74 (Silvanus and Nymphs); Ivan Pedišić, 'A relief of Silvanus from Ćulišić', *Diadora* (Zadar) 14 (1992), pp. 265–78 (Silvanus from Ćulišić)

97 Cambi, 'Kiparstvo (Sculpture)', pp. 132 and 169, pl. 72

98 M. Glavičić, *Proceedings of the 8th International Colloquium on Problems of Roman Provincial Art: Religion and Myth as an Impetus for Roman Provincial Sculpture*, Zagreb 2005, pp. 223–8

Catalogue of sites

Aenona (Nin): Mate Suić, *Antički grad na istočnom Jadranu* (Ancient Cities on the Eastern Adriatic), Zagreb 1976, p. 137 (plan); Jagoda Meder, *Podni mozaici u Hrvatskoj od 1. do 6. stoljeća* (Floor Mosaics in Croatia from the First to the Sixth Centuries), Zagreb 2003, pp. 78–9 and pl. XXX, 3 (mosaic)

Aequum (Čitluk, Sinj): Suić, *Antički grad*, pp. 131 (plan), 123 (gate), 159 (forum)

Arba (Rab): *CIL* III, no. 3116 (water supply in AD 173)

Asseria (Podgrađe, Benkovac): Suić, *Antički grad*, pp. 138 (plan), 158 (forum)

Burnum (Kistanje): S. Zabehlicky-Scheffenegger and M. Kandler, *Burnum I*, Vienna 1979, pp. 14–15 and pl. 5

Curicum (Krk): unpublished aqueduct inscription; Meder, *Podni mozaici*, pp. 71–2 and pl. XXVII, 1–3 (mosaic)

Delminium (Duvno): J. J. Wilkes, *Dalmatia* (History of the Roman Provinces), London 1969, pp. 371–2 and fig. 18

Iader (Zadar): Suić, *Antički grad*, pp. 128 and 198 (plan), 124–5 (gate), 150–2 (forum), 180–1 (house); Meder 2003, p. 151 and pl. XXXIII, 1–3 (mosaics)

Issa (Vis): Suić, *Antički grad*, p. 84 (plan); Meder, *Podni mozaici*, pp. 104–5 and pl. XLIII, 2 (mosaic)

Narona (Vid): *CIL* III, no. 1805 cf. P. 2328/119 (baths)

Pharos/Pharia (Hvar): Suić, *Antički grad*, p. 85 (plan); Meder, *Podni mozaic*, p. 158 and pl. XLI, 3–4 (mosaic)

Rider (Danilo): Tufi, *Dalmazia*, p. 80 (villa)

Salona (Solin): Suić, *Antički grad* (plan), pp. 122 (Porta Caesarea), 149, 153–5 (forum temple), 165–6 (baths), 171 (theatre), 175–8 (amphitheatre); Wilkes, *Dalmatia*, p. 372 (aqueduct); Meder, *Podni mozaici*, pp. 107–8 and pl. XLV, 5 (Sappho mosaic), 108 and pl. XLV, 1 (Apollo mosaic), 109 and pl. XLV, 2 (Triton mosaic), 109–10 and p. XLVI, 1 (Orpheus mosaic)

4. THE PALACE OF DIOCLETIAN AT SPLIT

I am very grateful to Jadranka Beresford-Peirse for giving me this opportunity to reconsider the palace in its original form and later manifestations. The symposium organized by Nenad Cambi in 2005 provided much stimulation. In Split, Vedrana Delonga, Sanja Buble and Katija Marasović generously shared the latest information from their continuing work. The last two have also helped me obtain illustrations. Živko Bačić and Ivan Sikavica kindly shared their photographs and advice. Jerko Marasović is as always a great inspiration. Oliver Nicholson and Nita Krevans provided essential criticism; Ivančica Shrunk assisted in critiquing and proofreading, and Carol Masters edited and proofread my text with her usual patient competence. Nancy Marten has done final editing, and overseen and corrected the restructuring of my citations.

1 For Diocletian's policies, see Stephen Williams, *Diocletian and the Roman Recovery*, New York 1985. For in-depth analysis of his contributions with ample bibliography and summaries of opinions, see Wolfgang Kuhoff, *Diokletian und die Epoche der Tetrarchie: das römische Reich zwischen Krisenbewältigung und Neuaufbau (284–313 n. Chr.)*, Frankfurt 2001. Recent assessments include the general summary of Alexander Demandt, 'Diokletian als Reformer', in *Diokletian und die Tetrarchie: Aspekte der Zeitwende*, ed. Alexander Demandt, Andreas Golz and Heinrich Schlange-Schöningen, Berlin and New York 2004, pp. 1–9, and the discussion of religion by Frank Kolb, 'Praesens Deus: Kaiser und Gott unter der Tetrarchie', in *Diokletian und die Tetrarchie: Aspekte der Zeitwende*, pp. 27–37. The best basic outline of ancient sources remains Timothy D. Barnes, *The New Empire of Diocletian and Constantine*, Cambridge MA 1982. Major documentation has been gathered and translated by Roger Rees, *Diocletian and the Tetrarchy*, Edinburgh 2004.

2 His retirement site is generally thought to have been called Aspalathos: see Jacques Zeiller, 'Sur l'origine de Spalato', in *Mèlanges Cagnat*, Paris 1912, pp. 419–42. Zeiller's conclusions have been recently queried by Tadeusz Zadawski, 'La residence de Diocletien a Spalatum: Sa denomination dans l'antiquite', *Museum Helveticum* 44 (1987), p. 230, n. 55. Recent archaeology has shown the site was more important than has been thought: see Wolfgang Kuhoff, 'Aktuelle Perspectiven der Diokletian-Forschung: Diokletian als Reformer', in *Diokletian und die Tetrarchie: Aspekte der Zeitwende*, p. 15, Demandt, 'Diokletian als Reformer', p. 8, and Vedrana Delonga, *Archaeological Research on Riva in Split in 2006–2007: Isječci iz fotografskog dnevnika Zorana Alabega*, Split 2007 (Croatian and English). Diocletian was born in Dalmatia, probably in Salona or even Split itself, so may have been returning to the scenes of his childhood. For the sources, see Barnes, *New Empire*, p. 31; cf. Nenad Cambi, 'Diocletian, tetrarchy and Diocletian's Palace on the 1700th anniversary of existence', in *Dioklecijan, Tetrarhija i Dioklecijanova palača, Split, Croatia, 19–22 Rujna 2005*, Split 2005, arguing that Dioklea was his birthplace. Recently, two authors have linked his choice of site to honouring his mother: see Slobodan Čurčić, 'Late antique palaces: the meaning of urban context', *Ars Orientalis* 23 (1993), p. 76, and Emanual Mayer, *Rom is dort, wo der Kaiser ist: Untersuchungen zu den Staatsdenkmälern des dezentralisierten Reiches von Diocletian bis zu Theodosius II*, Mainz 2002.

3 Scholars often argue that its building proves his retirement was planned, not sudden. That must be true, but does not also mean he had either set or announced a retirement date. To receive him in 305, construction must have begun at least by 300 and probably earlier: see Williams, *Diocletian and the Roman Recovery*, p. 186, and Kolbe, *Diokletien und die Erste Tetrarchie*, pp. 150–1. For summaries of several points of view, see Kuhoff, *Diokletian und die Epoche der Tetrarchie*, pp. 304–5, n. 800. Some analysts stress unfinished or awkward construction to argue that the abdication was a sudden decision, e.g., Goran Nikšić, 'The restoration of Diocletian's Palace – Mausoleum, Temple, and Porta Aurea (with analysis of the original architectural design)', in *Diokletian und die Tetrarchie: Aspekte der Zeitwende*, p. 168 (not universally accepted). It is often thought that major work would not have continued after Diocletian arrived, particularly if he was very ill, but the extent of his illness is also debatable; see Kuhoff, *Diokletian und die Epoche der Tetrarchie*. It is possible that he enjoyed overseeing final details.

4 On construction and workmen, see John J. Wilkes, *Diocletian's Palace, Split: Residence of a Retired Roman Emperor*, Sheffield 1993 (first published 1986); Sheila McNally, *The Architectural Ornament of Diocletian's Palace at Split*, Oxford 1996, pp. 38–9; Sanja Buble, 'Dioklecijanova palača – izvor poznavanja rimske tehnike građenja (Diocletian's Palace – a Source of Knowledge for Roman building Technology)', in Dioklecijan, Tetrarhija i Dioklecijanova Palača o 1700. obljetnici postojanja, ed. Nenad Cambi, Joško Belamarić, Tomislav Marasović, Split 2009, pp. 135-161,

5 I use the names commonly accepted for a century or more, such as Mausoleum, Temple (but not Temple of Jupiter), Peristyle and Vestibule, with capital letters. All seem more or less appropriate; the appearance and function(s) of each part will be considered later.

6 Sheila McNally, 'Split in the Byzantine Empire', *Acts, XVIIIth International Congress of Byzantine Studies*, ed. Ihor Sevčenko, Gennady G. Litavrin and Walter K. Hanak, Shepherdstown WV 1996, vol. 2, pp. 250–63; Ivančica Dvoržak Schrunk, 'Diocletian's Palace, Split: the role of Christianity and Romanitas in the rise of a city', in *Ancient Images, Ancient Thought: The Archaeology of Ideology. Proceedings of the Twenty-Third Annual Chacmool Conference*, ed. A. Sean Goldsmith et al., Calgary 1992, pp. 35–41.

7 For the relationship of later construction to the original palace, see Cvito Fisković, 'Srednjovjekovna izgradnja i identitet grada Splita', *Kulturna baština* 14 (1989), pp. 28–50, and Tomislav Marasović, 'Prilog istraživanju transformacije antičke jezgre u ranosrednjovjekovni grad', in *Gunjačin Zbornik*, Zagreb 1980, pp. 99–112 (Croatian with English summary). There are short popular introductions in Croatian, well illustrated and with full bibliographies, published by the Museum of Croatian Archaeological Monuments: Tomislav Marasović, *Split u starohrvasko doba*, Split 1996, and Željko Rapanić, *Split: grad u palači, palača u gradu*, Split 1997.

8 Hans Peter L'Orange, *Art Forms and Civic Life in the Late Roman Empire*, Princeton 1965, pp. 70–1.

9 Kuhoff, *Diokletian und die Epoche der Tetrarchie*; Kuhoff, 'Aktuelle Perspectiven der Diokletian-Forschung: Diokletian als Reformer', pp.10–26.

10 Cvito Fisković, 'Prilog proučavanju i zaštiti Dioklecijanove palače u Splitu', *Rad Jugoslavenske akademije znanosti i umjetnosti* (Jugoslavenska akademija znanosti i umjetnosti, vol. 279), Zagreb 1950.

11 These two buildings will finally be fully published by Sanja Buble; so far their identification has proved difficult, but clearly they add additional visual and functional energy to this temenos. Mannell's effort to restore the two buildings as monopteroi containing statues of the tetrarchs ignores the coffer blocks that required inner and outer supports, either a colonnade and wall as in the 1994 reconstruction or possibly two colonnades: Joanne Mannell, 'The monopteroi in the west precinct of Diocletian's Palace at Split', *Journal of Roman Archaeology* 8 (1995), pp. 235–44.

12 A finely illustrated summary of work through the early 1960s appeared in several languages, e.g. Jerko Marasović and Tomislav Marasović, *The Diocletian Palace*, Zagreb 1968.

13 This work was carried out jointly by the University of Minnesota and Town Planning Institute, co-directed by Jerko Marasović and myself, with John Wilkes as field director during the first seasons. We are very grateful for the generous funding by the Smithsonian Institution, then by the United States–Yugoslav Joint Board for Scientific and Technical Cooperation, with assistance from the Graduate School of the University of Minnesota.

14 Connection suggested by Frank Brown, conversations, 1970–2. Tajma Rismondo has since traced this bath to the north: see Tajma Rismondo, 'Unutrašnja dekoracija istočnih termi Dioklecijanove palače u Splitu 2002. Arheološka istraživanja 2000. godine', 'Interior Decoration eastern *Thermae* of Diocletian Palace in Split. Archaeological excavations in 2000', *Vjesnik za arheologiju i povijest dalmatinsku* 1 (2005) pp. 151-158, esp. plans 1 and 2 (open access journal http://hrcak.srce.hr/vapd). A point of access to the baths from the residential block has been discovered but not yet published (Katja Marasović, personal communication, July 2007).

15 On the date of the courtyard, Margaret Alexander, personal communications, 1970s; also Ivančica Dvoržak Schrunk,

'The palace in the light of new ceramic evidence', in *Diocletian's Palace: American–Yugoslav Joint Excavations*, vol. 5, Minneapolis 1989, p. 221. On the western bath, see Snježana Perojević, Katja Marasović, Jerko Marasović,., 'Istraživanja Dioklecijanove palače od 1985. do 2005. Godine (The research of Diocletian's Palace from 1985 to 2005)', in Dioklecijan, Tetrarhija i Dioklecijanova Palača, pp. 51-94. , and also Katja Marasović and Sanja Buble, personal communications, July 2007.

[16] For major discussions of military parallels, George Niemann, *Der Palast Diokletians in Spalato*, Vienna 1910; Ernest Hébrard and Jacques Zeiller, *Spalato, le palais de Dioclétien*, Paris 1912; Frane Bulić, *Palača cara Dioklecijana u Splitu* (with a contribution by Ljubo Karaman), Zagreb 1927; Frane Bulić, *Kaiser Diokletians Palast in Split* (shortened translation of Bulić 1927), Zagreb 1929; Wilkes, *Diocletian's Palace*. For the first mosaic, see Niemann, *Palast*, pp. 86–9, figs 113–14; Bulić, *Palača*, and Bulić, *Kaiser Diokletians Palast*, fig. 67; Wilkes, *Diocletian's Palace*, p. 41. For the second mosaic, see Jerko Marasović, 'Research in Diocletian's Place after 1974', in *Diocletian's Palace: American–Yugoslav Joint Excavations*, p. 225. Neither mosaic suggests particular importance for the space it floors.

[17] At one time it seemed possible that the large central spaces might have contained the gardens and fountains so necessary to a Roman's comfortable retirement, and until now so surprisingly lacking at Split. They would involve colonnades, water features, probably some complexity in plan and certainly some elaboration in decor. No such elements have appeared. Apparently the garden where Diocletian planted his vegetables lay outside the high perimeter walls (for his gardening, see *Epitome de Caesaribus* [Brief Accounts of the Emperors], 39.6).

[18] For discussion of the palace as a city, see Čurčić, 'Late antique palaces'; for discussion of a factory in the palace, see Joško Belamarić, 'The date of foundation and original function of Diocletian's Palace at Split', *Hortus Artium Medievalium* 9 (2003), pp. 173–85, and Joško Belamarić, 'Gynaecum Iovense Damatiae–Aspalatho', in *Diokletian und die Tetrarche*, pp. 141–63; cf. earlier suggestions on that topic by Wilkes, *Diocletian's Palace*, p. 41, and Ejnar Dyggve and Hermann Vetters, *Mogorjelo: Ein spätantiker Herrensitz im römischen Dalmatien*, Vienna 1966, pp. 42–4.

[19] Much recent work, including that in the north, must be omitted because of spatial constraints. Numerous institutions are active in the palace: (1) for work by Marasović on the north of the palace, on the water supply system and more, see Marasović, 'Research after 1974'; Jerko Marasović and Tomislav Marasović, 'Le ricerche nel Palazzo di Diocleziano a Split negli ultimi 30 anni (1964–1994)', *Antiquité tardive* 2 (1994), pp. 89–106; Jerko Marasović, 'Znanstveni projekt graditeljsko naslijeđe Splita', *Obnove povijesne jezgre* 2 (1997), pp. 27–93; (2) for work in the north by Helga Zglav Martinac, see Ivan Alduk, 'Lokalitet Split – Dioklecijanova palača (Carrarina poljana)', *Hrvatski arheološki godišnjak* 2 (2005), pp. 398–9; (3) for work in the south-east uncovering pre-palace architecture, see Vedrana Delonga and Maya Bonačić Mandanić, *Arheološka istraživanja u jugoistočnom dijelu Dioklecijanove palače 1992. Godine*, Split 2005; (4) for work in the south tracing various periods of harbour installations, see Delonga, *Archaeological Research on Riva in Split in 2006–2007*; (5) for studies of the construction methods, cf. J. Marasović et al., 'Istraživanja … od 1985. do 2005. Godine', and Buble, 'Dioklecijanova Palača'. Much conservation work is also going on, e.g. Marin Barišić and Sagita Mirjam Sunara, "Konzervatorsko-restauratorski radovi na Peristilu Dioklecijanove palače u Splitu', *Godišnjak zaštite spomenika kulture Hrvatske* 29/30 (2005/2006), p. 67. I regret skipping so swiftly over these manifold and enthusiastic contributions by various institutions, and hope to discuss them elsewhere.

[20] St Jerome, ann. Abraham 2332 (*Chronicon ad annum Abraham*, entry 2332); Zadawski, 'La residence de Diocletien', Zeiller, 'Sur l'origine'. This alternative meaning of the word villa had also occurred earlier.

[21] Duval argued for the term chateau first in Noël Duval, 'Le "Palais" de Dioclétien à la lumiere des récentes découvertes', *Bulletin de la societé nationale des antiquaires de France* 80 (1961), p. 90. An article that I have not seen will contribute to this question of continuity invoking the traditions of the maritime villa and the villa as castrum: Xavier Lafon, 'La Villa de Split et sa place dans l'évolution de la villa romaine', in Dioklecijan, Tetrarhija i Dioklecijanova, pp. 295-306.. On the urbanity of late Roman villas see Javier Arce, 'Otium et negotium: the great estates, 4th–7th century', in *The Transformation of the Roman World, AD 400–90*, ed. Leslie Webster and Michelle Brown, Berkeley 1997, pp. 19–32.

[22] On Konz, see most recently Thomas H. M. Fontaine, 'Das Trierer Umland im 4. Jahrhundert', in *Konstantin der Grosse: Ausstellungskatalog*, ed. Alexander Demandt and Josef Engemann, Mainz 2007, p. 340. On Mogorjelo, see Dyggve and Vetters, *Mogorjelo*; cf. Lynda Mulvin, *Late Roman Villas in the Danube-Balkan Region*, Oxford 2002, p. 50. Fontaine has expressed doubt that Konz was imperial, based on its relatively modest size, but we have no indication of any established standard. Mulvin notes that the portico plan (single or double) is rare in the Danube-Balkan region, a fact she tentatively attributes to its lack of security, not a problem within Split's high walls ('winged plan', Mulvin, *Late Roman Villas*, p. 50). The choice of a protruding single entrance was made for other reasons, discussed below. Additional access to the main floor came through stairways from the basements below, and there must have been minor exterior entrances on the south that have not yet come to light (see discussion above of access to the baths).

[23] Any two will do. Some mosaic depictions of towered facades with high arcades indicate a rectangular plan, e.g. Tadeusz Sarnowski, *Les reprèsentations de villas sur les mosaïques africaines tardives*, Warsaw 1978, figs 18–21; others do not. Some remains of rectangular structures with towers preserve indications of a second floor facade; most do not.

[24] For Gamzigrad, see Dragoslav Srejović et al., *Gamzigrad: Kasonantički carski dvorac* (with English summary), Belgrade 1983. For Mogorjelo, see note 22. Number and placement of towers in both stages at Gamzigrad resemble and may have imitated Split. Mogorjelo is smaller and simpler. Mulvin, *Late Roman Villas*, lists other examples from the Balkans, as well as free-standing villas with walls around them.

[25] Hermann Vetters, 'Zum Bautypus Mogorjelo', in *Festschrift für Fritz Eichler*, ed. Egon Braun, Vienna 1967, pp. 138–50.

[26] Wilkes, *Diocletian's Palace*, p. 3.

[27] See reconstruction in Wilkes, *Diocletian's Palace*, fig. 3.

[28] Marthe Aston, 'Diocletian's Palace gates, Split', in *SOMA 2001: Symposium on Mediterranean Archaeology*, ed. Georgina Muskett, Aikaterina Koltsida and Mercurios Georgiadis, Oxford 2001, pp. 132–7.

[29] Aston, 'Diocletian's Palace gates', p. 134.

[30] Satyrs: McNally, *The Architectural Ornament of Diocletian's Palace at Split*, p. 42; river gods: Monika Verzár-Bass, 'Figurate del Palazzo di Diocleziano a Spalato', in Dioklecijan, Tetrarhija i Dioklecijanova Palača, pp. 163-180.

[31] Dyggve and Duval originally concentrated disagreement on large apsed halls usually referred to as 'aulae' and connected by Dyggve to the development of 'architecture of power', meaning imperial power: see Ejnar Dyggve, *Ravennatum Palatium Sacrum: La basilica ipetrale per cerimonie: Studii sull'architettura dei palazzi della tarda antichità*, Copenhagen 1941; Ejnar Dyggve, 'O izvornom izgledu antičkog Peristila' (with English summary), *Urbs* 4 (1961–2 [1965]), pp. 53–60; Ejnar Dyggve, 'Nouvelles recherches au péristyle du Palais de Dioclétien à Split', *Acta ad archeologiam et artium historiam pertinentia* 1 (1962), pp. 1–6; Duval, 'Le "Palais"', pp. 76–117; and Noël Duval, 'La place de Split dans l'architecture aulique du Bas-Empire', *Urbs* 4 (1961–2 [1965]), pp. 67–95. It is now clear that such halls arose in private architecture, were adopted by palace architecture on a grand scale, and so expressed both imperial and non-imperial power (but see R. J. A. Wilson, Vivere in Villa" (review article), *Roman Journal of Archaeology* 21 (2008), p. 487.. It is also clear that they were often supplemented by multi-apsed rooms thought to be specifically for dining, so the term 'aulic' seems outdated.

[32] For various possibilities see Simon Ellis, 'Late antique dining: architecture, furnishings and behaviour', in *Domestic Space in the Roman World: Pompeii and Beyond*, ed. Ray Laurence and Andrew Wallace-Hadrill, Portsmouth, RI 1997, p. 42, At this period triclinium dining was giving way to stibadium dining where diners reclined in a semicircle around a table. Archaeologists have liked to place such dining in rounded areas: either in rooms with an apsed ending or in multi-apsed rooms to entertain larger groups. Identifying function by shape is, of course, not totally dependable. Stone stibadia (curved furnishings) or mosaic floor patterns often indicate that rectangular rooms, ranging from simple to grand (e.g. Faragola), were used for dining. Large rooms at the extreme east of this residential block could have also served for dining.

[33] For Pfalzel, see Fontaine, 'Das Trierer Umland', p. 341; for Konz and Mogorjelo, see above note 22. Minimal evidence that fortifications were built, or at least begun, around the villa at Piazza Armerina is mentioned by Mulvin, *Late Roman Villas*.

[34] Hébrard and Zeiller, *Spalato*, pp. 111–12; Bulić, *Palača*, and Bulić, *Kaiser Diokletians Palast*, pl. 62.

[35] Marasović and Marasović, 'Le ricerche … negli ultimi 30 anni', figs 10 and 11; Marasović, 'Znanstveni projekt', fig. 4 on pp. 37–8.

[36] The importance of servants to late antique stibadium dining is stressed in depictions, the importance of entertainment in literary sources; see Katherine Dunbabin, *The Roman Banquet: Images of Conviviality*, Cambridge 2003, and Ellis, 'Late antique dining'. Dunbabin thinks late antique depictions of dining reflect contemporary practice more closely than earlier pictures had.

[37] Jerko Marasović et al., 'Prostorni razvoj jugoistočnog dijela Dioklecijanove palače', *Prostor* 8 (2000), fig. 34.

[38] For the latter see Dragoslav Srejović, ed., *Roman Imperial Towns and Palaces in Serbia*, Belgrade 1994, pp. 146–7: 'building with the cruciform ground plan'. For pairings of apsed halls with triconches or multi-conches see e.g. R. J. A.Wilson, *Piazza Armerina*, London and New York 1983, p. 50; cf. Mulvin, *Late Roman Villas*, p. 42.

[39] Dyggve, *Ravennatum Palatium Sacrum*; Dyggve, 'Nouvelles recherches'; Dyggve, 'O izvornom izgledu'.

[40] Duval, 'Le "Palais"'; Duval, 'La Place de Split'; Noël Duval, 'Les résidences imperials', in *Usurpationen in der Spatantike*, ed. François Paschoud and Joachim Szidat, Stuttgart 1997, pp. 127–53.

[41] For Diocletion's abdication, see Lactantius, *De Mortibus. Persecutorum* (On the Death of the Persecutors), 19. The dedicatory inscriptions are in the *Corpus Inscriptiones Latinarum* (Corpus of Latin Inscriptions), VI, 1130=31242. For the coins, see Dragoslav Srejović, 'The representations of tetrarchs in Romuliana', *Antiquité Tardive* 2 (1994), p. 145. For the sarcophagus, see Heinz Kähler, 'Domkirche', in *Mansel'e armağan (Mélanges Mansel)*, Ankara 1974, vol. 2, pp, 809–20. For the veil, see Ammianus Marcellinus, *Res Gestae XVI*, 8.3–6.

[42] Demandt, 'Diokletian als Reformer', p. 8.

[43] If we can trust the *Historia Augustae*, he also offered the fruits of his political experience, presumably to visitors in a position to benefit (*SAH: vita Aurel.* XLIII, i.e. *The Imperial History: Life of Aurelian*, disputed authorship).

[44] Gamzigrad: Srejović, 'The representations of tetrarchs in Romuliana', figs 1–5, p. 145; cf. Frank Kolb, *Herrscherideologie in der Spätantike*, Berlin 2001; Luxor: Kolb, *Herrscherideologie in der Spätantike*. This attractive interpretation is unfortunately based on nineteenth-century watercolours rather than the paintings themselves, which are fast vanishing from the walls.

[45] Three not incompatible accounts of ageing with greater or less illness and depression, and the differing story of a sudden suicide: old age, Eutropius, *Breviarium Historiae Romanae* (Abridgement of Roman History), ix 2.8; illness, Eusebius, *Historia Ecclesiastica* (Church History), VIII.xvii (the authenticity of this passage has been disputed); despair, Lactantius, *De Mortibus. Persecutorum* (On the Death of the Persecutors), 42; sudden suicide, *Epitome de Caesaribus* (Brief Accounts of the Emperors, author unknown), 39.6.

[46] Dragoslav Srejović, 'Two memorial monuments of Roman palatial architecture: Diocletian's Palace in Split and Galerius' Palace at Gamzigrad', *Archaeologica Jugoslavica* 22–3 (1982–3 [1985]), pp. 41–9.

[47] See Wilkes, *Diocletian's Palace*, p. 71, stressing military observances. We may not be able to determine what occurred, but we can examine the effect created by the interaction of differing functions framing this porch; see below.

[48] Eugenia Bolognesi Recchi-Franceschini, 'Ravenna und Byzanz: Parallelen in der Nomenklatur der Paläste', in *Palatia: Kaiserpaläste in Konstantinopel, Ravenna und Trier*, ed. Margarethe König, Trier 2003, pp. 117–19, with bibliography.

[49] On Diocletian's camp at Luxor, see J. C. Deckers, 'Die Wandmalerei im Kaiserkultraum von Luxor', *Jahrbuch des deutschen archäologischen Instituts* 94 (1997), pp. 600–52. On the sphinxes in the palace, see Petar Selem, 'Stanje istraživanja sfingi carske palače u Splitu', *Adriatica praehistorica et antiqua: zbornik radova posvećen Grgi Novaku*, ed. V. Mirosavljević, D. Rendić-Miočević and M. Suić, Zagreb 1970, pp. 633–56. The sphinxes were certainly brought from Egypt, so probably the column shafts were as well. Importing cumbersome objects from Egypt was an imperial habit from Augustus to Theodosius, and not one often copied by lesser Romans. Sphinxes once contributed to the crowd of decoration in this area. There were certainly five or six, probably once eight to ten, several small in size. None are in their original positions, but most were found in the area of the tomb and the Temple. They could conceivably have all lined the steps leading up to the Mausoleum, or some might have been arranged in front of the Temple in the opposite temenos. Such arrangements, of course, would imitate the double rows of sphinxes that lead to Egyptian temples like the one at Luxor.

[50] Several generations of American students have learned from Jansen's *History of Art* that 'the architrave is curved, echoing the arch of the doorway below', when, of course, it is the much later doorway that echoes the architrave, as later builders fit their work into its ancient frame. For Diocletian's builders this porch was both an entryway and a part of the Peristyle; for the later builders it could only, and emphatically, be the latter.

[51] See, e.g., Sheila McNally, 'Introduction: state of scholarship', in *Diocletian's Palace: American–Yugoslav Joint Excavations*, and Sheila McNally, "The frieze of the Temple in Split', in *Dioklecijan, Tetrarhija i Dioklecijanova Palača*, pp. 279–294..

[52] Dragoslav Srejović and Čedomir Vasić, *Imperial Mausolea and Consecration Memorials in Felix Romuliana (Gamzigrad, East Serbia)*, Belgrade 1994. For two reactions to their views see Tomislav Marasović, review of J. J. Wilkes, *Diocletian's Palace, Split: Residence of a Retired Roman Emperor*, 1986, in *Journal of Roman Archaeology* 2 (1989), pp. 374–7, and Noël Duval, 'Le "Mausolée" de Dioclétien: Une appellation usurpée?' paper given in the symposium the proceedings of the symposium "Dioklecijan, Tetrarhija i Dioklecijanova

palača o 1700. obljetnici postojanja (18.–22. Rujna 2005)", not included in publication.

[53] On Galerius' intentions, see Timothy D. Barnes, 'Emperors, panegyrics, prefects, provinces and palaces (284–317)', *Journal of Roman Archaeology* 9 (1996), p. 552, and Kuhoff, *Diokletian und die Epoche der Tetrarchie*, n. 1492. For contrary opinions, see Srejović, 'Two memorial monuments of Roman palatial architecture', pp. 41–9, and Duval, 'Les résidences imperials', pp. 127–53. On Galerius' mother's beliefs, see Srejović and Vasić, *Imperial Mausolea*, p.127. Aston argues that Galerius could not be buried inside the walls at Gamzigrad because it was a city, which Split was not (Aston, 'Diocletian's Palace gates', p. 136). There is no clear evidence for city housing in either place.

[54] Mark J. Johnson, 'Late antique imperial mausolea', PhD thesis, Princeton University 1986; McNally, 'Introduction', pp. 22–3, and McNally, *Architectural Ornament*, p. 31.

[55] Kähler, 'Domkirche', vol. 2, pp. 809–20, vol. 3, p. 271. Additional evidence that there would have been such a sarcophagus comes from Ambrose's statement that Diocletian's colleague Maximian was buried in a porphyry sarcophagus (Ambrose, *Epistolae* [Letters] 53.4). On imperial inhumation, see Simon Price, 'From noble funerals to divine cult', in *Rituals of Royalty: Power and Ceremonial in Traditional Societies*, Cambridge 1987; Javier Arce, *Funus Imperatorum: Los funerales de los emperadores romanos*, Madrid 1988; Javier Arce, 'Imperial funerals in the later Roman Empire: change and continuity', in *Rituals of Power from Late Antiquity to the Early Middle Ages*, ed. Frans Theuws and Janet L. Nelson, Leiden 2000, pp. 115–29.

[56] For the friezes see McNally, 'The frieze of the Temple'; for the ceiling, see McNally, *Architectural Ornament*.

[57] McNally, *Architectural Ornament*, p. 32.

[58] The decoration carved on the buildings plays an important role in characterising sources of power; see McNally, *Architectural Ornament*.

[59] On later residents, see Bulić, *Palača*, p. 181. Srejović has suggested that both Gamzigrad and Split were intended as places of pilgrimage, anticipating the Christian practices of the next century. Griesbach's studies of developments in ancestor cult make that possibility seem more likely (Joseph Griesbach, 'Villa e mausoleo: transformazioni nel concetto della memoria nel suburbia romano', *Roman Villas around the Urbs: Interaction with Landscape and Environment*, ed. B. Santillo Frizell and A. Klynne, Rome 2005). Waurick's comment that the unprecedented placement of Diocletian's tomb beside a place of worship and near a palace prefigures Constantine's construction is more clearly applicable (Götz Waurick, 'Untersuchungen zur Lage der römischen Kaisergräber in der Zeit von Augustus bis Constantine', *Jahrbuch des Römisch-germanischen Zentralmuseums Mainz* 20 (1973), pp. 107–46); cf. R. J. A. Wilson, 'Vivere in villa,' note 3, p. 484.

5. ILLUMINATED MANUSCRIPTS IN CROATIA

[1] General reference books in Western European languages on manuscripts in Croatia are rare. I have used H. Folnesics, *Die Illuminierten Handschriften in Dalmatien* (Beschreibendes Verzeichnis der Illuminierten Handschriften in Österreich, VI), Leipzig 1917; *Minijatura u Jugoslaviji*, Zagreb 1964, with a summary in French (an exhibition catalogue of 158 items, lent to me by Nigel Morgan); *Riznica zagrebačke katedrale, the Treasury of Zagreb Cathedral*, Zagreb 1983; R. Katičić and S. P. Novak, *Two Thousand Years of Writing in Croatia*, Zagreb 1989; the exhibition catalogue for Trinity College, Dublin, November 2000 to February 2001, *Discovering the Glagolitic Script of Croatia*, Zagreb 2000, and the related catalogue for the Royal Library in Brussels, January–February 2004, *Trois Ecritures – Trois Langues: Pierres gravées, manuscrits anciens et publications croates à travers les siècles, Three

Scripts – Three Languages: Croatian Written Monuments, Manuscripts and Publications through Centuries, Zagreb 2004; and, most useful of all, A. Badurina, *Illuminirani rukopisi u Hrvatskoj*, translated by M. Paravić as *Illuminated Manuscripts in Croatia*, Zagreb 1995. In the Metropolitana of the Hrvatski Državni Arhiv (Croatian State Archives) in Zagreb, I was guided by Mirna Abaffy. Sister Lina Plukavec kindly showed me the treasury in Zagreb Cathedral. Ivan Kosić welcomed me to the Nacionalna i Sveučilišna knjižnica (National and University Library); and in Dubrovnik Dr Fra Stjepan Nošić generously gave me access to the books of the Franjevački Samostan (Franciscan convent) and Fra Kristijan Raić to those of the Samostan dominikanaca (Dominican convent). My wife and I owe incomparable accommodation in Dubrovnik to Captain Ante Jerković. Dr Ivan Mirnik has helped me especially, both with academic information and courteous improvement of my rapid Croatian spellings (I hope he can forgive me if I have missed some). I am indebted to Dr Stjepan Ćosić and Professor Tomislav Šola for assistance and kindness throughout Croatia. Above all, I am grateful to the arch-magician of this whole project, Lady Beresford-Peirse, whose name opens all doors and whose friendship has made this inquiry such a pleasure.

[2] E. A. Lowe, *Codices Latini Antiquiores: A Palaeographical Guide to Latin Manuscripts Prior to the Ninth Century*, XI, Oxford 1966, p. 26, no. 1669.

[3] W. Cahn, *Romanesque Bible Illumination*, Ithaca, NY 1982, pp. 101–7.

[4] M. Collon, *Catalogue général des manuscrits des bibliothèques publiques de France*, vol. XXXVII, Paris 1900, pp. 61–4; J. Tandarić and F. Šanjek, 'Juraj iz Slavonije (oko 1355/60–1416) profesor Sorbonne i pisac, kanonik i penitencijar stolne crkve u Toursu', *Croatia Christiana Periodica* VIII (1984), pp. 1–23; and *Discovering the Glagolitic Script of Croatia*, p. 99, no. M.1. There is a later but intriguing use of another Glagolitic manuscript in France. In 1574 a medieval Glagolitic Gospel book was brought to Reims, where it was regarded as strange and incomprehensible but so indisputably Christian in its unique script that it was used during coronations for the swearing of the oaths of each new king (L. P. M. Léger, *Notice sur l'Évangeliaire slavon de Reims, dit: Texte du Sacre*, Reims 1899).

[5] F. Avril, *Manuscrits Normands XI–XIIeme siècles*, Rouen 1975, pp. 70–1, no. 75; and J. J. G. Alexander in *The Splendor of the Word: Medieval and Renaissance Illuminated Manuscripts at the New York Public Library*, New York, London and Turnhout 2005, pp. 46–7.

[6] N. Golob, *Twelfth-Century Cistercian Manuscripts: The Sitticum Collection*, Ljubljana and London 1996.

[7] T. Kaeppeli and H.-V. Shooner, *Les manuscrits médiévaux de Saint-Dominic de Dubrovnik* (Institutum Historicum FF. Praedicatorum Romae ad S. Sabinae, dissertationes historicae, fasc. XVII), Rome 1995, pp. 80–1.

[8] G. Murano, *Opere diffuse per exemplar e pecia* (Fédération internationale des instituts d'études médiévales, textes et etudes du moyen âge, XXIX), Turnhout 2005, pp. 775–7, no. 890, and pp. 633–4, no. 667.

[9] F. Manzari, *La miniatura ad Avignone al tempo dei papi 1310–1410*, Modena 2006, pp. 92–5, figs 36–40.

[10] Murano, *Opere diffuse*, pp. 100–1, no. XXVI.

[11] R. Schilling, 'The *Decretum Gratiani* formerly in the C. W. Dyson Perrins collection', *Journal of the Archaeological Association*, 3rd ser., XXVI (1963), pp. 27–39; the manuscript described there is now in Los Angeles, J. Paul Getty Museum, MS Ludwig XIV.2.

[12] C. Fisković, 'Dubrovački sitnoslikari', in C. Fisković and K. Prijatelj, *Prilozi povijesti umjetnosti u Dubrovniku*, Split 1950, pp. 5–21; the documents concerning Marinus Kovačić are pp. 17–20, nos 19–20.

[13] L. M. C. Randall, 'Frontal heads in the borders of Parisian

and south Netherlandish Books of Hours', in *The Making and Meaning of Illuminated Medieval & Renaissance Manuscripts, Art & Architecture: Tributes to Jonathan J. G. Alexander*, ed. S. L'Engle and G. B. Guest, London and Turnhout 2006, pp. 249–68.

[14] Cited, with one small emendation, from W. M. Voelkle in J. J. G. Alexander, ed., *The Painted Page: Italian Renaissance Book Illumination, 1450–1550*, Munich and New York 1994, p. 246.

[15] W. Smith, *The Farnese Hours: The Pierpont Morgan Library, New York*, New York 1976, facsimile of fols 4v–5r and 26v–27r; J. J. G. Alexander, *The Towneley Lectionary, Illuminated for Cardinal Alessandro Farnese by Giulio Clovio*, [London] Roxburghe Club 1997, pls XI–XII.

[16] *Manuscrit enluminé d'un Prélat Hongrois à la Bibliothèque Beatty à Londres*, n.p., *c.* 1921, comprising G. Fraknói, 'La vie du Prélat Dominique Kálmáncsehi', pp. 5–14, and T. Gottlieb, 'Beschreibung der Kálmáncsehi-Handschrift in der Bibliothek Beatty', pp. 17–22. The Book of Hours described there was lot 65 in the Chester Beatty sale, Sotheby's, 9 May 1933, and lot 590 in the Wilmerding sale, New York, 29 October 1951. A breviary in Budapest with Kálmáncsehi's arms is illustrated in I. Berkovits, *Illuminated Manuscripts in Hungary, XI–XVI Centuries*, Shannon 1969, pls XXIV–XXX.

[17] Buda is the only late fifteenth-century city in Central Europe known to have produced gilt bindings in the Italian style (cf. P. Needham, *Twelve Centuries of Bookbindings, 400–1600*, New York and London 1979, pp. 112–14, no. 31).

[18] A. Schneider, '"Hans pictor Alemanus", Ein deutscher Maler in Zagreb von 1503–1526', *Neue Ordnung*, Zagreb (26 April 1942), pp. 10–11; the attribution is accepted by Badurina, among others.

[19] The same arms, identified as those of Erdödy-Bakócz, occur in a gradual in Esztergom (Berkovits, *Illuminated Manuscripts in Hungary*, pl. XLI).

[20] R. Flóris, 'Kalmanczai Domokos székes-fehérvái prépost codexe', *Magyar Könyv-Szemle, A Magyar Nemzeti Múzeum Könyvtóra*, Budapest 1876, pp. 169–73; Gottlieb, 'Beschreibung der Kálmáncsehi-Handschrift in der Bibliothek Beatty', pp. 17–22; and E. Hoffmann, *Régi Magyar Bibliofilek*, Budapest 1929, pp. 111–19.

6. GOTHIC ART AND THE FRIARS IN LATE MEDIEVAL CROATIA, 1213–1460

My first thanks are to Flora and Eric Turner for encouraging my Dalmatian interests and opening many doors in Croatia. Daniel Premerl and Milena Grabačić have provided invaluable guidance to the relevant Croatian language scholarship, while seminar audiences in Oxford, Nottingham, Warwick and the Courtauld Institute provided much-appreciated sounding boards. I am also grateful to Andreja Brulc, Roberto Cobianchi, Emil Hilje, Marijana Kovačević, Andrea De Marchi, Ivana Prijatelj-Pavičić, Cristina Guarnieri, Zoe Willis, and my companion on Jackson's 'mysterious, almost unknown shore', Annette Wickham. Most of all, I am indebted to Jadranka Beresford-Peirse for conceiving this project and supporting my research so generously and wholeheartedly.

[1] Thomas G. Jackson, *Dalmatia, the Quarnero and Istria*, 3 vols, Oxford 1887, III, p. 202.

[2] For a comprehensive survey of continental Croatia's Franciscan churches, see the catalogue for the exhibition at the Galerija Klovićevi dvori: *Mir i dobro, umjetničko i kulturno nasljeđe Hrvatske franjevačke provincije sv. Ćirila i Metoda (Artistic and Cultural Heritage of the Croatian Franciscan Province of the Saints Cyril and Methodius)*, Zagreb 2000.

[3] Lelja Dobronić, 'Lik sv. Timoteja na fresci (XIII st.) u sakristije zagrebačke katedrale' ('The figure of Saint Timotheus on the wall painting in the sacristy of the Zagreb Cathedral'), *Peristil* 38 (1995), pp. 27–30, has argued that Timotheus, bishop of Zagreb from 1263 to 1287, may have included his name

saint in the scheme. The programme of building work that included the sacristy commenced in 1275, and the paintings should be dated to the final decades of the century. The lunette with the mendicant saints is, however, only part of a larger fresco programme of standing saints. The restoration in the near future of the currently illegible figures on the vaults above will add considerably to our understanding of this important cycle.

[4] Recorded in the first life by Thomas of Celano, 'Vita prima', in *Analecta franciscana*, 12 vols, Quaracchi 1926–83, X (1941), p. 42 (cap. 20, n. 55). For a comprehensive discussion of this and other early textual references connecting Francis with Dalmatia, see Marijan Žugaj, 'San Francesco in Croazia e la protoprovincia croata (1217–1239)', *Miscellanea francescana* 82 (1982), pp. 247–310.

[5] See Žugaj, 'San Francesco in Croazia', pp. 252–3.

[6] For Paulinus's list of Dalmatian houses, see Conrad Eubel, *Provinciale Ordinis Fratrum Minorum vetustissimum secundum codicem vaticanum nr. 1960*, Quaracchi 1892, pp. 68–9.

[7] Purchased by the British Museum in 1858, the inscription reads: 'S[IGILLUM] MINISTRI: P[RO]VINCIE DALMATIE ORD[IN]IS FR[ATRU]M MINOR[UM]'. I am indebted to Bet McCleod of the British Museum for her generous help in researching this object.

[8] The work of the Dominican scholar Stjepan Krasić has been fundamental for our understanding of the history of the Preaching Friars in Croatia, and all dates here are taken from Krasić's *Congregatio Ragusina Ordinis Praedicatorum (1487–1550)*, Rome 1972.

[9] The fundamental work on the Zadar foundation is the anthology *Samostan Sv. Frane u Zadru*, ed. Justin Velnić, Zadar 1980. Carlo Cecchelli, *Zara: Catalogo delle cose d'arte e antichità*, Rome 1932, pp. 124–44, provides a useful guide to the artworks conserved in the church.

[10] See Atanazije J. Matanić, 'Franjevački počeci u Zadru' ('Origini francescane a Zara'), in Velnić, *Samostan*, pp. 7–23; for a more sceptical view of the Zadar tradition, see Žugaj, 'San Francesco in Croazia', p. 248, n. 8.

[11] For the inscription, which is much later in date, see Justin Velnić, 'Samostan Sv. Frane u Zadru, povijesni prikaz njegova života i djelatnosti' ('Il convento di San Francesco a Zara: sua storia e attività'), in Velnić, *Samostan*, pp. 25–101, at p. 48.

[12] The Gothic fenestration was restored in the 1970s; for photographs of the church before and during these interventions, see Velnić, *Samostan*, pls III–IX.

[13] For the Zadar antiphonaries and their illumination, see Lazar Mirković, *Miniature u antifonarima i gradualima manastira Sv. Franje Asiskog u Zadru (Les miniatures des antiphonaires et des gradueles du monastère de St Francois d'Assise à Zadar)*, Belgrade 1977; and now also Federica Teniolo's catalogue entries in the exhibition catalogue *Prvih pet stoljeća hrvatske umjetnosti (The First Five Centuries of Croatian Art)*, Zagreb 2006, pp. 266–73. A *terminus post quem* for this group of choir books is provided by the inclusion of the feast of St Clare (instituted 1292) and an *ante quem* by the absence of the feast of Corpus Christi (instituted in 1317).

[14] The principal point of reference for this panel remains Grgo Gamulin, 'Un crocifisso del Millecento e due Madonna duecentesche', *Arte Veneta* 21 (1967), pp. 9–20; see also Grgo Gamulin, *The Painted Crucifixes in Croatia*, trans. Ellen Elias-Bursać, Zagreb 1983, pp. 13–15; and more recently Igor Fisković's catalogue entry in *Prvih pet stoljeća*, pp. 262–5, who dates the panel to *c.* 1200.

[15] For the bell, see Ivo Petricioli, 'O važnijim umjetninama u franjevačkom samostanu u Zadru' ('Sulle più importanti opere d'arte nel convento francescano di Zara'), in Velnić, *Samostan*, pp. 109–27, at pp. 110–11 and pls XLVIII and XLIX. The inscription reads: '+ MAGISTER BELO ET VIVENCIUS ME FECIT ANNO D[OMI]NI MCCCXXVIII

AN[N]I CHE DIO VENE I[N] S. MARIA'. See also Sofija Petricioli, 'Zvono majstora Bela i Vivencija u Zadru' ('A bell cast by masters Belo and Viventius in Zadar'), *Prilozi povijesti umjetnosti u Dalmaciji* 21 (1980), pp. 246–51 (who also lists over a dozen other bells signed by these founders), and Velnić, 'Samostan Sv. Frane u Zadru', in idem, *Samostan*, pp. 59–60.

[16] Velnić, 'Samostan Sv. Frane u Zadru', in idem, *Samostan*, p. 58; the treaty was signed 'Jadrae in monasterio Sancti Francisci Ordinis Fratrum Minorum in sacristia ecclesiae suae'.

[17] For the identification of the donor figure on this cross, see Marijana Kovačević, 'Ophodni križ – još jedan anžuvinski *ex voto* u Zadru?' ('Processional Cross – Another Angevin *ex voto* in Zadar?'), *Radovi Instituta Povijesti Umjetnosti* 31 (2007), pp. 29–42. Iconographic analysis of this object now depends on old photographs as it was stolen in 1974 and has yet to be recovered.

[18] For this document, see Emil Hilje, *Gotičko slikarstvo u Zadru (Gothic Painting in Zadar)*, Zagreb 1999, pp. 204–5. Nikola promised to fashion 'duas cruces talis similitudinis, magnitudinis, longitudinis, latidunis, grossitudinis, pulcritudinis et bonitatis qualis est ad presens crux quam ipse Nicolaus vendidit fratribus minoribus de Iadra'. The text has also been published in the compendium of transcriptions from the Zadar archives made between the two world wars by the then archivist Giuseppe Praga and now deposited in the Biblioteca Marciana in Venice: Giuseppe Praga, *Documenti per la storia dell'arte a Zara dal medioevo al settecento*, ed. Maria Walcher, Trieste 2005, pp. 67–8 (doc. 82). This publication, however, does not give the collocations presently in use in the state archives in Zadar.

[19] In September 1366, Nikola was granted citizenship having travelled to Venice as a boy, working as a watchman, serving as a crossbowman in the Venetian army, and having trained with the painter Paolo Veneziano for five years, see Michelangelo Muraro, *Paolo da Venezia*, University Park, PA 1970, p. 85. This important document is found in Archivio di Stato di Venezia, *Grazie* XVI, fol. 62r, and a summary was published by Bartolomeo Cecchetti, 'Nomi di pittori e lapicidi antichi', *Archivio Veneto* 33 (1887), p. 61; see also p. 62 for the testament that Nikola made in Venice in 1374, presumably before he returned to Zadar.

[20] For a full discussion of this commission, see Ivo Petricioli, *Umjetnička obrada drveta u Zadru u doba gotike (Wood Carving of the Gothic Period in Zadar)*, Zagreb 1972, pp. 21–35. Giovanni's Tuscan origins were understood by Jackson, *Dalmatia*, I, p. 308.

[21] The 1394 and 1395 contracts are transcribed by I. Petricioli, *Umjetnička*, pp. 117–19 (docs 8 and 9). The 1394 document had earlier been published in truncated form by Donato Fabianich, *Storia dei Frati Minori dai primordi della loro instituzione in Dalmazia e Bosnia fino ai nostri giorni*, Zadar 1864, parte seconda, vol. II, p. 50. See also Praga, *Documenti*, pp. 108–9 (doc. 163) and p. 110 (doc. 167).

[22] The Matafaris family patronised the altar of St John in the Franciscan church, which occupied the vaulted side chapel to the north ('a parte boreali') of the high altar chapel. See Praga, *Documenti*, p. 240 (doc. 390), for Ludovik de Matafaris's bequest of 100 ducats in 1438 for the repair of the chapel and the execution of an 'anchona'. It may also reflect the fact that Petro de Matafaris was archbishop of Zadar from 1376 until his death in 1400, see Conrad Eubel, *Hierarchia catholica medii aevi*, Regensburg 1913, vol. I, p. 281.

[23] For these documents, see Donal Cooper and James Banker, 'The church of San Francesco in Borgo Sansepolcro in the Middle Ages and Renaissance', in *Sassetta: The Borgo Sansepolcro Altarpiece*, ed. Machtelt Israels, Florence and Leiden 2009, pp. 573-4. Of particular interest are two notarial acts of November 1400, where Giovanni and his brother

Angelo are contracted to fashion choir precincts for the Servite churches in Sansepolcro and Sant'Angelo in Vado in the Marches. Some caution must remain regarding the identification, as Giovanni's patronymic is given as Jacopo in the Zadar documents, whereas his (and Angelo's) father is named as 'Schiacto' in the Sansepolcro contracts. 'Schiacto', however, may have been a nickname, or may have been misunderstood by the Zadar friars.

24 I. Petricioli, 'O važnijim umjetninama u franjevačkom samostanu u Zadru' in Velnić, *Samostan*, pp. 114–15.

25 Paulus de Paulo's text, first cited by Giuseppe Praga, 'Alcuni documenti su Giorgio da Sebenico', *Rassegna Marchigiana* 7 (1928), pp. 73–80 (at p. 76, n. 1), survives in a corrupt version copied by Iohannes Lucius (Ivan Lučić), *De regno Dalmatiae et Croatiae*, Amsterdam 1666, p. 438. The two statues 'fuerunt portatae in Ecclesia fratrum minorum cum maxima solemnitate … cum magnis cantionibus ecclesiasticis et musicis instrumentis et cum multa effusione lachrymarum pro devotione, ubi consecratae fuerunt per ipsum dominum archiepiscopum'. For a more recent edition, see Ferdo Šišić, 'Ljetopis Pavla Pavlovića patricija zadarskoga', in *Vjesnik kr. hrvatsko-slavonskog-dalmatinskog zemaljskog arkiva*, 6 vols (1899–1904), VI, Zagreb 1904.

26 See I. Petricioli, 'O važnijim umjetninama u franjevačkom samostanu u Zadru', p. 115; and idem, 'From early Christianity to the baroque', in the exhibition catalogue *Sjaj zadarskih riznica (The Splendour of Zadar Treasuries)*, Zagreb 1990, p. 38.

27 For this commission, see I. Petricioli, *Umjetnička*, pp. 74–86.

28 I. Petricioli, *Umjetnička*, pp. 124–5 (doc. 18); Praga, *Documenti*, pp. 210–11 (doc. 315).

29 These fragments were first assembled by Cvito Fisković and Ivo Petricioli, 'Zadarski poliptij Petra de Riboldisa' ('Le polyptyque de Pierre de Riboldis à Zadar'), *Anali Historijskog Instituta u Dubrovniku* 4–5 (1956), pp. 153–80. The roofing of the church had been repaired shortly before; see the contract of 1439 with 'Magister Vidolus marangonus de Iadra' of 2 December 1439, published in Praga, *Documenti*, pp. 224–5 (doc. 352).

30 This contract of 11 January 1452 is transcribed in I. Petricioli, *Umjetnička*, pp. 127–8 (doc. 22); Praga, *Documenti*, p. 258 (doc. 394); Vučković was to 'inaurare unam totam et integram palam de lignamine sculptam pro maiori altare ecclesie Sancti Francisci predicti ipsamque palam optimis coloribus depingere, aptare et ornare'. The painter's name is often mistranscribed as Vušković, for the correct spelling, see Emil Hilje, 'Ikonografski program predele Ugljanskog poliptiha' ('Il programma iconografico della predella del "Polittico di Ugljan"'), *Prilozi povijesti umjetnosti u Dalmaciji* 36 (1996), p. 45, note 4.

31 Known as Giorgio Dalmata in Italy; these documents were first published by Praga, 'Alcuni documenti su Giorgio da Sebenico', pp. 73–80.

32 For the reconstruction of a number of choir screens in Franciscan churches in Dalmatia, see the important article by Igor Fisković, 'O unutrašnjem uređenju samostanskih crkava na istočnoj obali Jadrana' ('Sugli interni delle chiese conventuali lungo la costa orientale dell'adriatico'), *Prilozi povijesti umjetnosti u Dalmaciji* 39 (2001–2), pp. 227–67 (pp. 238–40 for the Zadar church). Praga, 'Alcuni documenti su Giorgio da Sebenico', p. 75, had not grasped the significance of the phrase 'in medio ecclesiae' and struggled to locate the chapels within the church.

33 The Ancona Loggia, although much altered, can therefore provide some indication of the richness of the Zadar capitals; for Juraj Dalmatinac's work in Zadar and Ancona, see Janez Höfler, *Die Kunst Dalmatiens vom Mittelalter bis zur Renaissance (800–1520)*, Graz 1989, pp. 205–9.

34 The contract with 'Magister Marco ab Organis de Venetiis' of 9 September 1443 was published by Donato Fabianich,

Il convento più antico dei Frati Minori in Dalmazia, Prato 1882, p. 118, n. 1; and more recently in Praga, *Documenti*, p. 230 (doc. 365). Marco was to be paid fifty-six ducats and undertook to send his assistant ('discipulus') from Venice with the organ to oversee its installation.

35 Blaž's testament is transcribed in the documentary appendix to the exhibition catalogue *Biagio di Giorgio da Traù*, ed. Zoraida Demori-Staničić with essays by Kruno Prijatelj, Igor Fisković, Joško Belamarić and Davor Domančić, Zagreb 1989, p. 86 (doc. 32), and also in Praga, *Documenti*, pp. 206–7 (doc. 309). Blaž's bequests indicate a particular devotion to the Franciscans; not only did he ask 'pro devotione sancti Francisci' to be buried 'in habitu fratrum minorum', he also left twelve ducats for a banner for the church, and absolved the friars of payment for a 'palla' (presumably an altarpiece) that he had been working on for the church. For the earlier payment to Blaž in 1445 'pro cantinellis pictis' for the church's organ, see *Biagio di Giorgio da Traù*, p. 84 (doc. 30).

36 Nikola Jakšić, 'Osnutak Franjevačkog samostana na Pašmanu 1392 godine' ('The founding of a Franciscan monastery on Pašman, 1392'), *Prilozi povijesti umjetnosti u Dalmaciji* 32 (1992), pp. 351–6.

37 For the Pašman panel, which measures 108 x 85 centimetres in its much reduced state, see Emil Hilje's entry in the exhibition catalogue *Stoljeće gotike na Jadranu: Slikarstvo u ozračju Paola Veneziana (The Gothic Century on the Adriatic: Painting in the Perspective of Paolo Veneziano and his Followers)*, ed. Joško Belamarić, Zoraida Demori Staničić and Biserka Rauter Plančić, Zagreb 2004, pp. 146–7. The figure of St John the Baptist was originally balanced by a now-lost St Francis on the other side of the Virgin and Child, recorded in 1878, see Grgo Gamulin, *Madonna and Child in Old Art of Croatia*, Zagreb 1971, p. 133.

38 For the Ugljan foundation, see Emil Hilje, 'Utemeljenje franjevačkih samostana na zadarskim otocima' ('The foundation of Franciscan monasteries on the Zadar islands'), *Radovi Zavoda za povijesne zanosti HAZU u Zadru* 45 (2003), pp. 7–19, esp. p. 15 for the church's consecration inscription: 'ANNO SALVTIS MCCCCXLVII DIE XXI MAII CONSECRATIO HVIVS ECCLESIAE DIVI HIERONYMI UCLEANI'. For the conventual church of St Jerome, which had a single nave terminating in a single vaulted high altar chapel, see Ivo Petricioli, 'Ostaci srednjovjekovne sakralne arhitekture na otoku Ugljanu' ('Restes d'architecture sacrée médiévale dans l'île d'Ugljan'), *Prilozi povijesti umjetnosti u Dalmaciji* 12 (1960), pp. 113–22.

39 See Joško Belamarić's catalogue entry in *Stoljeće gotike na Jadranu*, pp. 156–9, with preceding bibliography. For the Giovanni di Pietro attribution, see Hilje, *Gotičko slikarstvo u Zadru*, pp. 92–121; and idem, 'Dva popisa dobara splitskih slikara iz 15. Stoljeća', *Radovi Zavoda za povijesne znanosti HAZU u Zadru* 49 (2007), p. 292.

40 The two painters had legally annulled their collaboration in April 1446, see Praga, *Documenti*, p. 234 (doc. 377). Ivana Prijatelj, 'Još o Ivanu Petrovu iz Milana' ('Ancora su Giovanni di Pietro da Milano'), *Prilozi povijesti umjetnosti u Dalmaciji* 31 (1991), pp. 97-113, has argued that the two painters executed different areas of the Ugljan altarpiece, Giovanni being responsible for the predella and main register of standing saints, while Vučković painted the central image of the Virgin and the pinnacles.

41 For the iconography of the predella, see Hilje, 'Ikonografski program predele Ugljanskog poliptiha', pp. 43–58.

42 This figure's hat is reminiscent of pilgrim headgear, and he could be St Pellegrinus. A small church at the other end of Ugljan island was dedicated to the pilgrim saint, see I. Petricioli, 'Ostaci srednjovjekovne sakralne arhitekture na otoku Ugljanu', p. 117.

43 For St Platon, later known as St Dominic, see Emil Hilje, 'Marginalije uz obnovu crkve Svetog Dominika u Zadru',

Glasje: Časopis za književnost i umjetnost 1, no. 2 (1994), pp. 57–66; and idem, 'Combinations of Romanesque and Gothic forms in the architecture of Zadar', *Hortus Artium Medievalium* 2 (1996), pp. 65–76, esp. pp. 69–70.

44 Stjepan Krasić, 'Inventar umjetničkih predmeta u nekadašnjoj dominikanskoj crkvi u Zadru' ('Inventario degli oggetti d'arte nella già chiesa domenicana di Zadar'), *Prilozi povijesti umjetnosti u Dalmaciji* 27, 1988, pp. 227–48.

45 Krasić, 'Inventar umjetničkih predmeta u nekadašnjoj dominikanskoj crkvi u Zadru', p. 238. The picture seems to have been removed to Venice by the end of the eighteenth century, when it was described in the Manfrin collection, see Andrea De Marchi, 'Ritorno a Nicolò di Pietro', *Nuovi Studi* 3 (1997), pp. 5–24, esp. pp. 5, 14, nn. 8-9.

46 Krasić, 'Inventar umjetničkih predmeta u nekadašnjoj dominikanskoj crkvi u Zadru', p. 234. However, Nicolò di Pietro's panel is not the only altarpiece that is documented for the church. In 1391 Meneghello de' Canali agreed to paint an altarpiece of the Virgin for the Dominican church similar to one that he had already painted for the Zadar Franciscans, see Hilje, 'Marginalije uz obnovu crkve Svetog Dominika u Zadru', p. 64, idem, *Gotičko slikarstvo u Zadru*, pp. 52, 83, n. 25. We also know through a 1385 'modo et forma' contractual clause of an 'ancona' over the altar of St Jerome in St Platon by the sacristy door which had a central figure of the saint flanked by four scenes from his life, see Praga, *Documenti*, p. 75 (doc. 98). All of which suggests that the church had a rich array of altars by the end of the fourteenth century. Two further 'anconae' for St Platon are mentioned in the 1386 document concerning the Catarino cross, see below n. 47.

47 Hilje, *Gotičko slikarstvo u Zadru*, pp. 155–8; Praga, *Documenti*, p. 96 (doc. 140).

48 Ivo Petricioli, 'Jedno Catarinovo djelo u Zadru?' ('Un'opera di Catarino a Zara?'), *Peristil* 8-9 (1965-6), pp. 57–62; and idem, *Tragom srednjovjekovnih umjetnika (Traces of Medieval Artists)*, Zagreb 1983, p. 98. The cross had been moved to the basilica of St Chrysogonus following the suppression of St Platon in 1807.

49 The complex but important interconnections between these painters and wood sculptors have been greatly clarified by De Marchi, 'Ritorno a Nicolò di Pietro', pp. 5–24. Even before Krasić had identified the 'Belgarzone Madonna' in the Zadar inventories, De Marchi had emphasised the activity of Nicolò di Pietro and other Venetian painters across the Adriatic region in this period, see idem, 'Per un riesame della pittura tardogotica a Venezia: Nicolò di Pietro e il suo contesto adriatico', *Bollettino d'arte* 72 (1987), pp. 25–66.

50 The screen (or 'ballatorio'), which also incorporated the church's organ, is recorded in a testamentary bequest of 200 gold ducats of 3 February 1396 'pro refectione et reparatione ballatorii que est in medio ipsius Ecclesie Sancti Platonis ubi sunt organa', see Hilje, 'Marginalije uz obnovu crkve Svetog Dominika u Zadru', p. 62, n. 39; I. Fisković, 'O unutrašnjem uređenju samostanskih crkava na istočnoj obali Jadrana', p. 251.

51 The contract for the 'duo armaria de lingnaminibus cum uno banco a sedendo' was published by Petricioli, *Umjetnička*, p. 120 (doc. 11). In 1405, the Dominicans contracted the local carpenters Nikola Arbuzjanić and Franjo Disinich to repair the roof of the church, see Praga, *Documenti*, pp. 196–7 (doc. 286).

52 This notice is taken from Vitaliano Brunelli, *Storia della città di Zara*, Venice 1913, republished Trieste 1974, p. 501.

53 For the early history of the Franciscan community in Pula, see Ljudevit Anton Maračić, *Pulski sveti Franjo: Crkva i samostan sv. Franje u Puli*, Pazin 2005, esp. pp. 13–43.

54 Blessed Ottone was renowned for his ability to cure blindness. Paulinus would note of the Pula convent: 'ubi fr. Otho cecos et alios infirmos mirabiliter curavit', see Eubel, *Provinciale Ordinis Fratrum*, p. 69, n. 288.

55 Attilio Krizmanić, 'Sviluppo architettonico del complesso francescano a Pola', *Hortus Artium Medievalium* 7, 2001, pp. 77–100.

56 Krizmanić, 'Sviluppo architettonico del complesso francescano a Pola', p. 85, figs 15 and 16; p. 98, n. 20, establishes that the reconstruction of the pulpit in 1926–7 was based on convincing traces of the original arrangement visible on interior and exterior of the nave walls; I. Fisković, 'O unutrašnjem uređenju samostanskih crkava na istočnoj obali Jadrana', pp. 260–2.

57 Miljenko Domijan, *Rab: The City of Art*, Zagreb 2007, pp. 151–63.

58 Jackson, *Dalmatia*, III, p. 224.

59 Domijan, *Rab*, p. 142.

60 For the bishops of Rab prior to 1431, see Eubel, *Hierarchia catholica*, I, p. 101. The likely connection with Juraj Hermolais III was made by Muraro, *Paolo da Venezia*, pp. 119–20, and repeated by Igor Fisković and Miljenko Domijan in their respective catalogue entries for the Rab retable in *Il Trecento adriatico: Paolo Veneziano e la pittura tra Oriente e Occidente*, ed. Francesca Flores d'Arcais and Giovanni Gentili, Milan 2002, pp. 164–5; and *Stoljeće gotike na Jadranu*, p. 83. The panel may well have been originally commissioned for Rab Cathedral, passing to the church of St John when it was converted into an episcopal palace in the early nineteenth century. Muraro noted that the cathedral possessed a relic of St Tecla, who also appears on the altarpiece, as well as St Christopher, the patron of Rab.

61 Žugaj, 'San Francesco in Croazia', p. 249.

62 Milan Ivanišević, 'Nestajanje najstarijega hrvatskoga franjevačkog mjesta u Trogiru' ('The disappearance of the oldest Croatian Franciscan site in Trogir'), *Prilozi povijesti umjetnosti u Dalmaciji* 39 (2001–2), pp. 149–84. For both mendicant orders in Trogir, see Irene Benyovsky, 'Trogirsko prigrađe na prijelaza 13. u 14. stoljeće – utjecaj dominikanaca i franjevaca na oblikovanje prostora' ('The burg of Trogir at the end of the 13th and the beginning of the 14th century: the influence of Franciscans and Dominicans on the formation of the urban space'), *Croatica Christiana Periodica* 52 (2003), pp. 47–56.

63 The contract of 15 November 1437 is transcribed in *Biagio di Giorgio da Traù*, p. 85 (doc. 28). Blaž was to deliver by the following September 'unam anchonam seu palam ad altare maius dicte ecclesie Sancte Marie fratrum minorum', measuring four braccia across, divided by columns into five fields and incorporating a predella.

64 For this lunette, see Cvito Fisković, 'Skulpture mletačkog kipara Nikole Dente u Trogiru i u Splitu' ('Sculptures du sculpteur venitien Nicolas Dente dit Cervo a Trogir et a Split'), *Prilozi povijesti umjetnosti u Dalmaciji* 14 (1962), pp. 63–78. For the Dominican church in Trogir, see Stjepan Krasić, 'Crkva i samostan sv. Dominiku u Trogiru' ('The Church and Monastery of St Dominic in Trogir'), *Prilozi povijesti umjetnostri u Dalmaciji* 41 (2005-7), pp. 67-107.

65 See Eubel, *Hierarchia catholica*, I, p. 490; Nikola Kažotić was bishop of Trogir from 1361 until his death in 1372.

66 For this altarpiece, dated to 1436–9 on the basis of Blaž's documented activity in Trogir during those years, see *Biagio di Giorgio da Traù*, pp. 107–8.

67 Blaž was paid 'dipingere voltam lignaminis super altaris maius Sancti Francisci cum stellis et floribus de coloribus pulcro', see *Biagio di Giorgio da Traù*, p. 83 (doc. 1).

68 For the Split cross, see *Biagio di Giorgio da Traù*, pp. 94–5. However, De Marchi, 'Ritorno a Nicolò di Pietro', p. 18, n. 36, has argued that the cross should be dissociated from the 1412 document and should be dated later, probably to the 1430s.

69 See Kruno Prijatelj, 'Profilo artistico del pittore Biagio di Giorgio da Traù', in *Biagio di Giorgio da Traù*, p. 12.

70 Andrea De Marchi, 'Un polittico spalatino di Dujma Vušković a Hermitage', *Prilozi povijesti umjetnosti u Dalmaciji* 36 (1996), pp. 19–29.

71 De Marchi's reconstruction of the Hermitage panels was further developed by Joško Belamarić, 'Nove potvrde za Dujma Vuškovića' ('Nuove conferme per Dujam Vušković'), *Prilozi povijesti umjetnosti u Dalmaciji* 36 (1996), pp. 31–42. Belamarić linked the altarpiece with a bequest of eighty ducats to the Split Franciscans in 1437 'ut fiat in maiori altari una pala', and speculated that the central field of the polyptych may have framed an older icon that was venerated on the church's high altar, and which had earlier been restored by Meneghello de' Canali in Zadar in 1413. The contract with Meneghello, which specified the transfer of the icon from Split and Zadar and asked the painter to repaint ('repingere') the image, has been published by Hilje, *Gotičko slikarstvo u Zadru*, pp. 209–10 (doc. 13), and in Praga, *Documenti*, p. 25 (doc. 22).

72 See Kruno Prijatelj, 'Slikano Raspelo iz samostana Sv. Klare u Splitu' ('Il crocifisso dipinto del convento di S. Chiara a Spalato'), *Peristil* 4 (1961), pp. 8–15; and subsequently Grgo Gamulin, 'La pittura su tavole nel tardo medioevo sulla costa orientale dell'Adriatico', in *Venezia e il Levante fino al XV secolo*, ed. Agostino Pertusi, 2 vols, Florence 1974, II, p. 193, n. 2; and now Joško Belamarić's catalogue entry in *Prvih pet stoljeća*, pp. 277–9, dating the panel to *c*. 1270–90. For 'Adrio-Byzantinism', see Belamarić, 'Gothic culture in Dalmatia: the development of painting between the 13th and 15th centuries', in *Stoljeće gotike na Jadranu*, p. 28.

73 The identification of the lower terminal as an image of St Francis was first advanced in *Romaničko slikarstvo u Hrvatskoj*, ed. Igor Fisković, Zagreb 1987, pp. 87, 129, and confirmed by Joško Belamarić. The cross, therefore, probably vies with the fresco in Zagreb Cathedral as the earliest surviving depiction of St Francis in Croatia.

74 For the history of the Clarissan house in Split, see the special issue of *Kačić: Zbornik franjevačke provincije presvetoga otkupitelja (Acta Provinciae SS. Redemptoris Ordinis Fratrum Minorum in Croatia)* 26 (1994), especially the essay by Perislav Petrić, 'Novi prilozi topografiji samostana Sv. Klare u Splitu' ('Nuovi apporti alla topografia del convento di Santa Chiara a Spalato'), pp. 319–46, for the first Clarissan house in Split located by the harbour.

75 The most accessible introduction to the convent's history is Stjepan Krasić, *The Dominican Priory in Dubrovnik*, Dubrovnik 2002, esp. pp. 25–40.

76 Grgo Gamulin, 'Un crocifisso di Maestro Paolo ed altri due del Trecento', *Arte Veneta* 19 (1965), pp. 32–43, and also Gamulin, *The Painted Crucifixes in Croatia*, pp. 31–2; for a more recent treatment of the Dubrovnik crucifix, see Igor Fisković's catalogue entry in *Stoljeće gotike na Jadranu*, pp. 106–9.

77 The document was first published by Jorjo Tadić, *Građa o slikarskoj školi u Dubrovniku XIII–XVI vek*, 2 vols, Belgrade 1952, I, p. 13 (doc. 34): 'Anchora vollio che se acatti 1. crocifisso che costi perperi LXXX et che se metta ali frari predichatori aprovo al altar grande'.

78 Tadić, *Građa o slikarskoj školi*, I, p. 353; the Lukarić chapel was located on the south side of the church ('… in chava ex parte pelagi', i.e. on the side towards the sea).

79 Serafino Cerva, *Monumenta congregationis Sancti Dominici de Ragusio ordinis fratris praedicatorum*, Dubrovnik 1733, vol. II, pp. 42–3 (manuscript in the archive of the Dominican convent in Dubrovnik).

80 It does not seem possible, however, that this could refer to a high altarpiece (cf. Belamarić in *Stoljeće gotike na Jadranu*, p. 28). Lukarić's testament unambiguously links the altarpiece to his chapel ('supra altari infrascripta cappella'), and his other bequests specify that the altar was dedicated to St Nicholas. The friars were to sing 'omni die unam missam et unam missam de conventu in die sancti Nicolai ad quam cappella est nomenatum'; the testator's devotion to his name saint was also reflected in his desire to send a priest to Bari to sing a Mass at St Nicolas's shrine. These passages from Lukarić's will were not transcribed by Tadić, see Dubrovnik, Državni archiv, Testamenta de notaria 4, fol. 33v. The St Nicholas altar was probably located close to the high altar, see the bequest for a mass 'al'altar de Sancto Nicola apresso lo altar grande a Sancto Domenego' from 18 October 1436: Testamenta de notaria 12, fol. 151r.

81 For the San Samuele cross, see Muraro, *Paolo da Venezia*, p. 127, pls 84, 85.

82 Tadić, *Građa o slikarskoj školi*, I, p. 13 (doc. 34); 'Et vollio che debia fare 1. altare sotto el lector de Sancta Maria fronido et che abia una anchona cola croxe, et d'una parte la Donna dall'altro lato sancto Çovanni, et che coste 1. altar fronido perperi LX'; the other clauses in Restić's will (not transcribed by Tadić) clarify that this altar was located in 'Sancta Maria Grande', the city's cathedral, see Dubrovnik, Državni archiv, Testamenta de notaria 5, fols 5r–v.

83 Tadić, *Građa o slikarskoj školi*, I, p. 198 (doc. 412); Gamulin, 'Un crocifisso di Maestro Paolo ed altri due del Trecento', p. 42, n. 3. Dobričević was to 'facere et complere … duas figuras in ecclesia Sancti Dominici de Ragusio in loco ubi stant mulieres apud crucifixum, videlicet figuram domine nostre virginis Marie a latere dextro et figuram sancti Johannis a latere sinistro dicti crucifixi'.

84 See Serafino Razzi, *La storia di Ragusa scritta nuovamente in tre libri*, with notes and introduction by G. Gelcich, Dubrovnik 1903 (first published in Lucca, 1595), p. 204. In 1452, the Dominicans commissioned 'unam lanciam de lignamine et intaglio pro portando crucem ecclesie Sancti Dominici', although it is not possible to determine what sort of portable or processional cross this refers to; for the contract see Tadić, *Građa o slikarskoj školi*, I, p. 190 (doc. 397).

85 Tadić, *Građa o slikarskoj školi*, I, p. 13 (doc. 34); however, the supplementary bequest for '1. ancona che sia in essa designata la maestade et che sia posta sovra allo crocifisso ali frari predicatori' is hard to explain.

86 For the two Turin panels and the Museo Correr fragment, see Cristina Guarnieri's forthcoming article: 'Per la restituzione di due croci perdute di Paolo Veneziano: il leone marciano del Museo Correr e i dolenti della Galleria Sabauda', in *Circolazione di modelli, opere e artisti nell'Alto Adriatico tra VIII e XV secolo*, ed. Federica Toniolo and Giovanna Valenzano, Padua 2009. Guarnieri also raises important doubts as to whether the Restić bequest of 1348 should be connected to Paolo's crucifix. I am very grateful to the author for discussing her research in advance of publication.

87 For discussion of this point, see Gamulin, *The Painted Crucifixes in Croatia*, p. 53, n. 56: there is no record of Paolo in Venice between 1349 and 1355, and Gamulin suggests that the wording of the 1352 Lukarić bequest, 'diendi ad faciendum', may indicate Paolo's direct presence, and that he may have brought the Dominican crucifix to Dubrovnik or painted it *in situ* in that year. For a more sceptical view, see Filippo Pedrocco, *Paolo Veneziano*, Milan 2003, pp. 178–9.

88 For the San Severino altarpiece see Alessandro Marchi's catalogue entry in *Il Trecento adriatico*, pp. 166–7, and Hanna Kiel, 'Das Polyptychon von Paolo und Giovanni Veneziano in San Severino Marche', *Pantheon* 35 (1977), pp. 105–8. There is also a fragmentary altarpiece now in the Fogg Art Museum which is sometimes attributed to Paolo himself (Muraro, *Paolo da Venezia*, pp. 103–4, pls 66, 67) but more often to his workshop (Pedrocco, *Paolo Veneziano*, pp. 116, 209), where the presence of Saints Thomas Aquinas and Dominic indicates a Dominican commission.

89 See Tadić, *Građa o slikarskoj školi*, I, pp. 97–8 (doc. 223) for the second contract of March 1436, which refers back to an earlier commission of November 1432, and for subsequent payments to May 1437. Cerva, *Monumenta congregationis*, II, pp. 124–5, gives a description of the marble high altar,

funded by a bequest of 1400. The dedication was funded by a generous bequest of one thousand gold ducats on 12 June 1394 by 'Anne olim uxoris quodam Jacobi de Menze' who willed 'che se faza i. choncha sovra lo altar grande dentro de la gliexia de li fra predicatori de Ragusa tutta de priede vive sovra le chollone iiii. per plu bel modo che se po'; the bequest was triggered by Anna's death on 10 January 1400, see Dubrovnik, Državni archiv, Testamenta de notaria 8, fol. 136r.

90 Tadić, *Građa o slikarskoj školi*, I, pp. 133–4 (doc. 291) for the new contract of February 1443 with the goldsmiths 'Giucho Goyachovich' and 'Goanne Todescho', who were required to work with Pietro should he come back to Dubrovnik ('se per caxo vignera a Ragusa').

91 Razzi, *La storia di Ragusa*, pp. 205–6 (author's translation).

92 Razzi, *La storia di Ragusa*, p. 206 (author's translation).

93 Tadić, *Građa o slikarskoj školi*, I, p. 163 (doc. 347).

94 Tadić, *Građa o slikarskoj školi*, I, pp. 175–6 (doc. 371).

95 Razzi, *La storia di Ragusa*, p. 204.

96 See Fisković, 'O unutrašnjem uređenju samostanskih crkava na istočnoj obali Jadrana', pp. 262–6. However, Jackson, *Dalmatia*, II, p. 365, noted that 'the very fine triple arch' had recently been moved from the north side of the nave to the western counter facade, so it appears that the chapels would not have originally faced the choir screen across the lower nave. The dedications of the chapels to the Crucifix, St Michael and St Peter Martyr are recalled by Cerva, *Monumenta congregationis*, II, p. 140. Also, the design of the three Maravić chapels would not accord with Razzi's description of a wooden 'ponte' on eight macigno sandstone columns, see Razzi, *La storia di Ragusa*, p. 204.

97 For this and other tombs in the church, see Đurdica Petrović, 'Sepulkrani spomenici u srednjovjekovnom Dubrovniku' ('Sepulchral monuments of medieval Dubrovnik'), in *Likovna kultura Dubrovnika 15. i 16. stoljeća*, ed. Igor Fisković, Dubrovnik 1991, pp. 127–36. For Andrija, bishop of Dubrovnik from 1388 to 1393, see Eubel, *Hierarchia catholica*, I, p. 411.

98 Janez Höfler, 'Florentine masters in early Renaissance Dubrovnik: Maso di Bartolomeo, Michele di Giovanni, Michelozzo, and Salvi di Michele', in *Quattrocento Adriatico: Fifteenth-Century Art of the Adriatic Rim*, Florence 1994, pp. 81–102, esp. pp. 89–90 for the Dominican cloister.

99 Höfler, 'Florentine masters in early Renaissance Dubrovnik', p. 89.

100 The fundamental study for the Franciscan convent in Dubrovnik is the anthology *Samostan Male Braće u Dubrovniku*, ed. Josip Turčinović, Zagreb and Dubrovnik 1985.

101 For this rich description, see Philippi de Diversis, *Situs aedificiorum, politiae et laudabilium consuetudinem inclytae civitatis Ragusii*, ed. Vitaliano Brunelli, Zadar 1882, p. 35; and also the recent dual-text Latin/Croatian edition: Filip de Diversis, *Opis slavnoga grada Dubrovnika (Description of the Famous City of Dubrovnik)*, ed. and trans. Zdenka Janeković-Römer, Zagreb 2004, p. 148.

102 For the cloister see Cvito Fisković, 'Romansko-gotički slog samostana Male Braće' ('Le style roman et gothique du cloître du couvent franciscain a Dubrovnik'), in *Samostan Male Braće*, pp. 413–38. The inscription reads: '+ S[EPULCRUM] DE MAGISTER MYCHA PETRAR DANTIVAR QUI FECIT CLAUSTRUM CUM OMNIBUS SUIS'; the script was reproduced by Jackson, *Dalmatia*, II, p. 393, fig. 68.

103 Jackson, *Dalmatia*, II, p. 371.

104 For the Gučetić tomb, see Igor Fisković, 'Srednjovjekovna skulptura u samostanu Male Braće' ('Sculpture médiévale du couvent franciscain à Raguse'), in *Samostan Male Braće*, pp. 465–95, esp. pp. 478–9.

105 The drawing was identified by Cvito Fisković, 'Slika iz radionice Paola Veneziana u Prčanju' ('Une Madone d'atelier de Paolo Veneziano non encore publiée, dans les Bouches de Kotor'), *Prilozi povijesti umjetnosti u Dalmaciji* 18 (1970), pp. 53–9.

106 See Gamulin, *The Painted Crucifixes in Croatia*, pp. 33, pl. 42, 53–54, n. 56. For the St John panel, see Zoraida Demori Staničić's entries in *Il Trecento adriatico*, pp. 172–3, and in *Stoljeće gotike na Jadranu* 2004, pp. 98–9, see also Joško Belamarić's English text essay in the Zagreb catalogue: 'Gothic culture in Dalmatia', pp. 25–32, esp. p. 28.

107 The full text that accompanied the 1614 drawing was published by Justin Velnić, 'Samostan Male Braće u Dubrovniku: Povijesni prikaz života i djelatnosti' ('Il convento di San Francesco a Dubrovnik: storia ed attività'), in *Samostan Male Braće*, pp. 181–2 (doc. 11).

108 See Gamulin, *The Painted Crucifixes in Croatia*, p. 54: 'Judging by the style and the whole conception of the crucifix, it really belongs to the second half of the 15th century'; but see also the discussion in Kruno Prijatelj and Ivana Prijatelj-Pavičić, 'Minijature u misalu kneza Novaka' ('Miniatures in the missal of Duke Novak'), *Prilozi povijesti umjetnosti u Dalmaciji* 34 (1994), pp. 71-84, esp. p. 83, where the authors compare the Zagreb panel with the miniatures in the Prince Novak missal of 1368 (now in Vienna). A Ragusan noblewoman's will of 2 October 1437 already included the following bequest: 'Ancora lasso a Sancto Francescho yperperi xv, mezo per olio che arda avanti crucifixo e mezo per le messe per anima mia' (Dubrovnik, Državni archiv, Testamenta de notaria 12, fol. 196r); which may indicate that the crucifix was *in situ* by that date. Furthermore, an altar dedicated to the 'Sancta Croxie' existed in the Franciscan church by 1394, see Testamenta de notaria 8, fol. 51v.

109 De Diversis, *Situs aedificiorum*, p. 35; *Opis slavnoga grada Dubrovnika*, p. 148.

110 English translation taken from Margaret Newett, *Canon Pietro Casola's Pilgrimage to Jerusalem in the Year 1494*, Manchester 1907, p. 174.

111 For the 1388 contract and subsequent payments, see Tadić, *Građa o slikarskoj školi*, I, pp. 26–9 (doc. 74), and for Bartolomeo's testament of 1392 which refers to the outstanding work on the Franciscan altarpiece, see p. 42 (doc. 107).

112 Newett, *Canon Pietro Casola's Pilgrimage to Jerusalem*, pp. 174–5.

113 Tadić, *Građa o slikarskoj školi*, I, pp. 194–5 (doc. 407).

114 Miklòs Boskovits, 'Od Blaža Trogiranina do Lovre Kotoranina' ('Da Biagio da Traù a Lorenzo da Cattaro'), in I. Fisković, *Likovna kultura Dubrovnika*, pp. 155–67, esp. p. 166.

115 For the Prague saints, see Hana Hlaváčková, 'Paintings by the Vivarinis in the National Gallery', *Bulletin of the National Gallery in Prague/Bulletin Národní Galerie v Praze* 1 (1991), pp. 15–17.

116 Federico Zeri, 'Un appunto per il maestro dell'Annunciazione Ludlow', *Quaderni di Emblema* 1 (1971); reprinted in *Giorno per giorno nella pittura, scritti sull'arte dell'Italia settentrionale dal Trecento al primo Cinquecento*, Turin 1983, pp. 167–9.

117 Miklòs Boskovits, 'Appunti su un libro recente', *Antichità viva* 10 (1971), pp. 14–15 (Appendice). For more recent discussion of the Wernher Collection panel, see David Ekserdjian, 'Old Master paintings from the Wernher Collection', *Apollo* 156, no. 487 (September 2002), p. 12; Flora Turner-Vučetić, 'U potrazi za Renesansnim Navještenjem', *Kvartel* 4, no. 3 (2007), pp. 2–5.

118 It is doubtful if any altarpieces in the church could have survived the 1667 earthquake and fire. Cvito Fisković, 'Nekoliko podataka o starim Dubrovačkim slikarima' ('Quelques données sur les peintres de Dubrovnik'), *Prilozi povijesti umjetnosti u Dalmaciji* 10 (1956), pp. 138–152,

had already connected the 1455 document with a much-damaged panel of St Blaise attributed to Lovro Dobričević from the Franciscan monastery. The multiple altars in the adjacent chapter house may have faired rather better, but their recorded dedications do not easily match the Wernher *Annunciation*. An altar dedicated to the Annunciation is documented in the church in a *modo et forma* clause in an altarpiece contract from 1531, Tadić, *Građa o slikarskoj školi*, II, pp. 148–9 (doc. 1076): '… prout est in ecclesia Sancti Francisci in Rhagusio in altare Sancte Annunciationis'. It is, however, unlikely that Dobričević's panels would have been regarded as a desirable model by that date.

119 See Tadić, *Građa o slikarskoj školi*, II, pp. 8–9 (doc. 766) for Božidarević's contract for 'unam inchonam seu palam, sub qua claudatur inchona argentea altaris maioris in ecclesia dictus conventus, iuxta designum factum'.

120 Grgo Gamulin, 'Za Lovru Dobričevića' ('Pour Lovro Dobričević'), *Prilozi povijesti umjetnosti u Dalmaciji* 26 (1986-7), p. 371, identified this figure as St Catherine of Siena, despite the absence of a Dominican habit. The inscription on her halo leaves no ambiguity: '[SANC]TA ELLISABET MATER IOHANNIS BAPTIST'. I am grateful to Petr Pribyl, curator of Italian painting at the Národní Galerie, for confirming this transcription. Furthermore, the saint is clearly intended to be older than her companions St Clare and St Catherine of Alexandria.

121 For the church at Rožat, often referred to in contemporary documents as the convent of Umbla after the neighbouring village, see Frano Jurić, 'Franjevački Samostan u Dubrovačkoj Rijeci', Zagreb 1916; Anđelko Badurina, 'Sakralna arhitektura', in *Zlatno doba Dubrovnika XV. i XVI. stoljeće*, ed. Vladimir Marković, Zagreb 1987, pp. 122-3, 329. The church was badly damaged in the 1667 earthquake and finally rebuilt in 1702-4.

122 De Diversis, *Situs aedificiorum*, p. 23; *Opis slavnoga grada Dubrovnika*, p. 144: 'Est quaedam ora, quae dicitur Umbla … Ibi est quidam pulcher et ornatus conventus fratrum minorum vicariatus Bosnae et ecclesia devota, ubi degunt complures fratres pauperis vitae'.

123 For the Vicariates of Bosnia and Dubrovnik, see Marijan Žugaj, *I conventi dei Minori Conventuali tra i Croati dalle origini fino al 1500*, Rome 1989, pp. 30-47.

124 Two contracts between Dobričević and the Bosnian Franciscans survive, the first for two altarpieces on 14 April 1459 and a second for a single altarpiece on 19 May 1460 (it is not clear whether this referred back to one of the earlier pair or represented a third commission), see Tadić, *Građa o slikarskoj školi*, I, p. 205 (doc. 430); p. 213 (doc. 445).

125 Tadić, *Građa o slikarskoj školi*, I, p. 205 (doc. 430); Dobričević was to paint 'duas anchonas pulchras, firmas, bene intagliatas, de bono lignamine elaboratas, cum figuris intus bene pictis et bene colloratis de bonis coloribus, et maxime cum azuro ultramarino, bene auratis de bono auro … quarum debet esse alta brachia ragusea sex cum dimidio usque in septem, et lata brachia quinque, altera debet esse alta brachia tria cum dimidio et lata brachia duo cum dimidio, que debent esse bene sculta et intagliata et picta ad laudem cuiuslibet magistri'.

126 The Wernher Collection *Annunciation* is 66 cm wide without its nineteenth-century frame, the individual Prague panels are each 28 cm wide.

127 On 23 July 1459 Lovro agreed to split the work 'del anchona di Sancta Chiara et di quella di Bosna' with the painter Vuchaz Raianovich, see Tadić, *Građa o slikarskoj školi*, I, p. 208 (doc. 435). The 1459 contract with the Bosnian Francisans was accompanied by receipts from February and May 1460; the 1461 contract by receipts from November 1461 and October 1462.

128 In both contracts the name of the Bosnian convent is left blank ('mittere in Bosnam ad locum …'), see Tadić, *Građa o

slikarskoj školi, I, p. 205 (doc. 430); p. 213 (doc. 445).

129 On 18 September 1469 Dobričević was paid for completing 'unius anchonae … pro ecclesia beatissime virginis matris Marie de Rosato de Ombla', see Tadić, *Građa o slikarskoj školi*, I, p. 244 (doc. 510). The Franciscan church had been referred to as the church of the Virgin in a testamentary bequest of 1444, where money was left 'a Sancta Maria in Ombla dove abitano frati de San Francesco che se meta in fabricha de la deta giexia', see Dubrovnik, Državni archiv, Testamenta de notaria 18, fol. 81v. However, the fact that in 1469 Lovro was paid by the chaplain of the church ('dom Bernardo, cappellano dicte ecclesie'), rather than by a friar or lay procurators, suggests that he painted the altarpiece for the parish church at Rožat, also dedicated to the Virgin. Karl Kovač, 'Nikolaus Ragusinus und seine Zeit', *Jahrbuch des Kunsthistorischen Institutes der Kaiserlichen Königlichen Zentralkommission für Denkmalpflege* 11 (1917), Beiblatt, pp. 10, 47-48, drew the same conclusion.

130 For the contract with Slano, dated 28 February 1461, see Tadić, *Građa o slikarskoj školi*, I, p. 216 (doc. 449): 'Magister Laurentius Dobrichievich de Cataro … promisit ser Andree et sociis, procuratoribus ecclesie Sancti Hieronymi Slani, conficere et pingere unam palam seu anchonam pro altari magno dicte ecclesie'.

131 The likely provenance from Rožat has been discovered independently by Ivana Prijatelj-Pavičić, see her forthcoming article 'Prilog poznavanju Navještenja Ludlow', in *Sic ars deprenditur arte: Zbornik u počast 70. godišnjice rođenja akademika Vladimira Markovića*, Zagreb 2009. It is just possible that St Elizabeth could have been included on a Slano commission as a reference to the sister convent at Rožat. However, Dobričević's retable at Slano had already been replaced over the high altar by the middle of the sixteenth century by a large altarpiece of the *Adoration*, still extant in the church. It should also be remembered that some elements of the altarpiece's iconographic programme have been lost, for example the central panel of the upper register. For the suggestion that the altarpiece was instead painted for the Franciscan church of Sv. Bernardin in Lovro's native Kotor, see Rajko Vujičić, 'Djelatnost Lovre Dobričevića u Boki Kotorskoj' ('Lovro Dobričević in Boka Kotorska'), in I. Fisković, *Likovna kultura Dubrovnika*, pp. 182-4. This proposal, however, seems to rest solely on the presence of San Bernardino amongst the Prague saints, which would not be unexpected for a Franciscan commission in the 1460s, especially one for an Observant convent, and hardly provides a firm indication of a church dedication. Moreover, the Kotor church, a suburban foundation, was demolished as early as 1537 and its contents dispersed amongst the other churches in the town.

132 For this aspect of the panel's iconography, see Ingvar Bergström, 'Den fångna fågeln' ('The Caged Bird'), *Symbolista* 1 (1957), pp. 32–4, fig. 16. I am very grateful to Annie Kemkoran-Smith, curator of the Rangers House, and Adam Webster, senior conservator of paintings at English Heritage, for generously providing access to the painting and its object file during the collection's winter closure.

133 Lippi had deployed the motif in his *Annunciation* of c. 1443 now in Munich, originally painted for the Florentine nunnery of Le Murate, see Meghan Holmes, *Fra Filippo Lippi: The Carmelite Painter*, New Haven and London 1999, pp. 232–3.

134 For the *Belvedere Antinöus* link, see Ekserdjian, 'Old Master paintings from the Wernher Collection', p. 12. Either dependence would have implications for the relevant prototype. The second-century *Belvedere Antinöus* is first recorded in Rome only in 1543, see Francis Haskell and Nicholas Penny, *Taste and the Antique: The Lure of Classical Sculpture, 1500–1900*, New Haven and London 1982, pp. 141–3.

135 For Michelozzo's dates in Dubrovnik, see Harriet McNeal Caplow, 'Michelozzo at Ragusa: New Documents and Revaluations', *Journal of the Society of Architectural Historians* 31 (1972), pp. 108-119.

136 Ekserdjian, 'Old Master paintings from the Wernher collection', pp. 12, 15, n. 8, identifies seven scenes in this subsidiary narrative; Turner-Vučetić, 'U potrazi za Renesansnim *Navještenjem*', pp. 3–4, has suggested that the city reflects the topography of Dubrovnik itself.

137 For discussion of the state's relationship with the friars, see Robin Harris, *Dubrovnik: A History*, London 2003, pp. 232–4.

138 For the Čiovo convent see Stjepan Krasić, 'Dominikanski samostan Sv. Križa na otoku Čiovu (1432–1852)' ('Il convento domenicano di S. Croce a Čiovo, 1432–1852') *Prilozi povijesti umjetnosti u Dalmaciji* 31 (1991), pp. 79–95; and for the Gruž foundation, idem, 'Dominikanski samostan Sv. Križa u Gružu (1437–1987)' ('The Dominican Priory of Holy Cross in Gruž, 1437–1987: Historical overview'), *Croatica Christiana Periodica* 37 (1988), pp. 184–200.

139 For the remarkable rise of the Franciscan Observants in Dalmatia, see Stanko Josip Škunca, *Franjevačka renesansa u Dalmaciji i Istri: Opservantska obnova i samostani provincije Sv. Jeronima u 15. st.*, Split 1999.

140 Škunca, *Franjevačka renesansa u Dalmaciji i Istri*, pp. 104–5; the Observant Franciscans had earlier founded the suburban convent of Holy Cross by 1442, but were moved into the city due to the growing Ottoman threat in 1453, taking over the church of St Francis from a dwindling number of Conventual friars, and the next year Holy Cross was demolished.

141 For a useful guide to this foundation, see Denis Lešić, *Košljun: Spirituality, Culture, Nature*, Krk 2005; see also Škunca, *Franjevačka renesansa u Dalmaciji i Istri*, pp. 139–40.

142 The most extensive discussion of the convent is in Domijan, *Rab*, pp. 210–27; see also Škunca, *Franjevačka renesansa u Dalmaciji i Istri*, pp. 131–2.

143 The inscription reads: 'ANNIS D[OMI]N[I] CURENTIB[US] MCCCCXLVI NOBILIS VIR S. PETRUS DE CAR FECIT FIERI HOC OP[US] P[E]R FRATRIBUS DE OBSERVANTIA AD HONOREM DEI B[EA]TI FRANCISCI ET B[EA]TE EUFEMIE ET AD REMISSIONEM SU[O]R[UM] PECCARTORUM ET SU[O]R[UM] MORTUORUM'; transcription adapted from Domijan, *Rab*, pp. 214–16.

144 The church was consecrated by five unnamed Dalmatian bishops, see Domijan, *Rab*, pp. 216–18: 'UNA DIE QUINQUE VENERANDI PRAESULES OMNES DALMATES SACRARUNT HANC TIBI SANCTE DOMUM BERNARDINE PATER SUB MILLE BISQUE DUCENTIS SEX DENO ET SEXTO JUNII DENA DIE UT VICIIS PURGES MENTEM VIRTUTIBUS ORNES HANC ADEAS SACRAM PECCATOR SEDULUS AULAM'.

145 The inscription on the frame below St Bernardino, which is curious in giving the date in both Roman and Arabic numerals, reads: 'ANTON[IO] ET BA[R]TOLOMEO DE MURANO F[RAT]RES PIX[N]ERUNT MCCCCLVIII 1458'.

146 Domijan, *Rab*, pp. 218–20.

147 Domijan, *Rab*, pp. 225–7.

148 Domijan, *Rab*, p. 223.

149 For medieval Franciscan churches in continental Croatia, see the section compiled by Diana Vukičević-Samaržija, 'Srednjovjekovna umjetnost', in the catalogue *Mir i Dobro* 2000, pp. 346–53, esp. the architectural plans on pp. 347–9.

150 Jackson, *Dalmatia*, II, p. 364.

7. THE RENAISSANCE IN CROATIA AND ITALY: THE CHAPEL OF THE BLESSED GIOVANNI ORSINI

My supreme debt of gratitude is to Jadranka Beresford-Peirse for sending me to Croatia in the first place, and then to all my most generous hosts and helpers there: Ivan Mirnik in Zagreb, and in Trogir, Split and Šibenik Don Tomislav Ćubelić, Joško Belamarić, Radoslav Buzančić, Fani Celio Cega and Vanja Kovačić.

1 D. Ekserdjian, *Correggio*, New Haven and London 1997, and D. Ekserdjian, *Parmigianino*, New Haven and London 2006.

2 B. Berenson, *Italian Pictures of the Renaissance: Venetian School*, 2 vols, London 1957, I, pp. 195–203, for lists of works by Alvise, Antonio and Bartolomeo Vivarini, including works in Andria (Bari), Bari, Barletta (Bari), Polignano a Mare (Bari), Rutigliano (Bari).

3 A. Tempestini, *Giovanni Bellini: Catalogo completo dei dipinti*, Florence 1992, pp. 82–8. A *Pietà*, which originally crowned the altarpiece, is now in the Pinacoteca Vaticana. Another *Pietà* by Giovanni (Pinacoteca Comunale, Rimini), which must always have been an independent work of art rather than a part of a larger whole, was believed by Vasari to have belonged to Sigismondo Malatesta, the lord of Rimini, who died in 1468 (Tempestini, *Giovanni Bellini*, pp. 97–9).

4 P. Humfrey, 'Marco Zoppo: La pala di Pesaro', in *Marco Zoppo e il suo tempo: Atti del convegno internazionale*, ed. B. G. Vigi, Bologna 1993, pp. 71–8.

5 Tempestini, *Giovanni Bellini*, pp. 154–5.

6 Tempestini, *Giovanni Bellini*, pp. 154–5, following the opinions of Giles Robertson and Rona Goffen.

7 J. Steer, *Alvise Vivarini: His Art and Influence*, Cambridge 1982, pp. 137–8, no. 10, pl. 28, for the *Madonna*, which was originally in the church of San Bernardino at Pirano, and then in the convent of Sant'Anna at Capodistria; P. Humfrey, *Cima da Conegliano*, Cambridge 1983, pp. 91–2, pl. 158, for the polyptych, which was also in Sant'Anna at Capodistria.

8 R. Lightbown, *Carlo Crivelli*, New Haven and London 2004, p. 3.

9 I. Petricioli, 'Orme di Carlo e Vittore Crivelli a Zara: L'opera pittorica di Pietro Jordanić e le testimonianze archivistiche', in *Vittore Crivelli e la pittura del suo tempo nel Fermano*, ed. S. Papetti, Milan 1997, pp. 37–41, esp. p. 38.

10 For a good short biography of Giorgio Schiavone with full bibliography, see J. Turner, ed., *The Dictionary of Art*, 34 vols, London 1996, XXVIII, pp. 84–5 (entry by K. Shaw and T. Shaw).

11 M. Boskovits, 'Appunti su un libro recente', *Antichità Viva* X, no. 6 (1971), pp. 3–15, esp. pp. 14–15; and D. Ekserdjian, 'Old Master paintings from the Wernher collection', *Apollo* 156, no. 487 (September 2002), pp. 12–15.

12 For Schiavone in general, see F. L. Richardson, *Andrea Schiavone*, Oxford 1980, and p. 131, no. 193, fig. 13, for an example of a derivation from a drawing by Parmigianino.

13 A. E. Popham, *Catalogue of the Drawings of Parmigianino*, 3 vols, New Haven and London 1971, p. 30, where the first date is misprinted as 1538.

14 See respectively Richardson, *Andrea Schiavone*, p. 171, no. 284, fig. 171, and pp. 177–9, no. 297, fig. 73, for the Schiavones, and F. Hartt, *Michelangelo Drawings*, New York 1975, p. 39, no. 20 (illustrated on p. 41) for the relevant drawing.

15 For Clovio in general, see M. Giononi-Visani and G. Gamulin, *Clovio: Miniaturist of the Renaissance*, London 1993, and p. 77 for the *Passion of Christ*.

16 For the portrait and the *Farnese Hours*, see respectively Giononi-Visani and Gamulin, *Clovio*, p. 84 and pp. 43–59.

17 For Laurana, see H.-W. Kruft, *Francesco Laurana: Ein Bildhauer der Frührenaissance*, Munich 1995.

18 For accessible illustrations, see F. Celio Cega, *Trogir*, Zagreb 2006, unpaginated.

19 For accessible illustrations, see A. Travirka, *Split: History, Culture, Art Heritage*, Zadar 2000, pp. 34–5 and 38.

20 For an excellent reproduction of the *Flagellation* from this altar-tomb, see *Tesori della Croazia restaurati da Venetian*

Heritage Inc., exh. cat., Chiesa di San Barnaba, Venice 2001, pp. 40–1 (entry by I. Fisković) and fig. 9.6 in this volume.

21 For a good biography with full bibliography, see Turner, *The Dictionary of Art*, XII, pp. 666–8 (entry by S. Kokole).

22 For accessible illustrations, see M. Zenić, *Šibenik Cathedral*, Šibenik 2003, pp. 167–77, and S. Grubišić and M. Knežević-Grubišić, *Šibenik*, Zagreb 2006, unpaginated.

23 For a good short biography with full bibliography, see Turner, *The Dictionary of Art*, I, p. 604 (entry by S. Štefanac).

24 For an exhaustive account of its contents (to which my discussion is deeply indebted), see A. Markham Schulz, *Niccolò di Giovanni Fiorentino and Venetian Sculpture of the Early Renaissance*, New York 1978, pp. 82–5.

25 For accessible illustrations, see Cega, *Trogir*.

26 A. Markham Schulz, 'Niccolò di Giovanni Fiorentino in Venice: the documentary evidence', *Burlington Magazine* CXLI, no. 1161 (December 1999), pp. 749–52. It is worth noting that Markham Schulz's interpretation of the phrase 'corpore languens' in the will as indicating that the testator was 'gravely ill' is open to question: he may indeed have been, since that was an obvious reason for making a will, but in my experience it is the entirely standard form of words in any will where the testator does not make a point of stressing his or her rude good health.

27 Comparison with the angel-putti in the *Coronation* relief supports the traditional view that this putto is indeed by Niccolò, but this is as near as he comes to the sense of movement and animation attained by Giovanni Dalmata in his *Torch-Bearing Putto* from the entrance portal of Palazzo Cippico at Trogir, now in the Museo Civico there, for which see *Tesori della Croazia*, pp. 54–5 (entry by I. Fisković).

28 G. Vasari, *Le Vite…*, ed. G. Milanesi, 9 vols, Florence 1878–85, VII, p. 518: 'e in Dalmazia mandò pure di pietra Quattro Apostoli nel duomo di Treu, alti cinque piedi l'uno'. See also V. Kovačić, 'Kipovi Alessandra Vittorie za trogirsku katedralu' ('Le statue di Alessandro Vittoria per la Cattedrale di Traù'), *Prilozi povijesti umjetnosti u Dalmaciji* XL (2003–4), pp. 215–38 (with synopsis in Italian), where it is pointed out that the statues are inscribed with the names of Saints Andrew, Matthew, James (Minor) and Simon (Zelotes).

29 Markham Schulz, *Niccolò di Giovanni Fiorentino*, p. 62.

30 J. Röll, *Giovanni Dalmata*, Worms am Rhein 1994, p. 137, for a dating of 1495.

31 J. Belamarić, 'Il volto di San Giovanni Evangelista di Giovanni Dalmata (Ivan Duknović) nella Cattedrale di Traù', in *Michelozzo, Scultore e Architetto (1396–1472)*, ed. G. Morolli, Florence 1998, pp. 287–96, for these arguments.

32 Markham Schulz, *Niccolò di Giovanni Fiorentino*, pp. 82–5, for these payments, and for the unconvincing suggestion that the *St Thomas* 'shows the influence of Giovanni Dalmata' but is – by implication – by Niccolò.

33 *Tesori della Croazia*, pp. 47–9 (entry by A. Markham Schulz), who gives the *Angel* to Niccolò and tentatively ascribes the *Virgin* to Alessi.

34 Markham Schulz, *Niccolò di Giovanni Fiorentino*, p. 85.

35 A tablet in the chapel dated 1681 names 'Loelio Cippico' as an 'operario'. For the earlier chapel of the Blessed Giovanni Orsini, see R. Buzančić, '*Secundum Sacrarium Divi Joannis*: Stara kapela sv. Ivana trogirskog u katedrali sv. Lovrinca', *Prilozi povijesti umjetnosti u Dalmaciji* XL (2003–4), pp. 77–112 (with synopsis in English).

36 Lack of space has alas meant that a considerable number of outstanding works elsewhere by both Niccolò di Giovanni Fiorentino and Giovanni Dalmata have gone unmentioned.

8. NIKOLA BOŽIDAREVIĆ

1 Nikola of Dubrovnik was first identified by the then director of the Dubrovnik archives, Karlo Kovač, in his fundamental study, 'Nikolaus Ragusinus und seine Zeit, Archivalische Beiträge zur Geschichte der Malerei in Ragusa im XV.

und der ersten Hälfte des XVI. Jahrhunderts', *Jahrbuch des kunsthistorischen Institutes der K. K. Zentralkommission für Denkmalpflege* XI, Vienna 1917.

2 L. Karaman, 'O staroj slikarskoj školi u Dubrovniku', *Anali Historijskog instituta JAZU u Dubrovniku* 2 (1959), p. 104, finds a Božidarević family in Kručica above Slano, perhaps a distant branch of Nikola's brother Vladislav, also a painter. For Nikola's life and works, with an exhaustive review of all the references, see V. J. Đurić, *Dubrovačka slikarska škola*, Belgrade 1964, pp. 116–43.

3 R. Samardžić, *Veliki vek Dubrovnika*, Belgrade 1963, pp. 223–409.

4 J. Tadić, ed., *Građa o slikarskoj školi u Dubrovniku XIII–XVI v.*, Belgrade 1952, p. 907; Kovač, 'Nikolaus Ragusinus und seine Zeit', p. 21. For Božidarević's singing of lampoons see P. Kolendić, 'Premijera Držićeva Dunda Maroja', *Glas SAN* 201 (1951), p. 58.

5 Tadić, *Građa o slikarskoj školi u Dubrovniku XIII–XVI v.*, pp. 680, 961; Kovač, 'Nikolaus Ragusinus und seine Zeit', pp. 23–4, 33.

6 The first rounded stylistic and critical analysis of Božidarević's work, of the Dubrovnik and Dalmatian painting school, as it has become known, was produced by Ljubo Karaman in a series of articles and studies. See *Umjetnost u Dalmaciji, XV i XVI vijek*, Zagreb 1933; 'Stari dubrovački slikari', *Hrvatska revija* 3 (1943), pp. 125–38; 'O staroj slikarskoj školi u Dubrovniku', *Anali Historijskog instituta JAZU u Dubrovniku* 2 (1959), pp. 101–23. See the most telling assessment of Božidarević's stylistic formation in K. Prijatelj, *Dubrovačko slikarstvo XV–XVI. stoljeća*, Zagreb 1968.

7 V. Marković, 'Nikola Božidarević u Rimu', in *Likovna kultura Dubrovnika 15. i 16. stoljeća* (Zbornik znanstvenog skupa uz izložbu 'Zlatni vijek Dubrovnika'), Zagreb 1991, pp. 184–8.

8 V. J. Đurić, *Dubrovačka slikarska škola*, Belgrade 1964, p. 139.

9 L. Babić, *Coloque sentimentale*, Zagreb 1953, p. 75; L. Babić, 'Božidarević Nikola', *Enciklopedija likovnih umjetnosti* 1 (1959), p. 479.

10 F. de Diversis de Quartiagianis, 'Opis položaja, zgrada, državnog uređenja i pohvalnih običaja slavnog grada Dubrovnika' (translation from the Latin by Ivan Božić), *Dubrovnik* 3 (1973). See also I. Fisković, 'Djelo Filipa de Diversisa kao izvor poznavanju umjetnosti i kulture Dubrovnika', *Dubrovnik* 30, nos 1–3 (1987), pp. 232–49.

11 The cloth-making industry launched in Dubrovnik on the threshold of the modern age, with its technological demands and the concatenation of working operations that needed to be impeccably harmonised in order to produce fabric bearing the stamp 'panni ragusei' for the Mediterranean and Balkan markets, kept Dubrovnik in contact with all regions of the world as it then was. At the beginning of the fifteenth century, hundreds of weavers, dyers and tailors from Prato, Siena, Florence, Bergamo, Aachen, Catalonia, Savoy, Brabant and Brittany were drawn to the city. In little Dubrovnik, with its fifty weaving shops, everyone benefited – the citizens, landowners and commoners, rich and poor, men and women. They imported merino wool from Castille and Aragon, Abruzzo and Apulia, France and England, Turkey and northern Africa. Dyes were imported from just as many parts of the world. An aqueduct with mills was developed, a city sewage system was engineered, and two fountains were put up on Placa. The cloth industry that provided the city with enormous profit developed practically from nothing at a time when the empires, kingdoms, princedoms and duchies in the general Dubrovnik area were being totally overwhelmed. For more concerning this see J. Belamarić, 'Urbanistički aspekti prve dubrovačke industrije u 15. stoljeću', in P. Marković, ed., *Zbornik radova Dana Cvita Fiskovića II*, Zagreb 2008, pp. 341–72.

12 Đurić, *Dubrovačka slikarska škola*, p. 126.

13 Z. Demori-Staničić, 'Lik donatora u dubrovačkom slikarstvu

15. i 16. stoljeća', in *Likovna kultura Dubrovnika 15. i 16. stoljeća*, p. 197.

14 For a new reading of the figure of the donator on the predela of the Lopud painting see Demori-Staničić, 'Lik donatora u dubrovačkom slikarstvu 15. i 16. stoljeća'.

15 V. Marković, 'Slikarstvo', in *Zlatno doba Dubrovnika*, exh. cat., Zagreb 1987, pp. 169–76.

16 M. Boscovits, 'Od Blaža Trogiranina do Lovre Kotoranina', in *Likovna kultura Dubrovnika 15. i 16. stoljeća*, pp. 155–67; G. Gamulin, 'Položaj Lovre Dobričevića u slikarstvu Venecije i Dubrovnika', in *Likovna kultura Dubrovnika 15. i 16. stoljeća*, pp. 167–78; R. Vujičić, 'Djelatnost Lovre Dobričevića u Boki kotorskoj', in *Likovna kultura Dubrovnika 15. i 16. stoljeća*, pp. 179–83.

17 See an article by R. Tomić concerning the depiction of landscape in old Dubrovnik painting in *Likovna kultura Dubrovnika 15. i 16. stoljeća*, pp. 201–4.

9. ITALY AND DALMATIA: ARCHITECTURE, SCULPTURE, PAINTING AND THE DECORATIVE ARTS, *c.* 1400–1800

1 Literature in English on Croatian art during the period discussed here is limited. There are excellent brief introductions to the subject by Paul Tvrtković, Želimir Koščević and Flora Turner in *The Dictionary of Art*, 34 vols, ed. Jane Turner, London 1996–2002, vol. 8, pp. 174–81, with useful bibliographies. The most comprehensive information is contained in *Enciklopedija likovnih umjetnosti* (Encyclopaedia of Fine Arts), 4 vols, Zagreb 1959–66, and *Enciklopedija Hrvatske povijesti i kulture* (Encyclopaedia of Croatian History and Culture), Zagreb 1980. Essential are *Dalmazia*, Touring Club Italiano, Milan 1942; A. Horvat, *Između gotike i baroka: Umjetnost kontinentalnog dijela Hrvatske od oko 1500 do oko 1700* (Between Gothic and Baroque: The Art of Continental Croatia between *c.* 1500 and *c.* 1700), Zagreb 1975 (with German summary); K. Prijatelj, 'La pittura del rinascimento in Dalmazia e in Istria', in *L'Umanesimo in Istria*, ed. V. Branca and S.Graciotti, Florence 1983, and A. Horvat, R. Matejčić and K. Prijatelj, *Barok u Hrvatskoj* (The Baroque in Croatia), Zagreb 1982. Useful introductions are *L'Art en Yugoslavie de la préhistoire à nos jours*, exh. cat., Paris 1971, and R. Ivančević, *Art Treasures of Croatia*, Motovun 1986. Essential are *Quattrocento Adriatico: Fifteenth-Century Art of the Adriatic Rim*, papers from a colloquium held at the Villa Spelman, Florence, in 1994, Baltimore 1996, and the *Atti del Convegno, 'Homo Adriaticus': Identità culturale e autoscienza attraverso i secoli*, Ancona, 9–12 Novembre 1993, Progetto Adriatico, vol. 3, Reggio Emilia 1998; Danko Zelić, 'Renaissance art and architecture in Croatia: recent research', *Bulletin of the Society for Renaissance Studies* XX, no. 2 (April 2003), pp. 6–14; *La Renaissance en Croatie*, exh. cat., ed. Alain Erlander-Brandenburg and Miljenko Jurković, Musée de la Renaissance, Écouen, 8 Avril–12 Juillet 2004, Galerie Klovićevi Dvori, Zagreb 26 août–21 novembre 2004, Zagreb 2004.

2 A handsome electrotype is in the Victoria and Albert Museum, London and currently on display.

3 A. De Niccolò Samazo, 'Padova e Giorgio Schiavone', in *La Pittura nel Veneto*, 2 vols, ed. M. Lucco, Milan 1990, II, pp. 524–5, 765–6.

4 R. L. Richardson, *Andrea Schiavone*, Oxford 1980.

5 M. Cionini Visani and G. Gamulin, *Giorgio Clovio: Miniaturist of the Renaissance*, New York 1980. *Klovićev zbornik, Juraj Julije Klović i minijatura-crtež-grafika*, ed. Milan Pelc, Zagreb 2001 (international conference on Clovio held in Zagreb).

6 British readers are most familiar with the architect Robert Adam's *Ruins of the Palace of the Emperor Diocletian at Spalatro [sic]*, London 1764. The most recent authoritative account is J. J. Wilkes, *Diocletian's Palace, Split*, Sheffield 1993.

7 The history of Split is well told in the Split City Museum,

which is within the Papalić Palace complex. It has a good guidebook, Elvira Šarić, ed., *The Split City Museum Guide*, Split 2003.

8 B. della Chiesa and E. Baccheschi, 'I Pittori da Santa Croce', in *I Pittori bergamaschi dal XIII al XIX secolo: Il Cinquecento*, vol. II, Bergamo 1976, pp. 4–19, 28–35, 52–65.

9 Peter Humfrey, *Lorenzo Lotto*, London 1997, p.165. Bernard Berenson (*Lorenzo Lotto*, London and New York 1956, p. 96) describes this picture as being of a 'haughty and irate elderly man', certainly a description very wide of the mark.

10 Humfrey, *Lorenzo Lotto*, pp. 106–7.

11 Both *corpora* relate to the silver crucifix that appears to have been made by Giambologna for Giovanna d'Austria and given by her to the Santa Casa, Loreto, on her pilgrimage there between 18 April and 9 May 1573, see *Giambologna: Sculptor to the Medici*, exh. cat., Arts Council of Great Britain, Edinburgh, London and Vienna 1978–9, cat. no. 106, p. 144 (entry by Katherine J. Watson).

12 For Bicci see Bernard Berenson, *Florentine Painters*, 2 vols, London, 1963, I, pp. 27–32; and C. Frosinone, 'Il passaggio di gestione in una bottega pittorica fiorentina', *Antichità Viva* XXVI (1986), pp. 5–15; and *Antichità Viva* XXVI: no. 1 (1987), pp. 5–14.

13 I. Chiappini di Sorio, 'Giorgio da Sebenico', in *Scultura nelle Marche*, ed. P. Zampetti, Florence, 1993, with bibliography; *Tesori della Croazia: Restaurati da Venetian Heritage Inc.*, exh. cat., Venice, Chiesa di San Barnaba, 9 June–4 November 2001, pp. 40–1, cat. 6 (*Flagellation* relief).

14 K. Prijatelj, *Umjetnost 17 i 18 stoljeća u Dalmaciji*, Zagreb 1957, pp. 44–6. R. Tomić, *Barokni oltari i skulptura u Dalmaciji*, Zagreb 1995, pp. 131, 142. Andrea Bacchi, ed., *La scultura a Venezia da Sansovino a Canova*, Milan 2000, fig. 538, pp. 765–70.

15 K. Prijatelj, 'Le opere di Alvise Tagliapietra e della sua bottega in Dalmazia e in Istria', *Arte Veneta* XXIX (1975), pp. 227–31; Tomić, *Barokni oltari i skulptura u Dalmaciji*, pp. 125–30, 205; Bacchi, *La scultura a Venezia*, pp. 790–1.

16 Giovanni Lucio (Ivan Lucić), *Memorie istoriche di Tragurio o detto Traù*, Venice 1673; Paolo Andreis, *Storia della città di Traù*, ed. M. Perojević, Split 1909. These have been more recently translated into Croatian as I. Lucić, *Povijesna svjedočanstva o Trogiru*, Split 1979; and P. Andreis, *Povijest grada Trogira*, Split 1977. Also useful are Ivo Babić et al., *Trogir*, Zagreb 1987; Fani Celio Cega, *Trogir: History, Culture, Art*, Zagreb 2004.

17 'Kronološka analiza ranorenesanse kapele sv Ivana Orsinija u Trogiru' (A chronological analysis of the early Renaissance chapel of St John Orsini), *Prilozi povijesti umjetnosti u Dalmaciji* 25 (1986–7); S. Štefanac, 'Niccolò di Giovanni Fiorentino e la capella del beato Orsini a Traù: Il progetto, l'architettura, la decorazione scultorea', in *Quattrocento Adriatico*, pp. 123–41; Anne Markham Schulz, 'Further thoughts on Niccolò di Giovanni Fiorentino in Dalmatia and Italy', in *Quattrocento Adriatico*, pp. 143–62; J. Belamarić, 'San Giovanni Evangelista di Giovanni Dalmata (Ivan Duknović) nella Cattedrale di Traù', *Prilozi povijesti umjetnosti u Dalmaciji* 37 (1997–8), pp. 155–81; J. Belamarić, 'Il volto di San Giovanni Evangelista da Giovanni Dalmata (Ivan Duknović) nella cattedrale di Traù', in *Michelozzo: Scultore e Architetto (1376–1472)*, ed. G. Morolli, Florence 1998, pp. 287–96; A. Markham Schulz, 'Niccolò di Giovanni Fiorentino in Venice: the documentary evidence', *The Burlington Magazine* 141 (1999), pp. 749–52; Further references in Zelić, 'Renaissance art and architecture in Croatia', p. 11, n. 27. For the Vittoria Sculptures see: V. Kovačić, 'Kipovi Alessandra, Vittorije za trogirsku katedralu' (le statue di Alessandro Vittoria per la Cattedrale di Traù.) in *Prilozi povijesti umjetnosti u Dalmaciji*. XL, (2003–4), pp215–238.

18 Douglas Lewis, 'The plaquettes of "Moderno" and his followers', in *Italian Plaquettes*, Studies in the History of Art,

vol. 22, National Gallery of Art, Washington, DC 1989, pp. 105–40; for this model, pp. 131, 139, n. 252. The Trogir pax is discussed and reproduced by Nevenka Bezić Božanić in *Tesori della Croazia*, pp. 140–1.

19 *Tesori della Croazia*, cat. no. 56, p. 141, entry by Nevenka Bezić Božanić. Another similar is in the Victoria and Albert Museum, London (inv. M39–1923), which belonged to Cardinal Ricci, archbishop of Pisa 1567–74. For yet another see Antonella Capitanio, *Arte orafo e controriforma: La Toscana come Crocevia*, Livorno 2001, pp. 23–4, figs 16 and 17. I am currently writing a paper on Luzio's designs for metalwork.

20 J. Meyer zu Capellen, *Gentile Bellini*, Stuttgart 1985, pp. 140, 159–60, cat. A 25 and C 27; Anchise Tempestini, *Gentile Bellini*, Milan 1997, pp. 51, 52, 193, 194; *Tesori della Croazia*, cat. no. 32.

21 *Biagio di Giorgio da Traù*, exh. cat., Venice and Zagreb 1989; A. De Marchi, 'La Mostra di Biagio di Giorgio da Traù a Venezia', *Arte Veneta* XLIII (1989), pp. 178–81; *Tesori della Croazia*, pp. 92–4, cat. no. 29.

22 Markham Schulz, 'Further thoughts on Niccolò di Giovanni Fiorentino in Dalmatia and Italy', p. 144, n. 4; J. Belamarić, 'Il volto di San Giovanni Evangelista da Giovanni Dalmata', pp. 287–9; *Tesori della Croazia*, pp. 44–6, cat. no. 7.

23 *Tesori della Croazia*, pp. 87–8, cat. no. 26 (St Peter).

24 A handy guide with English translation is Mirjana Knežević-Grubišić, *Šibenik*, Zagreb 2006.

25 Giorgio Vasari, *Le vite de' più eccelenti pittori, sculturi ed architettori* (1550, rev. 1568), in *Le opere di Giorgio Vasari*, 9 vols, ed. G. Milanesi, Florence 1906, VI, p. 346. V. Brunelli, 'le pere fortificatorie del commune di Zara' in *Rivista Dalmatica*, III, Zara 1904, pp 246–247.

26 A. Deanović, 'Architetti Veneti del cinquecento impegnati nella fortificazione della Costa Dalmata', in *L'architettura militare Veneta del cinquecento*, Milan 1988, pp. 125–34; A. Deanović, 'Dalmazia fortificata: un concetto di Michele e Gian Girolamo Sanmicheli', in *Castelli e Città fortificante*, Udine-Trieste 1991, pp. 27–36; K. Prijatelj, 'Sanmicheli e la Dalmazia', in *Michele Sanmicheli*, ed. H. Burns, C. Frommel and L. Puppi, Milan and Venice 1995, pp. 222–7 and 319–320.

27 D. Frey, *Der Dom von Sebeniko und sein Baumeister Giorgio Orsini*, Vienna 1913; P. Kolendić, *Šibenska katedrala pre dolaska Orsinijeva (1430–1441)*, Zagreb 1924; R. Ivančević, 'Prilozi problema interpretacije djela Jurja Matejeva Dalmatinca', *Radovi Instituta za povijest umjetnosti* 3–6 (1979–82), pp. 25–64; I. Fisković, 'Utjecaji i odrazi Jurja Dalmatinca u Šibeniku', *Radovi Instituta za povijest umjetnosti* 3–6 (1979–82), pp. 116–42; R. Ivančević, *Šibenska Katedrala*, Šibenik 1998; J. Belamarić, 'Come Giorgio di Matteo ottenne in carica di protomaestro della Cattedrale di San Giacomo a Sebenico', in *Per l'arte da Venezia all'Europa: Studi in onore di Giuseppe Maria Pilo*, Venice, pp. 97–102, 301–2; M. Zenić, *Catedrale di Sebanico* Šibenik 2003, with excellent photographs.

28 Milan Pelc, *Horacije Fortezza, Šibenski zlatar i graver 16 stoljeća*, Institut Povijesti Umjetnosti, Zagreb and Šibenik 2004.

29 Milan Pelc, *Natale Bonifacio*, Institut Povijest Umjetnosti, Zagreb and Šibenik 1997; Milan Pelc, *Martin Rota Kolunić, život i djela Šibenskog bakroresca*, Zagreb 1997.

30 C. F. Bianchi, *Zara Cristiana*, vol. I, Zadar 1877; G. Sabalich, *I Dipinti delle Chiese di Zara*, Zadar 1906; G. Sabalich, *Pitture antiche di Zara*, Zadar 1912; C. Cecchelli, *Zara (Catalogo delle cose d'arte e antichità d'Italia)*, Rome 1932; Antun Travirka, *Zadar: History, Culture, Art Heritage*, ed. Đurđica Šokota, Zadar 2003.

31 See note 26. The design was clearly Michele's, while the execution was by his nephew.

32 Licia Ragghianti Collobi, *Il libro de' disegni del Vasari*, 2 vols, Florence 1974, I, p. 136, II, p. 237, no. 417. Pen and brown

ink, 31.7 x 31.8 cm. Inscribed on the verso: 'A Mo Polo de san Micheli cusin carissimo in Verona a San Tomaso rio dei Zerbi'. The inscription demonstrates that it was drawn by Michele and sent to Pietro Paolo, his cousin, who was the father of Gian Girolamo. Michele visited Zadar in 1537, and the gate was erected between 1543 and 1549, when Michele Salomon was 'capitan' whose stemma is carved on the gate flanking that of Diedo.

33 Ivo Petricioli, *Stalna izložba crkvene umjetnosti u Zadru: Katalog zbirke*, Zadar 2004.

34 *Vittore Carpaccio*, exh. cat., ed. P. Zampeti, Venice 1963, cat. nos 9–13; I. Petricioli, *Oko datiranja Carpacciova poliptiha u Zadru*, Zbornik za likovne umjetnosti, 21, Novi Sad 1985, pp. 287–91; Petricioli, *Stalna izložba crkvene umjetnosti u Zadru*, pp. 114–15, cat. no. RP 1.

35 Petricioli, *Stalna izložba crkvene umjetnosti u Zadru*, p.84, cat. no. R 3.1. Beaten silver over limewood, 44.5 x 47.5 x 26 cm.

36 Petricioli, *Stalna izložba crkvene umjetnosti u Zadru*, cat. no. M 13.

37 Petricioli, *Stalna izložba crkvene umjetnosti u Zadru*, p. 67, cat. no. MP 6, tempera on panel, 67.5 x 37.5 cm.

38 Petricioli, *Stalna izložba crkvene umjetnosti u Zadru*, p.117, cat. no. RP 5, for *Virgin and Child Enthroned*, oil on panel, 132 x 67 cm, and *Assumption of the Virgin*, p. 118, cat. no. RP 6, oil on panel, 246 x 137.5 cm. For Luzzo see Sergio Claut, 'Pittori Veneti del cinquecento in Dalmazia: Lorenzo Luzzo e Niccolò de Stefani,' *Antichità Viva* XXXIII, no. 1 (1994), pp. 23–9. I do not share Claut's belief that there is a stylistic relationship between Palma Vecchio's *Assumption* in the Accademia, Venice, and Luzzo's *Assumption* in Zadar.

39 Petricioli, *Stalna izložba crkvene umjetnosti u Zadru*, p. 128, cat. no. RS 2, marble; Tomić, *Barokni oltari i skulptura u Dalmaciji*, p. 113; Bacchi, *La scultura a Venezia*, pp. 739–40, pl. 394.

40 Petricioli, *Stalna izložba crkvene umjetnosti u Zadru*, p. 128, cat. no. RS 3, marble; A. Riccoboni, 'Sculture inedite di Antonio Corradini', *Arte Veneta* VI (1952), pp. 158–60; Tomić, *Barokni oltari i skulptura u Dalmaciji*, p. 113; Bacchi, *La scultura a Venezia*, pp. 726–30.

41 Bacchi, *La scultura a Venezia*, pp. 790–1, pls 613, 614.

42 See note 26.

43 Margaret Binotto, 'I Rubini e gli Albanesi', in *Scultura a Vicenza*, ed. Chiara Rigoni, Milan 1999, pp. 159–91, pls 6, 9 and 19.

44 Helga Zglav-Martinac, *Ulomak do ulomka … Prilog proučavanju keramike XIII–XVIII stoljeća iz Dioklecijanove palače u Splitu*, Muzej Grada, Split 2004; *Antiche ceramiche italiane tra le due sponde dell'Adriatico (dal Palazzo di Diocleziano a Spalato alla Fortezza di Pescara)*, exh. cat., 30 Luglio–30 Settembre 2001, Split and Pescara 2001; Silva Grković and Anita Lovrić, 'New findings of Venetian sgraffito ware at Split', in *The Heritage of the Serenissima: Proceedings of the International Conference Izola/Venezia*, 4–9 November 2005, ed. Mitja Gustin, Koper, Slovenia 2006, pp. 149–54; Liljana Koračić, 'Raccolta delle ceramiche dal XIV al XVII secolo del Museo Archeologico di Ragusa/Dubrovnik', in *The Heritage of the Serenissima*, pp. 161–9.

45 Hanno-Walter Kruff, entry in *Dictionary of Art*, pp. 859–61, with bibliography.

46 Francesco Paolo Fiore, entry in *Dictionary of Art*, pp. 861–2, with bibliography.

47 J. Belamarić, *Isola di Hvar*, Zagreb 2002.

48 Mirjana Kolumbić Šćeparović, *Katedrala, Biskupski Muzej, Hvar*, Zagreb 1979.

49 For Palma see K. Prijatelj, 'Le opera di Palma il Giovane e dei Manieristi Veneziani in Dalmazia', in *Venezia e l'Europa*, Atti del XVIII Congresso Internazionale di Storia dell'Arte a Venezia 1955, Venice 1956, pp. 294–6; G. Gamulin, 'Due dipinti di Palma il Giovane', *Paragone* (1959), n. 115; G. Gamulin, 'Ritornando su Palma il Giovane', *Arte antica e*

moderna (1961), pp. 250–66; Stefania Mason Rinaldi, *Palma il Giovane: L'opera completa*, Milan 1984.

50 Currently poorly displayed sandwiched between two sheets of glass, it is very difficult to photograph and apparently unpublished.

51 Dismissed by Mason Rinaldi as workshop: *Palma il Giovane*, p. 169, cat. no. A 32.

52 Aldo Čavić, *Stari Grad: A Guide to the History of the Town*, Stari Grad 2005. A delightful picture book of the town kindly given to me by the author: Aldo Čavić, *Stari Grad in Miniature*, photographs by Paweł Jaroszewski, Stari Grad 2006.

53 Tomić, *Tesori della Croazia*, cat. no. 34, p. 107.

54 For an English translation of *Fishing and Fishermen's Conversations* see E. D. Goy, *Croatian Review* no. 15, London 1979. Hektorović was very likely to have been familiar with the fishermen's eclogues by Jacopo Sannazaro which followed Virgilian conventions, see J. Belamarić, 'Kultura ladanja u Dalmaciji-slučaj Hektorovićeva Tvrdalja', *Prilozi povijesti umjetnosti u Dalmaciji* 34 (1994), pp. 180–92; J. Belamarić, 'Renaissance villas on the Dalmatian coast', in *Quattrocento Adriatico*, pp. 103–22.

55 See G. Mariacher, *La scultura Veneta del '600 e del '700*, Venice 1966, and A. Nava Cellini, *La scultura del Seicento*, Turin 1982, pp. 195–7.

56 Branko Kirigin, *Pharos: An Archaeological Guide*, Centre for Culture, Stari Grad 2003.

57 See leaflet, Anon. ('CZZKB'), *Vrboska and its Works of Art*, Vrboska 1984.

58 K. Prijatelj, 'La pittura in Dalmazia ai tempi del Veronese', in *Nuovi Studi su Paolo Veronese*, ed. M. Gemin, Venice 1990, pp. 108–9; T. Pignatti and F. Pedrocco, *Veronese*, vol. II, Milan 1995, pp. 524–5; the status of this picture with previous literature is discussed extensively by Vladimir Marković in *Tesori della Croazia*, pp. 108–10, cat. no. 35.

59 N. Gobbin, *Korčula, ein Beispiel dalmatinischen Städtebaus*, Berlin 1930; B. Kalogjera, *Korčula: Portret jednog grada na istočnom Jadranu*, Korčula 1995; J. Belamarić, 'Marsilio Zorzi e la fondazione della città di Curzola (Korčula) nell'anno 1256', in *Venezia, le Marche e la civiltà adriatica*, Arte Documento 17, 18, 19, Venice 2006, pp. 139–47.

60 Zbornik Radova, ed., *Korčulanske Biskupije, 700 Godona*, Korčula 2005; Don Božo Baničević, *Korčula: The Cathedral and the Episcopal Treasury of St Marco*, Korčula nd.

61 Katarina Kusijanović et al., *The Painting of Jacopo Tintoretto from Korčula in the Light of New Research*, exh. cat., Rector's Palace, Dubrovnik, 7 July–26 July 2006, cathedral of St Mark and church of Our Lady, Korčula, 28 July–7 September 2006; Katarina Kusijanović, 'Oltarna pala Jakoba Tintoretta iz Korčulanske Katedrale', in Radova, *Korčulanske Biskupije*, pp. 173–86.

62 Igor Fisković, 'Korčula Grad-Biskupija i starija njezina likovna baština', in Radova, *Korčulanske Biskupije*, pp. 135–94; both of these Leandro Bassano altarpieces are reproduced and discussed p. 184 and p. 185 respectively.

63 Fisković, 'Korčula Grad-Biskupija i starija njezina likovna baština', reproduced pp. 186–7.

64 Timothy Clifford, entry in Peter Humfrey et al., *The Age of Titian: Venetian Renaissance Art from Scottish Collections*, exh. cat., National Gallery of Scotland, Edinburgh 2004, p. 374, cat. no. 208, pp. 445–6, n. 209. This entry discusses in detail the variant cast with seahorses and the companion Venus with dolphins.

65 Damir Tulić, 'Djelo Antonija Corradinija u Korčuli', in Radova, *Korčulanske Biskupije*, pp. 64–73. For the sculptor see Bruno Cogo, *Antonio Corradini (1688–1752): Scultore Veneziano*, Este 1996.

66 R. Tomić, 'O slikama Francesca Maggiotta u Korčuli', *Mogućnosti* 79 (1995), pp. 32–5; Fisković, 'Korčula Grad-Biskupija i starija njezina likovna baština', reproduced pp.

192–4.

67 A prototype for this image is in the church of St Dominic, Split, reproduced in Prijatelj, *Umjetnost 17 i 18 stoljeća u Dalmaciji*, p. 129, fig. 52, with the wrong attribution to Palma il Giovane.

68 Tomić in Radova, *Korčulanske Biskupije*, reproduced pp. 181–2.

69 Tomić in Radova, *Korčulanske Biskupije*, reproduced pp. 190–2.

70 Andrija Vjenceslav Vlašić, *Franjevački Samostan, Orebić*, Zagreb 1990.

71 Uffizi, pen and brown ink wash, 27 x 19.5 cm, inv. 942E (recto), signed in ink lower right: 'Antonio del polaiolo/horafo'; Leopold D. Ettlinger, *Antonio and Piero Pollaiuolo*, London 1978, p. 162, cat. no. 39, pl. 3; Alison Wright, *The Pollaiuolo Brothers: The Arts of Florence and Rome*, New Haven and London 2005, pp. 49–52, pl. 34. Wright suggests that the Uffizi drawing may have been made originally for a silver thurible made for San Pancrazio, Florence in 1459.

72 Massimo Pulini, *Andrea Lilio*, Milan 2003, pp. 110–11, cat. no. 87, reproduced in colour.

10. DUBROVNIK: ITALIAN ART, C. 1400–1800

These two chapters could not have been written without the dynamic enthusiasm and support of Lady Beresford-Peirse and the detailed time-consuming advice of Joško Belamarić, who acted in Split as my cicerone. At Dubrovnik the staff of Villa Stay were most supportive and helpful. The typing has been done by my wife, Jane Clifford, and my secretary, Kay Henderson, and to both of them I am truly grateful. As these appear to be pioneering works in English on Italian art in Croatia I have had to struggle with the Croatian language, and a substantial quantity of the attributions made here are my own. I hope subsequent archival work in Croatia may substantiate these ideas. Finally, my thanks must go to Nancy Marten, who has been an extremely efficient copy-editor and Maria Charalambous, who has been responsible for the layout and final proofs.

Radoslav Buzančić, Ministry of Culture, Conservation Department, Trogir; Anthea Brooke, Witt Library, Courtauld Institute of Art, University of London; Zrinka Buljević, Archeological Museum, Split; Diana Bolanča, Ministry of Culture, Conservation Department, Šibenik; Aldo Čavić, Director of Museum, Stari Grad, Hvar; Dr Živan Filippi, Korčula; Vedrana Gjukić-Bender, Curator, Rector's Palace, Dubrovnik; Robin Harris, London; Vanja Kovačić, Ministry of Culture, Conservation Department, Trogir; Katarina Kusijanović, Conservator, Croatian Conservation Institute, Villa Stay, Dubrovnik; Neda Kuzek, Conservator, Croatian Conservation Institute, Villa Stay, Dubrovnik; Nada Lucić, Conservator, Croatian Conservation Institute, Villa Stay, Dubrovnik; Dr sc Vinicije B. Lupis, State Archivist, Dubrovnik; Anastasia Magaš, Zadar; Fra Stipe Nosić, Franciscan Church, Dubrovnik; Don Ivica Pervan, Bishopric Museum, Dubrovnik; Božena Popić-Kurtela, Ministry of Culture, Conservation Department, Dubrovnik; Vlaho Pustić, Head of Conservation Department, Croatian Conservation Institute, Villa Stay, Dubrovnik; Mara Pustić, Conservator, Croatian Conservation Institute, Villa Stay, Dubrovnik; Fra Kristijan Raić, Dominican Church, Dubrovnik; Danka Radić, Trogir; Relja Seferović, Institute for Historic Research of the Croatian Academy of Sciences and Arts (HAZU); Sanja and Samir Serhaltić, Paper Conservators, Croatian Conservation Institute, Villa Stay, Dubrovnik; Helga Zglav-Martinac, Curator, Split Museum and specialist on majolica.

1 Robin Harris, *Dubrovnik: A History*, London 2006; Antun Travirka, *Zadar: History, Culture, Art Heritage*, ed. Đurđica Šokota, Zadar 2003. Evidently important was the lively Ragusan cloth trade with many workers in the early 15th

century coming from Prato, Siena, Florence, an Bergamo (see ch. 8 ???).

2 Harris, *Dubrovnik*.

3 Philippus de Diversis de Quartigianis de Lucca, *Situs aedificorum, politiae et laudabilium consuetudinum inclytae civitatis Ragusii*, ed. Brunelli, Zadar 1882, pp. 41–7; Diversis was a Tuscan schoolmaster and humanist who lived in Dubrovnik between 1434 and 1441, and is the most informative and reliable historian/commentator on early Dubrovnik; I. Fisković, 'Kiparstvo', in *Zlatno doba Dubrovnika, XV i XVI stoljeće*, exh. cat., Zagreb and Dubrovnik 1987, pp. 127–8; Harris, *Dubrovnik*, pp. 300–3.

4 L. Beritić, *Utvrđenja grada Dubrovnika*, Zagreb 1959, p. 51; L. Beritić, *The City Walls of Dubrovnik*, Dubrovnik 1989, p. 8.

5 Harris, *Dubrovnik*, pp. 290–3.

6 Harris, *Dubrovnik*, pp. 123–45.

7 Harris, *Dubrovnik*, pp. 298–9.

8 Harris, *Dubrovnik*, p. 339.

9 Benedetta Montevecchi, 'Pietro Antonio Palmerini', in *Pesaro nell'età dei Della Rovere*, vol. III 2 (Historia Pisaurensis), Venice 2001, pp. 137–48, the Fossombrone *bozzetto*, fig. 4.

10 National Galleries of Scotland, inv. no. D1569; Keith Andrews, ed., *A Catalogue of the Italian Drawings: National Gallery of Scotland*, 2 vols, Cambridge 1968, I, p. 54, II, p. 69, fig. 388; a study for the *Risen Christ* in Genga's altarpiece in the oratory of Santa Caterina da Siena, Via Giulia, Rome, of *c.* 1519.

11 J. Tadić, *Gradja o slikarskoj Skoli u Dubrovnika XIII–XVII*, 2 vols, Belgrade 1952, II, pp. 128–9, 135; M. Gligorijevich, 'Pier Antonio Palmerini', in *Zbornik za likovne umjetnosti* 7 (1971), pp. 55–81; V. Marković, *Zlatno doba Dubrovnika XV i XVI stoljeće*, exh. cat., Zagreb 1987, pp. 354–5; Montevecchi, 'Pietro Antonio Palmerini', pp. 141–2, figs 5 and 6.

12 Very similar examples of *lavabo* are also in the Dominican monastery and in the summer villa of Petar Sorkočević at Lapad (now Institute of Historical Science of the Croatian Academy of Sciences and Arts).

13 The picture was first recognised by Roberto Longhi; see Emilio Negro and Nicoletta Roio, *Francesco Francia e la Sua Scuola*, Modena 1998, pp. 152–3, cat. no. 22, reproduced.

14 Robert Engass, *The Paintings of Baciccio*, Philadelphia 1964, pp. 122, 123, fig. 42.

15 *Giovanni Battista Gaulli 'Il Baciccio'*, exh. cat., Palazzo Chigi, Ariccia, 11 December 1999–12 March 2000, Ariccia 1999, cat. no. 51b, pp. 211–13, entry by Daniele Petrucci.

16 S. Krasić, *Stjepan Gradić, 1613–1683: Život i djelo*, Zagreb 1987.

17 *Bernini in Vaticano*, exh. cat., Vatican, May–July 1981, Rome 1981, cat. no. 241 (Gabinetto dei Disegni e delle Stampe, inv. no. FC 137. 506, as Studio of Bernini).

18 Stjepan Krasić, *The Dominican Priory in Dubrovnik*, Dubrovnik 2002.

19 G. Gamulin, *The Painted Crucifixes in Croatia*, Zagreb 1983, pp. 31–2; Radovan Ivančević, *Art Treasures of Croatia*, Belgrade 1986, p. 106, fig. 85; *Paolo Veneziano e la pittura del trecento in Adriatico*, exh. cat., Castel Sismondo, Rimini, Milan 2002 (entries by Francesca Flores D'Arcais and Giovanni Gentili); Filippo Pedrocco, *Paolo Veneziano*, Milan 2003.

20 The picture was rolled and folded when hidden from the French by a member of the Pucić family *c.* 1808, which resulted in heavy losses and abrasions. Then in 1859 Count Pucić sent it to Venice to be restored – or rather repainted – by Paolo Fabris. The new sensitive cleaning and retouching by the Croatian Conservation Institute at Zagreb has revealed the quality of the picture. It was exhibited 16 January–25 February 2007 at Zagreb and is now on permanent view in the museum of the Dominican monastery, Dubrovnik. J. A. Crowe and G. B. Cavalcaselle, *Titian: His Life and Times*, London 1872; Harold Wethey, *The Paintings of Titian, I: The*

Religious Paintings, London 1969. Both Grgo Gamulin and Rodolfo Pallucchini have apparently seen the picture after its recent conservation and recognise 'the hand of the master'.

[21] The picture is not by Lorenzo di Credi but by another follower of Verrocchio, perhaps the so-called 'Tommaso'. B. Berenson, *Paintings of the Florentine School*, 2 vols, London 1963, I, p. 207.

[22] Simona Lecchini Giovannoni and Marco Collareta, *Disegni di Santi di Tito (1536–1603)*, exh. cat., Gabinetto Disegni e Stampe degli Uffizi, Florence 1985, cat. no. 12, pp. 33–4, fig. 13 (inv. no. N 1348S).

[23] Krasić, *Dominican Priory*, pp. 36–8.

[24] R. Tomić, *Barokni oltari i skulptura u Dalmaciji*, Zagreb 1995, pp. 111–19, 204, with good bibliography; Andrea Bacchi, *La scultura a Venezia da Sansovino a Canova*, Milan 2000, pp. 740–1, figs 394–404.

[25] L. Beritić, *Urbanistički razvitak Dubrovnika*, Zagreb 1958; Harris, *Dubrovnik*, pp. 300–2. See also the entry by Paul Tvrtović, in *The Dictionary of Art*, 34 vols, ed. Jane Turner, London 1996–2002, p. 330 under Dubrovnik.

[26] Inv. 844; oil on panel, 66 x 57.5 cm. *Lelio Orsi 1511–1587, dipinti e disegni*, exh. cat., Teatro Valli, Reggio Emilia, 5 December 1987–30 January 1988, Reggio Emilia 1987, cat. no. 198, pp. 224–5, entry by Fiorella Frisoni.

[27] Pavica Vilać, 'Kabinetski ormarić iz Kneževa dvora u Dubrovniku', *Prilozi povijesti umjetnosti u Dalmaciji* 37 (1997–8), pp. 274–7 and 290.

[28] Alvar González-Palacios, *Il tempo del gusto*, Milan 1986, vol. II, pp. 223 and 231. Another similar cabinet offered to Sotheby's, London, *Important Continental Furniture, Ceramics and Clocks*, 2 December 2008, Lot 17.

[29] Timothy Clifford, 'Another clock painted by Baciccio', *The Burlington Magazine* (December 1976), pp. 852–5, figs 97–100; Vedrana Gjukić Bender, 'Noćni Sat u Dubrovniku u kućnoj upotrebi', *Prilozi povijesti umjetnosti u Dalmaciji* 33 (1992), pp. 297–304.

[30] C. Fisković, 'Umjetnine stare dubrovačke katedrale', *Bulletin JAZU* XIV (1967); K. Prijatelj, 'Barok u Hrvatskoj', in *Strani barokni arhitekti u Dalmaciji*, ed. K. Prijatelj, Zagreb 1982; Ante Dračevac, *Die Kathedrale in Dubrovnik*, Zagreb 1988; Don Stanko Lasić, *The Dubrovnik Cathedral*, Zagreb n.d.

[31] John Varriano, *Italian Baroque and Rococo Architecture*, Oxford 1986, esp. pp. 19–43.

[32] Harris, *Dubrovnik*, p. 338.

[33] G. Gamulin, 'Tizianov poliptih Uzašašća Marijina u Katedrali u Dubrovniku', *Zbornik Instituta za hist. nauke Filozofskog fakulteta u Zagrebu* I (1955).

[34] This painting is signed: 'STEPHANI SORGII VOTUM/ SOLUTUM A PAULLO FRATRE/ OPERA PEREGRINI BROCARDI/ INTERMELIENSIS MDLVIII RAGUSII'. Oil on canvas, 288 x 192 cm, published in K. Prijatelj, 'Uz biografiju Pellegrina Brocarda, slikara nabiskupa Ludovica Beccadellija', *Radovi Instituta zu povijest umjetnosti* 8 (1984). For the Perino, see Lichtenstein collection, inv. no. G24. Elena Parma Armani, *Perino del Vaga, l'anello mancante*, Genoa 1986, cat. BXIV, p. 170, fig. 202. *Perino del Vaga: tra Raffaello e Michelangelo*, exh. cat., Palazzo Tè, Mantua, 18 March–10 June 2001, Milan 2001, cat. no. 55, pp. 160–1. For the Beccadelli connection see also I. Fisković, 'Les arts figuratifs de la Renaissance en Croatie', in *La Renaissance en Croatie*,

exh. cat., ed. Alain Erlander-Brandenburg and Miljenko Jurković, Écouen and Zagreb 2004, p. 189; *Allgemeines Künstler Lexicon*, vol. 14, Leipzig 1996; and G. Fragnito, *In museo e in villa*, Venice 1988, pp. 109–58; *I Madruzzi e l'Europa 1539–1658*, exh. cat., Trento 1993, cat. no. 46, pp. 120–1.

[35] Grgo Gamulin, 'Poklonstvo Pastira od Luke Cambiasa u katedrali u Dubrovniku', in *Stari Majstori u Jugoslaviji, II*, Zagreb 1964, pp. 94–7, fig. 56. It reminds me much more of Sammacchini's sheet of studies in the Louvre (ex Giorgio Vasari), reproduced in Licia Ragghianti Collobi, *Il libro de' disegni del Vasari*, 2 vols, Florence 1974, I, no. 479, II, p. 299; another sheet with *Putti Disarming the Sleeping Cupid* in the Musées Royaux des Beaux Arts, Brussels, inv. no. 65A; and his oil, the *Coronation of the Virgin*, in the Picture Gallery, Bologna (reproduced in Vera Fortunati Pierantonio, *Pittura Bolognese del '500*, 2 vols, Bologna 1986, II, p. 670).

[36] Kruno Prijatelj, 'Pala Sebastiana Riccija u Dubrovniku', *Studije o umjetninama u Dalmaciji* I (1963), pp. 77–8, figs 50–2. Jeffery Daniels, *L'opera completa di Sebastiano Ricci*, milano 1976, p111, no 263. Zlatko Bielen, 'Conservation-restoration operations to the painting of Sebastiano Ricci: The Virgin with St. Theresa and Simon Stock' in *Restaurirane slike iz crkve Gospe od Karmena u Dubrovniku*, exh. cat., ed. Neda Kuzek, Zagreb 2007, pp. 57–60 (see note 35).

[37] These pictures have now all been cleaned by the Croatian Conservation Institute's Restoration Department (Hrvatski Restauratorski Zavod, Dubrovnik) and published by them in Kuzek, *Restaurirane*.

[38] Barbara Knežević-Kuzman, 'The Assumption of the Blessed Virgin Mary', in Kuzek, *Restaurirane*, pp. 51–6. Two old copies of this composition are at Mljet and Koločep demonstrating the great popularity of this picture at the time.

[39] Neda Kuzek, 'The restoration of the altarpiece by Angelo Canini', in Kuzek, *Restaurirane*, pp. 23–30. It was commissioned by Bernardo Ivanov Đurđević and the selection of the saints on the altar corresponds to names of members of Đurđević's family.

[40] Kruno Prijatelj, 'Dvije Slike Andree Vaccara u Dubrovniku', *Studije o umjetninama u Dalmaciji* I (1963), pp. 71–2, fig. 42. I am most grateful to Mara and Vlaho Pustić for showing me this picture during conservation. Mara Pustić, 'The altarpiece of Andrea Vaccaro from the church of Our Lady of Carmel', in Kuzek, *Restaurirane*, pp. 37–50. The Carmel Vaccaro must date from the same moment as the signed *Immaculate Conception* now in the museum at Salamanca. The Salamanca picture repeats the pose and drapery of the Virgin Mary, and we know it was bought from the artist by the count of Monterey, viceroy of Naples and founder of the Augustinian College at Salamanca.

[41] Kruno Prijatelj, 'Padovaninove Slike u Dalmaciji', in *Studije o umjetninama u Dalmaciji* I (1963), pp. 67–70, figs 37–40.

[42] Jennifer Montagu, *Alessandro Algardi*, New Haven and London, 2 vols, 1985, II, pp. 327–8, cat. no. L16, and pp. 329–30, cat. no. 16 c.4. The model appears very close, with the perizonum flying out to the left, but the corpus is fixed by three rather than four nails to the cross.

[43] Vinicije B. Lupis, 'Prilog poznavanju rimskog zlatarstva u Dubrovniku', *Radovi Instituta za povijest umjetnosti* 30 (2006), pp. 93–106.

[44] Vinicije B. Lupis, 'O napuljskom zlatarstvu u Dubrovniku i okolici', *Prilozi povijesti umjetnosti u Dalmaciji* 28 (2004), pp. 163–75.

[45] Harris, *Dubrovnik*, pp. 341–4.

[46] Kruno Prijatelj, 'Puligova Lokrumska Madona u Dubrovniku', *Dubrovnik* 1–2 (1981).

[47] Grgo Gamulin, 'Tri Slike Palme Vecchia', in *Stari Majstori u Jugoslaviji, II*, pp. 40–7, fig. 24.

[48] Grgo Gamulin, 'Doprinos Toskancima', in *Stari Majstori u Jugoslaviji, II*, pp. 98–106, figs 57, 58.

[49] Uffizi, inv. 1890.n 1556.

[50] Varriano, *Italian Baroque and Rococo Architecture*, pp. 167, 169, 172 and 174.

[51] Anna De Floriani, 'Nicolò Corso in Liguria e la pittura Genovese in Corsica nella seconda metà del quattrocento', in *Genova e l'Europa Mediterranea*, Genoa 2005.

11. CASTLES AND MANOR HOUSES OF CROATIA: WINNING OR LOSING?

This chapter is the result of a week's whirlwind tour of Croatian castles and manor houses. I cast a critical – and appreciative – eye at Croatia's remarkable legacy of grand aristocratic seats and smaller manor houses of many periods, assessing the problems, the threats, the possibilities and the achievements, looking not only at architecture and interiors but the all-important settings of these remarkable places. The ownership and future of some of these properties is uncertain; a few were for sale when I visited them.

I would like to thank the following people and institutions in Croatia who have assisted me during the journey, with thanks due especially to Professor Mladen and Dr Bojana Obad Šćitaroci: the Tourist Board of Croatia and Josip Lozić in their London office, the Ministry of Culture, Professor Ferdinand Meder and his staff from the Croatian Conservation Institute, Silvija Ladić from the County of Varaždin, Željko Trstenjak and Ivana Peškan from the Conservation Department of the Ministry of Culture in Varaždin, Zdenka Predrijevac from the Conservation Department of the Ministry of Culture in Osijek, and the following owners or directors of museums or houses which I visited: Adam Pintarić in Trakošćan, Davor Vlajčević in Golubovec, family Hellenbach in Marija Bistrica, Sister Miroslava Bradica in Lužnica, Lada Szabo Kajfež in Miljana, Siniša Križanec in Bežanec, Zdravko Šabarić in Đurđevac, Dubravka Sabolić in Virovitica, Melia Vidaković in Donji Miholjac, Biserka Vistica in Bilje, Mirela Hutinec in Vukovar, Dubravka Tomsik Krmpotić, Ružica Cerni and Ivica Miličević in Ilok, Ratko Ivanušec in Valpovo, Silvija Lučevnjak in Našice and the mayor of Kutjevo Ante Pavković, and above all to Jadranka Beresford-Peirse, who sent me on this fascinating mission.

[1] Mladen Obad Šćitaroci, *Castles, Manors and Gardens of Croatian Zagorje*, Zagreb 1996, and Mladen Obad Šćitaroci and Bojana Bojanić Obad Šćitaroci, *Manors and Gardens in Croatia*, Zagreb 2001.

12. MUSEUMS OF ZAGREB

[1] Laurence Kantner, *Fra Angelico*, New Haven and London 2005, p. 274.

[2] In *The British Art Journal* 6, no. 1 (Winter 2005).

LIST OF CONTRIBUTORS

JOHN JULIUS NORWICH has written histories of Norman Sicily, Venice, Byzantium and the Mediterranean. As a former member of HM Foreign Service, he was posted to the former Yugoslavia from 1955 to 1957 and knows Croatia well.

STJEPAN ĆOSIĆ graduated in history and sociology at the University of Zadar and completed his doctorate at the University of Zagreb in 1988. He worked as an archivist in the State Archives in Dubrovnik (1991–5) and as researcher in the Institute for Historical Sciences in Dubrovnik (1996–2004). Since 2004 he has been the Director of the Croatian State Archives in Zagreb. He lectures on graduate and doctoral studies in Zagreb and Dubrovnik. His main subject of interest is the social, cultural and demographic history of Dubrovnik and Dalmatia in the eighteenth and nineteenth centuries, including archival studies. He has published books and scientific papers.

ROBIN HARRIS is the author of *Dubrovnik: A History*. He is also a writer of biographies and contributes to British and American journals on politics and international affairs.

BRANKO KIRIGIN is Curator of Greek Antiquities at the Archaeological Museum, Split.

MICHAEL VICKERS is Professor of Archaeology at the University of Oxford, Senior Research Fellow in Classical Studies at Jesus College, Oxford, and Curator of Greek and Roman Antiquities at the Ashmolean Museum.

JOHN WILKES After studies in ancient history and archaeology at University College London and the University of Durham, John Wilkes taught these subjects in the universities of Manchester, Birmingham and London. At retirement in 2001 he held the position of Yates Professor of Greek and Roman Archaeology at University College London. He is a Fellow of the British Academy, and of the Societies of Antiquaries of London and Scotland, and is Honorary Vice-President of the Society for the Promotion of Roman Studies. He has undertaken historical and archaeological research in several regions of the Roman Empire, but his main focus has been the territory of the former Yugoslavia, and his principal publications relate to that area, including *Dalmatia* (1969), *Diocletian's Palace* (1986) and *The Illyrians* (1992).

SHEILA J. MCNALLY received her PhD in art history from Harvard University. She has taught at Ohio State University and Mt Holyoke College, and currently teaches at the University of Minnesota. Together with Jerko Marasović, she directed excavations at Diocletian's Palace and has also excavated in Akhmim, Egypt. Besides books and articles on those excavations, she has published studies of maenads and sleepers in Greek art, on monastic space, and on the Mary Silk in the Abegg Stiftung. She has served on the boards of the College Art Association and the Archaeological Institute of America.

CHRISTOPHER DE HAMEL has been Donnelley Fellow Librarian of Corpus Christi College, Cambridge, since 2000. From 1975 to 2000 he was responsible for all sales of medieval and illuminated manuscripts at Sotheby's, London. He has written many books on medieval manuscripts and the history of book collecting.

DONAL COOPER is Assistant Professor in the History of Art Department at the University of Warwick. A specialist in the artistic patronage of the Franciscan Order in the Middle Ages and Renaissance, he has published widely on the art and architecture of the friars in Italy, particularly in Umbria. Donal is currently preparing a book on the Basilica of San Francesco at Assisi.

DAVID EKSERDJIAN has been Professor of the History of Art and Film at the University of Leicester since 2004. Currently a Trustee of the National Gallery and of the Tate Gallery, and a member of the Reviewing Committee on the Export of Works of Art, he is the author of numerous publications, including *Correggio* (1997), *Parmigianino* (2006) and *Alle origini della natura morta* (2007). In 2004 he was made an honorary citizen of the town of Correggio.

JOŠKO BELAMARIĆ, art historian and director of the Conservation Department of the Ministry of Culture at Split since 1992, is the author of books, studies and papers on art of the later antiquity, the Middle Ages and the Renaissance in Dalmatia. He has held the post of Professor in Iconology at the University of Zadar since 1985 and travels widely as a lecturer. For his scholarly and professional work, he has received several prestigious prizes and awards.

GRAHAM MCMASTER read English at Cambridge, where he also received a doctorate. He had a teaching career in Yugoslavia, then Poland, Iran and Japan, after which, on the eve of the war in the 1990s, he and his Zagreb-born wife went to live in Croatia, where he started a second career as a translator.

SIR TIMOTHY CLIFFORD was formerly Director General of the National Galleries of Scotland for twenty-one years, and before that he was Director of Manchester City Art Galleries for six years. Previously he worked in the Victoria & Albert Museum (Ceramics Department) and the British Museum (Print Room). He has published widely in periodical literature on Italian art and collaborated in mounting monographic exhibitions in Scotland on Raphael, Titian, Bernini and Canova. He is now retired and divides his time between homes in Italy and Scotland.

MARCUS BINNEY CBE is Architecture Correspondent to *The Times* of London and founder and President of SAVE Britain's Heritage. He is also co-presenter of the thirty-nine-part television series, *Great Houses of Europe*. He has written frequently on country houses from Portugal to Poland.

BRIAN SEWELL read history of art at the Courtauld Institute and has worked ever since in the field of paintings by Old Masters. He is now the art critic of the London *Evening Standard*.

INDEX